LEARNING TO WRITE EFFECTIVELY: CURRENT TRENDS IN EUROPEAN RESEARCH

STUDIES IN WRITING
Series Editor: Gert Rijlaarsdam

Recent titles in this series:

VAN WAES, LEIJTEN AND NEUWIRTH
Writing and Digital Media

SULLIVAN AND LINDGREN
Computer Key-Stroke Logging and Writing

HIDI AND BOSCOLO
Writing and Motivation

TORRANCE, VAN WAES AND GALBRAITH
Writing and Cognition

ALAMARGOT, TERRIER AND CELLIER
Written Documents in the Workplace

HA AND BAURAIN
*Voices, Identities, Negotiations, and Conflicts: Writing Academic
English Across Cultures*

L'ABATE AND SWEENEY
Research on Writing Approaches in Mental Health

CASTELLÓ AND DONAHUE
University Writing: Selves and Texts in Academic Societies

Related journals:

Journal of Writing Research
Written Communication
L1 - Educational Studies in Language and Literature
Learning and Instruction
Educational Research Review
Assessing Writing
Computers and Composition
Journal of Second Language Writing

LEARNING TO WRITE EFFECTIVELY: CURRENT TRENDS IN EUROPEAN RESEARCH

EDITED BY

MARK TORRANCE
Nottingham Trent University, UK

DENIS ALAMARGOT
University of Poitiers, France

MONTSERRAT CASTELLÓ
Ramon Llull University, Barcelona, Spain

FRANCK GANIER
European University of Brittany and University of Brest, France

OTTO KRUSE
Zurich University of Applied Sciences, Switzerland

ANNE MANGEN
University of Stavanger, Norway

LILIANA TOLCHINSKY
University of Barcelona, Spain

LUUK VAN WAES
University of Antwerp, Belgium

United Kingdom • North America • Japan
India • Malaysia • China

Emerald Group Publishing Limited
Howard House, Wagon Lane, Bingley BD16 1WA, UK

First edition 2012

British Library Cataloguing in Publication Data
A catalogue record for this book is available from the British Library

ISBN: 978-1-78052-928-8
ISSN: 1572-6304 (Series)

ISOQAR certified
Management Systems,
awarded to Emerald for
adherence to Quality
and Environmental
standards ISO 9001:2008
and 14001:2004,
respectively

Certificate Number 1985
ISO 9001
ISO 14001

INVESTOR IN PEOPLE

Contents

SECTION 1: WRITING DEVELOPMENT

SECTION 2: LEARNING AND TEACHING WRITING

Subsection 2.01: Writing Instruction

Subsection 2.03: Text Assessment

SECTION 4: TOOLS FOR STUDYING AND SUPPORTING WRITING

List of Contributors

Denis Alamargot   Université de Poitiers-CNRS, France.
E-mail: Denis.Alamargot@univ-poitiers.fr

Riikka Alanen   Centre for Applied Language Studies, University of Jyväskylä, Finland.
E-mail: riikka.alanen@jyu.fi

María-Lourdes Álvarez   University of León, Spain.
E-mail: mlalvf@unileon.es

Margarida Alves   Instituto Superior de Psicologia Aplicada, Lisboa, Portugal.
E-mail: mmartins@ispa.pt

Barbara Arfé   Department of Developmental Psychology, University of Padova, Italy.
E-mail: barbara.arfe@univr.it

Olga Arias-Gundín   University of León, Spain.
E-mail: o.arias.gundin@unileon.es

Vicenta Ávila   University of Valencia, Spain.
E-mail: vicenta.avila@uv.es

Melina Aparici Aznar   Grup de Recerca Percepció, Comunicació i Temps, Universitat Autònoma de Barcelona, Barcelona, Spain.
E-mail: melina.aparici@uab.cat

Veerle Baaijen   Centre for Language and Cognition Groningen, University of Groningen, Netherlands.
E-mail: V.M.Baaijen@rug.nl

Céline Beaudet   Université de Sherbrooke, Québec, Canada.
E-mail: Celine.Beaudet@USherbrooke.ca

Lucie Beauvais   Université de Poitiers and CNRS, France.
E-mail: lucie.beauvais@etu.univ-poitiers.fr

Caroline Beauvais

Université de Poitiers and CNRS, France.
E-mail: caroline.beauvais@etu.univ-poitiers.fr

Michael Becker-Mrotzek

University of Cologne, Germany.
E-mail: becker.mrotzek@uni-koeln.de

Huub van den Bergh

Utrecht University; University of Amsterdam, Netherlands.
E-mail: Huub.vandenBergh@let.uu.nl

Freyja Birgisdóttir

School of Education, University of Iceland, Iceland.
E-mail: freybi@hi.is

Pietro Boscolo

Department of Developmental Psychology, University of Padova, Italy.
E-mail: pietro.boscolo@unipd.it

Martine Braaksma

University of Amsterdam, Netherlands.
E-mail: braaksma@uva.nl

Sandra Budde

University of Giessen, Germany.
E-mail: budde.sandra@googlemail.com

Marcel Burger

University of Lausanne, France.
E-mail: marcel.burger@unil.ch

José María Campillo Ferrer

Universidad de Murcia, Spain.
E-mail: arrobaj@hotmail.com

José J. Cañas

Cognitive Ergonomics Group, Department of Experimental Psychology, University of Granada, Spain.
E-mail: delagado@ugr.es

Inês Cardoso

Research Centre for Didactics and Technology in Teacher Education, University of Aveiro, Portugal.
E-mail: inescardoso@ua.pt

José Brandão Carvalho

University of Minho, Portugal.
E-mail: jabrandao@ie.uminho.pt

Montserrat Castelló

Ramon Llull University, Barcelona, Spain.
E-mail: montserratcb@blanquerna.url.edu

Nuria Castells

University of Barcelona, Spain.
E-mail: nuria.castells@ub.edu

Lucile Chanquoy

University of Nice-Sophia Antipolis, France.
E-mail: lucile.chanquoy@unice.fr

Vincent Connelly

Division of Psychology, Oxford Brookes
University, UK.
E-mail: vconnelly@brookes.ac.uk

Mariona Corcelles

SINTE Research Group, Barcelona, Spain.
E-mail: Marionacs@blanquerna.url.edu

Isabel Cuevas

Autonomous University of Madrid, Spain.
E-mail: isabel.cuevas@uam.es

Bruno De Cara

University of Nice-Sophia Antipolis, France.
E-mail: bruno.de-cara@unice.fr

Kees de Glopper

Centre for Language and Cognition Groningen,
University of Groningen, Netherlands.
E-mail: C.M.de.Glopper@rug.nl

Ana M. de Caso

University of León, Spain.
E-mail: amcasf@unileon.es

Isabelle Delcambre

Université Charles-de-Gaulle-Lille 3, France.
E-mail: isabelle.delcambre-derville@univ-lille3.fr

Carmen Díez

University of León, Spain.
E-mail: carmen.diez.gonzalez@unileon.es

Julie Dockrell

Institute of Education, University of London, UK.
E-mail: j.dockrell@ioe.ac.uk

Christiane Donahue

Dartmouth College, USA.
E-mail: christiane.k.donahue@dartmouth.edu

Gerardo Echeita

Autonomous University of Madrid, Spain.
E-mail: gerardo.echeita@uam.es

Sandra Espino

University of Barcelona, Spain.
E-mail: sespino@ub.edu

Inmaculada Fajardo

University of Valencia, Spain.
E-mail: infabra@uv.es

Monik Favart

Université de Poitiers and CNRS, France.
E-mail: monik.favart@univ-poitiers.fr

Antonio Ferrer

University of Valencia, Spain.
E-mail: Antonio.Ferrer@uv.es

Raquel Fidalgo

Psychology, Sociology and Philosophy
Department, University of León, Spain.
E-mail: rfidr@unileon.es

Mathias Fürer

University of Berne, Switzerland.
E-mail: mathias.fuerer@bluewin.ch

David Galbraith   Southampton Education School, University of
                          Southampton, UK.
                          E-mail: D.W.Galbraith@soton.ac.uk

Franck Ganier   Computer Science Laboratory for Complex
                          Systems, European University of Brittany and
                          European Centre for Virtual Reality, University of
                          Brest, France.
                          E-mail: franck.ganier@univ-brest.fr

Jesús-Nicasio García   Psychology, Sociology and Philosophy
                          Department, University of León, Spain.
                          E-mail: jn.garcia@unileon.es

Esther García-Martín   University of León, Spain.
                          E-mail: egarmr@unileon.es

Aleksandra Gnach   University of Berne, Switzerland.
                          E-mail: aleksandra.gnach@bluewin.ch

Joachim Grabowski   Leibniz University, Hannover, Germany.
                          E-mail: grabowski@psychologie.uni-hannover.de

Marta Gràcia   University of Barcelona, Spain.
                          E-mail: mgraciag@ub.edu

Helmut Gruber   Department of Linguistics, Vienna University,
                          Austria.
                          E-mail: helmut.k.gruber@univie.ac.at

Cecilia Gunnarsson   Laboratoire Octogone-Lordat, Université
                          Toulouse, France.
                          E-mail: gunnars@univ-tlse2.fr

Anne Håland   National Centre for Reading Education and
                          Research, University of Stavanger, Norway.
                          E-mail: anne.haland@uis.no

Marie-Claire Hazard   University of Nice-Sophia Antipolis, France.
                          E-mail: mc.hazard@free.fr

Kenneth Holmqvist   Humanities Laboratory, Lund University, Sweden.
                          E-mail: humlab@sol.lu.se

Birgit Huemer   Department of Linguistics, Vienna University,
                          Austria.
                          E-mail: birgit.huemer@univie.ac.at

Ari Huhta   Centre for Applied Language Studies, University
                          of Jyväskylä, Finland.
                          E-mail: ari.huhta@jyu.fi

Cornelia Ilie	Malmö University, Sweden. E-mail: cornelia.ilie@gmail.com
Anna Iñesta	Ramon Llull University, Barcelona, Spain and SINTE Research Group, Barcelona, Spain. E-mail: Ana.inesta@esade.edu
Tanja Janssen	Research Institute of Child Development and Education, University of Amsterdam, Netherlands. E-mail: T.M.Janssen@uva.nl
Roger Johansson	Centre for Languages and Literature, Lund University, Sweden. E-mail: Roger.Johansson@ling.lu.se
Victoria Johansson	Centre for Languages and Literature, Lund University, Sweden. E-mail: Victoria.Johansson@ling.lu.se
Jörg Jost	University of Cologne, Germany. E-mail: joerg.jost@uni-koeln.de
Paula Kalaja	Centre for Applied Language Studies, University of Jyväskylä, Finland. E-mail: paula.kalaja@jyu.fi
Sonia Kandel	Université Pierre Mendès France, Grenoble, France. E-mail: sonia.kandel@upmf-grenoble.fr
Joyce Karreman	University of Twente, Netherlands. E-mail: j.karreman@utwente.nl
Matthias Knopp	University of Cologne, Germany. E-mail: matthias.knopp@uni-koeln.de
Otto Kruse	Zurich University of Applied Sciences, Switzerland. E-mail: kreo@zhaw.ch
Nathalie Le Bigot	University of Poitiers, France. E-mail: nathalie.le.bigot@etu.univ-poitiers.fr
Mariëlle Leijten	University of Antwerp, Belgium. E-mail: marielle.leijten@ua.ac.be
Eva Liesa	Ramon Llull University, Barcelona, Spain and SINTE Research Group, Barcelona, Spain. E-mail: Evalh@blanquerna.url.edu

Eva Lindgren
Umeå University, Sweden.
E-mail: eva.lindgren@sprak.umu.se

Geoff Lindsay
Cedar, University of Warwick, UK.
E-mail: Geoff.lindsay@warwick.ac.uk

Marieke Longcamp
Laboratoire Adaptations Perceptivo-Motrices et Apprentissage, Paul Sabatier University, Toulouse, France.
E-mail: longcamp@cict.fr

Nicole Loorbach
University of Twente, Netherlands.
E-mail: n.r.loorbach@utwente.nl

Sonia López Serrano
Universidad de Murcia, Spain.
E-mail: lopezserrano@gmail.com

M. José Loureiro
Research Centre for Didactics and Technology in Teacher Education, University of Aveiro, Portugal.
E-mail: zeloureiro@ua.pt

Maria Luna
Autonomous University of Madrid, Spain.
E-mail: maria.luna@uam.es

Charles A. MacArthur
University of Delaware, USA.
E-mail: macarthu@udel.edu

Clare Mackie
Institute of Psychiatry, Kings College London, UK.
E-mail: clare.mackie@iop.kcl.ac.uk

R. Ignacio Madrid
Technosite, ONCE Foundation, Madrid, Spain.
E-mail: nmadrid@technosite.es

Anne Mangen
University of Stavanger, Norway.
E-mail: anne.mangen@uis.no

Katja Mäntylä
Centre for Applied Language Studies, University of Jyväskylä, Finland.
E-mail: katja.mantyla@jyu.fi

Maisa Martin
Centre for Applied Language Studies, University of Jyväskylä, Finland.
E-mail: maisa.martin@jyu.fi

Elena Martín
Autonomous University of Madrid, Spain.
E-mail: elena.martin@uam.es

Ana Martín
Autonomous University of Madrid, Spain.
E-mail: ana.martinmoreno@uam.es

Isabel Martínez   Autonomous University of Madrid, Spain.
                                    E-mail: isabel.martinezalvarez@uam.es

Reinaldo Martínez-Fernández   Autonoma University of Barcelona,
                                    Spain and SINTE Research Group,
                                    Barcelona, Spain.
                                    E-mail: JoseReinaldo.Martinez@uab.cat

Mar Mateos   Autonomous University of Madrid, Spain.
                                    E-mail: mar.mateos@uam.es

Marta Minguela   University of Barcelona, Spain.
                                    E-mail: martaminguela@ub.edu

Mariana Miras   University of Barcelona, Spain.
                                    E-mail: mariana.miras@ub.edu

Noreen S. Moore   The College of New Jersey, USA.
                                    E-mail: nmoore@tcnj.edu

Margunn Mossige   National Centre of Reading Education and
                                    Research, University of Stavanger, Norway.
                                    E-mail: Margunn.mossige@uis.no

Maarit Mutta   Department of French Language, University of
                                    Turku, Finland.
                                    E-mail: maamut@utu.fi

Nicole Nachtwei   Leibniz University Hannover, Germany.
                                    E-mail: nachtwei@psychologie.uni-hannover.de

Astrid Neumann   Institute for German Language and Literature
                                    Education, Leuphana University of Lüneburg,
                                    Germany.
                                    E-mail: aneumann@leuphana.de

Florentina Nicolás Conesa   University of Murcia, Spain.
                                    E-mail: florinc@um.es

Jun O'Hara   San Diego State University, CA, USA.
                                    E-mail: kurizaki@rohan.sdsu.edu

Rannveig Oddsdóttir   School of Education, University of Iceland,
                                    Iceland.
                                    E-mail: rannodd@hi.is

Thierry Olive   Centre de Recherches sur la Cognition et
                                    l'Apprentissage (CeRCA), Université de Poitiers
                                    and CNRS, France.
                                    E-mail: thierry.olive@univ-poitiers.fr

Gunn Helen Ofstad Oxborough   The Reading Centre, University of Stavanger, Norway.
E-mail: gunn.h.oxborough@uis.no

Deilis-Ivonne Pacheco-Sanz   University of León, Spain.
E-mail: dipacs@unileon.es

Åsa Palviainen   Centre for Applied Language Studies, University of Jyväskylä, Finland.
E-mail: asa.palviainen@jyu.fi

Gisella Paoletti   University of Trieste, Italy.
E-mail: paolet@units.it

Marta Pardo   Ramon Llull University, Barcelona, Spain and SINTE Research Group, Barcelona, Spain.
E-mail: Martape@blanquerna.url.edu

Jean-Michel Passerault   Centre de Recherches sur la Cognition et l'Apprentissage (CeRCA), Université de Poitiers and CNRS, France.
E-mail: jean-michel.passerault@univ-poitiers.fr

Luísa Álvares Pereira   Research Centre for Didactics and Technology in Teacher Education, University of Aveiro, Portugal.
E-mail: lpereira@ua.pt

Joan Perera   University of Barcelona, Spain.
E-mail: jperera@ub.edu

Daniel Perrin   Zurich University of Applied Sciences, Winterthur, Switzerland.
E-mail: daniel.perrin@zhaw.ch

Hrafnhildur Ragnarsdóttir   School of Education, University of Iceland, Iceland.
E-mail: hragnars@hi.is

Judy Reilly   San Diego State University, CA, USA; Université de Poitiers, Poitiers, France.
E-mail: reilly1@mail.sdsu.edu

Markus Rheindorf   Department of Linguistics, Vienna University, Austria.
E-mail: markus.rheindorf@univie.ac.at

Gert Rijlaarsdam   University of Amsterdam, Netherlands.
E-mail: g.c.w.rijlaarsdam@uva.nl

Patricia Robledo

Psychology, Sociology and Philosophy
Department, University of León, Spain.
E-mail: probr@unileon.es

Julio Roca de Larios

Universidad de Murcia, Spain.
E-mail: jrl@um.es

Silvia Sacilotto

Department of Developmental Psychology,
University of Padova, Italy.
E-mail: skatasil@gmail.com

Naymé Salas

University of Barcelona, Spain.
E-mail: naymesalas@yahoo.es

Ted Sanders

Utrecht University, Netherlands.
E-mail: T.J.M.Sanders@uu.nl

Michael Schanne

University of Applied Sciences, Winterthur,
Switzerland.
E-mail: michael.schanne@zhaw.ch

Markus Schmitt

University of Education, Heidelberg, Germany.
E-mail: markus.schmitt@ph-heidelberg.de

Lies Sercu

Department of Language and Education,
University of Leuven, Belgium.
E-mail: lies.sercu@arts.kuleuven.be

Cristina Silva

Instituto Superior de Psicologia Aplicada, Lisboa,
Portugal.
E-mail: csilva@ispa.pt

Astrid Skaathun

National Centre for Reading Education and
Research, University of Stavanger, Norway.
E-mail: astrid.skaathun@uis.no

Atle Skaftun

National Centre for Reading Education
and Research, University of Stavanger,
Norway.
E-mail: atle.skaftun@uis.no

Jamie Smith-Spark

Department of Psychology, London South Bank
University, UK.
E-mail: smithspj@lsbu.ac.uk

Isabel Solé

University of Barcelona, Spain.
E-mail: isoleg@ub.edu

Oddny Judith Solheim

University of Stavanger, Norway.
E-mail: Oddny.j.solheim@uis.no

Kristyan Spelman Miller

The University of Winchester, UK.
E-mail: kris.spelmanmiller@winchester.ac.uk

Michaël Steehouder

Department of Technical and Professional
Communication, University of Twente,
Netherlands.
E-mail: M.F.Steehouder@gw.utwente.nl

Kirk Sullivan

Umeå University, Sweden.
E-mail: kirk.sullivan@sprak.umu.se

Mirja Tarnanen

Centre for Applied Language Studies, University
of Jyväskylä, Finland.
E-mail: mirja.tarnanen@jyu.fi

Marion Tillema

Utrecht University, Netherlands.
E-mail: M.Tillema@uu.nl

Liliana Tolchinsky

University of Barcelona, Spain.
E-mail: ltolchinsky@ub.edu

Mark Torrance

Division of Psychology, Nottingham Trent
University, UK.
E-mail: mark.torrance@ntu.ac.uk

Per Henning Uppstad

National Centre for Reading Education and
Research, University of Stavanger, Norway.
E-mail: per.h.uppstad@uis.no

Hans van der Meij

Faculty of Behavioral Science, Twente University,
Netherlands.
E-mail: H.vanderMeij@utwente.nl

Herre van Oostendorp

Center for Content and Knowledge
Engineering, Institute of Information and
Computing Sciences, Utrecht University,
Netherlands.
E-mail: herre@cs.uu.nl

Elke Van Steendam

University of Antwerp/University of Leuven/
University College Brussels, Belgium.
E-mail: elke.vansteendam@telenet.be

Luuk Van Waes

University of Antwerp, Belgium.
E-mail: luuk.vanwaes@ua.ac.be

Daphne van Weijen

Dutch Department/UIL-OTS, Utrecht University,
Netherlands.
E-mail: d.vanweijen@uu.nl

Jean-Luc Velay   Mediterranean Institute for Cognitive
                        Neuroscience, CNRS, University of the
                        Mediterranean, Marseille, France.
                        E-mail: velay@incm.cnrs-mrs.fr

Olga Soler Vilageliu   Grup de Recerca Percepció, Comunicació i Temps,
                        Universitat Autònoma de Barcelona, Barcelona,
                        Spain.
                        E-mail: olga.soler@uab.cat

Ruth Villalón   Autonomous University of Madrid, Spain.
                        E-mail: r.villalon@uam.es

Swantje Weinhold   Institute for German Language and Literature
                        Education, Leuphana University of Lüneburg,
                        Germany.
                        E-mail: weinhold@leuphana.de

Christian Weinzierl   Leibniz University, Hannover, Germany.
                        E-mail: weinzierl@psychologie.uni-hannover.de

Åsa Wengelin   Centre for Languages and Literature, Lund
                        University, Sweden.
                        E-mail: Åsa.Wengelin@ling.lu.se

Marc Wildi   Zurich University of Applied Sciences,
                        Switzerland.
                        E-mail: marc.wildi@zhaw.ch

Darin Woolpert   San Diego State University, CA, USA.
                        E-mail: woolpert@rohan.sdsu.edu

Patricia Wright   School of Psychology, Cardiff University, Wales,
                        UK.
                        E-mail: Wrightp1@cardiff.ac.uk

Beverly Wulfeck   San Diego State University, CA, USA.
                        E-mail: wulfeck@crl.ucsd.edu

Vinzenz Wyss   University of Applied Sciences, Winterthur,
                        Switzerland.
                        E-mail: vinzenz.wyss@zhaw.ch

Foreword: Writing as a Societal Question in Europe

Knowledge sharing is the key to society's economic, social, scientific and cultural development. It is mainly through writing that knowledge is created, shared and acted upon across cultural boundaries. Research into writing in schools and the workplace contributes to the quality of the knowledge cycle. Writing is an extremely varied activity, ranging from jotting down shopping lists, writing school essays, designing blogs and websites to penning novels and monographs. It can be created in various ways (handwriting, keyboarding, dictation, speech synthesis) and contexts (text messages, letters, press releases, essays, poetry, scientific papers, company reports, legal texts, etc.). The common underlying factor is that writing involves the construction of knowledge objects which are shared, understood while the writer is absent, and stored for the future.

Advances in the study of writing can have far-reaching consequences for our understanding of writing processes, of evidence-based teaching methods and of democracy. The long-standing focus on reading skills is consistent with the official line that citizens must primarily be able to understand written information. However, to make their voices heard, readers must also be able to write. With the advent of new information technologies, new curricula and greater specialization in the workplace, written communication has become a vector for integration and success within our society.

In order to improve the teaching and use of writing, there must be continuous development in knowledge of the cognitive and linguistic processes associated with text production by skilled and developing writers, and by text users. Europe has an active and dynamic writing research community that makes a significant contribution to international scientific advances. Nevertheless, for historical, linguistic and cultural reasons, European research is not as unified as in the United States; researchers are relatively isolated and inter-country co-operation could be improved significantly. This means it is difficult to develop comparative studies of writing instruction and to share good practice and sharing knowledge across boundaries.

Overcoming this problem requires (i) the creation of a European platform that spans the gap between 'regional' research cultures, promoting co-operation and providing high-quality scientific data. This will permit (ii) the dissemination of recommendations on writing to a broad spectrum of end users — schools, universities, workplaces, citizens.

The COST Action IS0703 'European Research Network on Learning to Write Effectively' (ERN-LWE) represents an efficient and effective route to achieve this twofold objective. By co-operation between research teams from different states that are already investigating writing (or are planning to do so) ERN-LWE permits the development of an active, open network, based on the commitment of researchers and boosted by regular scientific events, meetings and junior researchers' training. ERN-LWE and its constitutive tools (working groups, short term scientific missions, conference, training schools, workshops) are of invaluable assistance and accelerate the emergence of a European writing network, bringing concrete results from studies already underway and stimulating new ones in countries which do not yet have structured writing research. Strong links between researchers and professionals (teachers, educators, technical writers, administrators, etc.) will ensure that recommendations about how to write effectively will penetrate many areas of European society.

The Action's research and innovation effort focuses on four areas, each associated with one of four working groups, and with the following aims:

– Early acquisition of writing skills in education: describing the acquisition of writing by pupils with or without learning difficulties in their mother tongue and a second language; understanding learning difficulties; analysing the impact of teaching situations.
– Improvements in written communication, in education and in the workplace: describing the development of different writing skills in two languages; understanding the factors favouring the development of expertise; comparing and designing specific and appropriate training situations.
– Design of written documents in the workplace: describing how professional writers manage their skills and knowledge; improving documents' communicative impact; modelling expertise.
– Technological advances in writing tools: developing and standardising technological tools for studying and fostering the writing process.

This book is an original and interesting presentation of the main research conducted by the COST Action 'ERN-LWE' inside these four areas. I hope that readers will find it interesting and through it they will discover the richness of European writing research and its contribution to broader European social issues.

Denis Alamargot
Chair of the COST Action IS0703
European Research Network on Learning to
Write Effectively – ERN-LWE
www.cost-lwe.eu

Introduction: Why We Need Writing Research

This volume gives an overview of a large number of research programmes spread across 15 European countries, each focused on understanding the nature of writing competence, how writing competence develops or how writing competence can best be taught. This volume of research is, in itself, testament to the perceived need for better understanding of writing and writing processes. Written production is, and is likely to remain, ubiquitous both as a learning and assessment tool in education and as a means of communication in the wider world. While the nature of media through which we gather and disseminate information is in rapid flux there is no evidence that text, as the mode of communication, has diminished in importance. If anything, its important is growing.

However, just because the large number of researchers who have contributed to this book (and their funders) perceive a need for greater understanding of written production, this does not mean that their perception is correct. People have been writing, in varying numbers, and with varying degrees of competence, since pre-history. Teachers tasked with teaching writing have, themselves, been able to write from a young age. Many millions of words are expended each year in discussing the merits or otherwise of particular texts. Many authors have documented their writing processes. In one sense, every literate person has first-hand understanding of the writing process. Writing researchers know this to their cost. Whatever findings may suggest, there is always someone in the audience happy to tell them that their own experiences differ.

So, do we need research exploring effective writing? The answer is yes (of course). There is a clear case for ongoing writing research, both from a basic-science perspective, and because we need to know how it is best taught.

The processes by which people produce coherent text are poorly understood. Arguably even if findings from this research did not have direct application to teaching policy and practice, it would still be worth investigating. The ability to write is both ubiquitous and not easily explained. It comprises a complex set of cognitive processes and mechanisms involving processing of meaning, vocabulary, syntax, spelling and movement. Only a small part of this processing is available to introspection (can be explored by asking writers to think about and report on their own cognitive processes). Understanding how people write is in itself a worthwhile scientific focus.

For some reason, however, writing has been largely ignored by the psychological and psycholinguistic research communities. Humans engage in four kinds of language activity: Language is comprehended either through listening or reading, and is produced either through speech or writing. Psychologists have explored textual input (reading) and spoken output (speech) but have given little attention to spoken input (listening) and have largely ignored textual output (writing). A quick search of all parts of the *Journal of Experimental Psychology* (one of the main outlets for high quality cognitive psychological research) between 1990 and 2010 yields 10 papers, out of a total of about 8100 that focus on motor processing during writing (handwriting or typing) and just two papers that focus on higher-level writing processes. This contrasts with upwards of 320 papers that focus on reading and a similar number that explore speaking. The spoken production literature reports a large body of empirical evidence and sophisticated and testable theories. The current consensus in the literature is that progress has been made, but many important questions still lack clear answers.

Study of basic processes in text production has not, by contrast, developed as a separate, clearly identified strand of psychological research. Within the experimental literature there are a number of studies exploring motor processing during typing (e.g. Gentner, Larochelle, & Grudin, 1988) and, more recently, research programmes exploring psycholinguist processes in single word production (Bonin, Peereman, & Fayol, 2001; Damian, Bowers, Stadthagen-Gonzalez, & Spalek, 2010). However, there is not, for example, a text-production parallel to the growing body of studies exploring planning scope in spoken sentence production (Martin, Crowther, Knight, Tamborello, & Yang, 2010; Smith & Wheeldon, 1999). When planning is discussed in the writing literature it has tended to be seen as a discrete, macro-level process which, historically at least, has been theorised as thinking and reasoning rather than as a psycholinguistic activity (Flower & Hayes, 1980 and subsequent papers).

One possible reason for the lack of attention given to basic writing processes in the psychological literature is that there isn't anything much to explain. It may be that findings from research exploring speech, which after all is an earlier-developing and therefore more fundamental language activity, also tell us what we need to know about writing. Speech researchers have a habit of using the terms 'language production' and 'speech production' interchangeably, suggesting that their findings are relatively independent of output medium. This may be the true, but it is not self-evidently so. Unlike speech, writing involves spelling and is created in the absence immediate audience feedback thus placing additional demands on the writer both in lexical retrieval (or post-retrieval processing) and in generating content and maintaining coherence. On the plus side writers can pause when they want to without damaging the final communicational effect of their text, and they have access to a permanent, visible record of their previous output. It is, therefore, at least plausible that the basic processes underlying text production are interestingly different from speech. Research is needed to establish whether or not this is actually the case and, where necessary, develop theories of language-via-writing that differ from theories of language-via-speech. Recent edited collections provide some pointers towards future development in this area (Berninger, 2011; Fayol, Alamargot, & Berninger, 2012).

The second reason that we need writing research, and the dominant motivation behind the research reported in this volume, is that we need to understand how best to teach students (children, adolescents and adults) how to communicate in writing. Cross-national research exploring achievement in written composition is made difficult by the fact that there is considerable variation across educational systems in the value placed on different aspects of the written product: What constitutes good text varies, to some extent, from country to country. Because of this the International Association for the Evaluation of Educational Achievement (IAE; Purves, 1992) concluded, after a large cross-national study of competence in written composition in school-age learners, that writing cannot be considered a general cognitive capacity or activity. The IAE survey also failed to find evidence that instructional practices within that classroom explained variation in students' performance.

The IAE's conclusions highlight the challenges faced by researchers seeking to make cross-national performance comparisons, or just to communicate their findings to audiences who are not familiar with the educational context in which the research was conducted. It also reflects negatively both on the quality of writing instruction at the time the study was conducted (or perhaps the value of any classroom intervention specifically focused on improving writing) and, more generally, on the potential for making any general claims about how writing instruction might be improved. If written composition in different contexts is associated with largely different underlying cognitive mechanisms, then findings from research exploring writing development and writing instruction will not have value to practitioners outside of the specific context in which that research was conducted.

This position is, however, overly pessimistic. There is evidence that some findings at least are surprisingly stable across educational contexts. This is even true for research exploring the efficacy of specific, whole-class interventions. Evaluations of interventions based in Self-Regulated Strategy Development (SRSD; Harris & Graham, 1996) illustrate this well. SRSD is a form of writing instruction that aims to teach general meta-cognitive (strategic, self-regulatory) skills that learners then apply to their own writing processes. It has proved very effective in developing writing competence in school children across a broad range of abilities and ages within the US educational system. Subsequent studies have shown that interventions based on SRSD are similarly effective in both Germany (Glaser & Brunstein, 2007) and Spain (Torrance, Fidalgo, & Garcia, 2007).

Findings of this kind suggest that, contrary to the IAE's conclusions, there are commonalities across educational cultures in the processes underlying written composition and therefore in the ways in which teachers should intervene to encourage better writing. It remains possible, of course, that findings from particular studies are highly context dependent. However, there is evidence for a core of underlying cognitive skills that are common across language and culture. Research that explicitly explores the dimensions on which writing instruction and students' texts vary across language and educational culture is valuable in this regard (e.g.

Tolchinsky & Perera, this volume) in that it informs when and how findings can be generalized across contexts.

Writing has been important focus of educationally oriented research over the last two or more decades. Of the 2176 papers in the *Journal of Educational Psychology* published between 1980 and 2010, 50 or more had a specific focus on written production. Educationally oriented writing research has explored two broad and overlapping research questions. One concerns the correlates of writing development. What skills, knowledge and cognitive capacities are present in children who write well (and absent in children who do not)? Findings from this research can generate hypotheses about basic processes in writing, and also inform writing instruction. For example, measures of language ability and of working memory capacity appear to independently predict writing performance in young writers (e.g. Swanson & Berninger, 1996). Despite (or even because of) thorough knowledge of what constitutes good text, developing writers may fail to write well because capacity restrictions limit their ability to apply this knowledge during production.

This kind of finding suggests that writing instruction (a) needs to avoid setting students tasks that overload their cognitive capacity (that involve thinking of too many things at once), and (b) should provide students with "divide and conquer" strategies that allow them to marshal relevant knowledge in a systematic and non-overloading way. This first point has been emphasized by Rijlaarsdam and co-workers (Rijlaarsdam & Couzijn, 2000) in their discussion of the 'double challenge' associated with the kinds of tasks typically used in writing instruction. Learner-writers find each new writing task intrinsically demanding. Expecting them to also consider and apply new, explicit, discourse knowledge — new rules about what is expected in their final text — may well be too much for them to the detriment both of their learning and of the quality of the text that they are writing. This is likely, in turn, to affect their beliefs about their writing self-efficacy, and therefore their motivation on subsequent tasks, particularly for students towards the bottom of the class. Findings of a meta-analysis by Graham and Perin (2007) of studies evaluating different forms of writing instruction can be understood in terms of this double-challenge idea. The most successful forms of instruction tend to (a) combine teaching discourse knowledge with strategies that make students structure and sequence their students writing processes, (b) give students simplified writing tasks (summary writing, sentence combining) or (c) involve classroom tasks that scaffold the writing process (peer assistance, word processing). Isolated teaching of grammar or of discourse models appears to be of substantially less benefit.

There is, however, a lot that we do not know both about the effects of writing instruction — what kinds of instruction work with children at which educational stage, and in which educational contexts — and about the mechanisms by which these results are achieved. Graham and Perrin identified 11 different forms of intervention, evaluated in upwards of 120 studies. These interventions included everything from simple one-session scaffolding (e.g. asking students to plan in advance of producing a text) to comprehensive classroom approaches that a teacher might adopt to the exclusion of most other writing instruction. The most successful of the latter approaches — the SRSD approach discussed above — involves a complex set of different instructional methods and classroom tasks. Little is known, to date, about which of these components are necessary and/or sufficient for intervention success. From a practical point of view this impacts efficiency of delivery. Do all components need to be included in all instruction for all students, or can some be omitted and others emphasized without detriment to the intervention's overall effect? From a theoretical point of view, it makes it difficult to unpick the mechanisms by which these interventions are effective. This in turn means that it is difficult to construct informed hypotheses that generalize the findings from evaluations to students in different age groups and educational contexts.

The above discussion is biased by my own interests as a writing researcher and gives only a selective overview of the kinds of questions that require answering about basic processes in writing and about how writing might best be taught. It notably omits mention of research exploring what constitutes effective text in different contexts, and of the ways in which children at the very early stages of writing development develop spelling knowledge. Both of these are important foci of the research described in this volume. Even with these omissions it should be clear that our understanding of the nature and development of writing skill is far from complete. This book provides a snapshot of current or recent research exploring a wide range of ideas, theories and practices around written text production. Readers will soon realize that considerable progress has already been made towards understand writing and writing instruction, and that extensive, serious and scientific effort is focussed on the many unresolved questions.

Our strategy in putting together this volume was to invite European researchers from a broad range of disciplines brought together under the EU COST IS0703 European Research Network on Learning to Write Effectively (ERN-LWE) to contribute short papers summarizing their current activity. The response was impressive and we were able to include 89 contributions. All papers had to deal with some aspect of the form or production of written text, and to show evidence of research rigour. We accepted papers that described completed research, ongoing research, or research that was just beginning. We allowed contributions of, at most, 1000 words and authors were not permitted to cite more than five publications. We specifically asked them to cite their own work in preference to that of others, where it was appropriate to do so. We adopted a light-touch approach to editing.

The resulting volume should, therefore, provide a tantalizing tour of the main themes in European writing research. We make no claims to completeness, although we believe that most European research groups who would identify written production as a main focus are represented. Also, the papers themselves will in most cases fall short of a full treatment of the authors' work. There should, however, be enough detail to awaken readers' interest. If this is the case then we encourage you to contact the authors directly to find out how their work is progressing. Author contact details are listed at beginning of the book. Doing so is particularly important given the greater-than-desired lag between our call for papers and final publication (probably an inevitable consequence of a project of this size).

Why specifically European writing research? Over and above the obvious reason that the network that brought together the researchers represented in this volume was funded by the EU taxpayer, there are positive reasons why a European-specific collection is valuable. Historically, there is a strong tradition of process-oriented writing research in Europe. The ERN-LWE network capitalized on existing relationships among European research groups brought together by the Writing special interest group of the European Association for Research on Learning and Instruction. This runs a long-established biannual conference that acts as a focus for research on writing both within and beyond Europe. More recently, this has spawned the *Journal of Writing Research* (www.jowr.org) as an outlet for high quality peer-reviewed scientific writing research. Interaction among writing researchers across different languages and educational cultures forces acknowledgement of these differences. Where findings from research in different countries agree, then this is a pointer towards underlying, fundamental characteristics of writing and educational processes. Where they do not, they this prompts further investigation of the culture-specific factors that mediate the nature and development of writing competence.

The papers in this volume are grouped around the four main themes that are the focus of the four workgroups of the ERN-LWE network. Each section is preceded by an introduction written by workgroup co-ordinators. These introductory chapters provide a detailed summary of section content, and I recommend them to readers wanting a general overview of the kinds of themes that European researchers are addressing. The first section deals with issues around the development of basic ('low-level') writing skills, mainly in the early years of education. The second section, which appropriately is by far the largest, focuses directly on issues around the teaching and learning of writing. This is divided into five parts that describe (1) evaluations of different forms of writing instruction, (2) research exploring the processes by which writers learn, (3) methods of text assessment in educational contexts, (4) research exploring the effects of various learner and teacher variables on the development of writing skill and (5) conceptions of and variation in educational text genres. The third section reports research exploring effective document design. The final section has a main focus on tools for exploring the writing process, illustrated with descriptions of process-oriented research.

As co-ordinating editor I would like to thank my co-editors for their time and patience in structuring and reviewing their sections and, of course, the very large number of researchers who contributed papers to this volume. This is also a good opportunity to express my gratitude, on behalf of the many people involved in the ERN-LWE network, to the various members of the steering committee, and particularly Denis Alamargot as chair, for the very considerable, difficult and often unrewarded work that they have put into making the network the success that it has been. The various and extensive activities of the network, this volume included, demonstrate that European writing research is in rude health, and offers considerable promise for the future.

Mark Torrance

References

Berninger, V. (Ed.) (2011). *Past, present, and future contributions of cognitive writing research to cognitive psychology*. New York, NY: Routledge.

Bonin, P., Peereman, R., & Fayol, M. (2001). Do phonological codes constrain the selection of orthographic codes in written picture naming? *Journal of Memory and Language, 45*(4), 688–720.

Damian, M. F., Bowers, J. S., Stadthagen-Gonzalez, H., & Spalek, K. (2010). Does word length affect speech onset latencies when producing single words? *Journal of Experimental Psychology-Learning Memory and Cognition, 36*(4), 892–905.

Fayol, M., Alamargot, D., & Berninger, V. (Eds.). (2012). *Translation of thought to written text while composing*. New York, NY: Routledge.

Flower, L. S., & Hayes, J. R. (1980). The dynamics of composing: Making plans and juggling constraints. In L. W. Gregg & E. R. Steinberg (Eds.), *Cognitive processes in writing* (pp. 31–50). Hillsdale, NJ: Erlbaum.

Gentner, D. R., Larochelle, S., & Grudin, J. (1988). Lexical, sublexical, and peripheral effects in skilled typewriting. *Cognitive Psychology, 20*(4), 524–548.

Glaser, C., & Brunstein, J. C. (2007). Improving fourth-grade students' composition skills: Effects of strategy instruction and self-regulation procedures. *Journal of Educational Psychology, 99*(2), 297–310.

Graham, S., & Perin, D. (2007). A meta-analysis of writing instruction for adolescent students. *Journal of Educational Psychology, 99*(3), 445–476.

Harris, K. R., & Graham, S. (1996). *Making the writing process work: Strategies for composing and self-regulation*. Cambridge, MA: Brookline.

Martin, R. C., Crowther, J. E., Knight, M., Tamborello, F. P., & Yang, C. L. (2010). Planning in sentence production: Evidence for the phrase as a default planning scope. *Cognition, 116*(2), 177–192.

Purves, A. C. (Ed.) (1992). *The IEA study of written composition II: Education and performance in fourteen countries*. Oxford: Pergamon Press.

Rijlaarsdam, G., & Couzijn, M. (2000). Writing and learning to write: A double challenge. In R. J. Simons (Ed.), *New learning*. Dordrecht: Kluwer.

Smith, M., & Wheeldon, L. (1999). High level processing scope in spoken sentence production. *Cognition, 73*(3), 205–246.

Swanson, H. L., & Berninger, V. W. (1996). Individual differences in children's working memory and writing skill. *Journal of Experimental Child Psychology, 63*(2), 358–385.

Torrance, M., Fidalgo, R., & Garcia, J. N. (2007). The teachability and effectiveness of cognitive self-regulation in sixth grade writers. *Learning and Instruction, 17*(3), 265–285.

SECTION 1

WRITING DEVELOPMENT

Chapter 1.00.01

Introduction: Writing Development

Liliana Tolchinsky

The study of writing from a developmental perspective inquires about the particular ways in which knowledge of writing evolves over time. The term writing, however, has multiple meanings. It can be employed for referring to a cultural practice that fulfills different functions — writing can be used, for example for mnemonic, religious or poetic functions. It can also refer to the notational system used in these practices (i.e. the writing system). For writing we may use alphabetic systems, abjads or logographic systems. Within each of these writing systems there are particular spelling systems such as French orthography or English orthography within the alphabetic system. Finally, the term writing can be applied to the discourse genres resulting from that practice (academic writing, narrative writing and so forth).

As a consequence of the multiple senses of writing its developmental study covers a wide range of topics, from socio-cultural considerations about the conceptualization of the functions of writing, through the study of the infra-lexical processes that are put into play for spelling in different orthographies, up to the lexical, syntactic and discourse concerns that are set in motion for composing a text. All of these diverse topics can be approached developmentally.

Moreover, writing is a cultural, institutionally supported practice; children learn to write at school. Their evolving notions about the functions of writing, the way in which they handle the spelling system of their language and their grasp of the different genres of discourse are unavoidably intertwined with schooling. Thus, a developmental approach to writing should also consider the role of the classroom context and the teaching practices on the various dimensions of writing.

In addition to the multiple topics that can be approached developmentally and to the need to consider the role of schooling in this development, we should also take into account the huge range of individual differences that appear in the process of learning how to write. Some of the individual differences have a recognized etiology,

Learning to Write Effectively: Current Trends in European Research
Studies in Writing, Volume 25, 3–6
Copyright © 2012 by Emerald Group Publishing Limited
All rights of reproduction in any form reserved
ISSN: 1572-6304/doi:10.1108/S1572-6304(2012)0000025005

but others result from still unknown causes. In any case, the study of atypical processes of learning offers a natural laboratory for exploring the many perceptual, motor and cognitive abilities that may account for learning the functions of writing, a particular spelling system or the features of a particular type of text.

The reports included in this section illustrate the diversity of topics that can be approached developmentally. Olga Soler Vilageliu, Sonia Kandel and Melina Aparici Aznar (*Early Development of Handwriting Motor Skills*) aim at investigating longitudinally how children acquire the basic handwriting skills in pre-school and early years at school. The studies were carried out in Barcelona, where the language taught at school is Catalan. Catalan has a transparent orthography and a syllabic structure. One of the main questions of the study is to find out the extent to which these two features, one orthographic the other one phonological, are reflected in the development of handwriting.

The following three chapters focus on spelling acquisition. The study reported by Marie-Claire Hazard, Bruno De Cara and Lucile Chanquoy (*Effects of Orthographic Consistency on Children's Spelling Development*) deals with the effect of a particular orthography not on the development of handwriting but on children's own spelling. In this article the selected orthography is French, a far less transparent system than Catalan. The study's main goal is to test whether children create an internal consistency in their own spelling (termed empirical consistency in this study) that differs from the consistency found in the spelling system (theoretical consistency). The results of the study showed that theoretical consistency had maximum effects on child's empirical consistency in grades 4 and 5 and was amplified for low-frequency words.

In the following chapter, *Acquisition of Spelling Skills with Regard to the Norwegian Language*, Astrid Skaathun and Per Henning Uppstad report several studies they have found developmental which rely as much on word frequency as on regularity. They stress the importance of studying spelling in the context of children's own composition — and therefore own word-choice — as well as in traditional writing-from-dictation, and suggest that studying spelling in the more authentic context provides a rather different picture of how spelling skills develop.

Cristina Silva and Margarida Alves (*The Impact of Open and Closed Vowels on the Evolution of Pre-School Children's Writing*) describe research in which children's spelling performance was evaluated not in terms of a simple correct/incorrect dichotomy, but whether after training they had developed skills for discriminating consonant sounds and matching them to their relevant graphemes, even when the spelling of the word as a whole might be invented. An intervention in which children wrote words with a specific set of initial consonants resulted in better performance than a reading-focused control. Importantly, effects generalized to consonants not taught in the intervention, suggesting that written production (and not reading-based instruction) can lead to developing more general skills for phoneme–grapheme mappings.

The next three chapters broadly concern the effects of different tasks on students' writing performance. The report by Christian Weinzierl, Joachim Grabowski and Markus Schmitt (*Copying Ability in Primary School: A Working Memory Approach*) focused on the analysis of one of the activities that are frequently used in schools in relation to writing, mainly with small children: copying. However, as the title of the chapter suggests, the researchers' goals are to explore the development of this ability from grades 2 to 4 to determine which parts of working memory are involved in the copying of patterns from different symbol systems (letters, numbers) and to identify the strategies used by students to efficiently employ their working memory capacity. The study demonstrates that copying strategies of primary school children are sensitive to the referential features of different symbol systems. Symbol systems that include semantic and phonological information are copied faster than symbol systems which contain less information.

The research reported by Lucie Beauvais, Monik Favart, Jean-Michel Passerault and Thierry Olive (*Acquisition of Linearization in Writing, from Grades 5 to 9*) was concerned with the ways in which manipulating task demands — specifically the requirement to pre-plan before writing full text, interacts with the genre of the text that is being produced and with the age of the writer. They found that only older children (ninth grade as compared to seventh grade and younger) benefited from this manipulation. This was shown both in their production fluency and in the quality of their final texts.

In *Construct-Relevant or Construct-Irrelevant Variance in Measures of Reading?* Oddny Judith Solheim and Per Henning Uppstad describe research that suggests that performance on tests that ostensibly measure reading performance, but that involve students writing about what they have read, is improved by increasing the salience of audience demands. However, early findings suggest that this affect seems to be limited to students who already have high reading self-efficacy.

Liliana Tolchinsky and Joan Perera in their chapter *Studying Written Language Development in Different Contexts, Languages and Writing systems* present three lines of work. The first centres on teacher practices for teaching literacy and shows that the encouragement of autonomous writing from the beginning of school is a main distinguishing feature between profiles of practices. The second discusses language specific influence in Moroccan and Chinese learning to write in an alphabetic system. Finally, the third line of work focuses on the development of the written lexicon of Catalan children throughout compulsory school and on the linguistic strategies used by French and Spanish speakers from age 9 to adulthood to create a detached discourse stance in expository texts.

The last three reports examine individual differences in learning to write and both are centred in text writing rather than on isolate words or sentences. Julie Dockrell, Vincent Connelly, Geoff Lindsay and Clare Mackie (*The Impact of Oral Language Skills on Children's Production of Written Text*) present a series of studies investigating how specific limitations in oral language skills such as vocabulary, phonology or grammar impact on children's written text production. These studies showed that restricted levels of vocabulary, poor phonological skills and language levels serve to constrain different aspects of composition. Vocabulary levels impact directly on idea generation both concurrently and overtime; grammatical understanding explained variability in text complexity while handwriting fluency remained a particular difficulty for our participants and directly affected writing performance.

This theme is continued in a paper by Judy Reilly, Jun O'Hara, Darin Woolpert, Naymé Salas, Beverly Wulfeck and Liliana Tolchinsky (*The Development of Written Language in Children with Language Impairment*) which explores the effects of specific language impairment — children showing very poor spoken language skills but normal IQ relative to typically developing peers — on the writing of narrative and expository text. They found that language impaired children's writing was more error prone with more morphological and phonologically improbable spelling errors. However, when writing narratives their use of syntax was no less complex than that found in the writing of typically developing peers.

Finally, Barbara Arfé, Pietro Boscolo and Silvia Sacilotto (*Improving Anaphoric Cohesion in Deaf Students' Writing*) focus on the use of devices for establishing and maintaining cohesion — in particular nominal referential systems. First and second year deaf students tend to prefer full lexical reference instead of the use of pronouns or ellipsis. The study presents preliminary results of an intervention study that shows how sentence-combining training, focused on inter-sentential cohesion, can be effective in fostering the use of mature anaphoric reference strategies in these young writers, who do not tend to benefit from more traditional interventions.

Taken together, papers in this section provide a snapshot of current European research in writing development.

Chapter 1.00.02

Early Development of Handwriting Motor Skills

Olga Soler Vilageliu, Sonia Kandel and
Melina Aparici Aznar

Most studies of children's handwriting acquisition focused on the elementary school years, and there is scarce information about the development of writing skills before that time. This study aimed at investigating how children acquire the basic handwriting skills in pre-school and early years at school. We ran two longitudinal studies on the development of handwriting skills. Both studies were carried out in Barcelona, where the language taught at school is Catalan. Catalan has a transparent orthography and a syllabic structure.

The first study concerned 18 children in a pre-school class over two academic years. The children (10 boys and 8 girls) were 4 years old when the study started. At that time they were able to write their names and knew most of the letters of the alphabet in upper case. None of them was able to read.

The children had to copy 10 familiar 6-letter words that appeared on a computer screen in upper case letters, on an unlined sheet of A5 paper attached to the surface of a digitizer (Wacom Tablet, Intuos2) using an ink pen. Half of the words were disyllabic and the other half were trisyllabic. We recorded data from seven different sessions from February 2008 to the end of May 2009.

The first analyses of the data included the first three sessions (February, April and June 2008). We used online graphomotor and perceptual measures taken while the participants copied words. These measures include temporal measures (time needed to write letters and words, time spent on movements in the air during the writing of a word); trajectory measures (writing length, number of segments); motor measures (dysfluency or number of velocity maxima, pressure exerted with the pen) and finally,

Learning to Write Effectively: Current Trends in European Research
Studies in Writing, Volume 25, 7–9
ISSN: 1572-6304/doi:10.1108/S1572-6304(2012)0000025006

the number of times the gaze is lifted to see the target word again, as a perceptual measure. The results indicated that the time needed to write a word decreased smoothly between February and June. The time spent on movements in the air was similar between February and April but decreased significantly in June, showing that children improved their motor planning. Furthermore, in June the children wrote the words using fewer segments and the dysfluency of their movements decreased. It is interesting to note that in June the average number of gaze lifts per word was less than five, that is the children did not need to look at each letter of the word in order to copy it. They learned to collect chunks of information by gathering more than one letter at each glance.

Globally, these results indicate an improvement in motor planning during handwriting, and consequently a better control in the handwriting movements, which become progressively smoother (Soler & Kandel, 2009b).

A second analysis was conducted of the inter-letter intervals (ILIs), that is the time that the pen is lifted between the letters of a word. It has been previously reported that children's handwriting movements are programmed according to linguistic units such as syllables (Kandel & Valdois, 2006a, 2006b) and graphemes (Kandel, Soler, Valdois, & Gros, 2006). In this analysis, we compared the production of disyllabic and trisyllabic words in the last three data collection sessions (January, March and May 2009). The results revealed that the syllable structure of the words progressively determines the timing of their motor execution. At the beginning, the words are mostly produced according to a letter-by-letter writing strategy. In contrast, during the last sessions the children start programming their handwriting movements according to the syllabic structure of the words. As elementary children, the inter-syllable intervals are longer than the inter-letter intervals. These results are in line with previous findings on the planning of handwriting movements (Soler & Kandel, 2009a).

A third analysis was done taking the data obtained in the first session (February), the middle session (November) and the last session (June). This analysis examined the percentage of time of writing, the percentage of time writing in the air, fluency, number of segments, number of gaze lifts and pressure. The results show a significant increase in the percentage of writing along the three sessions, with a decrease of the time In Air. The pressure decreases substantially, especially between November and June, and the number of gaze lifts shows a smooth slope. Interestingly, the fluency is lower in November than in June, suggesting that there is some factor that hinders the performance of writing. It is likely that this factor is the access to linguistic information, since at this time almost all the children are able to read. We are preparing the publication of these data.

We are carrying out a second longitudinal study that concerns children in their first and second years of elementary school, when they are 6 and 7 years old. The first year at elementary school is important for children's handwriting because they have to master the cursive characters. Cursive characters entail new difficulties for young learners, because they are not supposed to lift the pen between letters when writing a whole word. This implies that the movements for writing new letters have to be programmed in parallel while they are writing the previous ones. Our aim is to study the development of handwriting skills during this period of time, using the same measures as in the aforementioned study. The participants are 25 children at the same school in Barcelona, and they copy 20 familiar 6-letter words (10 disyllabic and 10 trisyllabic) that appear in upper case letters on the computer screen. They have to transcribe these words in cursive letters. We collected data in December 2008, March, June and November 2009, and March and June 2010. We are currently running analyses of the data.

Acknowledgement

This project is supported by a grant from the Spanish Ministry of Science and Innovation, ref. SEJ2007-64918.

References

Kandel, S., Soler, O., Valdois, S., & Gros, C. (2006). Graphemes as motor units in the acquisition of writing skills. *Reading and Writing*, *19*(3), 313–337.

Kandel, S., & Valdois, S. (2006a). French and Spanish-speaking children use different visual and motor units during spelling acquisition. *Language and Cognitive Processes*, *21*(5), 531–561.

Kandel, S., & Valdois, S. (2006b). Syllables as functional units in a copying task. *Language and cognitive processes*, *21*(4), 432–452.

Soler, O., & Kandel, S. (2009a). Factores lingüísticos en la programación del trazo en la escritura infantil: Importancia de la estructura silábica. *Infancia y Aprendizaje*, *32*(2), 189–198.

Soler, O., & Kandel, S. (2009b). Early development of writing skills: A longitudinal study with pre-school writers. Paper presented at the 14th Conference of the International Graphonomics Society, 13–16 September, Dijon, France.

Chapter 1.00.03

Effects of Orthographic Consistency on Children's Spelling Development

Marie-Claire Hazard, Bruno De Cara and
Lucile Chanquoy

Although French orthography is broadly viewed as an inconsistent mapping from sounds to letters (Caravolas, 2006), surprisingly little work has been done on the effects of orthographic consistency on the development of children's spelling in French. As part of lexical statistics, phoneme-to-grapheme inconsistency has been computed from a developmental perspective through children's reading books as a function of age (Manulex-infra: Peereman, Lété, & Sprenger-Charolles, 2007). The results showed that French children were early exposed to inconsistent words when acquiring literacy (Lété, Peereman, & Fayol, 2008).

   The aim of this study was to investigate variability that can be assigned to individual development in children's spelling consistency. Indeed, we assume that orthographic consistency or lexical statistics that can be computed from theoretical lexicons are under-specified in the child's mind, at least at the beginning. So, our goal was to follow the gap between theoretical lexicons and the child's empiric lexicon across spelling development. To do so, a new measure we called 'empiric consistency' for assessing child's consistency within her/his own spelling was created. This measure coded rime spelling consistency (i.e. similarity), within the same child, across pairs of words that had the same spoken rhyme. Pairs of words were dictated to children. When the same spelling was produced within the pair, child's empiric consistency was coded '1'; when different spellings were produced within the pair, it was coded '0' (this measure was irrespective of orthographic accuracy). Pairs of words were tested as a function of theoretical orthographic consistency computed from lexical statistics through three levels: (i) *fully consistent spelling* (i.e. only one

Learning to Write Effectively: Current Trends in European Research
Studies in Writing, Volume 25, 11–13
Copyright © 2012 by Emerald Group Publishing Limited
All rights of reproduction in any form reserved
ISSN: 1572-6304/doi:10.1108/S1572-6304(2012)0000025007

possible spelling in lexicon, as for k<u>it</u>/s<u>it</u>); (ii) *pseudo-consistent spelling* (i.e. same spelling within the pair but other possible spellings in lexicon, as for fl<u>eet</u>/str<u>eet</u>); (iii) *inconsistent spelling* (i.e. different spellings within the pair, as for b<u>oat</u>/n<u>ote</u>).

A cross-sectional study was carried out. Words were dictated within sentences to children aged from 6 to 14 (20 participants by age group). Words within a pair were dictated during two separate sessions (one-week break between sessions). The main prediction was the following: if children use grapheme-phoneme correspondence rules at the beginning of learning to read and spell, child's empiric consistency should approach the value '1' in beginning spellers (whatever response accuracy). Actually, the opposite trend was found: child's empiric consistency was much lower than expected (approx. mean 0.50) during the first year of spelling tuition for all pairs of words (cf. Figure 1).

In addition, the results showed that child's empiric consistency was higher for words with theoretical consistent spellings (only one possible spelling, e.g. kit/sit) than for words with theoretical inconsistent spellings (e.g. boat/note). Similarly, child's empirical spelling was more consistent for fully consistent pairs (e.g. kit/sit) rather for pseudo-consistent pairs (e.g. fleet/street). Generally speaking, theoretical consistency had maximum effects on child's empirical consistency in grades 4 and 5 and was amplified for low-frequency words.

Other experimental results equally revealed lexical effects on child's empiric consistency. Firstly, children were less consistent with their own spelling for pairs of pseudo-words rather than for pairs of words. Secondly, child's empiric consistency was higher within the same word rather than between two different words. These results were collected as part of the first author's PhD dissertation and need to be submitted for publication. However, at least two main conclusions can be drawn. Firstly, children showed early sensibility to inconsistent phoneme-to-sound mappings

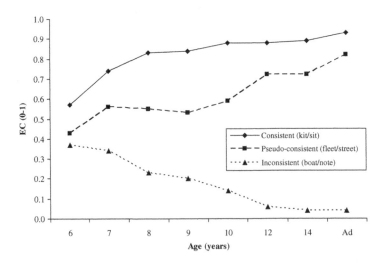

Figure 1: Child's empiric consistency in spelling as a function of age.

in French. They are able to replicate theoretical inconsistency in their own spelling as soon as the first year of spelling tuition. Secondly, developmental models of lexical acquisition should take into account both lexical statistics and child's empiric consistency in written production for a better understanding of lexical factors in spelling development (Pacton, Fayol, & Perruchet, 2005).

References

Caravolas, M. (2006). Learning to spell in different languages: How orthographies variables might affect early literacy. In R. M. Joshi & P. G. Aaron (Eds.), *Handbook of orthography and literacy* (pp. 498–511). Mahwah, NJ: Lawrence Erlbaum Publishers.

Lété, B., Peereman, R., & Fayol, M. (2008). Consistency and word-frequency effects on spelling among first- to fifth-grade French children: A regression-based study. *Journal of Memory and Language, 58*(4), 952–977.

Pacton, S., Fayol, M., & Perruchet, P. (2005). Children's implicit learning of graphotactic and morphological regularities. *Child Development, 76*(2), 324–339.

Peereman, R., Lété, B., & Sprenger-Charolles, L. (2007). Manulex-infra: Distributional characteristics of grapheme-phoneme mappings, and infralexical and lexical units in child-directed written material. *Behavior Research Methods, 39*(3), 579–589.

Chapter 1.00.04

Acquisition of Spelling Skills with Regard to the Norwegian Language

Astrid Skaathun and Per Henning Uppstad

Spelling is not learned at any particular occasion. Spelling skill is normally acquired and developed over a period of several years. It can be performed both orally and in writing, but the concept is in our connection used about the written mode and as synonym of word writing. Another complicating factor is that spelling skill, as it is expressed in authentic writing situations, comes out differently from the spelling that can be observed during dictation writing. We have therefore identified a useful skill concept which differentiates between acquired skill and the performed quality of the skill in question (Tønnessen, 1999). Acquired skill is relatively stable, whereas performed skill is more dependent on the context. For instance, cognitive attention can be directed towards single words in a dictation situation, whereas free text writing implies that attention must be directed towards other aspects. Since spelling as such adds little value in addition to the written communication, functional spelling skill will only be expressed in authentic writing situations. Dictations may, however, too a larger extent disclose spelling skill which is more in accordance with the acquired spelling skill.

In addition, Tønnessen (1999) claims that a skill always consists of a flexible combination of automatization and consciousness. In our opinion, this line of thinking represents a valuable addition to our understanding of spelling. Acquired spelling skill can be performed with a high degree of automatization as a consequence of experiences. Nevertheless, spelling will always contain elements of close watch and conscious actions by the performer if uncertainty concerning spelling arises.

A Norwegian longitudinal study of spelling acquisition followed an age cohort of pupils at a Norwegian rural school over the first 6 years of schooling (Skaathun, 2007). The annual data collection was based on authentic writing situations (writing

Learning to Write Effectively: Current Trends in European Research
Studies in Writing, Volume 25, 15–17
Copyright © 2012 by Emerald Group Publishing Limited
All rights of reproduction in any form reserved
ISSN: 1572-6304/doi:10.1108/S1572-6304(2012)0000025008

story paper at school), and all written words (both misspellings and orthographically correctly spelled words) formed the basis for the qualitative analysis. Further statistical analyses of data yielded no support for a stage-based spelling acquisition of the Norwegian written language. Analyses were done on a group level and showed that both alphabet-related and orthography-related spelling skills (language specific overruling of the alphabetical principle) were present in the written material throughout the study period. An unpublished review of the written material from the best and the poorest spellers in the cohort gave the same result on an individual level. The findings suggest that Norwegian spelling development takes on the shape of a parallel development of alphabetical and orthographic skills.

A cross-sectional study of spelling skills in a pupil cohort at a rural Norwegian primary school, using non-word and word dictation, yielded the same results (Gilja, 2009). Analyses of both misspelled and correctly spelled non-words and words showed that both alphabetical-related and orthographical-related spelling skills were present at all grade levels and were further developed over the 6 years of the study. The stage models are thereby not supported by this study where spelling skill was evaluated in the form of dictation writing.

A frequency analysis of all words in the authentic material in the first mentioned longitudinal study (Skaathun, 2007) showed that a small number of words were particularly frequent in all written material. These words turned out to be over-lapping with the most frequent words found in Norwegian newspaper texts. Without exception, these were short functional words (closed class) which served as glue in the language. Many of these words had an irregular alphabetical spelling format, but misspelling was seldom seen with regard to these particularly frequent words. The findings are in accordance with what has been found through investigations of language acquisition in children (Strömqvist, Ragnarsdóttir, & Richthoff, 2001) and suggest that word frequency in language plays an essential role in spelling acquisition in the same manner as in language acquisition. There is reason to believe that high word frequency leads to frequent exposure of the words in texts, which in turn leads to rapid acquisition of the orthography of the words.

Research on acquisition of spoken language has shown that not only word frequencies, but also frequencies attached to the inner structure of the word play a part in the progression of acquisition. The most usually reported spelling error with regard to alphabetical orthography is the spelling of words with alphabetically irregular spelling, that is the spelling of words is as if they were regular. The reported findings show that the letters and the alphabetical principle are acquired early and often dominate the spelling when word specific and orthographic skill is missing. Since the alphabetical connections between graphemes and phonemes, which dominate early spelling, simultaneously comprise an underlying inner structure in orthographic letter sequences in an alphabetical orthography, the regularization errors point in the direction that written language learning has common traits also in this area. In further development of theoretical frames of reference for Norwegian spelling development it therefore seems important to take frequencies in the language into consideration, as well as the impact frequency may have on the acquisition of spelling skill, both in relation to the general language principle and the language specific orthographic overruling. In our opinion, such an ambition requires that linguistic structures are given a stronger hypothetical status than what is traditional. That is to say that when focus is on development of spelling skill the linguistic structures must (only) serve as more or less purposive tools in order to obtain deeper insights. In this, there is also a constructive critique of models which also focus on frequency (e.g. connectionism), where the linguistic structures in our opinion are ascribed an unfortunate ontological status. A suggestion for the solving of this problem has been proposed by Uppstad (2006).

References

Gilja, T. (2009). *Utvikling av staveferdigheit — ei kvantitativ undersøking i ein norsk barneskole.* Mastergradsoppgåve. Det humanistiske fakultet, Universitetet i Stavanger, Stavanger.

Skaathun, A. (2007) *Staveferdigheit. Ei undersøking av stavetileigning i norsk barneskole.* Doktoravhandling. Det humanistiske fakultet, Universitetet i Stavanger, Stavanger.

Strömqvist, S., Ragnarsdóttir, H., & Richthoff, U. (2001). Input and production in acquisition of function words. In B. Höhle & J. Weissenborn (Eds.), *Approaches to bootstrapping: Phonological, syntactic and neurophysiological aspects of early language acquisition* (Vol. 2. pp. 157–177). Language Acquisition and Language Disorders. Amsterdam: John Benjamins.

Tønnessen, F. E. (1999). Awareness and automaticity in reading. In I. Lundberg, F. E. Tønnessen & I. Austad (Eds.), *Dyslexia: Advances in theory and practice* (pp. 91–100). London: Kluwer Academic Publishers.

Uppstad, P. H. (2006). The dynamics of written language acquisition. *L1 — Educational Studies in language and literature, 6*(1), 63–83.

Chapter 1.00.05

The Impact of Open and Closed Vowels on the Evolution of Pre-School Children's Writing

Cristina Silva and Margarida Alves

The scientific interest on invented spelling increased since the pre-school children's early spelling can be seen as a window onto their concepts and skills about literacy and about the written code (Quellette & Sénéchal, 2008). Pre-school children's writing activities act as a factor in the progress inasmuch as they induce meta-linguistic thinking practices that have consequences on the ability to analyse the oral segments of words and to discover the relations between those segments with the correspondent letters (using the repertoire of letter's names that children had acquired very often in informal contexts of learning). In this sense children seem to find it easier to develop alphabetic analytical procedures in writing activities rather than in reading ones, given that writing 'may prompt children to use more systematic methods of deriving the spelling from sounds' (Bowman & Treiman, 2002, p. 31).

Alves Martins and Silva (2006a, 2006b) confirmed this viewpoint in several experimental studies in which they compared the effect of programmes designed to lead pre-school age children to evolve in terms of the quality of their invented spellings. After writing a few words, the children were confronted with spellings by a child at a level immediately above their own (e.g. pre-syllabic or grapho-perceptive children that make no attempt to match the oral to the written language/syllabic children that produce syllabic writing where a letter represents one of the sounds of each syllable). They were asked to analyse the word in the oral form, to think about the two spellings, to choose one and to justify their choice. In other words, they were induced to engage in meta-linguistic reflection at the level of speech, writing and the relationships between the two. The main cognitive activities involved were predicting the number and type of letters to be written, comparing the child's own spelling with

Learning to Write Effectively: Current Trends in European Research
Studies in Writing, Volume 25, 19–21
Copyright © 2012 by Emerald Group Publishing Limited
All rights of reproduction in any form reserved
ISSN: 1572-6304/doi:10.1108/S1572-6304(2012)0000025009

spellings one level higher from an hypothetic child, evaluating which one was better and justifying the spelling.

Evolution towards phonetized writing, where the children began to use some conventional letter correctly, can be influenced by various types of linguistic factors such as the nature of the language, the characteristics of the phonemic sequences in the structure of a word (some words possess a phonological structure that makes it easier to mobilize letters, since include phonological sequences that matches letter's names); the articulatory properties of the initial phonemes influence the individualized perception of both the phonemes themselves and the characteristics of the letters that need to be mobilized. Another aspect that might influence the quality of children's writing is the pattern of accentuation of syllables on words and the characteristics of the vowels (open or closed) that integrate the syllable. In Portuguese language very often the syllables contain open vowels *a, e* and *o* that matches letters names, which makes the mobilization of letter for the representation of syllable's vowel more easier than the mobilization of the letter for representation of the consonant.

Our aim in this research was to analyse the impact of the characteristic of the words used in writing programmes on the phonetization of pre-school children's writing. In this study we analysed the effect that stressed vowels versus unstressed vowels of initial syllables of words can have on the nature of phonetization in children's writing. We formulated the following research question: Will two writing programmes (working grapho-phonetic correspondences of initial consonants followed by a stressed versus unstressed vowel) produce equivalent use of conventional letters to represent the initial phonemes in the post-test? Will children from both groups generalize the phonetization procedures to grapho-phonetic correspondences that were not worked on during the programmes?

The participants were 60 five-year-old grapho-perceptive children and who were familiar with the vowels and at least with the consonants *B, D, F, P, T* and *V*. Their intelligence, number of letters known and phonological skills were controlled. Their writing was evaluated in a pre- and a post-test by 36 disyllabic words beginning with B, D, F, P, T and V.

The children were divided in four groups. Experimental Group 1 and Experimental Group 2 were engaged in writing programmes similar to those described above, where they had to think about the relations between the initial letter and the corresponding phoneme of different words. (Exp. G1: wrote words where the initial consonant (P, T, F) was followed by a stressed vowel; Exp. G2: wrote words where the initial consonant (P, T, F) was followed by an unstressed vowel). Control Group 1 was engaged in a phonological training programme where grapho-perceptive children classified different words in function of their initial phonemes (P, T, F) and Control Group 2 classified geometric shapes in accordance with criteria such as identical shape, size or colour.

Both experimental writing groups produced phonetization writing in the post-test, whilst the control groups did not. There are no statistically significant differences between the two experimental writing groups concerning the consonants that were worked during the programme (PTF) but differences exist for the consonants that have not been worked during the programmes (BDV stressed vowels: $U = 64.50$,

$p = .045$; BDV unstressed vowels: $U = 58.00, p = .022.$). Experimental Group 1 that worked the grapho-phonetic correspondences between initial consonants followed by stressed vowels had better results in the post-test in the generalization of the phonetization procedures. The generalization of the phonetisation procedures in both experimental groups suggests that this type of programme leads children to acquire the notion that the phonemes they identify in words should be represented by letters which contain the applicable sound, and that they simultaneously acquire phonemic identification skills — the ability to perceive phonemes as stable identities within different words — which they then apply when they analyse new words.

References

Alves Martins, M., & Silva, C. (2006a). The impact of invented spelling on phonemic awareness. *Learning and Instruction, 16*, 41–56.

Alves Martins, M., & Silva, C. (2006b). Phonological abilities and writing among Portuguese preschool children. *European Journal of Psychology of Education, 21*, 163–182.

Bowman, M., & Treiman, R. (2002). The effects of letter names and word position on reading and spelling performance. *Journal of Experimental Child Psychology, 82*, 305–340.

Quellette, G., & Sénéchal, M. (2008). A window into early literacy: Exploring the cognitive and linguistic underpinnings of invented spelling. *Scientific Studies of Reading, 12*, 195–219.

Copying Ability in Primary School: A Working Memory Approach

Christian Weinzierl, Joachim Grabowski and Markus Schmitt

Although copying is an assignment often used during the primary school grades, it has been seldomly explicitly addressed hitherto. Apparently, there is no elaborate curriculum in the schools for the teaching of how to precisely and efficiently perform copy tasks. Rather, students are supposed to acquire their copying skills more or less 'along the job'.

Similarly, concerning research on the cognitive aspects of writing, the focus of interest has been predominantly on high level processes like planning or revision, compared to low-level processes like translating already formulated contents into handwritten (or typed) script. Since the performance of a copy task is a writing assignment that mainly involves low-level processes of writing (Grabowski, 2008), copying hasn't been investigated very often either. Rather, when copy tasks were addressed at all, they were mostly used as a method for the study of other phenomena. In contrast, we here report on a research project that makes copying a subject matter in its own right: How do copying skills develop from grade 2 to grade 4? Which parts of working memory are involved in the copying of patterns from different symbol systems? And what strategies do primary schoolers use to efficiently employ their limited working memory capacity?

Among the rare contributions to the study of copying skills and their development, Rieben and Saada-Robert (1997) found that primary school students through their first years in school seem to increasingly use linguistic properties of the text to be copied in order to hold larger (pronounceable and/or meaningful) chunks in their working memory, and thus copy more efficiently. This is consistent with recent

Learning to Write Effectively: Current Trends in European Research
Studies in Writing, Volume 25, 23–25
ISSN: 1572-6304/doi:10.1108/S1572-6304(2012)0000025010

process models of writing which claim that limited working memory capacity plays a major role in the writing process as a whole (Kellogg, 1996). Comparable limitations, thus, should also hold for writing tasks like copying, which almost exclusively involve low-level processes. These considerations led us to the main research questions set out above.

Method

In a first empirical approach to study copying skills across primary school and its dependency on working memory resources and symbol pattern characteristics, pupils of four classes of each second grade ($n = 87$) and fourth grade ($n = 70$) were supposed, in individual sessions, to copy 'texts' of different symbol systems under varying working memory conditions. Four symbol systems were used which varied with respect to their semantic and phonological characteristics: arbitrary graphical objects, unpronounceable consonant strings, numeral strings and meaningful text. Furthermore, participants performed different secondary tasks in parallel with the copying. These secondary tasks were designed such that they put selective load on the different components of working memory proposed by Baddeley and his colleagues (for an overview see Repovš & Baddeley, 2006) — phonological loop, visuospatial sketchpad and central executive. In conjunction, this led to 16 possible task combinations of the 4 symbol systems together with 4 working memory conditions (3 conditions with working memory load and 1 control condition). All participants performed copy tasks under each of the different task combinations, while writing time was held constant for all conditions. This ensured that the number of copied characters could serve as a measurement for copying speed, which we assumed would vary systematically with the different task combinations.

Results

Separate Analyses of Variance (ANOVAs) on the dependent variable copying speed were performed for both class levels. Results showed that copying speed differed significantly between the different symbol systems ($p < .001$ for both class levels). Moreover, the order of the symbol systems was the same for both class levels with all single comparisons also being significant: Meaningful text was copied the quickest, followed by numerals, which in turn were succeeded by consonant strings and finally by geometrical symbols. Furthermore, when the two class levels were compared, results showed that these differences were significantly more marked for fourth graders than for second graders ($p < .001$).

Regarding working memory load, the results showed that it was the copying of meaningful text which was affected the most. In both class levels there was a significant decrease in the copying speed of text when load on either the phonological loop or the central executive was imposed ($p < .001$ for both class levels). The copying of other symbol systems on the other hand was much less affected by secondary working memory tasks. Here it was load on the central executive which led to significant decreases in copying speed in all other three symbol systems. The only exception to this pattern was a small but nevertheless significant decrease when fourth graders were copying numerals under phonological load.

Discussion

Our results indicate that primary school children indeed seem to rely on linguistic features of the material to be copied: Symbol systems that to a larger extent include semantical and phonological information are copied faster than symbol systems which contain less of that information. Since these differences are larger for fourth graders, it could be concluded that, as the children grow older, linguistic features become increasingly important as a strategy for quicker copying. Regarding working memory, the effect patterns indicate that — besides a general effect of load on central attentional resources — it is also phonological aspects that play an important role. Imposing working memory load on the phonological loop disrupts the copying of symbol systems that include more linguistic information (meaningful text, numerals) while symbols with less of that information (letter strings, geometrical objects) are left unaffected.

Currently, a third phase of the project is in its planning stage where we will examine the copying abilities of even younger children in kindergarten. We believe that further research in this domain is necessary in order to come to a better understanding of how copying develops over the early school years. In a later step this basic knowledge could be used to derive interventions for teaching efficient copying skills in primary school.

References

Grabowski, J. (2008). The internal structure of university students' keyboard skills. *Journal of Writing Research, 1,* 27–52.

Kellogg, R. T. (1996). A model of working memory in writing. In C. M. Levy & S. Ransdell (Eds.), *The science of writing: Theories, methods, individual differences, and applications* (pp. 57–71). Mahwah, NJ: Lawrence Erlbaum Associates.

Repovš, G., & Baddeley, A. (2006). The multi-component model of working memory: Explorations in experimental cognitive psychology. *Neuroscience, 139,* 5–21.

Rieben, L., & Saada-Robert, M. (1997). Relations between word-search strategies and word-copying strategies in children aged 5 to 6 years old. In C. A. Perfetti, L. Rieben & M. Fayol (Eds.), *Learning to spell: Research, theory, and practice across languages* (pp. 295–318). Mahwah, NJ: Lawrence Erlbaum Associates.

Chapter 1.00.07

Acquisition of Linearization in Writing, from Grades 5 to 9

Lucie Beauvais, Monik Favart,
Jean-Michel Passerault and Thierry Olive

When writing a text, the writer should implement a linearization process, which serves to translate a conceptual message into a linguistic one. Referring to Hayes and Flower's (1980) model, two main components are involved in the linearization process: the organizing sub-process (i.e. a subcomponent of 'planning') and the translating process. On the one hand, organizing plays an important role in producing a coherent text: It enables the addressee to process the written text as a single and understandable unit. On the other hand, the translating process leads to set out propositions at a linguistic level and specifies their semantic relations. As such, it ensures textual cohesion to help the addressee to (re)construct the writer's mental representation. Therefore, connectives function as strategic indicators that express semantic relations between propositions. Moreover, both organizing and translating processes involve working memory, limited in capacity. Gradually, with acquisition of writing expertise, cognitive resources are freed up from lower level processes and can then be allocated to higher level ones. This enables children to deal with the difficulty on managing both the organizing and linguistic processes involved in the linearization process. In addition to the acquisition of writing skills, the impact of genre knowledge should also be considered. This is because it greatly influences the cost of linearization, due to the various demands different textual structures place on organizing. The increasing knowledge of genres through education, which increases students' ability to implement a discourse schema to guide the organization of ideas, provides a substantial benefit to the writing process. Such guidance improves the organizational task and results in a decrease in the cognitive cost allocated to

Learning to Write Effectively: Current Trends in European Research
Studies in Writing, Volume 25, 27–29
Copyright © 2012 by Emerald Group Publishing Limited
ISSN: 1572-6304/doi:10.1108/S1572-6304(2012)0000025011

composition. For example, this is the case when composing instructional genre, in which the strict chronology of sub-goals and actions dictates the way in which ideas need to be organized. However, it is often the case that the content is not easily expandable, warranting a reorganization to match the rhetorical aims of the genre to produce. This is particularly the case when composing an argumentative text, a genre which places heavy demands on the writers' executive capacity. For these reasons, the mastery of argumentative composition is improbable before the age of 15 or 16 (Bereiter & Scardamalia, 1987).

Given this framework, the aim of the study was to examine the improvement in the linearization process through grades as a function of genre. Accordingly, we studied the linearization process, with fifth, seventh and ninth graders, in comparing two genres (instructional and argumentative). Two experimental factors were crossed: conceptual ordering and genre. To test conceptual ordering, we used Favart and Coirier's (2006) scrambled ideas paradigm. Participants were asked to compose a coherent text on the basis of 11 ideas presented at random. This paradigm only implements the linearization process of composition. In addition to the scrambled ideas condition, we introduced a control condition, providing the same 11 ideas in the correct order (i.e. ordered ideas condition). The effect of genre was tested by comparing instructional versus argumentative structures.

Fifth, seventh and ninth graders composed one text on the digital tablet. This experimental device records writing activity as it progresses. Each participant's writing task was performed in one of the four writing conditions: two organizing conditions (ordered ideas condition vs. scrambled ideas condition) × two genres (instructional vs. argumentative). The management of linearization during writing was assessed using two complementary approaches.

We considered two quantitative measures concerning pausing during writing, using 'Eye and Pen' (Chesnet & Alarmargot, 2005):

- The percentage of time spent pausing while writing, which is considered a good indicator of the task complexity (Schilperoord, 2002), reflects the management of the writing processes involved in linearization.
- The percentage of time spent pre-planning reflects whether an organizing strategy is entailed before embarking on the actual writing, so reducing the demands associated to the organizing task in the course of composition (i.e. in the scrambled ideas condition).

Moreover, we qualitatively analysed the 'offline' measures of the written products. This approach focused on text quality in terms of coherence (organizing scores) and cohesion (diversity in the use of connectives).

Results show that, only ninth graders composed well-organized texts, all the while allocating quite little attention to the writing task. Fifth and seventh graders produced coherent instructional texts. However, they failed to compose as coherent argumentative texts as ninth graders, despise the greater amount of effort they devoted to the writing task. This result aligns with Bereiter and Scardamalia's (1987) conclusion that mastery of the argumentative genre is improbable before the age of

15–16 years. Moreover, only when organizing demands were imposed did differences emerge between grades: Ninth graders spent more time pre-planning than their younger counterparts in the scrambled ideas condition. This emphasis on pre-planning, specific to ninth graders, was not observed in the control condition. Pre-planning only seemed to be beneficial to ninth graders, insofar as they not only spent less time pausing than fifth and seventh graders, but also produced better-organized and more cohesive texts, especially in the argumentative genre. This strategic behaviour, which enables content to be reorganized in order to achieve communicative goals, can also be attributed to the meta-knowledge that expert writers acquire about the planning process. This knowledge makes writers aware of ways to manage writing processes when performing compositional tasks. Our results lead us to support the educational practice whereby novice writers are explicitly encouraged to adopt the pre-planning strategy in order to reduce the cost of planning while writing. These findings could be taken one step further by investigating the beneficial effect on text quality of a focus on organizing while pre-planning, and also by analysing the online management of the writing process in the context of standard writing tasks.

References

Bereiter, C., & Scardamalia, M. (1987). *The psychology of written composition.* Hillsdale, NJ: Erlbaum.

Chesnet, D., & Alarmargot, D. (2005). Analyse en temps réel des activités oculaires et graphomotrices du scripteur: Intérêts du dispositif "Eye and Pen". *L'Année Psychologique, 105*(3), 477–520.

Favart, M., & Coirier, P. (2006). Acquisition of the linearization process in text composition in 3rd to 9th graders: Effects of textual superstructure and macrostructural organization. *Journal of Psycholinguistic Research, 35*(4), 305–328.

Hayes, J. R., & Flower, L. S. (1980). Identifying the organization of writing processes. In L. W. Gregg & E. R. Steinberg (Eds.), *Cognitive processes in writing* (pp. 3–30). Hillsdale, NJ: Erlbaum.

Schilperoord, J. (2002). On the cognitive status of pauses in discourse production. In T. Olive & C. M. Levy (Eds.), *Contemporary tools and techniques for studying writing* (pp. 61–88). Dordrecht: Kluwer Academic Publishers.

Chapter 1.00.08

Construct-Relevant or Construct-Irrelevant Variance in Measures of Reading?

Oddny Judith Solheim and Per Henning Uppstad

Many reading comprehension assessments use constructed-response items where students write an answer to a comprehension question (for instance National reading tests, PIRLS and PISA). In a written response to a reading comprehension question the task is to demonstrate understanding of a text passage. The claim is that there is no evaluation of students' writing ability as part of the scoring criteria. It is argued that students can receive the highest score for comprehension on a particular question even if the written response contain awkward sentences, misspellings or poor word choices. At the same time the risk that scorers over-interpret responses provided by the students is highlighted. It is stated that the responsibility for demonstrating comprehension falls to the student, and that it is not for the scorer to assume what the student meant in his or her response.

Several studies have shown that scorers of written responses to reading comprehension questions in fact manage to ignore weaknesses in writing ability. Previous research has, however, not focused the ability of the writer to take another's perspective in regard to this problem. In order to ensure that a response is a satisfactory answer to a question, the student has to take the perspective of another. Taking another's perspective is regarded as an important prerequisite for the acquisition of language. For the young child, most modalities of writing forces new ways of achieving shared pre-understanding (Strömqvist, 2006). This might be a part of children's writing ability that affect their ability to demonstrate reading comprehension through written responses in a test situation. In a recent study we explored this problem by investigating whether taking the perspective of another predicted scores on written responses in reading comprehension tests.

Learning to Write Effectively: Current Trends in European Research
Studies in Writing, Volume 25, 31–33
Copyright © 2012 by Emerald Group Publishing Limited
All rights of reproduction in any form reserved
ISSN: 1572-6304/doi:10.1108/S1572-6304(2012)0000025012

We also included measures of self-efficacy in this study. Self-efficacy is defined by Bandura (1997) as 'individuals' confidence in their ability to organize and execute a given course of action to solve a problem or accomplish a task' (1997, p. 3). Based on a number of studies from different domains, Bandura (1997) has demonstrated how individuals' beliefs about their self-efficacy influence their performance, effort and persistence as well as their choices of what tasks to perform. A self-efficacious student will participate more readily, work harder, persist longer and have fewer adverse emotional reactions when encountering difficulties than a student who doubts his or her capabilities. Results have also shown that there is a relationship between self-efficacy in reading and writing and performance in these domains. The background for including measures of reading self-efficacy in the present study was findings in a recent study where we investigated the relationship between reading self-efficacy and answering reading comprehension questions in different item formats (Solheim, 2011). Results showed that, after controlling for variance associated with word-reading ability, listening comprehension and non-verbal ability through hierarchical multiple regression analysis, reading self-efficacy was a significant positive predictor of reading comprehension scores. For students with low self-efficacy in reading, reading self-efficacy was a significant positive predictor of multiple-choice comprehension scores but not of constructed-response comprehension scores. For students with high self-efficacy in reading, reading self-efficacy did not account for additional variance in either item format.

In the study focusing on taking another's perspective a total of 217 fifth graders from 12 classes in 5 schools participated. Each of the participants completed a test battery consisting of word reading, listening comprehension, non-verbal reasoning, spelling, taking another's perspective and reading comprehension. Taking another's perspective in writing was operationalized as a writing task focusing on a road description contextualized as an SMS.

Preliminary findings (Solheim & Uppstad, 2009) indicate that taking another's perspective predict reading comprehension when measured with short written responses for students with a high level of self-efficacy in reading, but not for students with a low level of reading self-efficacy. When reading comprehension is measured with a multiple-choice format, taking another's perspective does not predict reading comprehension. Preliminary findings also indicate that spelling is the strongest overall predictor for both MC and CR reading comprehension.

The fact that writing-related abilities predict reading comprehension scores does not necessarily imply a problem. Especially the fact that spelling predicts reading comprehension to a greater extent than word reading and listening comprehension for fifth graders opens up for new hypotheses about the relationship between reading and writing. Is the strong correlation an expression of amount of reading, a perquisite for both reading comprehension and spelling? Or is the crucial factor *the way* the text is read? Our colleague Tønnessen (1999) has proposed a continuum between automaticity and awareness to describe 'cognitive participation' in reading. Are good comprehenders characterized by a higher amount of awareness while reading? Is development in spelling also affected by this awareness? We intend to explore these questions in future research.

An important consideration is whether we regard variance associated with writing-related abilities as construct relevant or construct irrelevant. The relationship between reading and writing might also turn out to be very different at different stages of skill development. A central question in our approach to these issues is whether we instead of evaluating reading and writing separately should apply a concept of literacy that includes both reading and writing.

References

Bandura, A. (1997). *Self-efficacy: The exercise of control.* New York, NY: Freeman.

Solheim, O. J. (2011). Impact of reading efficacy on reading comprehension scores in different item formats. *Reading Psychology, 32*(1), 1–27.

Strömqvist, S. (2006). Learning to write: A window on language, communication and cognition. In Bernicot (Ed.). Pragmatique développementale: Perspectives européenne, special edition of *Le Langage et, 41*(2), 157–180.

Solheim, O. J., & Uppstad, P. H. (2009). Learning to write: The role of taking another's perspective. Paper presented at The 7th International Association for the Improvement of Mother Tongue Education International Conference, June 23–26, 2009, Toronto, Canada.

Tønnessen, F. E. (1999). Awareness and automaticity in reading. In I. Lundberg, F. E. Tønnessen & I. Austad (Eds.), *Dyslexia: Advances in theory and practice* (pp. 91–100). Dordrecht: Kluwer Academic Publishers.

Chapter 1.00.09

Studying Written Language Development in Different Contexts, Languages and Writing Systems

Liliana Tolchinsky and Joan Perera

Learning to write, as any act of learning, is the joint product of the learner and the environment. The learner's intellectual, linguistic and emotional characteristics, his/her cognitive abilities, capacities and strategies interplay with the socio-cultural and linguistic features of the many contexts in which writing is used to constrain not only the acquisition process but also text production at any level of expertise. Our research group is undertaking three lines of study that are aimed at understanding the contribution of these many factors/dimensions to the learning process. The first centres on teacher practices for teaching literacy, the second on the initial stages of learning both as a second language (L2) and a second writing system (WL2) and the third on discourse structures and strategies in different genres and modalities.

An important step is to detect *teacher practices for teaching reading and writing*. We applied a massive questionnaire throughout Spain to collect pre-school and first grade teachers' preferences in four areas of written language teaching: (a) organization of the class, (b) planning, (c) activities and content and (d) evaluation. The result of the questionnaire revealed three profiles of practice. The first gathers teachers' preferences for explicit *Instructional Practices*, highly focused on the learning outcomes but less concerned with autonomous writing and occasional learning. The second brings together *Situational Practices*, more concerned with spontaneous writing and occasional learning than with explicit instruction and learning outcomes. The third is called *Multidimensional Practices*, unites the two by focusing both on explicit instruction and leaning outcomes and on autonomous writing. That is, teacher's attitude towards autonomous writing in the early school

Learning to Write Effectively: Current Trends in European Research
Studies in Writing, Volume 25, 35–37
ISSN: 1572-6304/doi:10.1108/S1572-6304(2012)0000025013

years was a main distinguishing feature among teacher's practices. Close observation confirmed the questionnaire results. We are currently engaged in a follow up study to test the extent to which this early work on autonomous writing will affect levels of performance on later text production.

Multilingualism is an important feature of European communities and it presents a challenge for learning writing (Perera, Tolchinsky, Albert, & Salas, 2008; Tolchinsky & Salas, 2009; Tolchinsky, Salas & Perera, 2007). During the late 1990s the number of foreign students attending regular classes increased dramatically in Catalonia. There was a need to understand the learning processes of Catalan as an L2. Second-language learners in a literate community are immersed in the spoken and written varieties of the language(s) of the community; by necessity, they must cope with the two modalities simultaneously. A second line of studies in our group focuses on *learning to write in a foreign language*. We looked particularly at children who are learning both an L2 and a WL2. We focused on young — 5 to 8 years old — L2 learners' sensitivity to morphological marking in Catalan. Specifically, we assessed the acquisition of inflectional and derivational morphology. Both processes are explored in the spoken and written representations produced by recently arrived Moroccan and Chinese children in Catalonia. Central to our research interests was the typological distance between the languages involved in the study, as well as the inclusion of different writing systems, since we aimed at exploring possible first language (L1) and first language-system influences in the process of acquiring and becoming literate in Catalan as an L2. We were also interested in determining the extent to which the situations of diglossia, from which these children proceeded, affect their sensitivity to morphology and their awareness of the links between the WL2 and L2. Our findings show that there is a subtle influence of learners' L1 in their mastery of critical aspects of L2 nominal morphology. Also, the linguistic features of the L1s seem to influence the deviant strategies children deploy for describing changes in number or derivation of a locative noun from a base noun.

There are, however, some critical matters that reappear in all the study groups: Chinese, Moroccan and, to some extent, Catalan children were all reluctant to produce plural indefinite-article NGs, while being prone to produce singular ones, when required. Moreover, many children were still unaware of the basic representational feature of alphabetic writing. More studies are required to better understand the relations between children's initial and further literacy learning in a new language.

A third line of research centres on exploring the structures and strategies of written and spoken discourse determining the influence of register and modality on them. Two studies illustrate this line of research. The first aims at tracking the growth of Catalan written lexicon of children and adolescents throughout compulsory school, a time when the lexicon is assumed to grow exponentially. The lexicon has a strong influence on demanding cognitive tasks and academic achievement. There were 2436 participants from 5 to 16 years old attending compulsory school in Catalonia at the time of the study. They were asked to produce in writing as many names as they could remember in five different semantic fields: Food, Clothing, Leisure activities, Personality traits and Natural phenomena. The 242,404 *lexical forms* that were produced were lemmatized into 8498 different lemmas and coded according to different linguistic dimensions. The size and the conceptual under-pinning of the lexicon grow significantly throughout compulsory school and show an increase in the use of Catalan correct forms, a reduction in deviant forms and a steady use of words and constructions in other languages. The corpus is available for public access — http://clic.ub.edu/es/cesca-es-.

The last study focuses on the linguistic means used by children (9–10, 12–13 and 15–16 year olds) and university graduate students in French and Spanish in their attempt to create a detached discourse stance in expository texts (Jisa & Tolchinsky, 2009). Two types of linguistic means for encoding discourse stance are examined: local devices which call for the manipulation of morphology and the lexicon (e.g. use of collective nouns such as 'people', 'society') and phrase-level devices which require manipulation of argument structure (e.g. use of passive constructions). Our results show (1) that children in both languages are sensitive early on to the necessity of encoding a depersonalized discourse stance in expository texts; (2) that devices affecting morphology and the lexicon are productive before those affecting the whole phrase and (3) that with development and increasing interaction with academic texts the range of devices employed increases. The data reveal that for the phrase-level devices French speakers prefer passive constructions, while Spanish-speakers prefer *se*-constructions. Our results illustrate how later language develop-ment is influenced by language-specific facts and literacy interacting with universally shared communicative needs.

Acknowledgements

The *Research Group for the Study of Linguistic Repertoire* — GRERLI — Consoli-dated Research Group is supported by the Generalitat de Catalonia 2009 SGR555.

References

Jisa, H., & Tolchinsky, L. (2009). Developing a depersonalised discourse stance in typologi-cally different languages: Written expository texts. *Written language and Literacy*, *12*, 1–25.

Perera, J., Tolchinsky, L., Albert, M., & Salas, N. (2008). Estrategias de realización de la morfología nominal del catalán por parte de niños de origen chino y árabe. In R. Monroy & A. Sánchez (Eds.), *25 Años de Lingüística Aplicada en España: Hitos y Retos* [*25 years of applied linguistics in Spain: Milestones and challeges.*] (pp. 147–155). Universidad de Murcia, Murcia.

Tolchinsky, L., & Salas, N. (2009). Written representation of nominal morphology by Chinese and Moroccan children learning a romance language. In Ch. Bazerman, R. Krut, K. Lunsford, S. McLeod, S. Null, P. Rogers & A. Stansell (Eds.), *Traditions of writing research*. London: Routledge.

Tolchinsky, L., Salas, N., & Perera, J. (2007). Spoken and written representation of number in L2 Catalan indefinite DPs. Catalan review. *International Journal of Catalan Culture*, *XXI*, 321–350.

Chapter 1.00.10

The Impact of Oral Language Skills on Children's Production of Written Text

Julie Dockrell, Vincent Connelly,
Geoff Lindsay and Clare Mackie

Oral language skills are a fundamental underpinning to written text production. Difficulties in the production of written text have been reported both for children with continuing language difficulties and those with resolved language problems. Yet research on the writing problems of children with specific oral language difficulties is limited. Studies of children with language difficulties provide a basis for elucidating the ways in which oral language competencies underpin written text production and identify appropriate targets for intervention.

A series of research projects have addressed the ways in which specific limitations in oral language skills such as vocabulary, phonology or grammar impact on children's written text production. In conjunction the extent to which the impact of oral language skills is mediated by literacy and transcription skills has been considered (Connelly, Campbell, MacLean, & Barnes, 2006). Both cross-sectional studies, which compare the performance with children language difficulties with age and language matched peers (Mackie & Dockrell, 2004), and longitudinal studies (Dockrell, Lindsay, & Connelly, 2009; Dockrell, Lindsay, Connelly, & Mackie, 2007) have been completed.

Methods

Studies have involved different cohorts of children identified with specific language difficulties and their age and language matched peers. Participants have typically

Learning to Write Effectively: Current Trends in European Research
Studies in Writing, Volume 25, 39–41
ISSN: 1572-6304/doi:10.1108/S1572-6304(2012)0000025014

been aged 8–11 but studies into adolescence have also been completed. Standardized measures of oral language, literacy and non-verbal ability have been collected. In addition a standardized measure of writing has been completed by the participants and in one case transcription speed was examined (Dockrell et al., 2009). Additional narrative writing tasks have been available for analysis. Writing products have been examined for accuracy, productivity (amount of text produced) and idea generation.

Analysis

Writing data were analysed in a number of ways including fluency, numbers of errors and factor analyses of writing measures. Relationships between writing, language and literacy have been established through correlations, regression analyses and path analyses.

Findings

In general the children's writing is characterized by short texts, poor sentence structure and difficulties with ideas and organization (Dockrell et al., 2007, 2009). In comparison to language matched peers children with specific language difficulties show weaknesses in inflectional morpheme production for both nouns and verbs (Mackie & Dockrell, 2004). However, grammatical difficulties were not predictors of text accuracy or productivity.

To date our research suggests that restricted levels of vocabulary, poor phonological skills and language levels serve to constrain different aspects of writing. Vocabulary levels impact directly on idea generation both concurrently and overtime (Dockrell et al., 2007, 2009), grammatical understanding explained variability in writing complexity while handwriting fluency remained a particular difficulty for our participants and directly affected writing performance (Dockrell et al., 2009).

Path analysis indicated that the impact of participants' oral language skills on writing was mediated by previous levels of literacy, both reading and spelling. Spelling was an area of particular vulnerability for our participants and continued to impact on text production into late adolescence (Dockrell et al., 2009).

Ongoing Research

Our current research (Dockrell & Connelly) examines the writing processes of children with language problems across two time points by sampling real time writing using a writing tablet. This will provide a detailed framework of the ways in which oral language skills interact with the cognitive, linguistic and text features involved in writing production and the writing process.

References

Connelly, V., Campbell, S., MacLean, M., & Barnes, J. (2006). Contribution of lower-order letter and word fluency skills to written composition of college students with and without dyslexia. *Developmental Neuropsychology, 29*(1), 175–196.

Dockrell, J. E., Lindsay, G., & Connelly, V. (2009). The impact of specific language impairment on adolescents' written text. *Exceptional Children, 75,* 427–446.

Dockrell, J. E., Lindsay, G., Connelly, V., & Mackie, C. (2007). Constraints in the production of written texts of children with specific language impairments. *Exceptional Children, 73,* 147–164.

Mackie, C., & Dockrell, J. (2004). The nature of written language deficits in children with SLI. *Journal of Speech, Language and Hearing Research, 47,* 1469–1483.

Chapter 1.00.11

The Development of Written Language in Children with Language Impairment

Judy Reilly, Jun O'Hara, Darin Woolpert, Naymé Salas, Beverly Wulfeck and Liliana Tolchinsky

Typically developing children have mastered the majority of the morphosyntax of their language by age five, and as they begin school, they learn to write, using their spoken language as point of departure. However, children with Language Impairment (LI) are delayed in language development and show persistent deficits in spoken language, especially in morphology (Leonard, 2000). The goal of our study is to investigate the development of written language in children and adolescents with Language Impairment across different genres as a means to inform our understanding of normal development and to provide insight into the nature of language impairment.

Children with LI are of special interest from both a theoretical and clinical perspective: their language performance is poor, often resembling adults with aphasia, yet their IQ scores are in the normal range and they show no systematic neurologic dysfunction. Incidence is 5–7% of the population. Various explanations have been proposed for LI: Specific grammatical deficits (e.g. Gopnik & Crago, 1991; Rice, 1996); Processing accounts (e.g. Leonard, 2000) and Neuro-developmental perspectives (cf. Ullman & Pierpont, 2005). Such accounts imply the following hypotheses: Strictly grammatical accounts would predict persistent deficits with no contextual effects. A temporal processing approach would predict phonologically, but not necessarily discourse-related deficits, and a neuro-developmental approach would predict vulnerability leading to both contextual effects and variability in performance. We will test these different models by comparing performance in two written discourse genres: narratives and expository texts in children with LI and their typically developing peers (TD).

Learning to Write Effectively: Current Trends in European Research
Studies in Writing, Volume 25, 43–45
Copyright © 2012 by Emerald Group Publishing Limited
All rights of reproduction in any form reserved
ISSN: 1572-6304/doi:10.1108/S1572-6304(2012)0000025015

These discourse genres, narratives and expository texts, were chosen because they represent two distinct discourse contexts to explore both grammatical and pragmatic aspects of language. Specifically, children hear stories from infancy and have some notion of 'story' from about age three; narratives are temporally organized and centred around events produced by specific agents. In contrast, children are generally not required to produce expository texts until school age, and this kind of texts is logically structured and theme centred.

Methods

The children and adolescents (ages 10; 0–16; 0) participating in the study included 24 children with LI and 24 age- and gender-matched controls. Children were asked to tell and then write a story about 'a time when someone made you mad or made you sad'. For the expository task, they were asked to give a speech and then write an essay 'about problems and how to solve them'. All texts were treated using the CHILDES system and a mirror transcript was created for the written texts. Texts were coded for length, morphological errors, frequency and diversity of complex syntax, spelling errors and discourse structure.

Results and Discussion

Overall, we found that texts were significantly shorter for the LI group for both narrative and expository productions whether counted in words or in propositions, and for both groups, expository texts were shorter than the narratives. With respect to morphosyntax, as expected, the children with LI made more morphological errors than controls in both written genres, and these were variable across contexts. Interestingly, however, they performed better in expository texts than in the narratives, making fewer errors in this more challenging text type. An unexpected finding was that on measures of syntactic complexity and the frequency of complex syntax, for narratives, the LI group performed in the normal range; however, their performance in this area for the expository texts was below TD. With respect to discourse structure, both groups performed better in the narrative task, and the groups did not differ on measures of overall structure. However, in looking at structural aspects in more detail, the typically developing group had more elaborate settings in their narratives than the LI group, and they were more likely to use a distanced thematic stance in the expository texts than the LI group suggesting more detailed analyses will reveal additional distinctions. Finally, with respect to spelling, the children with LI not only made more errors, but they also produced proportionally more phonologically improbable errors than the control group.

In sum, for the narrative task, as expected, the children with LI made more errors; however, they used complex syntax in a manner comparable to the TD group, suggesting they have acquired a strategy to increase the coherence of their discourse.

The variability of the errors in the LI group and the significantly poorer perform-ance in expository texts suggest that a neuro-developmental rather than a strictly grammatical or temporal processing approach offers the most promising explanation of this disorder.

In conclusion, these data demonstrate that language deficits in these young people with Language Impairment persist well into adolescence but manifest differentially across development. Moreover, they suggest that development in this group is not a matter of 'catching up', but rather an iterative process, and that atypical development does indeed follow an atypical path.

Acknowledgement

This research was funded in part by National Institute of Health grant P50-NS22343 (JR).

References

Gopnik, M., & Crago, M. (1991). Familial aggregation of a developmental language disorder. *Cognition, 39*, 1–50.
Leonard, L. (2000). *Children with specific language impairment*. Cambridge, MA: MIT Press.
Rice, M. I. (Ed.) (1996). *Toward a genetics of language*. Mahwah, NJ: Lawrence Erlbaum Associates.
Ullman, M., & Pierpont, E. I. (2005). Specific language impairment is not specific to language: The procedural deficit hypothesis. *Cortex, 41*(3), 399–433.

Chapter 1.00.12

Improving Anaphoric Cohesion in Deaf Students' Writing

Barbara Arfé, Pietro Boscolo and
Silvia Sacilotto

Among deaf students' writing problems, difficulties in managing inter-sentential relations in written text present the greatest resistance to instructional intervention. These relations include the anaphoric. Deaf students have been found to have severe problems managing pronominal reference in discourse, as well as many other elements of morphology (Arfé & Perondi, 2008). This is especially critical in Italian, which has a particularly rich referential system, with a variety of pronominal forms, that even hearing children tend to master late, during their elementary school years.

In a recent study, Arfé and Perondi (2008) have shown that deaf students can use a variety of referential forms according to their appropriate referential functions in discourse. Despite this, they tend to avoid anaphoric strategies and prefer nominal reference (a repetitive reintroduction of nouns) when writing. This disproportionate use of nominal forms breaks the flow of discourse.

In this paper we outline an intervention study which tests the efficacy of a training programme designed to improve the use of anaphoric cohesion in deaf students' writing. Deaf students show poor grammatical knowledge of the Italian pronominal system; however, discourse rules and conventions are more accessible to them (Arfé & Boscolo, 2006; Arfé & Perondi, 2008). We assumed that exploring the specific textual function of pronominal devices in discourse may be an effective way to scaffold anaphoric cohesion in writing, and the construction of grammatical knowledge about pronouns.

Learning to Write Effectively: Current Trends in European Research
Studies in Writing, Volume 25, 47–50
Copyright © 2012 by Emerald Group Publishing Limited
All rights of reproduction in any form reserved
ISSN: 1572-6304/doi:10.1108/S1572-6304(2012)0000025016

Participants

Thirteen deaf high school students attending the first and second years of a special high school for the deaf participated (8 girls, 5 boys, mean age 16.6). All used sign language and showed severe difficulties in oral comprehension and poor grammatical verbal skills. Their average linguistic age, assessed by a standardized test of verbal receptive grammar, was 6 years at the time of the intervention. Their verbal working memory (Digit Span) was within the average.

Procedure

A pre-test–post-test design was used, with a control and a training group. The control ($N = 6$) and training ($N = 7$) groups were balanced as regards age, oral receptive grammar skills and verbal working memory (Digit Span scores). Groups were balanced for Digit Span, since, as Millogo (2005) suggests, the use of a linguistic anaphor implies the availability of the referent trace in the writer's memory, and thus verbal short term memory capacities.

Pre-test: Three sub-tests of the Test for the Grammatical Evaluation of Written Italian and a narrative writing task (the written narration of the events corresponding to the first 15 pictures of 'Frog, where are you?') were administered to all the participants to assess: (a) their ability to use Italian pronouns in written sentences (pronominal position and agreement) and (b) their ability to generate anaphoric relations in writing.

The assessment of anaphoric cohesion included scoring the (a) overall number of pronominals (personal pronouns, clitic pronouns, zero anaphors) and nominals (full nouns) used in the written texts, and (b) the overall number of pronominal forms and the overall number of nominal forms used to maintain and switch reference to the main protagonist of the story ('Frog, where are you?').

Full nouns are explicit forms of reference normally used to reintroduce reference in discourse. Pronominals are more implicit forms of reference, which presume the listener's or reader's knowledge of the referent. They are used anaphorically to maintain the reference. A mature referential strategy in written discourse implies the flexible use of diverse linguistic devices: nominal forms mainly used for reference switching and pronominal forms for reference maintenance. Sentence length, in terms of number of intelligible clauses written by each participant, was also considered.

Post-test: The same sub-tests and writing task were administered at the post-test, after intervention. Two language skills teachers, not involved in the study, were asked to assess on a six-point scale, the overall quality of the written texts (Frog, where are you?) produced by the control and training groups at the pre-test and at the post-test.

Intervention: The intervention took place at school, during school hours. The training group participated in six training sessions of one hour's duration, during language skills and Italian lessons. The control group followed the regular language and Italian programmes. The training included textual analysis tasks, to stimulate reflection on the appropriate use of various anaphoric devices in written discourse, and sentence-combining tasks (Saddler & Graham, 2005), to foster the generation of co-referential links in text production. The use of pronouns in discourse was illustrated in the first session. The students were invited to reflect on the different functions of nominal and pronominal forms in discourse. In this session two activities were proposed to students: (a) individuating pronominal forms and their referential antecedent in a short text (10 lines) and (b) a sentence-combining task: using pronominal and nominal devices to reconstruct a short narrative text from separate sentences. The following five sessions included: (a) sentence-combining tasks and (b) subsequent self-evaluation of the referential strategies that students used to reconstruct the texts.

Results

Non-parametric Mann–Whitney tests showed that the performance of the control and training groups did not differ at the pre-test in any of the measures considered (pronominal knowledge, anaphoric cohesion and text length). A negative correlation between the students' verbal short term memory scores and their use of nominal forms in writing emerged at the pre-test: $\rho(13) = -623, p < .05$. Students that showed a better performance at the verbal working memory task used nominal strategies less in writing.

Wilcoxon's pre-test–post-test comparisons highlighted, for the training group only, an increase in the use of pronominal forms for maintaining reference on the protagonist of the story, $Z = -1.48, p < .05$. No significant differences between pre-test and post-test evaluations emerged for the control group. A qualitative analysis of the students' referential strategies in writing underlined a shift in referential strategies for the training group that moved from a predominantly nominal to a more anaphoric strategy (Table 1). This positive shift is also reflected in teachers' perception of the quality of students' written texts, which improved significantly for the training group only, $Z = -2,07, p < .05$. No improvements in deaf participants' grammatical use of pronouns emerged.

Conclusions

The idea that a lack of grammatical knowledge was at the basis of deaf students' poor writing has led educators, and rehabilitators, to focus their literacy programmes primarily on grammar and morphology. This effort, valuable in principle, has led to interventions addressing grammatical exercises and focusing on the sentence level. The approach resulted largely ineffective in enhancing deaf children's grammatical skills, and even disruptive to the development of writing skills, reinforcing deaf

Table 1: Proportion of referential strategies at the pre-test and post-test.

	Training group			Control group		
	Maintain (%)	**Switch (%)**	**Total (%)**	**Maintain (%)**	**Switch (%)**	**Total (%)**
Pre-test						
Pronominal	21	6	27	27	12	39
Nominal	23	50	73	13	48	61
Total	44	56	100	40	60	100
Post-test						
Pronominal	50	26	76	28	0	28
Nominal	5	19	24	16	56	72
Total	55	45	100	44	56	100

writers' predisposition to focus on a sentence-by-sentence generation strategy in writing (Wilbur, 1977).

The use of linguistic anaphors has a high cognitive cost for deaf students (in particular those with poorer verbal short term memory), who prefer to generate the text as a sequence of separate sentences. The preliminary results of this study show how a sentence-combining training, focused on inter-sentential relations, can be effective in fostering the use of mature anaphoric strategies in these writers, who do not benefit from more traditional interventions. Further studies are needed to confirm these results and to assess the possible effects of the training programme on deaf students' knowledge of the grammatical rules governing the use of pronouns.

References

Arfé, B., & Boscolo, P. (2006). Causal coherence in deaf and hearing students' written narratives. *Discourse Processes, 42*, 271–300.

Arfé, B., & Perondi, I. (2008). Deaf and hearing students' referential strategies in writing: What referential cohesion tells us about deaf students' literacy development. *First Language, 28*, 355–374.

Millogo, V. E. (2005). The use of anaphoric pronouns by French children in narrative: evidence from constrained text production. *Journal of Child Language, 35*, 439–461.

Saddler, B., & Graham, S. (2005). The effects of peer-assisted sentence combining instruction on the writing of more and less skilled young writers. *Journal of Educational Psychology, 97*(1), 43–54.

Wilbur, R. B. (1977). An explanation of deaf children's difficulty with certain syntactic structures in English. *The Volta Review, 79*, 85–92.

SECTION 2

LEARNING AND TEACHING WRITING

Chapter 2.00.01

Introduction: Teaching and Learning Writing

Montserrat Castelló and Otto Kruse

In the multilingual context of European higher education, both the need to study new linguistic situations in diverse educational contexts and the pressure to meet the demands of contemporary teaching are challenging tasks for writing research. Over the past 30 years, the study of teaching and learning of writing constitutes a major field of interdisciplinary research which has compiled a substantial body of knowledge but still expands with respect to new research questions, new research fields and new methodologies.

This expansion is particularly evident in this section on the teaching and learning of writing, which contains a large number of contributions on writing and reading processes, teaching methods, learner characteristics and text genres. The perspectives of the studies vary, as do the subjects studied, the contexts, the purposes of writing and the educational situations. The section is organized into five major sections which have been defined on the basis of the main research lines or research perspectives followed:

- Focus on writing instruction
- Focus on writing process
- Focus on text assessment
- Focus on learner and teacher variables
- Focus on genre

This classification is somewhat arbitrary, as most studies touch on more than one field. Still, we feel that each of the following papers has a main focus that allows classification into one of the proposed subsections. Other variables and study characteristics were excluded from the classification, as, for example the participants' characteristics (e.g. with or without learning disabilities (LD)), the educational level

Learning to Write Effectively: Current Trends in European Research
Studies in Writing, Volume 25, 53–68
Copyright © 2012 by Emerald Group Publishing Limited
All rights of reproduction in any form reserved
ISSN: 1572-6304/doi:10.1108/S1572-6304(2012)0000025017

(primary, secondary or higher education), the methodological approach (descriptive, correlational or experimental) and the theoretical approach. Some of the papers may share several or even all of these characteristics but are placed in different sections on the basis of their main research focus.

Writing Instruction

The first section includes the major number of contributions which are mainly focusing on the impact of instructional patterns, writing programmes or didactic sequences, on text quality as well as other outcomes such as learning efficiency, different types of knowledge acquisition, meta-cognitive skills, writing strategies and motivation.

The section starts with two contributions which assess the effectiveness of what can be called *multicomponent programmes* to promote strategies and skills of composing in young children. The study of Budde (*Implementation of Self-Regulated Writing Strategies in Elementary Classes*) is based on the 'Self-Regulated Strategy Development' (SRSD) programme developed by Harris and Graham (1996) and aims at testing this model in the context of regular elementary classrooms. From the results, they conclude that teaching writing skills in conjunction with self-regulation procedures constitute both an effective and feasible tool of promoting young students' writing skills in upper elementary classrooms.

In their paper *Evaluating Cognitive Self-Regulation Instruction for Developing Students' Writing Competence*, Fidalgo, Torrance, Robledo and García used a similar self-regulatory instruction system, Cognitive Self-Regulation Instruction (CSRI), and summarized four of their own studies with children in Spanish primary education. They connected several instructional systems in order to understand how these affect writing behaviours and text quality. After declarative instruction of good writing, they used a self-instructional system to enhance meta-cognitive knowledge on writing and model learning with a teacher who 'thinks aloud'. They conclude that there are clear benefits of developing explicit (strategic) knowledge of the finished product, but that it is less clear whether there are benefits of instruction that focuses on developing strategies for planning and revision.

The next contribution from Arias-Gundín and García, both members of the same research team as the authors of the previous paper, focuses on revision. In their paper *Are Help Levels Effective in Textual Revision?* they aim to verify whether two programmes — one focused on surface and the other on deep level revision — both connected with different levels of help — improve text quality and text revision in primary education. The preliminary results indicate that both instructional programmes improve coherence and productivity, although the authors stress the need for further analysis and for replication in secondary education, claiming that the revision process is supposed to be different at primary and secondary school levels.

The next six contributions form a unit since they come from the same research team and are all devoted to writing instruction of Spanish students with learning disabilities. The first, from García and García-Martín, entitled *A Spanish Research Line Focused on the Improvement of Writing Composition in Students With and Without LD*, is an introduction to the research line and offers an overview of the writing programmes the authors have developed. Most of these projects are explained in more detail in the following papers.

de Caso and García, in two papers titled *Results of Writing Products After a Motivational Intervention Programme According to Students' Motivational Levels* and *Can Different Instructional Programmes Achieve Different Results on Students' Writing Attitudes and Writing Self-Efficacy?*, explore writing productivity and text quality with respect to the students' motivational level. In the first paper, they present a study where they develop a motivational programme addressed to children with learning disabilities. Results lead the authors to confirm that participating in a motivation programme influences the quality and productivity of learning in disabled students' writings. This influence, however, varies depending on the initial degree of motivation and the type of task. In the second study, the authors analyse the motivational components of three different writing training programmes. The first programme focused on the training of planning strategies for writing, the second on the training of reflective processes and the third one on improving writing skills by motivational strategies. The results suggest that not only the text quality improves with any explicit intervention, but also the attitudes and self-efficacy towards writing are modified as a result of participating in different interventions.

In the next contribution, the same authors — de Caso and García — report an intervention study aimed to improve both the written product and the writing processes of Students with learning disabilities. A 10-session programme was designed to foster the students' self-efficacy. Results show the enhancement of the writing processes as well as of the products (text productivity, coherence, structure and quality) in the experimental group; some relationships between processes and products in the experimental group were observed although the authors point out that additional studies are necessary to confirm the nature of these process–product relationship in writing.

In the fifth paper in this group, *Comparative Studies of Strategy and Self-Regulated Interventions in Students with Learning Disabilities*, Fidalgo and García present a synthesis of two intervention studies with students with LD from the fifth and sixth grades of primary school. In the first one, they compare the effects of two types of strategy-focused writing intervention programmes in developing LD students' writing competence with each other, one being the social cognitive model of sequential skill acquisition, the other the SRSD model. They used online measures of writing process, written product measures based on reader and text, and measures of writing modulation variables, such as self-efficacy, and self-regulation skills. They found almost no differences between these two programmes but clear differences between both of them and the control group. In the second study, they compare the effects of these intervention programmes on writing development of students with and without LD. Both groups profited from the training but LD students seemed to overestimate their writing abilities and their ability to transfer the learning effects to other writing situations seemed limited. Still, the authors suggest that the effects of this kind of self-regulation instruction are stable enough to be used in regular classes with students with LD.

In the next paper, *Instructional and Developmental Online Approaches of Writing Composition in Students With and Without Learning Disabilities*, García, Álvarez, Díez, and Robledo outline the characteristics of a future research project which aims to investigate the use of the cognitive resources directly related to the writing of younger students with and without LD, using online methodology with a new adaptation of the writing log technique.

In the final contribution of this group, *Effective Characteristics of Intervention Programmes Focused on Writing and Agenda*, García and García-Martín reflect on the need to compile a guide to establish the key components of effective interventions with the final aim of sharing the principal effective elements with other researchers.

The contribution of Mossige and Uppstad, *Improving Struggling Writers Via Digital Recordings*, focuses on dyslectic writers. Searching for adequate methods to guide older students with writing difficulties, they use case studies to gain insight into processes. The first part of their interventions was devoted to the modelling of the planning phase for the students, while the second part was devoted to text production. The authors analysed the students' completed texts and also the writing process and the habits of the writer (trough ScriptLog-recordings). This information was used to give the student feedback on how to improve the writing. Results show the usefulness of key-logging for reflecting on and improving writing. They base their work on the assumption that observational learning is effective, particularly observation of digital recordings of one's own behaviour.

Observational learning is also the focus of the following two papers. In the first, *Non-Fiction Writing in Lower Secondary School*, Håland reports an ongoing project in which she explores the impact of reading model texts on the quality of students' text quality and on their development as writers in school. Following the students during one academic year, the study focuses on three different types of texts: logs, lab reports and topic texts. Class interactions of students and teachers, text quality and students' perceptions were assessed. Preliminary results indicate that pupils not only apply patterns learned from model texts but that the use of model texts diminished the differences between weak and strong writers. In addition, it seems that the students were able to '*position themselves relevantly in* relation to *the semiotic domain under which they write*'.

The second paper on observational learning, *Observational Learning in Argumentative Writing* by Braaksma, Rijlaarsdam and van den Bergh, studies the effects of observational learning in argumentative writing. Using a multimethod approach, the study explores in depth how observational learning affects writing process and how learner characteristics influence the way students make use of observational learning. Results show that observation of writing leads to more meta-cognitive awareness of writing processes than learning by doing. Students profited from observation because '*their cognitive effort is shifted from executing writing tasks to learning from writing processes of others*'. Furthermore, weak learners seemed to use the observation experience differently from better learners and both learner groups profit from the observational situations differently when it is a familiar task than when it is unfamiliar. The authors also discuss the effects of learners' characteristics on the effects of instructions.

The same authors Braaksma, Rijlaarsdam and van den Bergh shift to a hypertext writing task in the next paper, entitled *Hypertext Writing: Learning and Transfer Effects*, with the purpose of showing that hypertext writing could have beneficial effects on writing skills and strategies. Their results stress the differences in process characteristics between hypertext writing and linear writing especially about the distribution of pauses in the course of the production. At least some of the process characteristics connected with linear writing were negatively related to text quality, while those found in hypertext writing — more planning and analysing activities — were positively related.

Focusing on the potential and characteristics of observation as an instructional method, the research study reported by Van Steendam, Rijlaarsdam, Sercu and van den Bergh (*Effective Instructional Strategies in Collaborative Revision in EFL: Two Empirical Studies*) aimed at investigating the more effective instructional method to improve both revision and writing skills of foreign language learners of English. The study focuses on different research questions such as what is the impact of different instructional strategies and of their combination on the quality of individually and collaboratively revised texts, what is the most effective instructional method to obtain a transfer effect from revising other students' writing to writing one's own text, and finally exploring the impact of different instructional strategies on both below- and above-average writers and on different types of ability dyads in terms of writing proficiency.

Two semi-experimental studies with undergraduate foreign language learners were developed in which different forms of strategy instruction were implemented in collaborative revision to determine the impact of each separate approach. Central to the two studies under review are observation and practising to instruct a revision strategy.

Among the results, one of the more salient findings is the interaction between pair composition and instructional strategy. In this sense, pair composition moderates the effect of observation: homogeneous dyads in terms of writing proficiency seem to profit more from observation than from practising, whereas weak, heterogeneous dyads made up of two initially weak writers benefit significantly more from dyadic practising.

Besides, results also show that revision of other students' texts is a powerful pedagogical method in writing instruction as students in all experimental conditions in both studies progressed significantly from pre- to post-test writing.

Collaborative revision but in this case at university is also the focus of the paper of Castelló, Iñesta, Pardo, Liesa and Martínez-Fernández, *Tutoring the End-of-Studies Dissertation: Helping Psychology Students Find Their Academic Voice When Revising Academic Text*, in which students' difficulties to write academic complex texts such as research projects are the starting point of an intervention study designed to help undergraduate students to make their academic voice visible in their texts. The intervention aimed to enhance students' reflection on the strategic use of the discursive mechanisms which allow writers to establish their own positioning, to maintain intertextuality and keep conventional scientific text structure through collaborative revisions in two different learning environments: online and face-to-face tutorial meetings. The variables analysed were the students' knowledge of the characteristics of academic texts, the students' satisfaction with their writing strategies and with the intervention, the nature of collaborative text revision process and the quality of the final texts. Results indicate firstly that text quality was significantly better for both intervention groups than for control group and, secondly, that better texts were related with higher rates of revisions and more students' knowledge and satisfaction with the course.

Teaching students to use writing as an epistemic tool is the aim of the study of Corcelles and Castelló, entitled *Learning Philosophy by Writing in a Community of Learning*. Its goal is to study the learning of philosophy by writing in a community of learners. For this, a collaborative context to learn Philosophy in secondary education was created in which writing is used as a dialogic tool to think, talk and discuss the philosophy content. Stable and heterogeneous work teams of three or four students were created. The academic course was divided into three didactic units, each with the same sequence of activities regarding individual and collaborative writing. All individual and collaborative texts produced during the academic year and in the work teams were assessed. Patterns of discussion when writing collaboratively were also analysed. Results show that students were able to use this setting to improve not only their philosophical reasoning competences but also their text production skill.

Still focusing on writing in different disciplines, but this time at the university, the paper of Gruber, Huemer and Rheindorf, *Improving Students' Academic Writing: The Results of Two Empirical Projects*, reports two related projects. The first one aimed at establishing an empirical basis for the development of writing courses for humanities students and the second one at developing and testing a prototype of such a course in a blended learning framework. In the first study, Austrian university students' writing practices in three social science disciplines (social history, business studies and business psychology) were investigated. Following a multidisciplinary approach, the study combined text analysis with interviews and participant observation during three courses. In the second study, an academic writing course for advanced students of linguistics, social history and economic history was developed in a blended learning framework. The course was composed of general and discipline-specific modules, and results were used to redesign both types of modules.

The work of Pereira, Cardoso and Loureiro (*Classroom Teaching of Writing Throughout Schooling*) is a summary of projects the authors have carried out in Portuguese schools and universities. The common aim of these projects is their interest in developing teaching/learning and educational devices which may lead teachers to reflect on and renew their teaching practices as well as their own relationship with writing. The authors report in some detail three examples which include the implementation of a specific didactic sequence, the use of writing notebooks and a writing workshop, emphasizing in each case the characteristics of these educational devices and some results derived from studies to assess their effectiveness.

The next two contributions stress the relationship between reading and writing. In the first, *Teaching Reading and Writing to Learn in Primary Education*, Martínez,

Martín and Mateos describe an intervention for improving the use that sixth-year primary school pupils (11- and 12-year-olds) make of reading and writing, in particular in producing a written synthesis based on various texts. The intervention focuses on organizing contents, selecting the relevant ideas from the source texts, integrating prior and new knowledge, and integrating information from different sources. All these processes were taught by means of a model provided by the tutor, by joint activity, by guided activity and by pupils' individual activity. Results show that written group products in the experimental situation were better than control ones, especially in selecting ideas to be included in their syntheses and in integrating those ideas from the source texts. Moreover, students in the experimental situation used more sophisticated procedures both when reading (underlining, note-taking) and writing (drafting, revising). Analysis of the relation between the procedures used and the quality of the products also reveals that making and modifying rough drafts was associated with producing better text.

In the second reading- and writing-focused paper (*Effects of Being a Reader and Observing Readers on Argumentative Writing*), Moore and MacArthur investigate the effects of observing the reading and discussion of texts on subsequent improvement in argumentative writing. Fifth-grade students wrote persuasive letters to a teacher or a principal. Subsequently, some students (the Readers) met in small groups to read the letters and discuss whether they were persuasive and why. A second group (the Observers) listened to the discussion and then listed criteria for convincing argumentation. A control group wrote an additional persuasive letter on a new topic. One week later, all students revised their original letters and wrote a new letter. The reader group produced higher-quality letters than the control group and showed greater evidence of audience awareness. Unlike observation of other writers, the observation of reading in this study did not improve text production.

Early writing skills and genre acquisition is the focus of the following paper (*Writing and Text Genre Acquisition Among 4- to 8-Year-Old Icelandic Children*) in which Oddsdóttir, Birgisdóttir and Ragnarsdóttir, taking into account the fact that the acquisition of writing has hardly been investigated in Iceland, focus on the emergence and development of both early writing skills and genre knowledge. The study is connected to a larger longitudinal project on the development of language, literacy and self-regulation. The main questions concern the development of children's oral and written text production skills and how these are related to other development aspects, such as oral language skills, emergent literacy and subsequent academic achievement. Authors also want to explore the possibility of teaching children about text genres in order to improve their ability to work with different kinds of texts.

The participants are divided into two different age groups which will be followed up during three years. The younger group includes 50 four-year-old pre-school children and the older group includes an equal number of six-year-old children at their first year of primary school.

The section on writing instruction ends with two papers studying special interventions to support writing in school. In the first (*Parental Intervention in Improving Children's Writing and Their Achievement*), Robledo-Ramón and García try to verify whether it is possible to improve students' writing competence and achievement through a programme including parents in the teaching. The study is still in progress and includes providing instruction to parents on writing procedures, guiding and encouraging their children with their written homework.

In the second (*Supporting Children in Improving Their Presentation of School Reports*), van der Meij describes tutorials aimed at enhancing students' knowledge and skills in report writing. In Dutch schools, the author notes, reports on history, biology, geography or internet searches are quite common but teachers are not well prepared to support students with report writing. The author constructed a self-administered manual with guidelines for report writing helping students to detect and format text elements such as paragraphs, enumerations, citations and headings. The study shows that while students profit from such a tutorial, not all kinds of tutorials fit all students. The author also tests the hypothesis, that a 'pedagogical agent' (a virtual figure expressing thoughts and emotions) included in such a manual is helpful only for good readers. Poor readers, however, are rather distracted from it.

Writing Process

The second set of papers in this section are contributions focusing on the analysis of activities and variables connected with the process of writing as well, including discussion of writing strategies and self-regulation. Most of these studies are concerned with the relationship between writing processes and specific writing tasks, contextual conditions or text qualities. Most studies work under the premise that knowledge of how to control writing processes and/or of the conditions under which they take place can improve the efficacy of educational practices and activities. Eight papers are included in this section, each focusing on specific aspects and topics related to writing processes. The last two also explore reading processes.

In *Explaining Knowledge Change Through Writing*, Baaijen, Galbraith and de Glopper investigate how writing processes relate to knowledge change. Based on the assumption that outlining can reduce, rather than enhance, the development of ideas and that the effects of outlining vary as a function of individual differences in self-monitoring, the authors try to find out whether the development of ideas varies as a function of planning and self-monitoring. One of the most important findings of the study is that writers' knowledge increased after unstructured 'synthetic' planning but not after more formal outline planning. The authors argue that the synthetic planning condition imposes less control on text production, thus allowing participants to develop their understanding of the topic without restrictions. This is considered within the framework provided by Galbraith's dual process model.

In *Patterns of Meta-Cognitive Processing During Writing: Variation According to Reported Writing Profile*, Tillema, van den Bergh, Rijlaarsdam and Sanders also explore the relationship between the two main organizational patterns that have regularly emerged in the research on writing processes: a strong focus on planning activities and a strong focus on revising activities and meta-cognition during writing.

It was expected that a typical Planner-type behaviour would be characterized by a peak of meta-cognitive activity at the start of writing tasks while typical Reviser-type behaviour, on the other hand, would involve a peak of meta-cognitive activity towards the end of task execution. Sixteen secondary students wrote three argumentative essays under think-aloud conditions and completed a questionnaire measuring reported writing behaviour.

In short, results support the authors' hypothesis. The higher the reported Planning-type behaviour, the more meta-cognition peaks at the start of task execution. The higher the reported Revising-type behaviour, the more meta-cognition peaks at the end of the writing process.

Formulating activities during writing is the focus of the following contribution (*Formulating Activities in L1 and L2 and Their Relation With Text Quality*) in which van Weijen, Tillema and van den Bergh focus on a relatively unexplored question, namely the orchestration of formulating activities during writing in L1 and L2, and their relation with text quality. First-year university students of English ($N = 20$) wrote eight short argumentative essays — four texts in their L1 (Dutch) and four texts in their L2 (English). Thinking-aloud protocols were analysed in terms of cognitive activities while writing and text quality were rated in a holistic grade. Results show that the occurrence of formulating activities differs between L1 and L2 and follows a more complex pattern in L1 than in L2. Furthermore, the correlation between formulating activities is more complex in L1 than in L2 and appears to be highly task dependent in L1 but not in L2.

The focus of the following contribution is the regulation and adjustment to goals. In *Relationship Between Text Quality and Management of the Writing Processes*, Beauvais, Olive and Passerault explore how the online management of the writing process during composition differs when genres are varied and when quality instructions are given to writers. They report two experiments examining this question. Results of the first study confirm that narrative and argumentative texts are composed with different strategies. The second experiment investigates in detail how text quality and online management of the writing processes change when writers receive instructions on the desired text quality. In this case, besides confirming that strategies to write both types of texts are different, results show that students who receive instructions on quality actually compose better texts. Nonetheless, no change was observed in the orchestration of the writing processes, suggesting that students use the same strategies to compose their texts regardless of what quality level they are seeking to achieve. The authors discuss the educational implications of these results.

Writing strategies are also the focus of Campillo Ferrer, López Serrano and Roca de Larios' paper *Spanish Children's Use of Writing Strategies When Composing Texts in English as a Foreign Language*, this time related to composing texts in English as a foreign language. The authors are interested in learning to what extent the L2 writing strategies of primary school children depend on their level of L2 proficiency. Interview data and thinking-aloud protocols were analysed as well as texts written in English by students of different levels of proficiency. Results show that children with an identical amount of language training may spontaneously activate different L2 writing strategies as a function of their L2 proficiency. The authors discuss the nature of these differences and point out implications for instructional approaches in L2 learning.

In their paper *The Effects of Dyslexia on the Writing Processes of Students in Higher Education*, Galbraith, Baaijen, Smith-Spark and Torrance deal with questions about whether dyslexic students' difficulties with low-level processes lead to differences in high-level planning processes. They made dyslexic and non-dyslexic undergraduate students write an article in three phases. In the first one, students were asked to list all ideas relevant to the topic; in the second one, they were asked to construct an organized outline; in the third one, they were asked to write their paper. Findings suggest that the problems dyslexics have with writing are not restricted to low-level processes related to spelling and punctuation. They appear to have greater difficulties than non-dyslexics in constructing a stable outline of their ideas before writing, and thus need to reconstruct content during writing, rather than relying on what they had generated during outlining. They also seemed to have greater difficulty in coordinating their initial goals with appropriate levels of text production.

The following two papers are interested in the study of literacy and the development of expertise, at which both look from a different perspective and within a different framework. In the first one, *Subcomponents of Writing Literacy: Diagnosis and Didactical Support*, Grabowski, Becker-Mrotzek, Knopp, Nachtwei, Weinzierl, Jost and Schmitt set out to identify abilities — or subcomponents — that play a role in across writing processes. They analyse three of these subcomponents: (a) the ability to take a partner's perspective and to adapt to the addressee's needs, (b) the differentiated and thematically adequate use of vocabulary and (c) the creation of coherence by the use of the respective linguistic means of cohesion. The long-term aim of the project is to look for skills that are relevant across all text types. Authors start from the assumption that such subcomponents of literacy may exist in students' writing development prior to their ability to generate complete texts of a certain quality.

The paper of Skaftun and Uppstad, entitled *What Expert Writers Do When they Don't Solve Problems? Literate Expertise Revisited*, aims at exploring the commonly accepted claim that expertise in writing, unlike expertise in other skill domains, is characterized by *greater* effort than 'novicehood'. Based on the crucial role of genre, Skaftun and Uppstad's hypothesis is that, when controlling for familiarity with the task or genre and keeping the complexity of the performance in mind, literate expertise is characterized by less time and less effort on the task as compared to novice writers. This is in accordance with expertise in other skill domains.

The two final papers in this section explore the interrelationship of reading and writing processes. In her paper *Effects of Creative Writing on Students' Literary Response*, Janssen follows the hypothesis that creative writing may positively influence students' reading comprehension and reading recall, and she provides a creative writing assignment (writing a story in the pre-reading stage) to test it. Subjects were asked to predict the content of a story-to-be-read by writing their own story first. The effects of this type of pre-reading activity on two outcome variables were examined: reading process and story appreciation, which are considered to shape what the author calls the 'literary response'. Two conditions of the literary response were compared with each other: one with and one without writing in the pre-reading phase. Results indicate that the creative writing task influences not only students' literary reading process but also the students' story appreciation. Tentative explanations of these results are provided.

A second paper by Solé, Miras, Gràcia, Castells, Espino, Mateos, Martín, Cuevas and Villalón (*Writing Summaries and Syntheses to Learn in Secondary and Higher Education*) explores how students use reading and writing as tools for learning in secondary and higher education. The authors are interested in the cognitive processes students from different educational levels activate when they carry out tasks involving reading and writing to learn. They collected data on students' prior topic knowledge, their writing process, their written products and their learning achievements. Four groups of students, ranging from early secondary to higher education, had to write a summary and a synthesis after reading one or more texts respectively. The main results indicate that the best products (summaries and syntheses) were associated with more recursive and a more flexible use of reading and writing as opposed to a more typical linear approach. The authors also note that very different products were generated by students using quite similar cognitive and meta-cognitive processes.

Text Assessment

The third set of papers focuses on the development of reliable and valid criteria for evaluating text quality and, therefore, students' written proficiency. With a few exceptions, the studies in this section deal with the assessment of texts and degrees of proficiency in text production in students' second or other languages.

The two first contributions are linked to the same project. In the first one, entitled *CEFLING: Combining Second Language Acquisition and Testing Approaches to Writing*, Martin, Alanen, Huhta, Kalaja, Mäntylä, Tarnanen and Palviainen present the CEFLING project which explores how second language skills in a given language develop from one functional level to the next. This brings together two usually separate research fields: the study of second language acquisition and the study of language testing. The influence of six-level scale of language proficiency of the Common European Framework of Reference for Languages: Learning, Teaching, and Assessment (CEFR) is at the origin of the reported project. Preliminary results from 671 texts from adults and 825 from young learners in Finish and 562 from young learners in English are discussed.

In the second paper about the CEFLING project, entitled *Designing and Assessing L2 Writing Tasks Across CEFR Proficiency Levels*, Alanen, Huhta, Martin, Tarnanen, Mäntylä, Kalaja and Palviainen focus on the characteristics of the tasks designed for eliciting L2 data from younger language learners. After discussing the conditions that they should accomplish — being communicative and authentic, familiar to students and adjusted to L2 proficiency level — the final tasks are explained and the criteria for their assessment discussed in the light of results from pilot research.

French as a second language is the focus of the next paper (*What Is 'Improvement' in L2 French Writing?*). In research analysing changes in the L2 writing of a group of 6 students over 30 months, Gunnarsson raises once again the question of how to measure improvement in intermediary L2 writing. She defined indicators to account for changes in complexity and accuracy of language. The examples and data discussed provide evidence that some learners concentrate on accuracy in terms of simple structures which are easier to control when writing, while others concentrate on grammatical complexity. Gunnarsson closes with the same question she started: What is 'improvement' in L2 writing?

The next two papers are devoted to an analysis of text production in German. In the first one, entitled *DESI — Text Production*, Neumann reports results of a study testing writing competencies in German secondary education as part of the DESI research programme (International German English Student Assessment). After explaining the coding schema and offering evidence that objective comparison was possible by using standardized coding procedures, Neumann discusses the results about competence levels. Among other things, she stresses the importance of considering writing competence as a two-dimensional construct thus confirming the results of many earlier studies and of the role of language awareness for an increase in writing competence.

In the second paper, *Indicator Model of Students Writing Skills (IMOSS)*, Neumann and Weinhold explain the characteristics and the rationale of a project designed to develop an empirically based indicator model of students' writing skills in the German school system. The project will explore factors influencing writing achievements of pupils on different levels of instruction, using both qualitative and quantitative data.

Palviainen's study *Assessment of Written Proficiency: Finnish-Speaking University Students Writing in Swedish* presents ongoing research focusing on the Swedish language proficiency of Finnish university students, and their attitude and motivation towards learning Swedish. One aim of the study is to examine whether Finnish-speaking students reach the proficiency level requested by the Finish state, which is at least level B1 on the CEFR scale. The second aim is to find the linguistic features and textual characteristics underlying teachers' judgements when assessing student performances. Results, based on analysis of 490 essays from seven university faculties, confirm that a relatively large group of Finnish-speaking university students do not have the required Swedish writing skills. An analysis of the assessments showed that the length of texts and their accuracy in terms of lexical and grammatical correctness played a major role in differentiating between different performance levels.

The following paper, *Development of Written and Spoken Narratives and Expositories in Icelandic* from Ragnarsdóttir, is part of ongoing research aimed at studying the development of text construction proficiency from late childhood to adulthood, in different genres (narratives and expository texts) and modalities (written and spoken). The findings reported in this paper are derived from the Icelandic part of a cross-linguistic study including six other languages (Dutch, English, French, Hebrew, Spanish, Swedish) and show that modality (written vs. oral) affects the scores on semantic and syntactic density while genre affects only some scores (not, e.g. vocabulary).

Learner Variables

This section is mainly shaped by studies exploring students' and teachers' conceptions and beliefs about writing as well as by studies relating writer variables (such as knowledge or domain expertise) to their performance and to characteristics of their writing in different educational contexts. All educational levels are covered, though secondary school and university writing dominates.

This is the case of the first paper of the section, entitled *What Do Portuguese University Students Say About Their Writing in Exams?*, in which Brandão Carvalho reports the results of a questionnaire administered to a sample of about 1700 first- and fourth-year Portuguese students from different disciplines exploring their writing habits when answering questions in exams. Results suggest that experienced writers tend to transform their knowledge while novices tend to simply tell their knowledge. Differences between disciplines allow the author to draw tentative conclusions about the existence of different literacy practices.

Still at university but focusing on L2, the contribution of Nicolas Conesa (*The Impact of Educational Experiences on Writing Processes and Products*) aims to deepen our knowledge about the development of a number of learners' internal variables which are thought to be related to the successful composition of academic texts. These variables include students' beliefs about the writing task, use of L2 writing strategies, goals about composing, L2 proficiency level and writing ability. It should be noted that both writing beliefs and students' writing goals have not been analysed in relationship with L2 writing strategies. Participants will be fourth-year students in a five-year-English Philology degree at a Spanish University in Murcia enrolled in an English for academic purposes (EAP) writing course. Data collection procedures will include interviews with students and teachers of the degree, learners' journals, proficiency tests, timed-essays and assignments produced by students, learners' background questionnaires and classroom observation.

Espino and Miras in their paper *Taking and Using Notes and Learning Approach in University Students* aim to understand how notes are used as a means of learning. In particular, the study focuses on the relationships between the type of notes taken, the uses they make of them and their learning approach when writing a synthesis from various source texts, including their lecture notes. Preliminary results indicate that students with a deep learning approach tend to have a constructive representation, while students with a surface learning approach have different types of representation (constructive, mixed and reproductive).

Mateos and co-workers, in *The Effect of Beliefs on Writing Synthesis from Multiple Texts*, explore the role that epistemological beliefs, reading beliefs and writing beliefs play in the way secondary and university students approach tasks in which they have to integrate, in a written composition, conflicting or complementary information on a particular issue obtained from reading various sources. Two different studies are reported; in the first one, general epistemological beliefs are related to beliefs about reading and writing and to the way students integrate conflicting positions in a synthesis statement. In the second one, reading and writing beliefs are related to the quality of a written synthesis, and to the learning benefits resulting from this activity. After discussing different findings which confirm their hypotheses, the authors give a tentative explanation for the relationship between reading and writing beliefs and the degree to which information from different sources is integrated into a new text.

Only one study in this section is devoted to learner variables of L2 students. It is Nicolás Conesa' paper *The Dynamics of Writing Beliefs and Composing Strategies* looking on how learner beliefs about L2 writing and about composing strategies are influenced by experience. Students' beliefs about L2 writing and self-reported use of writing strategies were analysed and related to their previous writing instruction and experience. Two questionnaires — on beliefs and on the use of strategies — were used. Results show that beliefs and strategies vary depending on students' previous experience.

The paper by Pacheco-Sanz, García and Díez is devoted to the study of teachers' beliefs and self-efficacy. In *Does the Quality of Teaching Determine Students' Achievement in Writing?* the authors develop a questionnaire on self-efficacy for teachers. Results are compared to their students' achievement on writing and measures of general intelligence. Authors discuss the results that, taken together, suggest that there are no significant differences either in teachers' self-reported theoretical assumptions or in their teaching practice with regard to the teaching of students with and without learning difficulties.

Each of the last four papers in this section deals with a different variable: the first one with perspective taking, the second one with fluency, the third one with personal opinion or stance and the last one with social perceptions.

In the contribution *Perspective Taking: A Prerequisite of Communicative Writing*, the authors Schmitt and Grabowski assume that the ability to take a reader's perspective can be regarded as a necessary condition for communicative writing. Their goal is to prove the predictive power of perspective taking for partner-oriented writing performance. Like most of the studies in this section, a questionnaire was developed and data regarding accuracy and response time were assessed. Results show that response time on the questionnaire is related with less time to write instructional texts. Moreover, those texts have a significantly better quality with respect to an appropriate use of language. Authors discuss some methodological and theoretical implications of these findings.

The second paper is *Development of Fluency in First and Foreign Language Writing* by Lindgren, Sullivan and Spelman Miller. In two longitudinal studies, the authors examined fluency and revision behaviour in young adolescents' first (L1) and foreign language (FL) writing. Students of 13 years of age at the onset of the study wrote an argumentative text in each language in each school year over a 3-year period. Results illustrate how L1 and FL writing fluency increases as learners become more experienced, how quality is closely related to fluency, and how L1 and FL writing can feed into each other. One of the most interesting findings is related to the idea that learners are able to transfer knowledge of writing between languages in order to produce texts of sufficient quality, and, under suitable writing conditions, this may compensate for a lack of fluency in the FL.

In the third paper of this last block, Alamargot and Beaudet address the impact of opinion on the temporal and linguistic characteristics of the texts produced. In their study *Writing Counter to Personal Opinion: Can Advanced Communication Students Set Aside Their Own Understanding of a Field?* they asked university students to write two different texts on the same subject — the threat to the environment — after providing them two contradictory documents dealing with economy and environment. In one of their texts written, students were instructed to position themselves in favour of the environment and in the other in favour of the energy companies. Among other findings, they observed that in texts defending the writer's own opinion and understanding of the field, content was more emphatically developed, whereas texts that defended an opposing position were more encyclopaedic and factual, based on a limited number of ideas that were more strongly articulated by a greater number of connectors. At the same time, contrary to what might be expected from previous research, results showed no effect of opinion on time invested in writing, so the two texts were produced with the same temporality and ease.

In the last study of this section from Díez, Pacheco and García (*Peer Interaction in Students With/Without Learning Disabilities in Writing*), social skills, anxiety and other emotional variables were assessed through a questionnaire and related to writing performance of students with or without learning disabilities (LD). Besides confirming that students without LD achieve better grades in writing than those with LD, results show that their perceptions concerning future grades are more optimistic. Results were partly dependent on the nature of the disability.

Genre

The last field of study represented in this section is genre research. Three studies from three different European countries explore genre use und genre practices in higher education. Different from most studies presented so far, this research is mainly naturalistic, not experimental. Under study are writing practices that are actually under way at different universities.

Delcambre and Donahue report in their paper *Academic Genres in French Humanities* on a project carried out at two French universities (Lille and Grenoble) to study disciplinary differences in academic genres and in student writing. A questionnaire survey among 600 students in five disciplines was accompanied by focus group and interview studies with students at the master level. The results show considerable differences in genre use between the disciplines. Every discipline seemed to rely on its own set of genres, whereas only the master thesis seemed to be used by all. Differences were also found with respect to the emphasis on personal expression versus linguistically correct texts and with respect to the amount of reading expected to be done for a good paper. Expectations towards the assumed standards of writing seemed to vary according to the discipline and the level of education.

In her contribution on *Comparing Genres of Academic Writing: Abstracts and Summaries*, Ilie talks about an ongoing Swedish project examining the differences between abstracts and summaries, exploring in particular focus, audience orientation and contextualization in time and space. The author also found differences with regard to lengths and selectivity, authorial presence and evaluative attitude, time-related framing, position slots, and content/scope of the text.

A Swiss project on studying different writing cultures is reported by Kruse in his paper *Writing Cultures and Student Mobility*. He sees a lack of genre knowledge as an important obstacle to student mobility as the kinds of educational genres used vary from country to country. Genre conventions and genre practices are hard to infer and are not well communicated by academic teachers. Students having to react to writing assignments in another culture are likely to miss important aspects of writing when trying to transfer experiences from their own to the guest culture. The project's main goal is to develop multilingual questionnaires for students and faculty as a tool for intercultural writing research and use it for a comparative study of writing cultures. The questionnaires focus on writing competences and attitudes towards student writing.

Finally, Ruth Villalon and Mar Mateos describe three studies that explore students' conception of academic writing. They distinguish between an understanding of writing as simply a means by which ideas can be transmitted or reproduced, and an "epistemic" understanding of writing as means for developing and transforming knowledge. They identify a trend from reproductive to epistemic conceptions as writers mature. Students with an epistemic conception of writing are likely to have higher writing self-efficacy. They tend also to produce better texts, and to report learning more as a result of writing.

Reference

Harris, K. R., & Graham, S. (1996). *Making the writing process work: Strategies for composing and self regulation.* Cambridge, MA: Brookline.

Subsection 2.01

Writing Instruction

Chapter 2.01.01

Implementation of Self-Regulated Writing Strategies in Elementary Classes

Sandra Budde

Based on the 'Self-Regulated Strategy Development' (SRSD) programme developed by Harris and Graham (1996) to promote young students' skills of composing, the purpose of the present research was to test the feasibility and effectiveness of a self-regulated writing strategies programme in elementary classrooms. Several meta-analytic reviews have found that SRSD produces strong and lasting effects on the writing skills of primary- and secondary-level students, but especially on the writing skills of children with learning disabilities (Graham, 2006; Graham & Harris, 2003) who were mostly trained in small-group settings. In our own research project, we sought to extend this approach to the context of regular classrooms. In doing so, we addressed the following two issues: (a) Are self-regulated writing strategies still effective when students are taught writing skills within the natural context of regular classroom settings? (b) To what extent are self-regulation procedures essential to the successful teaching of writing strategies to elementary-school students?

Initial Test of the Effectiveness of Teaching Self-Regulated Writing Strategies in Elementary Classes

Method

Participants and design Participants were 156 fourth graders from eight intact classes in five elementary schools located in a medium-sized German town. Their average age was 9.9 years. Study variables were assessed at pre-test (one week before instruction), post-test (one week after instruction) and maintenance (six weeks after

Learning to Write Effectively: Current Trends in European Research
Studies in Writing, Volume 25, 71–74
Copyright © 2012 by Emerald Group Publishing Limited
All rights of reproduction in any form reserved
ISSN: 1572-6304/doi:10.1108/S1572-6304(2012)0000025018

post-test). Classes were randomly assigned to one of two conditions: (a) self-regulated writing strategies instruction (37 girls and 39 boys) and (b) writing strategies workshop (40 girls and 39 boys). Instructions were delivered in whole classroom contexts by four trained instructors. Over six consecutive weeks, students received one 90-minute lesson each week. Each instructional assistant taught one class in each of the two conditions.

All students received the same writing strategies instructions. They were taught a general writing strategy to help them carry out planning, writing and revising activities while producing picture stories (see Glaser & Brunstein, 2007). In addition, they were taught a genre-specific story grammar strategy (see Stein & Glenn, 1979) to produce complete, illustrative and cohesive stories. The only difference between the two conditions was that in the self-regulated writing strategies condition, writing strategies were taught in tandem with three self-regulation procedures: (a) self-monitoring of strategy use; (b) self-assessment of strategy outcomes; (c) criterion setting with respect to the development of one's writing achievement (see Glaser & Brunstein, 2007, for a detailed description of these procedures). No such procedure was taught to students participating in the writing strategies workshop.

Fidelity to treatment Before the start of the training, instructors were taught how to implement each of the two instructional conditions. During the training period, independent judges observed each session held and assessed its instructional quality using a number of standardized scales. All instructors reached high scores on these assessments and were found to have successfully completed 100% of the planned instructional units.

Measures All outcome variables were scored by the first author. One trained graduate student who was unfamiliar with the purpose and design of the study independently scored 30% of the material. Interscorer reliabilities were satisfactorily high. On each measurement occasion, wordless pictures were used as writing prompts. All stories were scored for the inclusion and stylistic embellishment of seven major story elements (see Glaser & Brunstein, 2007; Harris & Graham, 1996). We also assessed students' knowledge about how to write a good story (strategy-related knowledge) and examined their ability to transfer the learned skills to a related but untrained task (writing a personal narrative).

Results

To explore treatment effects on the dependent variables, we conducted one-way ANCOVAs with treatment condition as between-subjects factor and the appropriate pre-test variable as covariate (see the appendix for an overview of statistical results). For each of the dependent measures, the effect of treatment was significant, indicating that the self-regulated writing strategies programme was more effective in promoting students' writing skills than the writing strategies workshop. The strength of these effects (as assessed with Cohen's coefficient *d*) was large. These results corroborated our hypotheses by showing that (a) trained instructors were able to successfully implement the self-regulated writing strategies programme in regular classrooms and (b) self-regulation procedures augmented the effects of the writing strategies workshop on students' strategy-related knowledge and the quality of their written stories.

Teacher-Guided Implementation of Self-Regulated Writing Strategies in Elementary Classes

In a second study, we used teachers, instead of instructional assistants, to implement the self-regulated writing strategies programme in 6 fourth-grade classes. Five different teachers implemented a writing strategies workshop in which students were taught the same strategies for planning and revising narratives in the absence of self-reflective practices. The effectiveness of the two programmes was assessed with the same measures as those reported above. The size and direction of effects obtained from this teacher implementation study were almost identical to those obtained from the above study with trained instructors.

Conclusion

From these findings, one may conclude that teaching writing skills in conjunction with self-regulation procedures constitute an effective and feasible tool of promoting young students' writing skills in upper elementary classrooms.

References

Glaser, C., & Brunstein, J. C. (2007). Improving fourth-grade students' composition skills: Effects of strategy instruction and self-regulation procedures. *Journal of Educational Psychology, 99,* 297–310.

Graham, S. (2006). Strategy instruction and the teaching of writing: A meta-analysis. In C. A. MacArthur, S. Graham & J. Fitzgerald (Eds.), *Handbook of writing research* (pp. 187–207). New York, NY: Guilford Press.

Graham, S., & Harris, K. R. (2003). Students with learning disabilities and the process of writing: A meta-analysis of SRSD studies. In H. L. Swanson, K. R. Harris & S. Graham (Eds.), *Handbook of learning disabilities* (pp. 323–344). New York, NY: Guilford Press.

Harris, K. R., & Graham, S. (1996). *Making the writing process work: Strategies for composition and self-regulation* (2nd ed.). Cognitive Strategy Training Series. Cambridge, MA: Brookline Books.

Stein, N., & Glenn, C. (1979). An analysis of story comprehension in elementary school children. In R. O. Freedle (Ed.), *Advances in discourse processes: New directions in discourse processing* (Vol. 2, pp. 53–120). Norwood, NJ: Ablex.

Appendix

Means, standard deviations, means adjusted by pre-test scores, *F*-scores from ANCOVAs and effect sizes (Cohen's *d*) by measurement occasion and treatment condition.

	Pre-test		Post-test			Maintenance		
	M	SD	*M*	SD	$M_{adjusted}$	*M*	SD	$M_{adjusted}$
Story grammar scale (picture stories)								
Self-regulated writing instruction	2.99	1.59	8.52	2.51	8.53	7.40	2.50	7.41
Writing strategies workshop	3.08	1.58	4.58	1.78	4.58	3.97	1.81	3.97
F-score	0.12		129.77[*]			98.21[*]		
d			1.81			1.57		
Strategy-related knowledge								
Self-regulated writing instruction	2.10	1.28	6.01	2.70	6.17	5.70	2.42	5.84
Writing strategies workshop	2.94	1.53	3.58	1.36	3.43	3.26	1.45	3.12
F-score	13.53[*]		62.30[*]			70.60[*]		
d			1.14			1.23		
Story grammar scale (personal narratives)								
Self-regulated writing instruction	3.62	1.46	7.14	2.70	7.13	6.18	2.30	6.17
Writing strategies workshop	3.53	1.54	3.97	1.80	3.99	3.92	1.51	3.94
F-score	0.15		77.83[*]			53.30[*]		
d			1.38			1.16		

Note: Self-regulated writing strategies, *n* = 77. Writing strategies workshop, *n* = 79.
[*]*p* < .001.

Chapter 2.01.02

Evaluating Cognitive Self-Regulation Instruction for Developing Students' Writing Competence

Raquel Fidalgo, Mark Torrance,
Patricia Robledo and Jesús-Nicasio García

Cognitive Self-Regulated Instruction (CSRI) is a strategy-focused whole-class intervention designed to develop writing skills in older primary school students. We conducted several studies evaluating the effectiveness of this intervention in Spanish sixth-grade (11- to 12-year-old) students.

The CSRI programme aims to develop students' discourse knowledge and procedural knowledge about specific writing strategies. As a result of the intervention, students should develop meta-cognitive knowledge and skills that allow them to regulate their own writing processes. These skills are intended to generalize across most or all writing tasks and contexts. CSRI has three phases. The first phase involves declarative (as opposed to experiential) learning about features of good writing products — with a particular focus on structure and global coherence, and of writing processes, focusing on the need for planning and revision. Planning is taught using the 'vowels' mnemonic: Objective, Audience, Ideas, Unir (link ideas), Esquema (structure ideas using an appropriate schema). Revising is taught around the mnemonic RED: Read, Evaluate, Do. The second and third phases implement the observation and emulation advocated by, amongst others. In the second phase, the teacher 'thinks aloud' (based partly around a pre-prepared script) while writing in front of the class so as to model specific writing strategies. In the third phase, students emulate what they have seen, first working in pairs and later individually. Students think aloud throughout this phase.

Learning to Write Effectively: Current Trends in European Research
Studies in Writing, Volume 25, 75–77
Copyright © 2012 by Emerald Group Publishing Limited
ISSN: 1572-6304/doi:10.1108/S1572-6304(2012)0000025019

We have evaluated CSRI in a series of studies. In the first of these (Fidalgo, García, Torrance, & Robledo, 2009; Torrance, Fidalgo, & García, 2007), we used a combination of online measures of writing process and detailed analysis of writing products. We sampled 95 normally achieving Spanish sixth-grade primary school students, 71 of whom participated in an implementation of CSRI spread over ten 90-minute sessions. The remainder formed the control group which continued with their normal literacy curriculum, completing a similar number of writing tasks during the period. We assessed performance prior to the intervention, immediately following the intervention and after 12 weeks. Writing process was assessed by writing log technique that involves students composing compare-contrast expository text whilst logging their writing activities at frequent, random intervals, which allows us to estimate mean time spent in different possible activities whilst writing process. Written products were assessed through holistic measures of coherence, structure and quality, and text-analytic measures of coherence.

Findings of this study suggested that CSRI results in a substantial increase in the amount of time that students spend planning but does not increase their tendency to revise. There was also a substantial improvement in text quality. These effects were maintained at 12 weeks. In a second study (Fidalgo, Torrance, & García, 2008), we tested the long-term effects of this CSRI intervention. Fifty-six eighth-grade students who had received CSRI in sixth grade were compared with 21 matched peers who had studied in the same school and same classes with the same traditional-curriculum writing for two previous years. As in the previous study, we collected both process and product data. The quality of the texts produced by students who had previously experienced CSRI remained significantly, and substantially, higher than that of the control group, and again, the CSRI group showed a greater tendency to plan their text.

Although these studies suggest the CSRI is effective, they do not give a clear idea of the effective elements within the intervention. CSRI, as with other strategy-focused intervention (e.g. Self-Regulated Strategy Development (SRSD); Graham, Harris, & Macarthur, 1993), has several components. It is not clear which of these are essential to its success. In particular, although there are post-intervention improvements in writing quality and increases in time spent planning, there is only a very weak correlation between these factors.

In a third study (Fidalgo, Torrance, Robledo, & García, 2009), we examined whether students' writing improvement after CSRI instruction resulted from instruction in cognitive strategies per se or simply from an increased understanding of what a good text looks like. The four groups of between 21 and 25 typically developing sixth-grade students, all from the same school, completed one of (a) planning-focused instruction (five sessions), followed by revision-focused instruction (five sessions), (b) the same intervention but with planning and revision components reversed, (c) a product-focused intervention in which writing strategies were not explicitly taught and (d) an ordinary writing curriculum checking the same number of writing tasks practice as control group. In all conditions, apart from the control, instruction was based on the same materials as used in the full CSRI intervention. Process, product, self-efficacy and self-knowledge of writing measures, which have been validated previously, were taken before the intervention, after the first part of the intervention and after the second part, and at similar times for the control. The process-focused interventions resulted in an increased tendency for students to pre-plan their text (i.e. they were partially successful in modifying students writing processes). However, there was no evidence that process instruction provided additional benefits over strategic teaching about product. We found similar (large) positive effects from all three interventions.

Finally, in a fourth study we specifically explored the extent to which modelling and emulation are important to the success of CSRI. Different students (again, three groups of around 24 from the sixth grade in the same school as previous studies) were sampled. One of these groups was taught the planning using the full CSRI method (the vowels mnemonic plus observation and emulation). A second group observed an expert writer (the teacher) and then emulated her performance, but no explicit reference was made to planning. The third group was a normal curriculum control. Both of these interventions appeared to result in improved text quality. However, we did not find any statistically significant increase in students' tendency to plan in any of the three groups.

We are left, therefore, with strong evidence of the effectiveness of observation and emulation methods for teaching writing to 11- and 12-year-olds. However we have not, as yet, found convincing evidence for the efficacy of explicitly teaching meta-cognitive strategies for planning and revision.

References

Fidalgo, R., García, J. N., Torrance, M., & Robledo, P. (2009). Cómo enseñar composición escrita en el aula: Un modelo de instrucción cognitivo-estratégico y auto-regulado. *Aula Abierta*, *37*(1), 105–116.

Fidalgo, R., Torrance, M., & García, J. N. (2008). The long term effects of strategy-focussed writing instruction for grade six students. *Contemporary Educational Psychology*, *33*, 672–693.

Fidalgo, R., Torrance, M., Robledo, P., & García, J. (2009). Dos enfoques metacognitivos de intervención: Auto-conocimiento del producto textual frente a auto-regulación del proceso de escritura [Two approaches to metacognitive intervention: Metalinguistic knowledge of the written product compared to self-regulation of the writing process]. *Revista de Psicología INFAD, International Journal of Developmental and Educational Psychology*, *1*(1), 303–312.

Graham, S., Harris, K. R., & Macarthur, C. A. (1993). Improving the writing of students with learning-problems: Self-regulated strategy development. *School Psychology Review*, *22*(4), 656–670.

Torrance, M., Fidalgo, R., & García, J. N. (2007). The teachability and effectiveness of cognitive self-regulation in sixth grade writers. *Learning and Instruction*, *17*, 265–285.

Chapter 2.01.03

Are Help Levels Effective in Textual Revision?

Olga Arias-Gundín and Jesús-Nicasio García

Text revision is probably one of the most complex skills in writing. The inclusive definition articulated by Fitzgerald (1987) has been generally accepted in the research community: Revision means making any change at any point in the writing process (p. 484). Moreover, the Hayes' revision model (1996) can be suited to describe both the revising of texts as they are being created and the revising of texts that already exist. For text revision to be effective, it is necessary to detect the problems that exist in the text to correct them. Thus, the ability to detect problems is necessary for correcting them, but the ability to correct problems is not necessary for their detection (Hayes, 2004). Likewise, there are children who may have difficulty generating alternative language to correct a problem, even once they detect it. It has been observed that novice writers detect a smaller percentage of text problems than expert writers do. Therefore, it is necessary to redirect students' attention in the revision process for conducting effective revision. According to this affirmation, we have created an instructional programme in textual revision with four help levels.

This study has two main aims: (i) to verify whether the instruction with help levels improves textual quality and textual revision in students of primary education and (ii) to determine what is the most effective textual revision programme in primary education.

In this study, 44 students from two classes of sixth-grade Spanish primary education, belonging to the same school, took part. Their age was between 11 and 12 years. It is important to note that none of the participant students presented education special needs, and all demonstrated educational levels within the normal standards established for sixth grade. The allocation of the groups to each condition was realized at random, without taking into consideration either the Castilian Language subject timetable or the yield of each class.

Learning to Write Effectively: Current Trends in European Research
Studies in Writing, Volume 25, 79–81
ISSN: 1572-6304/doi:10.1108/S1572-6304(2012)0000025020

For this study, we used an experimental design with two groups: one group received instruction in surface aspects of revision and another group received instruction in deep aspects of revision. The effects of implementing the programme with help levels were assessed using a repeated-measures design. Three tasks were used from the Instrument of Revision of the Written Composition (IRCE) (Arias-Gundín, 2005; Arias-Gundín & García, 2007): writing task, rewriting task and selection of strategies. The assessment included text-based measures: productivity, coherence, structure and revision aspects. All these measures were also used with texts written by students in each session.

The first author provided the instruction for the intervention and administered all the writing probes. The instructional programme consisted of nine sessions, each one lasting 45–50 minutes. Each week, the instructor had to check each of the students' texts to determine the help level that each student required for the following session. We used the same general procedure in each of the nine sessions. We started by revising the knowledge gained in the previous session. We continued with the activation of prior knowledge related to the specific contents of the session. Following that, we carried out the instruction with whole class in the specific contents of the session. And finally, the students had to rewrite the proposed text with the following process: (a) careful reading of the proposed text, (b) detection of problems in the text, (c) thinking and/or suggesting improvements, (d) rewriting the text, and (e) repeating steps a, b, c and d with their own text. Two versions of the instructional programme were elaborated: one which emphasized the surface aspects of revision and another which was aimed at the deep aspects of textual revision. For these programmes, we created four help levels and each level was used during two sessions (the first and the ninth sessions were the same; thus, we could also use the texts of these sessions to assess the effectiveness of the programme). At the first help level, the student directly rewrites the text only with the assistance of several self-questions. At the second level, the text is rewritten with the help of revision guides. At the third level we provide students with a list of revision strategies as a prompt for the student to choose one or more of these when revising their text. In the last stage, students are asked to indicate, from a list, which strategies they used when revising their text, as a prompt to use these for their next writing assignment.

We only show the results of the preliminary analysis, because it is necessary to complete the data collection and to realize more specific analysis of each of the revision aspects and for each level of help. We have not found *a priori* differences between the conditions on the three tasks. We show as an example some of the results found so far. In general, between moments, in the writing task we have found statistically significant differences [$\lambda_{(42,1)} = .555$; $F_{(42,1)} = 4.224$; $p \leq .000$; $\eta^2 = .445$], in particular in productivity [$F_{(42,1)} = 38.537$; $p \leq .000$; $\eta^2 = .293$; $M_{\text{pre}} = 1.78$; $M_{\text{post}} = 3.39$] and in coherence [$F_{(42,1)} = 6.981$; $p \leq .010$; $\eta^2 = .070$; $M_{\text{pre}} = 11.35$; $M_{\text{post}} = 14.46$]. In the post-test also, there are significant differences in rewriting task [$\lambda_{(42,1)} = .287$; $F_{(42,1)} = 4.965$; $p \leq .000$; $\eta^2 = .713$], and the findings show differences in productivity [$F_{(42,1)} = 7.682$; $p \leq .008$; $\eta^2 = .149$; $M_{\text{surface}} = 121.63$; $M_{\text{deep}} = 86.86$]

and in coherence [$F_{(42,1)} = 22.351$; $p \leq .000$; $\eta^2 = .337$; $M_{\text{surface}} = 20.38$; $M_{\text{deep}} = 10.36$]. Finally, in the selection of strategies, there also are differences [$\lambda_{(42,1)} = .868$; $F_{(42,1)} = 2.789$; $p \leq .022$; $\eta^2 = .132$].

At the moment, we can affirm that both instructional programmes are effective because they improve coherence and productivity. Likewise, we noted a decrease in the frequency of students to choose the strategies or to ignore the problem and to solve the problem later, and it has increased the frequency of the strategy to rewrite. Nevertheless, it is necessary to determine which of the two programmes is more effective and what is the best help level in primary education; and then, to replicate the study in secondary education, because the revision process is different in both educational levels.

Acknowledgement

During this research, we received competitive funds from the MICINN — The Ministry of Research, Science and Innovation — from the Spanish Government; project SEJ2007-66898-EDUC (2007–2010), and European Union FEDER funds.

References

Arias-Gundín, O. (2005). *Revision in the writing to reorganize knowledge and to learn through changing habits: Development and instruction.* Unpublished doctoral dissertation, University of León, Spain.

Arias-Gundín, O., & García, J. N. (2007). The re-writing task to assess the textual revision. *Boletín de Psicología, 90,* 33–58.

Fitzgerald, J. (1987). Research on revision in writing. *Review of Educational Research, 57,* 481–506.

Hayes, J. R. (1996). A new framework for understanding cognition and affect in writing. In C. M. Levy & S. Ransdell (Eds.), *The science of writing: Theories, methods, individual differences and applications* (pp. 1–27). Mahwah, NJ: Lawrence Erlbaum Associates.

Hayes, J. R. (2004). What triggers revision? In L. Allal, L. Chanquoy & P. Largy (Eds.), *Revision: Cognitive and instructional processes* (pp. 9–20). Norwell, MA: Kluwer.

Chapter 2.01.04

A Spanish Research Line Focused on the Improvement of Writing Composition in Students With and Without LD

Jesús-Nicasio García and Esther García-Martín

We briefly review the characteristics of our instructional approach and the interventions we have implemented. The data are derived from more than 20 studies focused on writing carried out by our research team (for a review, see García, de Caso, Fidalgo, Arias, & Torrance, 2010). We review some of the major research projects carried out by our team and summarize them into an overview of characteristics of the writing programmes, and the components of the different writing programmes for both learning disabilities (LD) students and for typically achieving students. Finally we include a paragraph on deliverables (see our other papers from this book).

Our instructional approach comprises several different characteristics. In each intervention we introduce planning of the text; the consideration of writing as a process in which students plan, edit and review recursively; a perspective on the knowledge which stems from the psychology of writing and instruction; a focus on both the nuclear processes — planning, syntactic, lexical and motor — and on the modulating components of writing — cognitive, motivational, meta-cognitive, the role of practice (Pacheco, García, & Díez, 2009); the use of a strategic orientation and self-regulatory instructions, learning from instructional models; developing and building assessment devices and intervention programmes. The basis referent in all these studies is a curricular relevance and educational focus. Our interest is for instructional and school achievement improvement, in the line of competence development in writing communication.

Learning to Write Effectively: Current Trends in European Research
Studies in Writing, Volume 25, 83–85
ISSN: 1572-6304/doi:10.1108/S1572-6304(2012)0000025021

Interventions in Students with LD

We have implemented different instruction programmes to improve the writing composition in students with LD. The first training programme included the components of planning the text and the process, as one part of the remaining intervention programmes with the idea that writing is a recursive process, writing implies rewriting. In other instructional studies we added writing reflexivity, or writing achievement motivation focusing on value of the task, achievement standards, self-efficacy and attribution of cause to success and failure; or a writing self-efficacy component (García & de Caso, 2006). We also included meta-cognition comparing two self-regulatory models, SRSD and SCM (García & Fidalgo, 2006). Finally, in another study we added the component of revision. In general, we found an improvement in the quality and the productivity of the composition writing products and in students' orchestration of processes. Moreover, we found some improvement and calibration in other psychological variables, such as self-efficacy in writing.

Contextual Interventions with Regular Students

With typically achieving students we followed some intervention programmes conducted by the teacher as part of the ordinary curriculum. To the planning of the text and of the processes we added a meta-cognition component (CSRI model) (Torrance, Fidalgo, & García, 2007), or revision. We found improvement in the quality and the productivity of the writing composition products, and in the orchestration of the process, and even in different psychological variables. And, most importantly, the gains were maintained two years later and were transferred and generalized to other texts (for a review, see García et al., 2010).

Deliverables

We also carried out other developmental and comparative and descriptive studies concerning the composition writing of students between 8 and 16 years old (about 8000 students). We compared the orchestration of the process and the calibration of self-efficacy in writing in students with and without writing LD identifying the main characteristics of difficulties that people with LD have in writing composition; and even, the differences in genre in this type of orchestration and calibration (García et al., 2010).

Moreover, we also produced different valid and reliable assessment devices, for example to assess the product and process of writing (see García & Fidalgo, 2006), writing motivation (see García & de Caso, 2006), writing self-regulation (see Fidalgo & García, this volume) or the revision processes in writing composition.

Furthermore, we are building an open and active corpus, for the creation of an active computerized tool for the automatic analysis of texts.

Finally, we have designed entire programmes developed and implemented for the above mentioned interventions (for a review, see García et al., 2010). For example, we have developed and validated (empirical-based intervention) numerous programmes focused on students with and without writing LD concerned with the following: planning the text and the process, writing reflexivity, writing motivation, writing self-efficacy, writing self-regulation or processes of revision in writing. All of them were implemented in schools with 11th- and 12th-grade student levels, whether by an expert instructor or by the students' own teachers.

Acknowledgements

During this research project, we received competitive funds from the Ministry of Research, Science and Innovation — from the Spanish Government; project EDU2010-19250 (EDUC) for 2010–2013, in addition to European Union FEDER funds. Excellence Research Group funds from Junta de Castilla y León (GR259) and European funds for 2009–2011 (BOCyL 27, April 2009) were awarded to the Director/Principal Researcher (J.-N. García). We are very grateful to Rubén García-Martín for the data analysis of the orchestration processes and to Jenny Gunn for the English correction.

References

García, J.-N., & de Caso, A. M. M. (2006). Comparison of the effects on writing attitudes and writing self-efficacy of three different training programs in students with learning disabilities. *International Journal of Educational Research*, *43*, 272–289.

García, J.-N., de Caso, A. M., Fidalgo, R., Arias-Gundín, O., & Torrance, M. (2010). Spanish research on writing instruction for students with and without learning disabilities. In C. Bazerman, R. Krut, K. Lunsford, S. McLeod, S. Null, P. Rogers & A. Stansell (Eds.), *Traditions of writing research* (pp. 71–81). New York, NY: Routledge.

García, J.-N., & Fidalgo, R. (2006). Effects of two types of self-regulatory instructions programs on students with learning disabilities in writing products, processes and self-efficacy. *Learning Disability Quarterly*, *29*(3), 181–211.

Pacheco, D. I., García, J.-N., & Diez, C. (2009). Self-efficacy, approach, and teacher's practice in the writing teaching. *European Journal of Education and Psychology*, *2*(2), 5–23.

Torrance, M., Fidalgo, R., & García, J.-N. (2007). The teachability and effectiveness of strategies for cognitive self-regulation in sixth grade writers. *Learning and Instruction*, *17*(3), 265–285.

Results of Writing Products After a Motivational Intervention Programme According to Students' Motivational Levels

Ana M. de Caso and Jesús-Nicasio García

In recent decades it has been stated that students' motivation influences their writing compositions (Hayes, 2006), but although many researchers corroborate this fact, few of them risk designing interventions which include these motivational components. The question itself may be 'how do we motivate our students?' de Caso and García (2006a) established four motivational determinants: task value, standards of performance, student attitudes, self-esteem and self-efficacy, and attributions of their successes and failures. At the same time they designed and carried out an instructional programme to improve the writing composition of children with learning disabilities, trying to enhance their motivation towards writing (García & de Caso, 2004). The aim of this study is to determine if writing productivity and quality varies depending on the students' motivational level.

Method

Participants comprised 127 fifth- and sixth-grade primary school students with learning disabilities (from 10 to 12 years old) who were randomly allocated to either the experimental group (66 students) which received the instructional programme or the control group (61 students) which attended normal classes.

All participants were assessed with writing and motivation measures before and after the instructional programme was applied to the experimental group. Writing measures involved the EPPyFPE of García, Marbán, and de Caso (2001) whereas

Learning to Write Effectively: Current Trends in European Research
Studies in Writing, Volume 25, 87–89
ISSN: 1572-6304/doi:10.1108/S1572-6304(2012)0000025022

motivation towards writing was assessed through four different questionnaires (MOES I, MOES II, MOES III and MODEMO) which aim to measure task value, self-esteem, standards of performance, attributions and goals of writing. All of them were designed and validated to carry out this research.

The instructional programme comprises 25 sessions of approximately 50 minutes each. During 16 sessions we teach the process that the participants have to follow in writing (planning the process), incorporating the planning the text strategies useful for learning disabled students. The remaining sessions are dedicated to specific instruction for description, narration and essay structure, at the same time all the writing process is reviewed.

The motivational components are included in all sessions through graphic organizers, revision lists, games and interactive dialogues which are new, comic and accessible to the students, at the same time they have the possibility to choose different materials to work with.

Results

It was proved that belonging to one group or another and the student motivational level produce statistically significant influence in productivity, structure and coherence of texts written by students with learning disabilities. We found statistically significant differences and a large effect size with multivariate contrasts in the interaction group $\times$ MOES I design [$F_{(10,112)} = 2.670$; $p = 0.000$; $\eta^2 = 0.193$]; also in the interaction group $\times$ MOES II design [$F_{(26,218)} = 1.659$; $p = 0.028$; $\eta^2 = 0.165$]; and finally, in the interaction group $\times$ adapted MODEMO design [$F_{(18,226)} = 3.048$; $p = 0.000$; $\eta^2 = 0.195$].

Regarding to the description task, we found that students with a low or high motivational level according to the MOES II achieved better scores in the coherence indicators, which means that these students have benefited more by the specific instruction. In the narration task, students with low or high motivational levels according to the MOES I are again those who scored better in structure and coherence indicators, although students with medium motivational levels used more functional words (productivity indicator). Finally, we only found one statistically significant difference in the essay task regarding the determinants the participants used when writing, with the students with a high motivational level according to the MODEMO being those who showed greatest improvement after the instruction programme.

Discussion

It seems clear that motivation influences learning disabled students' writing compositions, so that if we create interventions to foster writing motivation, a positive attitude towards writing, realistic self-efficacy towards writing or adequate attributions about students' success and failures, those could improve the quality of their writing compositions (de Caso & García, 2006b).

Furthermore, this study has demonstrated that the intervention did not affect every student in the same way, but it rather depended on the level of motivation towards writing so we need to know our students' motivational level to ensure the efficacy of the programme. In fact, students with a high motivational level are the ones who benefited most from the motivational instruction, while students with a medium motivational level are those who showed least improvement on writing productivity and coherence after the intervention.

Acknowledgements

During this research, we received competitive funds from the MICINN — Ministry of Research, Science and Innovation — from the Spanish Government, project SEJ2007-66898-EDUC (2007-2010), and European Union FEDER funds. Excellence Research Group funds from Junta de Castilla y León (GR259) and European non FEDER funds for 2009–2010–2011 were awarded to the Director/Principal Researcher (J.-N. García). We are very grateful to Jenny Gunn for the English correction.

References

de Caso, A. M., & García, J.-N. (2006a). Relación entre la motivación y la escritura. *Revista Latinoamericana de Psicología, 38*(3), 477–492.

de Caso, A. M., & García, J.-N. (2006b). What is missing from current writing intervention programmes? The need for writing motivation programmes. *Estudios de Psicología, 27*(2), 221–242.

García, J.-N., & de Caso, A. M. (2004). Effects of a motivational intervention for improving the writing of children with learning disabilities. *Learning Disability Quarterly, 27*, 147–159.

García, J.-N., Marbán, J. M., & de Caso, A. M. (2001). Evaluación colectiva de los procesos de planificación y factores psicológicos en la escritura. In J.-N. García (Ed.), *Dificultades de aprendizaje e intervención psicopedagógica* (pp. 151–155). Barcelona: Ariel.

Hayes, J. R. (2006). New directions in writing theory. In C. A. McArthur, S. Graham & J. Fitzgerald (Eds.), *Handbook of writing research* (pp. 28–40). New York, NY: Guilford Press.

Chapter 2.01.06

Can Different Instructional Programmes Achieve Different Results on Students' Writing Attitudes and Writing Self-Efficacy?

Ana M. de Caso and Jesús-Nicasio García

Self-efficacy beliefs about writing have received modest attention from researchers in the field of composition; while there have been several findings which demonstrate that students' confidence in their writing capabilities influences their writing motivation as well as the various writing outcomes in school. The same occurs with students' attitudes towards writing as only a few researchers have measured them but none have attempted specific training programmes to improve them (de Caso & García, 2006).

It is also been proved that learning disabled students misinterpret their self-efficacy beliefs (García & de Caso, 2006), so it may be necessary to render these self-efficacy beliefs more realistic in this kind of students in order to bring about improved achievements in writing.

As self-efficacy and attitudes determine motivation and motivation influences the writing composition of students with learning disabilities (García & de Caso, 2004), the aim of this study is to investigate the importance of these motivational components in writing training programmes.

Method

Participants comprised 191 fifth- and sixth-grade learning disabled students, ranging from 10 to 13 years old. Three experimental groups were selected, one trained in planning strategies for writing (28 students), another group incorporated training

Learning to Write Effectively: Current Trends in European Research
Studies in Writing, Volume 25, 91–93
Copyright © 2012 by Emerald Group Publishing Limited
ISSN: 1572-6304/doi:10.1108/S1572-6304(2012)0000025023

the reflexive processes (49 students) and the third one was trained in writing skills using motivational strategies (66 students). The control group comprised 48 students who received no specific instruction.

All participants were assessed with the EPPyFPE of García, Marbán, and de Caso (2001) before and after the instructional programmes were applied to the experimental groups. This instrument includes both a writing attitudes questionnaire of 10 items, and writing self-efficacy questionnaire of 15 items.

The three training programmes were carried out in three different years, but each of them consisted of 25 sessions lasting approximately 55 minutes each. These interventions were conducted in small groups of two to four children in their standard school settings but not during timetabled classes.

The first programme purported to teach students the processes to be realized when writing compositions and the necessary skills to control these processes before, during and after writing (García & Marbán, 2003). The second programme included how to think when writing to the first aim in order to enhance students' reflexive style. The final programme had the purpose of improving writing of learning disabled students using motivational strategies (García & de Caso, 2004).

Results

After ensuring the homogeneity of all groups through a multivariate contrast with the pre-test data, finding no significant difference for Wilks' lambda [$F_{(162,402)} = 1.106$; $p = 0.214$]; we found significant differences for Wilks' lambda [$F_{(162,390)} = 16.22$; $p = 0.001$; $\eta^2 = 0.430$] with post-test data, which means that the differences are due to the effects of the different training programmes.

When carrying out an analysis which accounted for the interaction between treatments and time (pre and post measures) we find statistically significant differences in all variables of totals in the writing products, showing that the planning group improves the most, followed by the motivational group and the reflexive group being the one which showed less improvement. With regard to the self-efficacy variables, the motivational training is that which apparently most improves students' self-beliefs, having into account that these self-efficacy variables are been measured with the questionnaire mentioned above.

On the whole, however, we observed few improvements in self-efficacy and attitudes towards writing as only item 11 from the self-efficacy questionnaire, and items 4 and 5 plus the attitudes total were statistically significant. Anyway, whereas only one item has been significant in the data analysis, we can observe the tendency mentioned before.

Discussion

The results suggest not only that writing outputs improves with explicit interventions, but also that motivational variables such as attitude and self-efficacy towards writing can be slightly affected by different interventions, showing that they can be modified, although they also seem to be stable over time.

Another finding concerns how self-efficacy and attitudes towards writing changes differently depending on the type of training given, with motivational instruction programme as the only programme which leads to afford the greatest benefits.

In summary, this study has implications both for an understanding of the components of the writing process and also for classroom practice as they show the influence that specific and explicit training has on composition.

Acknowledgements

During this research project, we received competitive funds from the Ministry of Research, Science and Innovation — from the Spanish Government; project EDU2010-19250 (EDUC) for 2010–2013, in addition to European Union FEDER funds. Excellence Research Group funds from Junta de Castilla y León (GR259) and European funds for 2009–2011 (BOCyL 27, April 2009) were awarded to the Director/Principal Researcher (J.-N. García). We are very grateful to Jenny Gunn for the English correction.

References

de Caso, A. M., & García, J.-N. (2006). What is missing from current writing intervention programmes? The need for writing motivation programmes. *Estudios de Psicología, 27*(2), 221–242.

García, J.-N., & de Caso, A. M. (2004). Effects of a motivational intervention for improving the writing of children with learning disabilities. *Learning Disability Quarterly, 27*, 147–159.

García, J.-N., & de Caso, A. M. (2006). Changes in writing self-efficacy and writing products and processes through specific training in the self-efficacy beliefs of students with learning disabilities. *Learning Disabilities: A Contemporary Journal, 4*(2), 1–27.

García, J.-N., & Marbán, J. M. (2003). Writing composition processes in LD/LA students: An instructional study on planning. *Infancia and Aprendizaje: Journal for the Study of Education and Development, 26*(1), 97–113.

García, J.-N., Marbán, J. M., & de Caso, A. M. (2001). Evaluación colectiva de los procesos de planificación y factores psicológicos en la escritura. In J.-N. García (Ed.), *Dificultades de aprendizaje e intervención psicopedagógica* (pp. 151–155). Barcelona: Ariel.

Chapter 2.01.07

Enhancing Writing Self-Efficacy Beliefs of Students With Learning Disabilities Improves Their Writing Processes and Writing Products

Ana M. de Caso and Jesús-Nicasio García

Different studies suggest that the texts of students with LD are generally shorter, poorly organized, with more superfluous data and mistakes in their structure (see Graham & Perin, 2007). It is possible that these differences in the writing products were caused by differences in writing processes, given that students with LD are considered to carry out little planning in their writing (García & Fidalgo, 2008). Besides, we know that the orchestration of writing processes is significant in contributing to text quality, so good and weak writers differ in the way they distribute cognitive and meta-cognitive activities throughout the writing process. Besides, motivational variables are important determinants of writing (e.g. Hayes, 2006). The question is if we can improve, through intervention, not only the writing product but the processes involved, and their relationship.

We present an intervention study focused on the improvement of the writing product and the writing processes fostering self-efficacy in writing. We assessed pre- and post-test results, comparing an experimental and a control group of students with LD. Results show improvement, not only in the process, but in the product of writing (productivity, coherence, structure and quality) in the experimental group, and in the relationship of process and product in the experimental group but not in the control one. We need more instructional and experimental studies to confirm the nature of the process-product relationship in writing.

Learning to Write Effectively: Current Trends in European Research
Studies in Writing, Volume 25, 95–98
Copyright © 2012 by Emerald Group Publishing Limited
All rights of reproduction in any form reserved
ISSN: 1572-6304/doi:10.1108/S1572-6304(2012)0000025024

Method

Sixty Spanish students with LD participated in this research. They were randomly assigned either to the experimental ($N = 40$) or the control-ordinary curriculum ($N = 20$) condition.

All participants wrote a narration before and after the instructional programme. While performing this writing task, the students heard a one-second tone played at random with a mean interval of 45 seconds. On hearing the tone, the students responded by indicating in a writing log the activity in which they were engaged (reading references, thinking content, outline, text, reading text, changing text, unrelated).

The ten-session programme designed was based on Bandura (1997), and it purported to enhance self-efficacy: psychological and affective state, verbal persuasion, enactive mastery and vicarious experience as described in de Caso and García (2007).

Results

We carried out a general lineal model 2×1 comparing the data from the post-test. First, we found that the multivariate contrast in the writing task taken jointly is statistically significant giving high effect size differences [$F_{(26,33)} = 2.55$; $p = 0.006$; $\eta^2 = 0.668$].

When we analysed the inter-subjects effects we found statistically significant differences in 24 of the 31 writing variables, always in favour of the experimental group and with a size effect ranging from 0.17 to 0.41: for example, in total productivity, referential and relational coherence, in total structure; or in quality ($p < 0.001$, $\eta^2 = 0.67$).

For the post-test, we used a general lineal model, for which we counted the number of processes students used, the time and the percentages that students spent on each writing process.

Related to the total time the students spent on their narration, while the students in the experimental group doubled the time from the pre-test to the post-test, the control students spent approximately the same time on pre-test and in post-test (from 285.75 seconds to 211.5 seconds) [$F_{(2,57)} = 10.91$; $p < 0.001$; $\eta^2 = 0.28$].

We observed statistically significant correlations, in the post-test, between writing product and process in both control and experimental groups, in text-based measures (productivity, coherence, but in structure only in the experimental group).

We did not find statistically significant correlations in the pre-test. However, we found statistically significant correlations in the experimental group, for the reader-based measures of the post-test (structure, coherence and quality). For example, we observed statistically significant correlations between structure with the categories making an outline ($\rho = 0.36$), changing text ($\rho = 0.44$) and time and frequency in carrying out the task. Statistically significant correlations were also observed between coherence with time and frequency of changing text ($\rho = 0.45$), time devoted to it

($\rho = 0.42$), the category of thinking about content in a 2nd time ($\rho = -0.31$). Also we found statistically significant correlations between the quality of text with the categories of frequency and time of making an outline ($\rho = 0.37$), changing text ($\rho = 0.37$).

Discussion

We investigated whether a specific training programme in writing self-efficacy is effective in improving the writing products and writing processes of children with learning disabilities and/or low achievement.

Enhancing the writing self-efficacy through the increment of Banduras' four sources of self-efficacy has a powerful impact on the writing processes and products. Trained students improved not only the writing product (structure, coherence, quality) (de Caso & García, 2007; Graham & Perin, 2007), but also in different writing processes such as the total process frequency, time writing, frequency and time spent on reading, writing and checking the essay, after the training programme. We can question if the improvement of the process affect its quality. One approach would be to study the relationship between process and product. We found significant relations between product and process for the post-test, in the experimental but not in the control group, suggesting the influence of some type of training.

We can highlight the effectiveness of the treatment, not only in processes involved (frequency, time and moment), but also in the product (structure, coherence and quality).

Acknowledgements

During this research project, we received competitive funds from the Ministry of Research, Science and Innovation — from the Spanish Government; project EDU2010-19250 (EDUC) for 2010–2013, in addition to European Union FEDER funds. Excellence Research Group funds from Junta de Castilla y León (GR259) and European funds for 2009–2011 (BOCyL 27, April 2009) were awarded to the Director/Principal Researcher (J.-N. García). We are very grateful to Rubén García-Martín for the data analysis of the orchestration processes.

References

Bandura, A. (1997). *Self-efficacy: The exercise of control.* New York, NY: W. H. Freeman and Company.
de Caso, A. M., & García, J.-N. (2007). Programa dirigido a la mejora de la auto-eficacia en la escritura en niños con discapacidad intelectual límite. In J. N. García (Coor.), *Instrumentos y programas de intervención en las dificultades del desarrollo* (cap. 3, CD-ROM). Madrid: Pirámide.

García, J.-N., & Fidalgo, R. (2008). Orchestration of writing processes and writing products: A comparison of sixth-grade students with and without learning disabilities. *Learning Disabilities: A Contemporary Journal, 6*(2), 77–98.

Graham, S., & Perin, D. (2007). *Writing next. Effective strategies to improve writing of adolescents in middle and high school.* New York, NY: Alliance for Excellent Education.

Hayes, J. R. (2006). New directions in writing theory. In C. A. MacArthur, S. Graham & J. Fitzgerald (Eds.), *Handbook of writing research* (pp. 28–40). New York, NY: Guilford Press.

Chapter 2.01.08

Comparative Studies of Strategy and Self-Regulated Interventions in Students With Learning Disabilities

Raquel Fidalgo and Jesús-Nicasio García

This chapter presents a synthesis of intervention studies developed in Spanish students with learning disabilities (LD) from the fifth and sixth grade of primary school. In the first study, we analysed the comparative effects of two types of strategy-focused writing intervention programmes in developing LD students' writing competence. We assessed their effects using online measures of writing process, written product measures based on reader and text and measures of writing modulation variables, such as, self-efficacy and self-regulation skills. In the second study we explored the effects of these intervention programmes in the writing development of students with LD, compared with that of their typically achieving peers. We assessed the students both prior to as well as post-intervention.

Study 1

In this study (see García & Fidalgo, 2006) we examined the differential effects of two patterns of cognitive and self-regulatory strategy interventions based on two intervention models: the social cognitive model of sequential skill acquisition (SCM intervention) and the self-regulated strategy development model (SRSD intervention). The sample included 121 (78 males and 43 females) Spanish primary students from the fifth and sixth grades between the ages of 10 and 12 years. All the students had been diagnosed with LD. They were distributed into three groups, two experimental groups and a control group. The first experimental group comprised

Learning to Write Effectively: Current Trends in European Research
Studies in Writing, Volume 25, 99–102
ISSN: 1572-6304/doi:10.1108/S1572-6304(2012)0000025025

48 students who followed the SRSD intervention programme. The second experimental group was formed by 31 students who received the SCM intervention. The control group was made up with the remaining 32 students who followed the ordinary curriculum. The participants performed pre-test and post-test writing tasks using a time-sampled self-report method, thus obtaining online writing process measures. The written products were assessed using two types of measurements: reader-based measures concerning structure, coherence and quality, and text-based measures regarding productivity, coherence and structure. Moreover, writing self-efficacy beliefs were assessed through a self-report scale that included eight items about students' confidence to complete a writing task and to achieve specific writing skills.

After the interventions both experimental groups showed a significantly higher improvement in writing achievement than the control group. In general, students in the experimental groups demonstrated improvement in all reader- and text-based written product measures with a large effect size. There were no differences between the experimental groups. As for the effects on the writing process, for both intervention groups, the full time spent on writing text, and on revising activities such as reading and changing text was significantly higher than for the control group at post-test. There were no significant differences between the experimental and control groups in the planning process. We only found a tendency towards significance in the SRSD experimental group versus the others in time spent on planning activities such as reading references, or thinking about content. Finally, in relation to the modulation variables such as self-efficacy, only the SCM intervention group showed a significant improvement compared with the control group in post-test. Subsequently, we developed a more detailed analysis considering the role of gender in the different effects of these strategy interventions in the calibration of LD students' writing self-efficacy (see García & Fidalgo, 2008b). This additional analysis suggested different effects of strategy interventions depending on gender. At post-test girls from the experimental groups achieved a more realistic calibration of their writing competence than boys after strategy interventions. The girls' post-test writing self-efficacy measures significantly predicted all the writing performances measures, quality, productivity, coherence and structure. However, there were no significant changes in LD boys' writing self-efficacy or their calibration after intervention.

In general, the findings of this former intervention study suggested the efficacy of this kind of intervention in improving the writing competence of students with LD. However, it raised questions concerning how this type of strategy interventions acts in the writing development of students with LD, compared with that of their typically achieving peers which was the objective of the purpose of the second study.

Study 2

We explored the effects of cognitive and self-regulation strategy interventions across a range of writing abilities in students with LD, in an attempt to shed light on the relationship between instructional factors and the writing development of students with LD compared with that of their typically achieving peers (García, Fidalgo, & Robledo, 2010). For this study the sample was comprised of 51 sixth-grade Spanish primary students with LD, and 73 typically achieving students from the same school year. All the students were aged between 11 and 12 years. The students with LD received specific cognitive and self-regulation strategy writing instruction. We compared the general writing competence of LD students with that of their typically achieving peers prior to and after the strategy and self-regulated intervention programmes. The differences in writing competence were broadly assessed through measurements of the written products and also using online measurements of the writing process, as well as measurements of modulation variables of writing, such as, self-efficacy and self-regulation strategies. The findings of this study suggested, as regards the comparison prior to the interventions, similar general patterns of differences which had been observed in previous research studies (see García & Fidalgo, 2008a). Students with LD spent more time on the task, but this generally included more interruptions and less involvement in the translating and revising processes. However, there were no differences between the two groups with regard to the planning process. As for the modulation variables of writing, students with LD displayed less self-knowledge and self-regulation in composition writing, with higher writing self-efficacy beliefs than typically achieving students. These factors probably influence the resulting written products of LD students, which showed poorer quality, structure and coherence than their peers without LD.

However, the comparison between the students with and without LD after the self-regulation interventions supposed the following changes. Students with LD demonstrated significant improvement in the written products compared to their non-LD peers, only in the specific genre trained during the instructional programme. As for differences in the writing process between the LD and non-LD students there were no significant changes from the patterns obtained prior to the instructional programmes. As for self-regulation strategies, although the students with LD slightly improved their self-regulation strategies of planning and monitoring in their compositions, they continued to show poorer self-regulation strategies than their typically achieving peers. There may be limitations about the transfer to other textual genres. Finally, with regard to the writing self-efficacy measures, after the instructional programmes, LD students continued to demonstrate a significant overestimation of their writing self-efficacy beliefs, higher than that of their non-LD peers.

In conclusion, from these studies it seems appropriate to advocate the effectiveness of this kind of self-regulation instruction in writing to improve the writing outcomes of students with LD. Teachers should be aware of the importance of this kind of instructional programmes and should try to continually incorporate them into the curriculum, helping students with LD to become strategic and self-regulating writers across various domains and genres, promoting the generalization of their effectiveness for developing writing competence.

Acknowledgements

During this research, we received competitive funds from the MICINN — The Ministry of Research, Science and Innovation — from the Spanish Government, project SEJ2007-66898-EDUC (2007–2010), and European Union FEDER funds. Excellence Research Group funds from Junta de Castilla y León (GR259) and European non FEDER funds for 2009–2010–2011 (BOCyL 27 on April 2009) were awarded to J.-N. García. We are very grateful to Jenny Gunn for the English correction.

References

García, J.-N., & Fidalgo, R. (2006). Effects of two self-regulatory instruction programs in students with learning disabilities in writing products, process and self-efficacy. *Learning Disability Quarterly, 29*(3), 181–213.

García, J.-N., & Fidalgo, R. (2008a). The orchestration of writing processes and writing products: A comparison of learning disabled and non-disabled 6th grade students. *Learning Disabilities: A Contemporary Journal, 6*(2), 77–98.

García, J.-N., & Fidalgo, R. (2008b). Writing self-efficacy changes after a cognitive strategy intervention in students with learning disabilities. The mediational role of gender in calibration. *Spanish Journal of Psychology, 11*(2), 414–432.

García, J. N., Fidalgo, R., & Robledo, P. (2010). The influence of two self-regulatory instructional programs in the development of writing competence in students with and without learning disabilities. In J. de la Fuente & A. E. Mourad (Eds.), *International perspectives on applying self-regulated learning in different settings* (pp. 595–614). New York, NY: Peter Lang Publishers.

Chapter 2.01.09

Instructional and Developmental Online Approaches of Writing Composition in Students With and Without Learning Disabilities

Jesús-Nicasio García, María-Lourdes Álvarez,
Carmen Díez and Patricia Robledo

Writing is an indispensable tool for learning because it makes it possible to gather, preserve and transmit information, with great detail and accuracy. Writing is the most common means by which students demonstrate their knowledge. They use it to gather, remember and share subject-matter knowledge as well as to explore, organize and refine their ideas about a topic.

One of the main components of writing involves the cognitive processes that provide a description of the mental operations employed during writing. This includes: planning what to say and how to say it, translating plans into written text and reviewing to improve existing text. In this regard, the study of the cognitive processes involved in writing composition has a long history, from both psychological and instructional perspectives, but with the use of offline methodologies. Only recently has the scientific research emphasized the need to address the issue using online methodologies, although most studies have focused on adult students without learning disabilities (LD), with the exception of the studies realized by Braaksma, Rijlaarsdam, van den Bergh, and van Hout-Wolters (2004) and by our research team (García & de Caso, 2006; García & Fidalgo, 2006; Torrance, Fidalgo, & García, 2007). However, currently there are no available systematic data concerning the emergence, acquisition, expertise, efficacy and any relationships with the productivity and quality of the writing, etc., in the use of the writing processes (recursivity,

Learning to Write Effectively: Current Trends in European Research
Studies in Writing, Volume 25, 103–106
Copyright © 2012 by Emerald Group Publishing Limited
ISSN: 1572-6304/doi:10.1108/S1572-6304(2012)0000025026

orquestration) in a wide sample of students, as well as including other relevant psychological variables.

The aim of this paper is to present the research project which employs online methodology involved in the cognitive processes in writing and their relationship with other important psychological variables, such as self-efficacy, motivation, attitudes, attention and working-memory. This research was carried out through the implementation of one differential study comparing samples of students with LD with students without LD, matched by age and by writing level (age and level designs) and through a developmental study which focused on the development of online processes. Both studies were used to create a new system of recording the categories of the processes involved in writing, both of a general type (related to the planning, writing and review processes), and of a specific types (only focusing on either planning or revision), comprising a very wide sample of students.

Method

A random sampling procedure, stratified by grade level, will be used to identify approximately 1100 students from the 4th year of primary education to the 4th year of secondary education.

For the differential study, three samples of students from the 6th year of primary education to the 4th year high education will be selected. Students will be closely matched for (1) students with LD, (2) students without LD of the same age and (3) students without LD with the same writing level. To identify students with writing LD, we will assess their spontaneous writing composition, according to subjective reader-based criteria, and also by more formal text-based criteria, we will also evaluate general intelligence, and finally we will value performance through the students' grades and teacher evaluations.

In a quiet place in the participating schools, each child independently completed several tasks, divided over two group sessions.

Writing Process

Students' writing processes is explored using an adaptation of the writing-log technique. While performing the writing task students hear a 1-second tone, with a mean interval of 45 seconds. On hearing the tone students have to indicate the activity in which they are currently engaged, chosen from the nine listed in the writing-log booklet: reading references (reading information and data about the topic), thinking about purpose and audience, thinking about content (thinking about things to say in the essay), outlining (making a scheme or notes about the essay that I am going to write), writing text, reading text (reading through part or all of the text), correcting text (correcting spelling mistakes), making changes to the writing (changing words, adding words, change order ...), and unrelated (doing or thinking something unrelated to the text). Prior to completing the writing task students are trained in the activity categories and then practice with 25 examples.

Written Products

The compare-contrast essays and argumentative texts will be assessed according to subjective reader-based criteria, and also by more formal text-based criteria (García & Fidalgo, 2008).

Self-Efficacy

We measure self-efficacy by asking students to provide self-judgments and beliefs about their capability to perform writing processes, implied in the writing task. The writing self-efficacy scale consist of 20 items, asking students how certain they are that they can perform cognitive processes on a scale from 1 to 7. The scale is divided into 9 subscales according to the different writing processes considered in our online register.

Attitudes and Motivation

These variables are evaluated using the Scale of Attitudes towards writing and is comprised of 10 questions and the students must answer according to their preferences. On the other hand, motivation is assessed using a scale of degrees (from 1 to 5) for 32 items.

Attention

To assess this variable we apply the D2 tool.

Working Memory

We use the Spanish adaptation of the Working Memory Battery; concretely we assess the phonological loop and central executive components.

Discussion

The purpose of our future research is to shed some light on the use of the cognitive resources directly related to the writing of younger students with and without LD, using online methodology with a new adaptation of the writing log technique, and it also considers other relevant psychological variables. This objective is based on the fact that although the study of online writing processes has been carried out in adult students without difficulties, the studies focused on younger students with or without LD are still scarce.

Acknowledgements

During this research project, we received competitive funds from the Ministry of Research, Science and Innovation — from the Spanish Government; project EDU2010-19250 (EDUC) for 2010–2013, in addition to European Union FEDER funds. Excellence Research Group funds from Junta de Castilla y León (GR259) and European funds for 2009–2011 (BOCyL 27, April 2009) were awarded to the Director/Principal Researcher (J.-N. García). We are very grateful to Rubén García-Martín for the data analysis of the orchestration processes; and to Jenny Gunn for the English correction.

References

Braaksma, A. H., Rijlaarsdam, G., van den Bergh, H., & van Hout-Wolters, H. A. M. (2004). Observational learning and its effects on the orchestration of writing processes. *Cognition and Instruction*, *22*(1), 1–36.

García, J.-N., & de Caso, A. M. (2006). Comparison of the effects on writing attitudes and writing self-efficacy of three different instructions in students with learning disabilities. *International Journal of Educational Research*, *43*, 272–289.

García, J.-N., & Fidalgo, R. (2006). Effects of two self-regulatory instruction programs in students with learning disabilities in writing products, process and self-efficacy. *Learning Disability Quarterly*, *29*(3), 181–211.

García, J.-N., & Fidalgo, R. (2008). The orchestration of writing processes and writing products: A comparison of learning disabled and non-disabled 6th grade students. *Learning Disabilities. A Contemporary Journal*, *6*(2), 77–98.

Torrance, M., Fidalgo, R., & García, J.-N. (2007). The teachability and effectiveness of strategies for cognitive self-regulation in sixth grade students. *Learning and Instruction*, *17*(3), 265–285.

Chapter 2.01.10

Effective Characteristics of Intervention Programmes Focused on Writing and Agenda

Jesús-Nicasio García and Esther García-Martín

The general aim is to contribute to the knowledge gained from our research studies as regards the effective interventions which are known to improve the writing processes and/or writing skills. In this sense, we have the conviction as well as the evidence that we can improve not only the students writing, but also the processes and the self-regulation involved in the product, whether the students have learning difficulties or are normally achieving students (Fidalgo, Torrance, & García, 2008; García & de Caso, 2006; García & Fidalgo, 2008; Pacheco, García, & Díez, 2009; Torrance, Fidalgo, & García, 2007).

Our specific aim is to compile a guide to establish the key components of effective interventions on the basis of all the studies carried out by our research group. Furthermore we aim to share the principal effective elements with other research projects by the other different teams from Europe and America. This will allow us to create a guide on the basis of such taxonomy and to always conduct empirically based interventions (EBIs) research studies. Consequently, this process will guarantee the best and most effective practices in writing. In short, this course of action is the basis for an agenda for the future in research and instruction in writing.

Key Characteristics of Efficacy Programmes in Writing

We are aware of the different factors that are responsible for the efficacy of a program, but we need to understand the specific role of each and, more importantly, why they work. For example, we know that recursivity is one strong factor in mature

Learning to Write Effectively: Current Trends in European Research
Studies in Writing, Volume 25, 107–113
Copyright © 2012 by Emerald Group Publishing Limited
All rights of reproduction in any form reserved
ISSN: 1572-6304/doi:10.1108/S1572-6304(2012)0000025027

writing; as is the orchestration of the processes; or the use of a more process oriented focus versus a product oriented one; or strategic use. However, we need to include, not only the cognitive aspects, but also the meta-cognitive, and motivational ones; some of which have been studied by our team. Moreover, we have identified a nuclear question that refers to the use of EBIs or empirically supported treatments, as a guide to indicate the correct and incorrect ways to proceed in the field. With the development of this guide, we would promote the use of those interventions which were deemed best as opposed to other specific ones. Other important factors to be considered relate to the role of direct versus observational instruction, or considering the characteristics of the students or the cultural context. Distinguishing the differential effects and roles of the characteristics between the programs constitutes the main shortcoming in identifying the efficient factors in writing instruction. In general, few studies compare instructional models and when this does occur, for example comparing the SRSD and SCM, we found similar results in writing quality and productivity (García & Fidalgo, 2008).

For example, if we analyse some intervention research in writing, we can identify key components or elements that must be taken into account (see Table 1): target learners, goals, instructional activities, assessment, professional development, implementation of groups, fidelity of the treatment, durability and generalization, length, empirical-based intervention and description of the interventions. This will allow in the future for the establishment of a rigorous and useful core agenda.

Agenda for the Future in Research and Instruction in Writing

Besides, when these key factors are understood and identified we can include the effective characteristics in every instructional study. For example, the recursivity aspect, the orchestration of the processes, the planning of the texts and the processes, the strategic and self-regulatory ways to proceed, or the motivational and observational approaches. Given that it is necessary to use EBIs we need to compare groups with different types of interventions and strategy models. In general, very few studies contrast different strategies. They focus on one unique model. This reduces our knowledge about the most effective ones.

Moreover, we can develop a guide which includes the elements of the best practices in writing intervention, as evidenced in the research and in instruction programmes. Some key components are concerned with the implementation of studies comparing the efficacy of direct versus the observational instructions in writing; or to compare the contextual versus the professional interventions; or to consider the level, the typology, the culture or the language of the students. We need to develop research and instruction patterns for different educational levels or student typology. And, finally, we need to know not only if the interventions are effective, and if they constitute an empirically supported treatment (EBI), but also we need to know why they work.

Table 1: Main elements that any guide for effective intervention in writing has to have, illustrated by a research project by García and de Caso (2006).

Target learners	Goals	Instructional activities (-teacher/-student)	Assessment as part of the instruction	Professional development/ teacher's training	Implementation control groups	Fidelity of treatment	Durability and generalization	Length, amount of time	To do an empirical-based intervention (EBI)	How to describe the interventions in the future?
Participants • N = 191 [5th/6th grade Students with LD/LA (10–13 years old) (131 males; 73 females)]	Training on planning • To teach the processes to be realized when writing and the skills to control these processes (before, during and after). Training in reflexivity • To teach the writing processes with their phases and strategies and how to think when writing. Training on motivation • To improve productivity and quality of compositions written by	Planning group • Writing processes • Processes prior to writing • Processes directly involved with writing • Revision processes in writing • Instruction on draft processes • All processes applied to descriptive, narrative an to essay texts	Writing measures • Product: EPPyFPE Description and essay: productivity and coherence Narration: productivity, coherence and structure	Training teachers in their final year of a master's programme in psychology and pedagogy	Students of the same educational level	Teacher training	Durability: Only post/not explored	25 sessions per group (3-4 times a week/ never 2 sessions on the same day) 55 minutes each	Training affected both self-efficacy and the attitudes towards writing and the other psychological aspects measured as well as the quality and productivity of the composition writing	Follow-up Durability

Table 1: (Continued)

Target learners	Goals	Instructional activities (-teacher/-student)	Assessment as part of the instruction	Professional development/ teacher's training	Implementation control groups	Fidelity of treatment	Durability and generalization	Length, amount of time	To do an empirical-based intervention (EBI)	How to describe the interventions in the future?
	students through motivational strategies									
Selection criteria: • Teachers or psychologist identified students with writing specific LD or LA • DD/Special Educational Needs	Writing tasks pre-test • 1 descriptive text • 1 narrative text • 1 essay	Reflexivity group: • Same work in writing + Color stop signal (definition approximation problem, attention focusing, answer selection and self-evaluation and self-reinforcement) • Teacher modelled, students had to do the exercises by themselves, initially aloud and finally through internalized thought.	Writing self-efficacy, attitudes towards writing and meta-cognition in writing EPPyFPE	Each teacher was trained in: • How to administer the different assessments • Specific intervention programme that they would have to carry out	To assign students to control or experimental groups not take into account whether the student had either LD or LA (IQ no significant differences)	Counterbalanced number of training sessions per week and the number of students in the small groups	Generalizability to other textual genres: Not explored, but worked 3 textual genders	Small groups each session (2-4 students)	Differences between experimental groups and control group (writing processes, productivity and quality) Better experimental group	

Design (groups)	Interventions / Writing tasks	Sampling	Administration	Differences between intervention groups
Design (groups): • Planning intervention (N = 28) • Reflexivity intervention (N = 49) • Motivation intervention (N = 66) • Ordinary curriculum (N = 48)	Writing tasks post-test: • 1 descriptive text • 1 narrative text • 1 essay Motivation group: • Same work in writing + motivation strategies (task value, standards of performance, students' attitudes, expectations, self-esteem and self-efficacy and attributions concerning success and failure Standard curriculum group (ordinary lessons): • Not process/cognitive/strategy oriented • Specific instruction: teacher talked about specific structural characteristics that texts; students read one example, composed their own text and the teacher corrected its; students did not have to revise their texts	The sampling was intentional (difficulties in access to schools). The sampling was neither random nor stratified, but group homogeneity. Control group: • Not specifically trained • Not receiving any process-oriented or cognitive-strategy instruction • Followed the ordinary curriculum	Administered in an equivalent manner across all participating schools In the students standard settings but not during timetabled classed	Differences between intervention groups • Planning vs. reflexivity + motivation in productivity, planning and self-efficacy. • Planning group better in productivity. • Reflexivity group moderate improvements in productivity and quality. • Motivational group better in self-beliefs. • Few improvements in self-efficacy and attitudes towards writing.

Table 1: (*Continued*)

Target learners	Goals	Instructional activities (-teacher/-student)	Assessment as part of the instruction	Professional development/ teacher's training	Implementation control groups	Fidelity of treatment	Durability and generalization	Length, amount of time	To do an empirical-based intervention (EBI)	How to describe the interventions in the future?
		• Specific instruction: organization, breadth of content, grammar, spelling, and the presence of the required structural features		.						

EPPyFPE: Evaluación de los Procesos de Planificación y otros Factores Psicológicos de la Escritura (Assessment of Planning Processes and other Writing Psychological Factors).

Conclusions

The first step for planning effective instruction and research in writing, is to identify key elements, as (i) recursivity of the process oriented, (ii) or consideration not only of the cognitive aspects but motivational ones, (iii) or accomplish to be EBIs. On that basis, the second step has to consider the relevant focus of research (see Table 1), as (i) the fidelity of the treatment, (ii) or the comparisons between groups and strategy models, (iii) or the generability and durability of the treatment effects. And last, with above questions answered, the building of a useful guide as agenda for the future in research and instruction in effective writing.

Acknowledgements

During this research project, we received competitive funds from the Ministry of Research, Science and Innovation — from the Spanish Government; project EDU2010-19250 (EDUC) for 2010–2013, in addition to European Union FEDER funds. Excellence Research Group funds from Junta de Castilla y León (GR259) and European funds for 2009–2011 (BOCyL 27, April 2009) were awarded to the Director/Principal Researcher (J.-N. García). We are very grateful to Rubén García-Martín for the data analysis of the orchestration processes; and to Jenny Gunn for the English correction.

References

Fidalgo, R., Torrance, M., & García, J.-N. (2008). The long-term effects of strategy-focussed writing instruction for grade six students. *Contemporary Educational Psychology*, *33*, 672–693.

García, J.-N., & de Caso, A. M. (2006). Comparison of the effects on writing attitudes and writing self-efficacy of three different training programs in students with learning disabilities. *International Journal of Educational Research*, *43*, 272–289.

García, J.-N., & Fidalgo, R. (2008). The Orchestration of writing processes and writing products: A comparison of 6th grade students with and without learning disabilities. *Learning Disabilities: A Contemporary Journal*, *6*(2), 77–98.

Pacheco, D. I., García, J.-N., & Díez, C. (2009). Self-efficacy, approach, and teacher's practice in the writing teaching. *European Journal of Education and Psychology*, *2*(2), 5–23.

Torrance, M., Fidalgo, R., & García, J.-N. (2007). The teachability and effectiveness of strategies for cognitive self-regulation in sixth grade writers. *Learning and Instruction*, *17*(3), 265–285.

Chapter 2.01.11

Improving Struggling Writers via Digital Recordings

Margunn Mossige and Per Henning Uppstad

Poor readers are normally characterized as being non-strategic and performing poorly on meta-cognition. The instructional approach to this group of students has largely been to help them to become more strategic and to improve their meta-cognitive abilities. The present project represents a different approach in providing individuals with a more concrete starting point for change in reading and writing performance.

Searching for adequate methods to guide elder students with writing difficulties to improve their writing, Mossige (2004) explored a method where the student should work top-down with text production and get so much insight in his own approach to writing that he might be able to evaluate his own writing strategies and writing habits. This was tested through training studies of four 16- to 17-year-old, dyslectic students (Mossige, 2004). In this study all students changed their approach of working to a varying degree, and improved that part of their text production which was focused in each case. All four students also improved their grades during the process.

Problems with word coding is considered the main problem for dyslectic writers, however, they show difficulties concerning all aspects of the writing process. Wengelin (2002) found, for example that grown-up dyslexics are extremely worried about word-coding problems, so much that it affects all other aspects of the writing process. While their peers are able to concentrate on higher levels of writing, such as the meaning, the style and the coherence, we assumed that the dyslectic writers were struggling with the basic skills.

Mossige's approach took as starting point that it would be fruitful to divide the writing process in three parts: planning, writing and revision. By planning as

Learning to Write Effectively: Current Trends in European Research
Studies in Writing, Volume 25, 115–117
Copyright © 2012 by Emerald Group Publishing Limited
All rights of reproduction in any form reserved
ISSN: 1572-6304/doi:10.1108/S1572-6304(2012)0000025028

thoroughly as possible and by postponing the work on spelling to a later stage, these students should be able to concentrate on higher text levels as content, context, formulations, style and the recipient of the writing during the moment of the text creation.

The first part of the experiment was to model the planning phase for the students.

The second part of text production, the writing, was analysed on the grounds of the students' drafts, and by statistics and replays of the ScriptLog-recordings in order to find out as much as possible about the writing process and the habits of the writer. This information was used to give the student focused and fine-grained feedback on how to improve the writing.

Mossige's work portrays two illustrating cases. The student O had written a long text with an interesting content, but he had great problems with the structure, the coherence and the syntax. The playback of the text production showed the cursor moving back and forth in the text, the student changing the orthography, key errors, formulations and content. Discussing these findings with O himself, he explained that he had developed a technique he called mini-draft, which consisted of writing a fast, preliminary draft, which ought to be filled out and changed a lot before the text was finished. This way of writing was partly a habit, partly a clever way of writing, he thought. He had to write fast to avoid forgetting the ideas he wanted to put on paper, he said, and he also liked to move backwards in the previously written text to expand or complete it.

Becoming aware of the bad result in his finished text, he agreed upon trying to avoid this mini-draft method, he would try to write continuously. Using good planning prevented the problem of forgetting his ideas. The replay and statistics in ScriptLog was used to control if he managed to change his habits, which he did, with good results.

The playback of L's writing process showed much the same cursor behaviour as O had. But in contrast to O' first text, L's finished text had a good coherence on all levels and a quite correct syntax. The assumption that writing without correcting orthography was good for the coherence and syntax, didn't quite fit here. L gave the explanation that he wrote slowly, and might correct the orthography or key errors during the writing, but improved words and phrases, coherence and content during these interruptions, too. He also read what he had written, and planned his next steps before moving on, he told. He sampled words he had used, trying to find the most precise word. We found that he worked on the higher text levels, which we had assumed a dyslexic wouldn't, and he wanted to go on that way, which we agreed in. We had to admit that the theory of cognitive overload did not fit L, but maybe the slowness of writing was his way to handling the complexity of the task?

Key-logging obviously has a potential both for guiding the students and for correcting the teacher's assumptions about the struggling writer. Maybe poor writers need such tutoring through their struggle with literacy more than others? The approach in our further research on the role of key-logging in improving writing relies on four assumptions: (1) observing one's own behaviour through digital recordings gives the individual a very fine-grained feedback, (2) the feedback is largely non-conscious or not verbalizable, (3) the feedback is open to the individual's own level of understanding and (4) the dynamic recording has a potential for personal involvement. Recent research has demonstrated the effectiveness of observational learning on the writing process (Braaksma, Rijlaarsdam, Van den Bergh, & Van Hout-Wolters, 2004) and we assume that this framework is fruitful also in the context of learning from digital recordings of one's own behaviour.

References

Braaksma, M. A. H., Rijlaarsdam, G., Van den Bergh, H., & Van Hout-Wolters, B. H. A. M. (2004). Observational learning and its effects on the orchestration of the writing process. *Cognition & Instruction, 22*(1), 1–36.

Mossige, M. (2004). *Å bruke det en har – å vite hva en mangler: Bruk av metakognisjon og top-down-metode for å fremme skriving hos dyslektikere i videregående skole.* Unpublished master-thesis, University of Stavanger.

Wengelin, Å. (2002). *Text production in adults with reading and writing difficulties.* Ph.D. thesis. Department of Linguistics, Göteborg University, Göteborg.

Chapter 2.01.12

Non-Fiction Writing in Lower Secondary School

Anne Håland

The aim of the study *Non-Fiction Writing in Lower Secondary School* is to explore and analyse the impact of model texts on written texts from pupils, and on their development as writers in school topics. I hope to find answers to the question whether model texts and the teaching offered by the teachers can be traced in the texts from the pupils: what the traces might be, and whether these model texts promote writing development in any significant way. Others have conducted similar controlled effect studies without being able to identify any substantial effects (Bereiter & Scardemalia, 1984). However, this study was carried out over a very limited period of time.

Method

I have chosen to follow a group of fifth graders for one school year. Different writing contexts are staged together with the teacher. The writing contexts have as a common denominator to be included in what we call non-fiction writing. Reading of model texts is an important part of the teaching in all writing contexts.

The three areas that the pupils will work in are logging, lab reports and topic texts. The model texts used are adapted from different domains (Gee, 2003). The model texts of log writing are adapted from working life, lab reports are constructed by us and belong to the natural science domain, whereas topic texts are adapted from different topic books written by authors of children's books.

Pupil texts and model texts are our main material. In addition, the reading of each new model text and work with the text in the classroom is videotaped. The teacher

Learning to Write Effectively: Current Trends in European Research
Studies in Writing, Volume 25, 119–121
ISSN: 1572-6304/doi:10.1108/S1572-6304(2012)0000025029

also writes a reflection log after each teaching session. The pupils are interviewed twice; the first time in the middle of the project and the second time when the project has ended. Two pupils are interviewed at the same time and the interview is semi-structured. The teachers are also interviewed twice.

The material consists of texts from 44 pupils, but I have 12 focus pupils who are followed particularly closely. The focus pupils are both boys and girls representing both weak and strong pupils.

Preliminary Results

A pilot study from the project shows that the pupils apply patterns from model texts and from the teaching given by their teachers in their own texts (Håland, 2009). A preliminary analysis of the pupil logs indicates that model texts yield patterns that erase differences between weak and strong pupils (Håland, 2010). In addition, it seems that the pupils position themselves relevantly in relation to the semiotic domain under which they write (Gee, 2003; Håland, 2009, 2010).

Conclusion

I will seek answers to the question whether model texts and the teaching offered leave traces in the texts of the pupils, and not least if these are traces that promote learning. In this work I need to define what developing as a writer implies. The material also makes a diversity of texts written by the pupils in fourth grade available. I can thus look at the development of the pupils not only during the project period, but also over an extended period of time.

Since the model texts are adapted from different domains, both specialized and not I intend to utilize different analytic tools to answer my research questions in a best possible way. A text linguistic approach to the written material from the pupils will be part of the analysis tools, and the way pupils position themselves as writers will also be an adjunct (Ongstad, 2004). In addition, it is logical to analyse the relevance of the texts within the domain in which they are written (Gee, 2003).

References

Bereiter, C., & Scardemalia, M. (1984). Learning about writing from reading. *Written Communication, 1*(2), 163–188.

Gee, J. P. (2003). Opportunity to learn: A language-based perspective on assessment. *Assessment in Education, 10*(1), 27–46.

Håland, A. (2010). Modelltekstar gir rammer! Skriving av biotoploggar på 5. trinn med utgangspunkt i autentiske loggar frå arbeidslivet [Model texts give a framework! Writing of biotoplog from the fifth grade, derived from authentic logs from work life]. In J. Smidt, I. Folkvord & A. J. Aasen (Eds.), *Rammer for skriving. Om skriveutvikling I skole og yrkesliv*

[*Frameworks for writing. Referenced to writing development in school and work life*]. Trondheim: Tapir Akademisk Forlag.

Håland, A. (2009). "Skriv slik at nokon får lyst til å lesa teksten din!" Fagtekstskriving på mellomtrinnet ["Write in a way that make others want to read your text!" Expository writing in lower secondary school]. In S. Knudsen, D. Skjeldbred & B. Aamotsbakken (Eds.), *Lys på lesing. Lesing av fagtekster i skolen* [*Focus on reading. Reading of non-fiction texts in school*]. Oslo: Novus Forlag.

Ongstad, S. (2004). *Språk, kommunikasjon og didaktikk. Norsk som flerfaglig og fagdidaktisk ressurs* [*Language, communication and didactic. Norwegian as multi disciplinary and didactic resource*]. Bergen: Fagbokforlaget.

Chapter 2.01.13

Observational Learning in Argumentative Writing

Martine Braaksma, Gert Rijlaarsdam and
Huub van den Bergh

In this research project about observational learning in argumentative writing, three issues in observational learning were addressed: the observational process itself, the role of learners' characteristics on the effect of different types of observational learning and the effect of observational learning on the mediating variable 'writing processes'. By studying these three issues, we aimed to contribute to the theoretical framework of observational learning. Using different methodologies — post-hoc analysis, experimental research and a case study — we tried to gain a better insight into the details of observational learning in argumentative writing.

Processes in Observational Learning

From the studies that are reported in Braaksma, Van den Bergh, Rijlaarsdam, and Couzijn (2001) and Braaksma, Rijlaarsdam, Van den Bergh, and Van Hout Wolters (2006), some insights are inferred on the processes involved in observational learning. We found that observers are strongly involved in meta-cognitive activities. They observe the writing of the models, identify and conceptualize the models' writing strategies, evaluate the performance of the models and reflect explicitly on the observed performances. The performance of these activities suggests that observers have developed, applied and internalized criteria for effective writing.

Two of these activities were found to be crucial for the effectiveness of observational learning: evaluation and elaboration. We established that these activities

Learning to Write Effectively: Current Trends in European Research
Studies in Writing, Volume 25, 123–126
Copyright © 2012 by Emerald Group Publishing Limited
All rights of reproduction in any form reserved
ISSN: 1572-6304/doi:10.1108/S1572-6304(2012)0000025030

are indeed already performed when observers are observing the performance of the models, and that observing the models' writing processes is sufficient to perform these activities. This is an important finding, because it refutes the alternative explanation of the effects of observational learning that the effect might also be attributed to the observation and comparison of the resulting texts, not of processes.

The results support the theoretical framework where we hypothesized that meta-cognitive activities construct the knowledge about writing, and where we assumed that these activities were stimulated in observational learning.

Effects on Writing Processes

We examined the effects of observational learning on the orchestration of writing processes (see Braaksma, Rijlaarsdam, Van den Bergh, & Van Hout Wolters, 2004). We found that observational learning influenced the writing processes differently than learning-by-doing. Writers who learned by observation performed relatively more meta-cognitive activities (Goal-orientation and Analysis) at the start and relatively more executional activities (Writing and Re-reading) in the second part of the writing process than writers who learned by doing. Over the whole writing process, writers who learned by observation showed more Planning activities than writers who learned by doing. Moreover, in the middle and last part of the writing process, writers who learned by observation performed increasingly more Meta-analysing activities, indicating monitoring and regulating processes, than writers who learned by doing. Furthermore, writers who learned by observation showed for some activities a changing execution over time, whereas writers in doing-writing condition performed these activities at a constant rate during the writing process (i.e. a monotonous process). Finally, we found that the orchestration of writing processes performed by the students who learned by observation was positively related to the quality of the writing product.

These effects from observational learning on writing processes are in line with the theoretical framework. Through adopting the orchestration examples the models provide, moving cognitive effort from writing to learning to write, and practicing meta-cognitive strategies, students in an observational learning environment may develop richer knowledge about writing. This knowledge influences writing processes in the direction we found: more knowledge about the task, the genre, the procedure, leads to more planning and analysis.

Effects of Learners' Characteristics on the Effects of Instructions

We have established that the same instructional method is not the most effective for every learner (Braaksma, Rijlaarsdam, & Van den Bergh, 2002). Moreover, task familiarity seemed to play an important role in this finding.

When a task is new, weak students benefited more from observational learning (focusing on weak models) than from performing writing tasks as they are less likely to use meta-cognitive strategies such as monitoring, evaluating and reflecting. Moreover, they profited from observational learning because their cognitive effort is shifted from executing writing tasks to learning from writing processes of others. They can thus focus on the learning task, providing themselves with a learning opportunity to acquire new understanding about writing. However, weak learners benefited only from observational learning when they reflect on weak models, they did not profit from reflecting on good models. Our explanation of this finding is that it is much easier to evaluate the weak model because the performance of the better model can be used as a reference. Besides, the performance of the observed weak model is probably more matched with the cognitive processes of a weak learner.

When a task is new for better learners they benefited not only from observational learning (focusing on good models) but also from performing writing tasks. They are probably able to divide their attention between writing task and learning task, and thus generate enough input for their learning by evaluating and reflecting on their own performance. However, good learners benefited only from observational learning when they reflect on good models, they did not profit from reflecting on weak models. Probably, the performance of a good model is more matched with the cognitive processes of a good learner. Moreover, good learners are able to identify and comment on the qualities of the good model, because they already have their own internal set of evaluation criteria available.

When a task is familiar, weak students benefited from performing writing tasks as much as they profited from focusing their observations on weak models' writing. Because the learners had already experienced successes with the tasks, they had a chance to construct knowledge about good writing, and thus were better equipped to learn from the writing task themselves. Reflecting on the performance of the better model however, was still not effective for these weak students.

When a task is familiar, good students profited only from observational learning with the focus on good models, not from focusing on weak models or from performing tasks themselves. Maybe, they need the challenge of explaining why the better model performed well.

The results concerning the observational conditions contribute to the research about the role that model-observer similarity plays in children's behavioural change (see Schunk, 1987).

References

Braaksma, M. A. H., Van den Bergh, H., Rijlaarsdam, G., & Couzijn, M. (2001). Effective learning activities in observation tasks when learning to write and read argumentative texts. *European Journal of Psychology of Education*, *1*, 33–48.

Braaksma, M. A. H., Rijlaarsdam, G., & Van den Bergh, H. (2002). Observational learning and the effects of model-observer similarity. *Journal of Educational Psychology*, *94*, 405–415.

Braaksma, M. A. H., Rijlaarsdam, G., Van den Bergh, H., & Van Hout Wolters, B. H. A. M. (2004). Observational learning and its effects on the orchestration of writing processes. *Cognition and Instruction, 22*(1), 1–36.

Braaksma, M. A. H., Rijlaarsdam, G., Van den Bergh, H., & Van Hout Wolters, B. H. A. M. (2006). What observational learning entails: A case study. *L1-Educational Studies in Language & Literature, 1,* 31–62.

Schunk, D. H. (1987). Peer models and children's behavioral change. *Review of Educational Research, 57,* 149–174.

Chapter 2.01.14

Hypertext Writing: Learning and Transfer Effects

Martine Braaksma, Gert Rijlaarsdam and
Huub van den Bergh

In the Netherlands the position of writing tasks in secondary education is twofold. Within the school subject Dutch, writing tasks are used in the context of 'learning-to-write': writing for communication. Students have to (learn to) write several text types, regularly in a communicative setting (e.g. writing an opinion article). In other subject domains, writing is focused on 'writing-to-learn', and is used as a learning or assessment tool. In all writing tasks, information and communication technology (ICT) plays an important role in information retrieval and in text composition and revision. Students can choose to produce a hypertext (i.e. a non-linear text in which information is organized as a network in which nodes are text chunks and links are relationships between the nodes; Rouet, Levonen, Dillon, & Spiro, 1996).

Nevertheless, there is a large gap between the possibility of constructing hypertexts at school and the current practice at schools. An analysis of textbooks and a questionnaire and interviews with students showed that within the subject Dutch, students do not write hypertexts. However, it is suggested that hypertext writing might enhance students' writing abilities (e.g. Lohr, Ross, & Morrison, 1995) and learning outcomes (Haas & Wickman, 2009).

We also suppose that hypertext writing could have beneficial effects on writing skills (writing processes and writing products). These proposed effects build on research by Braaksma, Rijlaarsdam, Couzijn, and Van den Bergh (2002). They observed that students who performed hypertext-like tasks executed more planning and analysing activities during writing than students who performed linear text-tasks. These planning and analysing activities were positively related to text quality,

Learning to Write Effectively: Current Trends in European Research
Studies in Writing, Volume 25, 127–130
ISSN: 1572-6304/doi:10.1108/S1572-6304(2012)0000025031

both in the hypertext-tasks and in the linear text-tasks. Therefore, it was concluded that writing hypertexts might stimulate the use of writing activities that are positively related to writing proficiency.

Method

We set up an experimental study in which 102 participants (10th grade) followed a lesson series in argumentative writing in two versions: a hypertext version (HYP) for the experimental hypertext writing condition, and a linear version (LIN) for the linear writing control condition. The two versions of the lesson series were similar in many aspects: same text type (argumentative text), theme, documentation materials, instruction time, etc. The first three lessons were exactly the same. Only the fourth and the fifth lesson differed between the conditions. Then, students in the HYP-condition ($N = 41$) wrote their argumentative text in a hypertext format. In contrast, students in the LIN-condition ($N = 61$) wrote a linear text (for more information about the lesson series see Braaksma, Rijlaarsdam, & Janssen, 2007).

Pre-tests (aptitude, computer skills) and post-tests (writing of a linear text) were administered. For a sample of participants ($N = 59$) logfiles of (linear) post-test essays were collected as well, providing indicative data for writing processes. For another sample of participants ($N = 16$), the writing of their hypertexts ($N = 8$) and linear texts ($N = 8$) in the intervention was logged as well.

Results

No *a priori* differences between conditions on computer skills and aptitude were observed. The quality of the linear writing post-test was coded globally. Regression analysis showed no differences between conditions on linear text quality for students with a medium aptitude. However, an aptitude-treatment interaction was found. The regression slopes differed significantly between the two conditions showing that students with a higher aptitude wrote a linear text of a higher quality in the post-test when they were in the hypertext-condition during the intervention than students in the linear condition. In future analyses, the logfiles of the (linear) post-test writing tasks will be related to the quality of the writing task to see whether we can find a relation between (some) process characteristics and text quality.

In regression analyses on the logfiles scores administered during hypertext writing and linear writing, we focused on different pause locations during writing and on production activities. Table 1 shows whether a (positive or negative) relation was found between the duration of time and number of pauses or production activities and text quality. For instance, for pausing between words a positive relation was found between the amount of time that was devoted to pausing and text quality in the middle of the writing process. A negative relation was found for the amount of

Table 1: Significant relations for duration and amount and text quality in three phases of the writing process.

	Start		Middle		End	
	Duration	**Amount**	**Duration**	**Amount**	**Duration**	**Amount**
Pausing within words						
Pausing between words			+		−	
Pausing between sentences	+		−	+		
Pausing between paragraphs						−
Production				+		

time devoted to pausing between words and text quality at the end of the writing process.

Furthermore, we tested whether we could find differences between conditions (HYP vs. LIN) on the different locations of pausing and production activities. Regression analysis showed that students in the linear condition devoted significantly more time to pausing between words in the beginning of the writing process than students in the hypertext condition and also spent more time in pausing between sentences in the middle of the writing process than students who wrote a hypertext. Students in the hypertext condition performed more frequently production activities and performed these for a longer period than students in the linear condition.

Conclusions

With our study we aimed to show that hypertext writing could have beneficial effects on writing skills. We found some differences in process characteristics between hypertext writing and linear writing. Linear writing showed more time spent in pausing between words in the beginning of the writing process and in pausing between sentences in the middle part than hypertext writing. Contrasting, students in the hypertext condition showed more frequently and during a longer time production activities during the whole writing process than students in the linear condition. Furthermore, it was found that (some of) the process activities that were mainly performed by students in the linear condition (much time devoted to pausing between sentences in the middle part) were negatively related with text quality and the activities that were mainly performed by students in the hypertext condition were positively related with text quality (executing frequently production activities in the middle part of the writing process). We might conclude that we found similar results as in our earlier study (Braaksma et al., 2002). However, one should realize that the earlier study was conducted with think aloud protocols and in the current study process characteristics were assessed with logfiles (which give no information about the content of the process) so we cannot compare these two studies entirely.

Acknowledgement

This project is funded by Netherlands Organization for Scientific Research (Grant 411-03-115).

References

Braaksma, M. A. H., Rijlaarsdam, G., Couzijn, M., & Van den Bergh, H. (2002). Learning to compose hypertext and linear text: Transfer or interference? In R. Bromme & E. Stahl (Eds.), *Writing hypertext and learning: Conceptual and empirical approaches* (pp. 15–38). London: Elsevier Science.

Braaksma, M., Rijlaarsdam, G., & Janssen, T. (2007). Writing hypertexts: Proposed effects on writing processes and knowledge acquisition. *L1 — Educational Studies in Language and Literature, 7*(4), 93–122.

Haas, C., & Wickman, C. (2009). Hypertext and writing. In R. Beard, D. Myhill, J. Riley & M. Nystrand (Eds.), *The SAGE handbook of writing development* (pp. 527–544). London: Sage.

Lohr, L., Ross, S. M., & Morrison, G. R. (1995). Using a hypertext environment for teaching process writing: An evaluation study of three student groups. *Educational Technology Research & Development, 43*(2), 33–51.

Rouet, J-F., Levonen, J. J., Dillon, A., & Spiro, R. J. (Eds.). (1996). *Hypertext and cognition.* Mahwah, NJ: Lawrence Erlbaum.

Chapter 2.01.15

Effective Instructional Strategies in Collaborative Revision in EFL: Two Empirical Studies

Elke Van Steendam, Gert Rijlaarsdam, Lies Sercu and Huub van den Bergh

Various methods have been suggested to teach novice revisers to improve their revision and writing skills such as peer interaction and collaborative revision, and strategy instruction. One form of strategy instruction which has proven to be particularly effective as far as learning-to-write and learning-to-revise is concerned is observational learning (Braaksma, Rijlaarsdam, & Van den Bergh, 2002). The research reported on in this paper, conducted in the context of a PhD study, combines insights from research on these various instructional methods. Its main purpose was to investigate the more effective instructional method to improve both revision and writing skills of foreign language learners of English. Two major research questions were investigated. A first question studies the impact of different instructional strategies and of their combination on the quality of individually and collaboratively revised texts (= Research Question 1). A second research question explores what the more effective instructional method is to have a transfer effect from revising other students' writing to writing one's own text (= Research Question 2). Apart from answering these two questions for the average student, we also explored the effect of the instructional strategies on both below- and above-average writers and on different types of ability dyads in terms of writing proficiency.

Learning to Write Effectively: Current Trends in European Research
Studies in Writing, Volume 25, 131–134
ISSN: 1572-6304/doi:10.1108/S1572-6304(2012)0000025032

Methodology

The two research questions were explored in two relatively large-scale semi-experimental studies with undergraduate foreign language learners. In the two studies different forms of strategy instruction were implemented in collaborative revision to determine the impact of each separate approach. Central to the two studies under review are observation and practising (so-called 'learning-by-doing') to instruct a revision strategy. In the experimental design of both studies based on Schunk and Zimmerman's Cognitive Model of Sequential Skill Acquisition (1997), each condition has two distinct phases: an instruction phase and an emulation phase. In the Instruction phase students were instructed in the use of a revision strategy in different ways. Either students watched a mastery peer dyad model the use of the revision strategy (= Observation) by applying it to a formal business letter containing higher-order errors on the structural and content level or they practised the revision strategy themselves by applying it to the same business letter (= Practising) with or without the use of a procedural facilitator. This first instruction phase was followed by an Emulation phase during which students exercised the strategy either in dyads or individually (cf. Van Steendam, Rijlaarsdam, Sercu, & Van den Bergh, 2010). Ultimately then, by contrasting different conditions in both studies, we were able to test the impact of experimental variables such as Observation versus Practising and Individual versus Dyad, on revision skill (cf. Van Steendam et al., 2010).

In both studies, near transfer to writing was measured by administering students an individual writing post-test after the experimental intervention. Through analysing this post-test we wanted to test which of the conditions was more effective in bringing about a transfer effect from revising other students' writing to writing one's own text.

In each study the impact of the instructional strategies was thus tested on two dependent variables: (1) revision quality comprising the detection, diagnosis and revision of structural and content problems (= Learning variable) and (2) writing quality including both holistic and primary-trait scores (= Transfer variable).

The written genre subject to both studies is a formal business letter. The studies combine both product and process measures (log files of revision and writing processes and of collaborative processes) and data are analysed both quantitatively and qualitatively. Product measures have been analysed using multilevel analyses. The analysis of process measures is ongoing at the moment of writing.

Results

Research Question 1: Effect of instructional methods on Learning variable. Salient results for revision quality reported in Van Steendam et al. (2010) mainly showed a statistically significant interaction effect: the effect of instruction depends on the setting of a subsequent exercising or emulation session and the effect of emulation type depends on the preceding instruction type. Observation is a powerful instructional method if the consequent emulation is a collaborative undertaking. However, a more traditional practice-only treatment proves to be as productive if followed by individual emulation (Van Steendam et al., 2010). Dyadic practising turns out to be least effective as preparation for collaborative revision. Additionally, analyses revealed a statistically significant interaction effect between instruction and pair composition. Pair composition moderates the effect of observation: homogeneous dyads in terms of writing proficiency seem to profit more from observation than from practising, whereas weak, heterogeneous dyads made up of two initially weak writers benefit significantly more from dyadic practising (Van Steendam, 2008).

Research Question 2: Effect on instructional methods on Transfer variable. The second research question investigates what the more optimal implementation of learning-to-write through learning-to-revise is. Both experimental studies show that revision of other students' texts is a powerful pedagogical method in writing instruction as students in all experimental conditions in both studies progressed significantly from pre- to post-test writing. Additionally, salient results showed statistically significant interaction effects between learner characteristics such as writing proficiency and instructional effectiveness: especially initially stronger writers benefited significantly more from observation than their counterparts in a practising condition irrespective of the fact if they revised collaboratively or individually. Initially more proficient writers write significantly more structured and reader-oriented letters after having observed a collaborative revision model. Observation thus seems to be a powerful instructional strategy for stronger writers to induce a transfer effect from revising the content and structure of other students' writing to generating and structuring one's own text. That observation of an expert peer model has a positive impact on text quality for stronger writers confirms prior research by Braaksma et al. (2002).

Conclusion

The studies conducted enabled us to look at issues which have remained relatively unexplored in research on strategy instruction and observational learning:

(1) the dichotomy individual versus collaborative revision and the effect of observation on collaborative revision;
(2) 'the combination ... of different instructional components ... of highly effective strategy instruction packages', in this case of observation or practicing followed by collaborative or individual emulation in revision (Van Steendam et al., 2010, p. 319) and
(3) the more optimal implementation of learning-to-write through learning-to-revise.

These issues were investigated with (4) foreign language learners, a target group which has not been studied frequently in research on cognitive strategy instruction in writing and on observational learning. The results further attest to the importance of differentiation in writing instruction for different types of learners (cf. Kieft, Rijlaarsdam, & Van den Bergh, 2008). One of the more salient findings is the interaction between pair composition and instructional strategy as few studies in collaborative writing and revision study the interaction between pair composition and instruction.

References

Braaksma, M. A. H., Rijlaarsdam, G., & Van den Bergh, H. (2002). Observational learning and the effects of model-observer similarity. *Journal of Educational Psychology, 94*, 405–415.

Kieft, M., Rijlaarsdam, G., & Van den Bergh, H. (2008). An aptitude-treatment interaction approach to writing-to-learn. *Learning and Instruction, 18*(4), 379–390.

Schunk, D. H., & Zimmerman, B. J. (1997). Social origins of self-regulatory competence. *Educational Psychologist, 32*, 195–208.

Van Steendam, E. (2008). *Effective instructional strategies in collaborative revision in EFL: Two empirical studies.* Unpublished doctoral dissertation, University of Leuven, Leuven, Belgium.

Van Steendam, E., Rijlaarsdam, G., Sercu, L., & Van den Bergh, H. (2010). The effect of strategy instruction on the quality of peer feedback in ESL/EFL. *Learning and Instruction, 20*, 316–327.

Chapter 2.01.16

Tutoring the End-of-Studies Dissertation: Helping Psychology Students Find Their Personal Voice When Revising Academic Texts

Montserrat Castelló, Anna Iñesta, Marta Pardo,
Eva Liesa and Reinaldo Martínez-Fernández

Students' difficulties to write academic complex texts such as research projects at the university have been pointed out by several recent studies (Castelló, Iñesta, & González, 2008) and consequently, an important number of research applied proposals have been developed to teach students those strategies which will allow them to manage the complexity of writing those texts.

Among the strategies which intervention studies have been recently focusing on are those aimed to teach students the discursive mechanisms linked to making voice and authorship visible in their academic texts. According to these premises we have designed an intervention because the possibility to teach undergraduate students how to manage the discursive mechanisms useful to make their own voice visible in texts without neglecting the requirements and conventions of academic texts, still remains hardly explored.

The intervention proposal had the general aim to help graduate students' use the discursive mechanisms to make visible their academic voice in texts through collaborative revisions in two different learning environments: online and face-to face tutorial meetings, and also to avoid plagiarism practices.

Learning to Write Effectively: Current Trends in European Research
Studies in Writing, Volume 25, 135–139
ISSN: 1572-6304/doi:10.1108/S1572-6304(2012)0000025033

Method

We have used a quasi-experimental design where the two conditions have been compared. The variables analysed were the students' knowledge of the characteristics of academic texts, the students' satisfaction with their writing strategies and with the intervention, the nature of collaborative text revision process and the quality of the final texts.

The sample was formed by 58 undergraduate Psychology students (21–22 years old), originally grouped in four classes (seminars). Those students have to write a brief dissertation explaining a research project they have carried out in previous semester. The text should fulfil the requirements of a scientific paper and this implies a real challenge for undergraduate students.

Those students were organized in two conditions. Condition 1, which was formed by 28 students, distributed in two modalities, online (12 students) and face-to-face intervention (16 students). Condition 2 where 30 students didn't receive writing tutorial (control group).

The intervention was led by 'seminar' teachers and researchers and took place in the natural classroom setting (in the case of the face-to-face condition) and in the Moodle website environment (in the case of the online condition).

Objectives

The intervention had the general aim to help graduate students' use the discursive mechanisms to make visible their academic voice in texts through collaborative revisions, in two different learning environments: online and face-to-face tutorial meetings.

More precisely, the proposal had the following objectives:

Facilitate students' revision strategies of academic texts
Improve the students' overall text quality

Improve the students' use of specific discursive mechanisms:

To maintain a stance and to make visible their academic voice
To dialogue with other voices and authors
To organize the information according to the expected characteristics of scientific papers in the field of psychology
To analyse the impact of virtual and face-to-face environments in the accomplishment of former objectives

The Course

We developed a course in which we combine the students' reflection and collaborative revisions (Castelló, 2008; Castelló, Iñesta, & Monereo, 2009). The course was incardinated in the already ongoing weekly tutorial meetings and was shaped by two different types of sessions; the first ones were devoted to increase students' knowledge and in the second type of sessions students revise their texts (drafts) collaboratively with their peers and with the help of the tutor.

The course content focused on:

The discursive mechanisms useful to maintain their stance all along the text.
The scientific paper structure and the way in which the organization of the information contributes to clarity and to make the author's position visible.
The different way in which citations and references can be used in scientific texts to discuss and dialogue with other authors.

The activities sequence consists of the following steps:

The students select their research topic.
The students read the necessary literature.
The students write a first version of their end-of-studies dissertation.
The students receive lessons about discursive resources necessary to make their voice visible in their texts.
The students revise the text of a peer with a writing guideline and did some suggestions to improve the text.
In peers, students discuss the revisions and suggestions to improve their text.
The students modify the text according to the suggestions received.

Guidance and Feedback

Tutors usually focus on how and where to search relevant databases and select readings and they also guide the process of identifying key concepts, mapping authors and organizing information. Regarding writing, tutors have developed a system of guidance in order to guarantee students' accomplishment of academic formal requirements

However tutors have problems trying to help them make their voice visible in their texts, to establish a personal but justified point of view, to maintain a stance all along the text and to progress in the argumentation without losing this stance. This was the focus of our intervention in which students, working in dyads, revised their peers' texts with the help of a writing guideline. Before the tutorial session, students also thought of suggestions to improve it and in the tutorial session students shared and discussed those suggestions. The teacher helped them to improve revision strategies and using guidelines, and offered their own suggestions about what need to be revised (Castelló, 2008).

Assessment

Students' activity is continuously monitored during instruction, both by seminar teachers and by the researchers. The teachers' assessment takes into account: the content of the text, length of paragraphs, references or notes, as well as interest and motivation. The researchers' assessment takes into consideration whether and in what ways students use the resources related with stance, intertextuality and information organization and gives some orientation or corrections when students need some help.

Regarding the quality of the final text, we used an assessment grid which includes different dimensions and aspects to be evaluated following the analytical approaches in written text quality assessment. Factorial analysis of this assessment grid (Main components with Varimax rotation for SPSS) revealed two highly related components ($r = .857$; $p < .001$) explaining text quality. We labelled these factors text organization (F1) and author's voice (F2).

To assess students' knowledge of the characteristics of scientific and academic texts in the field of psychology, we developed a questionnaire consisted of 12 items addressing the contents of the course, that is the discursive mechanisms useful to make author's voice visible in texts ($\alpha = .75$).

We also analysed the type of suggestions students or the tutor made when collaboratively revising the two successive versions of the final text. In this case, the three first authors of this paper transcribed and discussed all the suggestions in order to group them in categories which were fully revised until consensus was reached. Then three trained judges analysed data of suggested changes in texts using the categories and the ratio of agreement was of 98%. In those few cases in which there wasn't agreement, the adscription to one of the categories was discussed until consensus was reached.

Finally, the students' course degree of satisfaction and involvement was assessed by a 10 items questionnaire and an open-ended survey (5 questions) that they answered at the end of the intervention

Results

Taking into account the qualitative and quantitative analysis it seems possible to confirm that our students learnt to revise peers' texts, and, they were also able to make changes in their own texts, especially at the end of the intervention, taking advantage of collaborative revision. Text quality was significant better for both intervention groups than for control group, and better texts were related with higher rates of revisions and more students' knowledge and satisfaction with the course.

References

Castelló, M., Iñesta, A., & González, L. (2008). Socially shared regulation in writing. Paper presented at the Sig-Writing Conference, Lundt. Retrieved from http://sig-writing.publication-rchive.com/public?fn = enter&repository = 1&article = 410. Accessed on October 22, 2008.

Castelló, M. (2008). Escribir trabajos de investigación con alumnos de grado. *Textos de didàctica de la lengua y de la literatura, 50,* 21–29.

Castelló, M., Iñesta, A., & Monereo, C. (2009). Towards self-regulated academic writing: an exploratory study with graduate students in a situated learning environment. *Electronic Journal of Research in Educational Psychology, 9*(3). Retrieved from http://www.investigacion-psicopedagogica.org/revista/new/english/ContadorArticulo.php?367

Chapter 2.01.17

Learning Philosophy by Writing in a Community of Learning

Mariona Corcelles and Montserrat Castelló

Studies on collaborative writing, writing to learn in specific subjects and writing across curriculum have shown that writing mediates knowledge construction (Bazerman et al., 2005). Writing and collaborative writing especially give students opportunities to participate in disciplinary dialogues to negotiate their voice and position into a particular community (Lemke, 1997; Prior, 1998). Collaborative writing also enables to create a multivocal and dialogic context in which teachers can promote learning by juxtaposing these voices (Dysthe, 1996).

According to these premises, we have created a collaborative context to learn Philosophy in secondary education where writing is used as a dialogic tool to think, talk and discuss the philosophy discourses. This context tries to develop the philosophical competences described by Tozzi (2008): problematization (formulating relevant philosophical questions and problems); conceptualization (defining and using philosophical concepts) and argumentation (arguing one's own point of view).

The classroom was organized as a learning community with stable and heterogeneous work teams of three or four students. The academic course was divided into three didactic units with the same sequence of activities regarding individual and collaborative writing:

Beginning of the didactic unit: Students write (individually) an argumentative philosophical text grounded on their previous ideas on the topic to be studied. This activity is useful not only to collect previous knowledge about the topic but also to know about students' argumentative skills.

Development of the didactic unit: These individual texts are discussed until all the philosophical concepts are introduced and, if necessary, explained by the teacher (multivoiced and dialogic classroom).

Learning to Write Effectively: Current Trends in European Research
Studies in Writing, Volume 25, 141–143
ISSN: 1572-6304/doi:10.1108/S1572-6304(2012)0000025034

Writing instruction: Think-sheets are used to analyse readings and to negotiate the characteristics of argumentative philosophical texts. Good samples are analysed with the teacher's guidance and modelling.

End of the didactic unit: To synthesize the content learned, students write an argumentative philosophical text collaboratively to publish their reflections about the topic studied in the School's Journal. These collaborative texts are co-assessed by other teams and the teacher (guidelines provided).

Finally, students rewrite their first individual text.

The writing intervention was implemented by the Philosophy teacher over an academic year. Prior to the intervention, the teacher was trained during one year since he plays a key role in transforming the classroom into a learning community.

The aim of the present case study is to analyse how students learn to develop philosophical competences by means of individual and collaborative writing. Qualitative and quantitative methodologies are combined.

Data were collected in the natural classroom setting along the academic year (2008–2009). Participants were 4 work teams (15 students). We collected 12 collaborative texts and 69 individual texts (27 initials and 42 revised). The whole writing sequence was not possible to follow in the third didactic unit for contextual reasons. The students couldn't start the unit with the individual text, had less time to do the collaborative text, didn't have the co-assessment session but did the individual text at the end of the unit.

The students' texts were assessed taking into account two dimensions of analysis related to philosophical competences:

Problematization: clear definition of a philosophical problem using philosophical questions.

Argumentation: clear author's position (thesis), provision of arguments and examples, provision of counterarguments, presence of coherent conclusion.

The conceptualization competence is included in the problematization and argumentation competence analysis because, in order to have a high punctuation in both dimensions, students need to use philosophical concepts. We included two more dimensions: one, related to a linguistic aspects such as coherence and cohesion properties of the text and a second, related to a global evaluation of the text.

All dimensions were assessed qualitatively in a range of 1–5 by two trained researchers. Examples of each punctuation were provided and interjudge agreement was 87%.

Results showed that the second collaborative texts improved in all the dimensions. This was not the case for the third texts. This could be explained by the conditions of the educational context, since, as we said, students didn't have time to plan and revise this third collaborative text.

Results regarding quality of the individual texts showed that there are improvements in the four dimensions along the academic course. This means, that revised texts were better than the first ones and the overall quality of those texts increased all along the academic year.

In conclusion, on the one hand, students developed the philosophical competences by participating in the community using the philosophical genre (Lemke, 1997). We collected empirical evidences that they learned to formulate philosophical questions, to analyse problems of the contemporary world and to argue their point of view in relation to the philosophical content. On the other hand, this study also highlights the relevance of the learning context conditions and the writing sequence (learning and having time to plan, elaborate and revise the text both collaboratively and individually) as predictors of text quality.

References

Bazerman, C., Little, J., Bethel, L., Chavkin, T., Fouquette, D., & Garufis, J. (2005). *Writing across the curriculum. Reference guides to rhetoric and composition.* Parlor Press and WAC Clearinghouse. Retrieved from http://wac.colostate.edu/books/bazerman_wac/

Dysthe, O. (1996). The multivoiced classroom: Interaction of writing and classroom discourse. *Written Communication, 13*(3), 385–425.

Lemke, J. L. (1997). Aprender a hablar ciencia. Lenguaje, aprendizaje y valores. BCN. Paidos.

Prior, P. (1998). *A sociohistorical account of literate activity in the academy.* Mahwah, NJ: Lawrence Erlbaum.

Tozzi, M. (2008) De la question des competénces en philosophie. *Diotime*, 36.

Chapter 2.01.18

Improving Students' Academic Writing: The Results of Two Empirical Projects

Helmut Gruber, Birgit Huemer and Markus Rheindorf

In this paper, we report the results of two projects (FWF projects P14720-G03 and L 179-G03) which were conducted during the last years at the Linguistics department of Vienna University and which aimed (a) at establishing an empirical basis for the development of writing courses for humanities students and (b) at developing and testing a prototype of such a course in a blended learning framework.

In the first study (Gruber et al., 2006), Austrian university students' writing practices in three social science disciplines (social history, business studies, business psychology) were investigated. Following a multidisciplinary approach, the study combined textual analyses with interview analyses and participant observation of three courses. In the theoretical framework which combined Bourdieu's concepts of habitus and field (Bourdieu, 1992) with the academic literacies approach (Jones, Turner, & Street, 1999), a text production model was developed which differentiates between 'text types' (abstract units on a rather general level) which are mainly influenced by the social and institutional purposes they serve and 'genres' which are (semiotically enriched) realizations of text types in certain institutional and social contexts. Text types and genres are related to field-specific habitus of persons insofar as the knowledge which text types and genres are appropriate for which kind of task in a field are relevant symbolic capitals. One general goal of the project was to investigate if students already develop a discipline-specific habitus and hence if they produce texts which realize discipline-specific genres. A further major goal was to investigate if and which linguistic features of a seminar paper correlate with the grade it receives.

Quantitative and qualitative text analyses of all linguistic characteristics (generic and rhetorical structures, meta-communication, intertextuality, argumentation,

Learning to Write Effectively: Current Trends in European Research
Studies in Writing, Volume 25, 145–147
Copyright © 2012 by Emerald Group Publishing Limited
ISSN: 1572-6304/doi:10.1108/S1572-6304(2012)0000025035

modality, lexis) which were analysed showed that students in the three seminars produced different genres which, however, belonged to one abstract text type which was coined 'academic qualification text'. This text type is located at the intersection of two social fields, namely the field of academia and the field of the university respectively (Bourdieu, 1992).

The results of the interview analyses showed that students are aware of this doubled institutional purpose of the text type in differing, yet systematically varying ways. Whereas social history students mainly oriented towards the academic purpose of a seminar paper and thus display the habitus of 'apprentice scholars', management students and most of the business psychology students orient towards the assessment character of the texts they produce and thus display a 'student habitus'.

The relationship between linguistic features of the texts and the grades the papers received was not straightforward. Most linguistic features of the micro-textual level do not show any correlation with the grades the papers received. Many features of the meso- and macro-textual level, however, do show rather systematic correlations with grades.

In the second project (Gruber, Huemer, & Rheindorf, 2009), an academic writing course for (advanced) students which was based on the results of the previous project was developed in a blended learning framework (Apel & Kraft, 2003). The course design comprised the development of (a) a web-based entrance module which consists of a self assessment of students' writing skills, and an investigation of the extent of their demand of assistance; (b) a general (discipline-independent) module containing information on academic writing; (c) two discipline-specific modules offering information on and training in academic writing (developed for Linguistics and Social and Economic History students). The entrance module consists of a series of questions and tasks that students have to complete and is designed to detect the individual students' level of previous writing experience and knowledge. This module was implemented on Vienna University's learning platform. The results of the entrance module were used to decide whether individual students were advised to work through one (or several) chapters of the general module before attending the writing course, or if they could attend the writing course without additional pre-course instruction. For the purpose of developing didactic applications of the linguistic results of the previous projects, the linguistic concepts and categories (see above) were 'translated' into 'everyday concepts' of scholarly work with which students were expected to be familiar. The general module covers seven broad areas which are relevant for a functional understanding of the specifics of academic language and academic genres in the humanities and social sciences: 'What is science?'; 'Scholarly work'; 'Academic language'; 'Differences between everyday language and academic language'; 'Structuring a paper'; 'Perspective'; 'Describing, Explaining, and Argumentation'. The module was designed as a hypertext and is available online at http://www.univie.ac.at/linguistics/schreibprojekt/Grundlagen. The two discipline specific courses elaborate the language-related aspects of the general module and comprise the following broad areas: 'Structuring a paper', 'Perspective', 'Explanation and argumentation' and 'The thematic thread'. Their development followed a blended learning approach, which integrates face-to-face and online learning phases, and draws on theories of communication, computer-mediated communication, cognitive psychology and education. In order to keep dependence on the e-learning platform to a minimum, course materials were mainly developed as written manuals and as MS-PowerPoint presentations, the learning platform was only used for communication with and between students and for exercises. The first instalment of the writing course was taught by two research assistants during the summer semester of 2008 at Vienna University and the whole course was evaluated by course participants via online feedback, questionnaires and oral feedback at the end of the semester. Results of this feedback were used to redesign the entrance module and to implement slight changes in both the general and the two discipline-specific modules.

References

Apel, H., & Kraft, S. (Eds.). (2003). *Online lehren*. Bielefeld: Bertelsmann Verlag.

Bourdieu, P. (1992). *Homo academicus*. Frankfurt: Suhrkamp.

Gruber, H., Huemer, B., & Rheindorf, M. (2009). *Wissenschaftlich Schreiben. Ein Praxisbuch für die Geistes- und Sozialwissenschaften*. Wien: Böhlau.

Gruber, H., Muntigl, P., Reisigl, M., Rheindorf, M., Wetschanow, K., & Christine, C. (2006). *Genre, Habitus und wissenschaftliches Schreiben*. Münster: LIT Verlag.

Jones, C., Turner, J., & Street, B. (Eds.). (1999). *Students writing in the university. Cultural and epistemological issues*. Amsterdam: John Benjamins.

Chapter 2.01.19

Classroom Teaching of Writing Throughout Schooling

Luísa Álvares Pereira, Inês Cardoso and M. José Loureiro

In this paper, by presenting some results of the research we have conducted on the learning of writing and on its underlying teaching practices (Pereira, Aleixo, Cardoso, & Graça, 2010), we aim at providing an important contribution to the first and second working groups — (i) early acquisition of writing skills and (ii) improvements in written communication. Up until now, our work has focused mainly on the three cycles of Compulsory Education in Portugal (covering nine school years) and has allowed us to observe that (a) the teaching of writing put into practice is frequently simplistic and reductive; (b) there is a huge gap between classroom practices and principles emanated from research conducted in this domain (Pereira, 2004). Bearing in mind this scenario, we have aimed at conducting research which allows us to intervene in the classroom work in order to produce knowledge either about the students' writing practices and their relationship with writing or about the teachers' practices concerning the development of students' writing skills. More specifically, we have tried to develop teaching/learning and educational devices which may lead teachers to reflect upon and renew their teaching practices as well as their own relationship with writing.

Furthermore, this group has also developed a study on academic writing, in both online and face-to-face contexts, which focused especially on the argumentative text and on writing-from-sources.

It is important to notice that all our studies consisted in qualitative and interpretative case studies — data was collected by the means of interviews, classroom video recording and questionnaires — which were also complemented by quantitative analyses.

Learning to Write Effectively: Current Trends in European Research
Studies in Writing, Volume 25, 149–152
Copyright © 2012 by Emerald Group Publishing Limited
All rights of reproduction in any form reserved
ISSN: 1572-6304/doi:10.1108/S1572-6304(2012)0000025036

Focusing specifically on the Portuguese Language 'classroom', our aims are to understand how students develop academic literacy and to analyse teachers' contributions towards that development. Teachers usually consider that the transposition reading-writing is immediate; such representation has motivated the development and testing of learning materials for classroom intervention. For the purpose of this report, we have selected, from a number of PhD and Master research projects, three examples which include the implementation of a Didactic Sequence, the use of Writing Notebooks and a Workshop about Writing. Each one of these didactic tools focuses on one of the three important dimensions of written production which we believe to be complementary in the teaching/learning process of such a complex competence as writing: the cognitive/procedural dimension of written production; the dimension of the subject's relationship with writing; and the social dimension of written language.

Thus, the Didactic Sequence (Pereira & Cardoso, 2011) joins together a social dimension of the written production — given that the writing choices are dependent from the communicative contexts and from the text genres concerned — and a more procedural dimension. Indeed, the Didactic Sequence aims more at the teaching/learning of a specific text genre, by putting into practice teaching modules particularly focused on the development of the skills implied in the writing process of that particular genre and which students are expected to learn how to handle.

This is a teaching/learning device which privileges (i) the recursive nature of the writing process, (ii) the insertion of the written productions in real or virtual communicative contexts, (iii) rewriting and (iv) the hard task of revision. We highlight a set of studies focused on the development of textual revision, whose results stress the relevance of the strategies of collaboration, interaction and verbalization in the construction of knowledge about written production (Pereira, Cardoso, & Graça, 2009).

In relation to the Writing Notebooks, they are specially conceived for allowing the emergence of the students' personal writing. Additionally, they provide students with the opportunity to have readers for their texts and contributions to improve them. Thus, these notebooks focus on the emergence of an author-subjects relationship, which school is also responsible for fostering.

By making students verbalize their personal relationship with writing, the Workshop about Writing also aims at making learner/individual (re)discover significations for the writing production which may favour a higher individual commitment in the process of appropriation of written production.

As far as higher education is concerned, a specific platform was validated for the development of online argumentation, by providing different digital tools such as Structured Chats, Graph Tool — for mapping arguments — and note taking (Loureiro, Pinho, Pereira, & Moreira, 2008).

In conclusion, our research has attempted to validate teaching/learning devices which (a) incorporate the main theoretical frameworks concerning the teaching/learning of written language and (b) foster teachers' contribution towards the improvement of the student's relationship with writing — from an identitarian relationship (which already seems to exist) to an epistemic relationship. Although the latter does not exclude the former, it acquires a crucial importance within the school context, given that it is a privileged context for knowledge-telling and knowledge construction.

Our studies have raised some problems/issues related to the teaching of different text genres and the importance of understanding students' individual relationships with writing as a global subject. Results suggest that the pedagogical approaches mentioned above, the production of texts based on students' personal/own motivation and the understanding of the triad activity/student/subject's motivation contribute towards the improvement of the written teaching/learning processes and can help each student use writing as citizens with full rights. Moreover, the use of specific text genre online platforms and the process of note-taking promote students' knowledge of the text genre under study, their self-confidence as writers and their capacity to use specific language features of online interaction.

As future research, we highlight the national research project 'PROTEXTS' — 'Teaching of Texts Production in Compulsory Education', financed by the Foundation for Science and Technology (PTDC/CPE-CED/101009/2008), which was recently launched and whose main aims are:

- to design valid criteria for the promotion and control of progression in the written production of textual genres, according to different levels of education — 1st, 2nd and 3rd cycles of Compulsory Education;
- to verify the evolution of the fourth-, sixth- and ninth-grade students, throughout one school year, in the experimental and control groups, concerning their written expression and reviewing skills;
- to compare didactic interventions designed according to the same didactic principles, with and without resorting to Information and Communication Technologies, in order to develop more specific guidelines for their effective operationalization within the classroom context;
- to become acquainted with school and extra-school writing practices, at a national level, of students who are in the final grades of each cycle of Compulsory Education.

References

Loureiro, M. J., Pinho, A., Pereira, L. A., & Moreira, A. (2008). Arguing on-line in order to learn how to argue. In A. J. Mendes, I. Pereira & R. Costa (Eds.), *Computers and education: Towards educational change and innovation* (pp. 251–261). London: Springer.

Pereira, L. A. (2004). Des discours sur les pratiques aux pratiques d'enseignement [From words about practices to teaching practices]. In C. Barré-De Miniac, C. Brissaud & M. Rispail (Eds.), *La littéracie: conceptions théoriques et pratiques d'enseignement de la lecture-écriture [The literacy: theoretical concepts and practices of reading and writing teaching]* (pp. 319–333). Paris: L'Harmattan.

Pereira, L. A., Aleixo, C., Cardoso, I., & Graça, L. (2010). The teaching and learning of writing in Portugal: The case of a research group. In C. Bazerman, R. Krut, K. Lunsford, S. McLeod, S. Null, P. M. Rogers & A. Stansell (Eds.), *Traditions of writing research* (pp. 58–70). Oxford, UK: Routledge.

Pereira, L. A., & Cardoso, I. (2011). A Sequência de ensino como dispositivo didáctico para a aprendizagem da escrita num contexto de formação de professores. In L. A. Pereira (Ed.), *O ensino de diferentes géneros textuais-IV Encontro de reflexão sobre a escrita*. Aveiro: Universidade de Aveiro.

Pereira, L. A., Cardoso, I., & Graça, L. (2009). For a definition of the teaching/learning of writing in L1: Research and action. *L1: Educational Studies in Language and Literature*, *9*(4), 87–123.

Chapter 2.01.20

Teaching Reading and Writing to Learn in Primary Education

Isabel Martínez, Elena Martín and Mar Mateos

Research on reading and writing has traditionally looked at these processes separately. However, various studies have shown that the combined use of reading and writing as learning tools is more powerful than when they are used separately. As research in this field has also revealed, students have difficulties in performing complex tasks in which they are required to write something based on reading multiple texts (Lenski & Johns, 1997; Mateos, Martín, Villalón, & Luna, 2008). These limitations might be due, in part, to the intrinsic difficulty of such tasks, as they require the students to carry out complex processes (selection, organization and integration) and, in part, to students' lack of familiarity with this type of tasks, which are seldom set by teachers and lecturers (Solé et al., 2005).

Against this background, we carried out a study whose overall aim was to assess the effectiveness of an intervention programme for improving the use sixth-year primary school pupils (11 and 12 year olds) make of reading and writing, in particular in producing a written synthesis based on various texts.

The participants in this study were 32 sixth-year students at a state-run primary school and their respective tutors, with 15 of the pupils in the experimental group and 17 in the control group. The participants performed three written synthesis tasks using three pairs of texts providing complementary information on the subject 'knowledge of the environment'. We controlled for the pupils' reading comprehension level and their prior knowledge of the topics dealt with in the texts. The differences between the experimental and the control group on these two measures were not significant.

In the experimental group, intervention began with the performance of the second task. During eight 75-minute sessions, the experimental group's teacher

Learning to Write Effectively: Current Trends in European Research
Studies in Writing, Volume 25, 153–155
ISSN: 1572-6304/doi:10.1108/S1572-6304(2012)0000025037

implemented the programme which she had been previously trained to employ. The processes on which work was done during the intervention were: organizing contents, selecting the relevant ideas from the source texts, integrating prior and new knowledge, and integrating information from both sources. Basing ourselves on previous studies such as the one by Wray and Lewis (1997), all these processes were taught by means of a model provided by the tutor, joint activity, guided activity and pupils' individual activity.

The effectiveness of the intervention was assessed by analysing the changes that took place between the initial and the final written synthesis tasks in relation to:

- The procedures employed by a subsample of six experimental group students who were video recorded while performing the task. We also looked at the influence of the intervention by means of interviews before and after the intervention in which the tutor who implemented the programme was asked about her ideas concerning reading and writing and her degree of satisfaction with the programme.
- The synthesis task products and procedures, and the teacher's ideas, were assessed using appropriately adapted forms of the criteria and instruments employed in previous studies (Mateos et al., 2008; Mateos & Solé, 2009; Solé et al., 2005).

The most important results of this study show that the pupils to whom the intervention programme was applied generated better written products. In particular, they made greater progress than expected in the selection of the ideas they included in their syntheses, the coherence of their written texts, the integration of ideas from the two source texts and the sophistication of the titles they gave to their own texts. Moreover, an analysis of the procedures they employed while performing the tasks showed that they carried out more elaborate reading activities (underlining, note-taking) and writing activities (more elaborate rough drafts and a greater number of them drafts), and revised their texts more on the final than on the initial task. Analysis of the relation between the procedures employed and the quality of the products revealed that the pupils who made rough drafts which they then modified when writing out their final text produced better quality texts that those who did not make rough drafts, or did so, but simply copied them out when writing their final text. These results are consistent with those found in a previous study (Mateos et al., 2008). Lastly, the tutor who implemented the programme was very positive about it and said she had learned about how to teach reading and writing to learn specific contents.

In conclusion, our results seem to point to the usefulness and relevance of teaching primary school pupils to synthesize in writing information from different sources as a means of helping them to make good use of reading and writing as learning tools. Nevertheless, we must be cautious in interpreting these results, mainly because of the small size of the study sample. We aim to develop this line of research further in the near future by expanding our sample and extending the duration of the intervention, and by expanding the analysis of the procedures with other methodologies such as interviews, and examining the relation not just between the procedures employed in reading and writing to learn and the quality of the texts generated, but also among the procedures, the written products and the degree of learning of the contents dealt with.

References

Lenski, S. D., & Johns, J. L. (1997). Patterns of reading-to-write. *Reading Research and Instruction, 37,* 15–38.

Mateos, M., Martín, E., Villalón, R., & Luna, M. (2008). Reading and writing to learn in secondary education: Online processing, activity and written products in summarizing and synthesizing tasks. *Reading and Writing, 21,* 675–697.

Mateos, M., & Solé, I. (2009). Synthesising information from various texts: A study of procedures and products at different educational levels. *European Journal of Psychology of Education, 24,* 435–451.

Solé, I., Mateos, M., Miras, M., Martín, E., Castells, N., Cuevas, I., & Grácia, M. (2005). Lectura, escritura y adquisición de conocimientos en educación secundaria y educación universitaria. *Infancia y Aprendizaje, 28,* 329–347.

Wray, D., & Lewis, M. (1997). *Extending literacy. Children reading and writing non-fiction.* London: Routledge.

Chapter 2.01.21

Effects of Being a Reader and Observing Readers on Argumentative Writing

Noreen S. Moore and Charles A. MacArthur

Cognitive and social perspectives on writing emphasize the importance of audience awareness. Proficient writers attend to audience while composing and understand that writing is an interactive meaning-making process between readers and writers. Argumentative writing, in particular, requires writers to consider the perspectives of readers who may hold different positions on an issue. Learning to consider audience is challenging for developing writers.

One approach to teaching audience awareness is to give learners experiences as readers. For example, Holliway and McCutchen (2004) had students write and revise descriptions of tangram figures. Before revision, students in the read-as-a-reader group read others' descriptions and selected the correct tangram from a set; other students read others' descriptions and evaluated them on criteria for description. Students in the read-as-a-reader group revised their own descriptions more successfully.

Another approach is to have students observe readers trying to comprehend texts. Observation may be more effective for learning than actual practice writing in some circumstances because it provides information on the task and the opportunity for reflection while freeing the learner from the cognitive burdens of doing the writing task (Rijlaarsdam & Van den Bergh, 2006). For example, Couzijn and Rijlaarsdam (2004) asked high school students to observe a peer read a description of a science experiment and try to carry out the experiment while thinking aloud. Students in this observation condition revised their own science manuals more effectively than students directed to re-read and comment on their own manuals.

The current study investigated the effects of being a reader and observing readers on a less concrete, and more common, writing task than conducting an experiment or

Learning to Write Effectively: Current Trends in European Research
Studies in Writing, Volume 25, 157–159
Copyright © 2012 by Emerald Group Publishing Limited
All rights of reproduction in any form reserved
ISSN: 1572-6304/doi:10.1108/S1572-6304(2012)0000025038

describing a tangram. Fifth-grade students wrote persuasive letters to a teacher or principal. Subsequently, some students (Readers) met in small groups to read three letters written by other students and discuss whether they were persuasive and why. Other students (Observers) listened to the discussion and then met to discuss the criteria that the Readers had used to evaluate the letters. A control group wrote an additional persuasive letter on a new topic. All students revised their original letters and wrote a new letter a week later. We hypothesized that the Reader and Observer groups would perform better on both tasks than the Control group, and that the Observer group would perform best.

Methods

A total of 87 fifth graders from five classrooms participated (average age: 10.7 years; ethnic background: 80% Caucasian, 20% minority). Socioeconomic status data at the district level identified about 46.9% of all fifth graders as low income. Average standardized test scores were slightly above average on reading and slightly below average on writing.

Students were randomly assigned within classroom to the three conditions (Reader, Observer, Control). The study included six 45-minute sessions on six days. First, students wrote a persuasive letter to their teacher on an assigned topic. Next, Reader and Observer groups practiced their roles using narrative texts while Control students wrote a narrative text. Third, students engaged in the experimental activities. The Reader group participants read, discussed and evaluated other students' argumentative letters. The Observer group participants listened to the Reader group discussions and then discussed and generated a list of the evaluation criteria used by the Readers. Meanwhile, the Control group practiced writing another argumentative letter. Fourth, all students revised the writing they did during the first session. During revision several students from each condition participated in think alouds. One week later, students wrote another persuasive letter, this time to the school principal, which they revised the next day. The same students who participated in think alouds during session four did so again.

The essays were analysed quantitatively for (a) overall persuasive quality; (b) revision activities; and (c) inclusion of argumentative elements. In addition, think-aloud data were analysed using constant comparative analysis in order to understand the rationale for students' revisions. Finally, Reader and Observer group discussions were analysed using constant comparative analysis to understand the discussion topics and characteristics during the activity.

Results and Discussion

The analyses indicated that the Reader group produced higher quality writing than the Control group immediately after participation in the experimental activity. In addition, the Reader group showed greater evidence of audience awareness than the control group. This was evidenced by their revision activities, inclusion of argumentative elements, and think-aloud protocols. The Reader group included more evidence of alternative proposition elements in each of these analyses than the Control group. The Observer group did not differ from the other groups on writing quality or process measures. The analysis of Reader and Observer discussions revealed that whereas the groups discussed similar topics related to evaluation criteria for persuasive writing, they discussed these topics in different ways. The Reader discussions were elaborate and specific and the Observer discussions were list-like and lacked elaboration. Finally, there were no differences among groups on measures of quality or inclusion of argumentative elements during the transfer task.

The argumentative writing of students from elementary school to college often fails to consider potential opposing positions (Felton & Kuhn, 2001; Midgette, Haria, & MacArthur, 2007). In this study, role-switching, or writers stepping into the shoes of readers, helped young students recognize the importance of considering audience when writing persuasively. However, observation of reading did not help students consider audience and improve the quality of their writing. This latter finding is inconsistent with previous research. Future research must re-examine the nature of observational tasks to determine the characteristics that make it effective. For example, are the differences in results due to the type of writing task, the observational activity, the age of students, or the fact that peers were observing known peers instead of unknown peers, older students or adults? Finally, the lack of transfer of learning is most likely due to the short duration of the experimental activities. Future research should examine the efficacy of these instructional activities over a longer period of time.

References

Couzijn, M., & Rijlaarsdam, G. (2004). Learning to write instructive texts by reader observation and written feedback. In G. Rijlaarsdam, H. van den Bergh & M. Couzijn (Eds.), *Studies in writing: Vol. 14. Effective learning and teaching of writing: A handbook of writing in education* (2nd ed., pp. 209–240). Boston, MA: Kluwer Academic Publishers.

Felton, M., & Kuhn, D. (2001). The development of argumentative discourse skill. *Discourse Processes, 32*, 135–153.

Holliway, R. D., & McCutchen, D. (2004). Audience perspective in young writers' composing and revising. In L. Allal, L. Chanquoy & P. Largy (Eds.), *Revision: Cognitive and instructional processes* (pp. 157–170). Boston, MA: Kluwer Academic Publishers.

Midgette, E., Haria, P., & MacArthur, C. (2007). The effects of content and audience awareness goals for revision on the persuasive essays of fifth- and eighth-grade students. *Reading and Writing, 21*(1/2), 131–151.

Rijlaarsdam, G., & Van den Bergh, H. (2006). Writing process theory: A functional dynamic approach. In C. A. MacArthur, S. Graham & J. Fitzgerald (Eds.), *Handbook of writing research* (pp. 41–53). New York, NY: The Guilford Press.

Chapter 2.01.22

Writing and Text Genre Acquisition Among 4- to 8-Year-Old Icelandic Children

Rannveig Oddsdóttir, Freyja Birgisdóttir and Hrafnhildur Ragnarsdóttir

Over the past decades a growing number of studies have concentrated on the development of early writing. The results of these studies have provided us with an increasingly detailed picture of how young children's writing skills develop and have enabled us to describe how their initial scribbles transform to the ability to produce continuous texts of various kinds (Clay, 1975; Donovan & Smolkin, 2002). Research indicates that from early on children start differentiating between text genres (Zecker, 1999) and that direct training in oral and written text production skills results in a significant improvement in the ability to structure different kinds of texts (Williams, Hall, Lauer, Stafford, & DeSisto, 2005). However, despite these findings, tuition in text genre acquisition generally plays a limited role in the initial stages of schooling and early reading materials seem largely confined to stories or other kinds of narratives (Duke, 2000). Consequently, when children start their secondary education and have to rely on their reading and writing skills to acquire and mediate their knowledge, many of them may run into difficulties because they are unfamiliar with the kind of texts that they are required to work with. Thus, it must be of great importance to introduce children to different sorts of texts as early as possible and acquire an understanding of how their early writing skills can be improved.

The acquisition of writing has hardly been investigated in Iceland. Consequently, we have limited understanding of the way in which Icelandic children's writing skills develop, and we know little about the factors that influence their emergence. This research aims to address these issues. The study is ongoing and is connected to a larger longitudinal project on the development of language, literacy and self-regulation

Learning to Write Effectively: Current Trends in European Research
Studies in Writing, Volume 25, 161–163
ISSN: 1572-6304/doi:10.1108/S1572-6304(2012)0000025039

and is part of the doctoral thesis of Rannveig Oddsdóttir at the University of Iceland. The main questions concern the development of children's oral and written text production skills and how these are related to other parts of development, such as oral language skills, emergent literacy and subsequent academic achievement. We also want to explore the possibility of teaching children about text genres in order to improve their ability to work with different kinds of text.

The participants comprise a sub-sample of 100 children who are already enrolled in the longitudinal project mentioned above. The sample is divided into two different age groups which will be followed up for three years. The younger group includes 50 4-year-old pre-school children and the older group an equal number of 6-year-old children at their first year of primary school.

There will be three main test points for each group. For the younger group, the first two test points will take place at the two final years of pre-school, during which their emergent literacy skills, letter knowledge, phonological awareness and initial writing abilities will be assessed. The children will also be asked to produce two kinds of oral texts (i.e. narratives and informational texts), first at the two pre-school sessions and then again towards the end of their first year at primary school.

The three test points for the older group will take place once a year during the first three years of primary school. The testing sessions will consist mainly of repeated assessments of their ability to produce oral and written texts of various kinds. As part of the larger longitudinal project mentioned above, both groups will also receive measures of vocabulary knowledge, oral comprehension and literacy skills at each of the three test points.

During their third year at school, half of the older group will participate in an intervention in which they receive a direct tuition in working with a variety of oral and written texts. The training will last over a few week period and will be delivered to a whole class, as part of the children's daily classroom activities. The effect of the intervention will be assessed by comparing the performance of the intervention group on a set of pre- and post-test measures to that of another group who has not received similar training.

Data collection for the first test point is still in progress. The children's scores in each of the measures will be analysed by comparing the mean scores of the two groups at the three test points, as well as by analysing the performance of each group longitudinally, across different testing sessions. The longitudinal and concurrent relationship between measures will also be assessed. These analyses will provide an overview of the children's ability to produce variety of written and oral texts at different age levels and at different stages of formal schooling. They will also demonstrate how text genre acquisition is related to other aspects of development and academic achievement.

References

Clay, M. M. (1975). *What did I write? Beginning writing behavior.* Portsmouth, NH: Heinemann Educational.

Donovan, C. A., & Smolkin, L. B. (2002). Children's genre knowledge: An examination of K-5 students' performance on multiple tasks providing differing levels of scaffolding. *Reading Research Quarterly, 37*(4), 428–465.

Duke, N. K. (2000). 3.6 minutes per day: The scarcity of informational texts in first grade. *Reading Research Quarterly, 35*(2), 202–224.

Williams, J. P., Hall, K. M., Lauer, K. D., Stafford, K. B., & DeSisto, L. A. (2005). Expository text comprehension in the primary grade classroom. *Journal of Educational Psychology, 97*(4), 538–550.

Zecker, L. B. (1999). Different texts, different emergent writing forms. *Language Arts, 76*(6), 483–490.

Chapter 2.01.23

Parental Intervention in Improving Children's Writing and Their Achievement

Patricia Robledo and Jesús-Nicasio García

In Spain, the achievement levels of learning goals and requirements has significantly increased as a result of the Organic Education Law (2006) which was adapted to meet the proposals made by the European Union. As a result, the impact of any extrinsic factor or agent, such as the family, on their process of teaching-learning is particularly important to the student.

With the implementation of European educational guidelines, young people must have acquired eight competences on completion of their compulsory education. The importance of the linguistic communication competence, which refers to the use of language as a tool for oral and written communication is emphasized. The school must prepare competent communicators who can successfully navigate in different communicative contexts and conditions. However, the empowerment of linguistic communication from schools frequently focuses especially on oral language and reading, relegating writing to the background (Torrance, Fidalgo, & García, 2007), although this is a task with high cognitive demands requiring explicit instruction, approached from the socio-cognitive perspective. Thus, the family could prove to be an effective alternative for its teaching. The habit of writing is more common in students whose families provide models and positive attitudes towards writing tasks and depending on the different parental variables (education level and degree of involvement in education) can also contribute to higher quality textual productions in children (Robledo, García, & Díez, 2009). Therefore, we propose that the family actively contribute to the students' successful acquisition of this competence.

The objective of the study in progress is to verify whether it is possible to improve students' writing competence and achievement through a specific programme for parents. The purpose of the programme is to raise parents' awareness about their

Learning to Write Effectively: Current Trends in European Research
Studies in Writing, Volume 25, 165–168
Copyright © 2012 by Emerald Group Publishing Limited
ISSN: 1572-6304/doi:10.1108/S1572-6304(2012)0000025040

influence on their children's academic performance and to prepare them to adjust various aspects of the home environment and to get involved in assisting and encouraging their children with their homework, especially in the area of language and specifically in written composition.

Method

The sample consists of students, enrolled in the fifth and sixth grade (10–12 years old) and their parents, who exemplified different structural or functional characteristics, like age, education level, profession or family typology and size.

The programme consists of 15 sessions for parents, carried out weekly according to the families' availability. The programme covered two themes: the family variables and written composition. The written composition contents to be addressed are: knowledge and positive assessment of writing; writing capacities; the importance of writing; writing and achievement; daily behavioural modelling and indirect modelling; planning, editing and revision process; enhancing writing process; generalization to other texts. The home tasks that parents should carry out with their children once the sessions were completed are: stimulating positive assessment of writing; stimulation-modelling of writing daily tasks (shopping lists, letters, Christmas cards); natural help in writing homework: motivation; declarative knowledge of writing processes: mnemonic techniques PER-didos (in Spanish) 'lost' = planning, editing and revising; self-activation planning strategy Plan-L (in Spanish): P = thinking objective, L = brainstorming, A = grouping ideas, N = child outline, L = reader; graphic organizer for editing; notebook teacher-parent; REC (R: re-read, E: evaluation, C: correct) self-regulatory strategy; reinforcement learning and cooperative work; implementation of procedural self-knowledge in relation to the whole process of writing (descriptive text).

For the development of the writing sessions with the families we apply techniques, with previously demonstrated effectiveness (García, Fidalgo, & Robledo, 2010; Torrance et al., 2007), such as cognitive modelling, thinking aloud, self-instruction, role-playing, pictures or graphic organizers, mnemonic devices. The goal is that parents learn these techniques and learn to teach their children with them.

Teachers also participate in the research at different levels of voluntary involvement in written composition instruction (application of the same writing contents worked on by the parents, previous training), which will determine the study design.

We will test the effectiveness of the programme on students' achievement and of the improvement in the home environment through the application (pre-/post-test and follow-up) of the appropriate evaluation procedures for parents (record sheets, interviews, Family opinions — Robledo & García, 2007) and for children (grades; Child Family Opinions; IQ). We will also analyse the parents' textual productions and their assessment of the written compositions. Also the effects of home writing sessions on the students' texts will be assessed. The evaluation of the textual product (in essay, description, comparison-contrast) will be done through the protocol designed by García and collaborators (text-based and reader-based measures), and the writing process through online records (Writing Log).

The author researcher will develop the intervention with families (and teachers) to ensure that all receive the same instructional treatment. In addition, through record sheets and regular meetings she will discuss any corrections to be made in the implementation of learning at home (or class) to verify the reliability of the intervention.

Results

The students' pre-test and post-test results in achievement and writing performance will be assessed according to the type of instruction they have received: (i) through families (experimental group 1), (ii) family-teachers (experimental group 2) (iii) instruction by teachers (experimental group 3), (iv) ordinary curriculum (control group). Students were tested as whole-class groups.

We expect to demonstrate the potential role of the family in education, their capacity to contribute to the improvement of students' performance by adjusting various personal and contextual variables and their ability to contribute to the teaching of written composition, both by themselves and in cooperation with the teachers It is anticipated that we can verify exponential improvements resulting from school-family coordination (Robledo & García, 2009).

Acknowledgements

During this research project, we received competitive funds from the Ministry of Research, Science and Innovation — from the Spanish Government; project EDU2010-19250 (EDUC) for 2010–2013, in addition to European Union FEDER funds. Excellence Research Group funds from Junta de Castilla y León (GR259) and European funds for 2009–2011 (BOCyL 27, April 2009) were awarded to the Director/Principal Researcher (J.-N. García). P. Robledo received a grant to finance the hiring of recently graduated research staff from the Junta de Castilla y León. We are very grateful to Jenny Gunn for the English corrections.

References

García, J.-N., Fidalgo, R., & Robledo, P. (2010). The influence of two self-regulatory instructional programs in the development of writing competence in students with and without learning disabilities. In J. de la Fuente & A. E. Mourad (Eds.), *International perspectives on applying self-regulated learning in different settings* (pp. 595–614). New York, NY: Peter Lang Publishers.

Robledo, P., & García, J.-N. (2007). Instrumento de evaluación de las necesidades de las familias con hijos con dificultades del desarrollo: FAOP [Instrument for assessing needs of families with developmental difficulties children: FAOP]. In J.-N. García (Coor.), *Instrumentos y programas de intervención en las dificultades del desarrollo* [*Instruments and intervention programs in development difficulties*] (cap. 34, CD-ROM). Madrid: Pirámide.

Robledo, P., & García, J.-N. (2009). The family environment's influence on the academic performance of students with learning disabilities: A review of empirical studies. *Aula Abierta*, *37*(1), 117–128.

Robledo, P., García, J.-N., & Díez, C. (2009). The role of parents implication in teaching writing in relation to writing products in students with and without learning disabilities. 31st international conference on learning disabilities, October 2nd & 3rd, Council for Learning Disabilities (CLD), Dallas, TX.

Torrance, M., Fidalgo, R., & García, J.-N. (2007). The teachability and effectiveness of strategies for cognitive self-regulation in sixth grade writers. *Learning and Instruction*, *17*(3), 265–285.

Chapter 2.01.24

Supporting Children in Improving Their Presentation of School Reports

Hans van der Meij

Students from all school levels in the Netherlands must write reports as the outcome from an inquiry (usually on the internet). In elementary schools reports are made for language as well as for history, biology, geography and the like. There tends to be very little teacher guidance and guidelines for doing so. The children can often select a topic of their own choice and they are expected to work on their own and at home.

In the absence of clear guidelines, reports vary considerably in quality, both for content and presentation. This study set out to advance a set of criteria for presentation and to train children in their application. It did so by engaging children in a hands-on training for developing their knowledge and skills on formatting their report. During the training the children worked independently with a tutorial about Word's formatting options. The tutorial acquainted the children with the following concepts: paragraphs, enumerations, citations, headings and a table of contents. These concepts were explained in a just-in-time fashion, namely immediately before the instructions on how to format a paragraph, enumeration and so on. Unlike the fancy stuff that children typically employ to spice up their reports (e.g. various colors, fonts, font sizes and pictures), the formatting guidelines in the tutorial concentrate on their functional nature. Paragraph formatting helps identify these as such, headings are formatted so that they appear in an automatically created table of contents and so on.

One of the tutorials in the study paid special attention to student motivation by including a virtual person, a pedagogical agent (PA) that shared motivation and feelings with the user. The PA in that tutorial was presented as a boy from the same age as the target group. On various places in the tutorial the PA visually and verbally expressed his feelings and emotions about task progress. In a recent study with

Learning to Write Effectively: Current Trends in European Research
Studies in Writing, Volume 25, 169–172
Copyright © 2012 by Emerald Group Publishing Limited
All rights of reproduction in any form reserved
ISSN: 1572-6304/doi:10.1108/S1572-6304(2012)0000025041

elementary school favourable effects of the PA were found for motivation after training (i.e. perceived relevance and self-efficacy beliefs) as well as for presentation skills (Van der Meij, Op de Weegh, & Weber, 2009).

The present study examines Clark and Choi's (2005) argument that PAs can tax the user beyond a level that is functional. Their complexity claim is studied by having an audience with low reading skills process the PA tutorial that was successful in the earlier study. The tested hypothesis is that this audience needs to muster all its reading skills to process the basic instructions and that, consequently, the PA distracts. The possible negative effects of the PA should be reflected in a higher cognitive load and lower motivation and learning when compared with a tutorial without PA.

Method

Participants

The 40 participants (mean age 11 years and 10 months) of grades 5 and 6 came from three different classrooms from an elementary school. This public school has a large population of disadvantaged children. Special governmental funding helps reduce the teacher-pupil ratio in these schools. Because the language skills of these children are often one or two years lower than those of their counterparts in regular schools, the funding is also used for additional language lessons. Participants were randomly distributed over the two conditions.

Procedure

One week before training users completed a motivation questionnaire (answers were given on a 10-point Likert scale with a lower score indicating lower processing demands) and a hands-on pretest for the to-be-trained tasks. Training took place in a computer room. Users were asked to work on their own using only the tutorial for support. During training users regularly answered questions about cognitive load ('I found the task difficult' — answers were given on a 7-point Likert scale with a lower score indicating lower processing demands). Maximum training time was 2 hours. Immediately after training users answered a motivation questionnaire and completed a post-test on trained tasks in hands-on fashion without access to the tutorial. Three weeks later users completed a retention test.

Data Analysis

The study is experimental with a control and experimental (PA) condition. Data are analysed with ANOVAs. Tests for predicted effects are one-sided with alpha set at 0.5. For effect size Cohen's d statistic is reported.

Results

Cognitive Load

The average score of 2.09 for cognitive load shows that students generally did not feel taxed. The presence of the agent also had no influence on this perception. The 2.02 score for the control condition was only slightly lower than the 2.14 score for the experimental condition, $F(1,38) = 0.18$, n.s.

Motivational Effects

There was a marginally significant increase of perceived task relevance, $F(1,33) = 3.79$, $p = 0.06$. The positive change is largely found in the control condition. In the PA condition the difference over time was small, rising from a (mean) score of 5.43 to a score of 5.64. In the control condition the change is much stronger, with a starting (mean) score of 4.88 resulting in an end score of 6.27. A comparison of the scores for perceived task relevance after training showed that the two conditions differed significantly, in favour of the control condition, $F(1,33) = 4.71$, $p<.018$, $d = 0.73$. This finding confirms the prediction.

There was a significant decrease in self-efficacy beliefs, $F(1,33) = 4.64$, $p = 0.039$ which tended to interact with condition, $F(1,33) = 3.40$, $p = 0.078$. The biggest change is found in the PA condition where the initial score decreased from 6.96 to 5.74. In the control condition the starting level was considerably lower and the decrease was minimal. That is self-efficacy beliefs decreased from 5.98 to 5.87. After training the two conditions did not differ in their scores for self-efficacy, $F(1,33)<1$, n.s.

Learning Effects

Table 1 shows that both groups have made significant progress. Before training participants hardly could solve any of the formatting tasks (8.5% correct for the whole group). After training this score rose to 53%. Three weeks later the average retention score was 49%.

Table 1: Learning outcomes (% correct) for the two conditions in the experiment.

	Pre-test Mean (SD)	Post-test Mean (SD)	Retention Mean (SD)
Control condition	9.5 (18.3)	54.4 (34.4)	60.8 (27.0)
PA condition	7.7 (15.7)	52.9 (33.5)	39.7 (39.8)

Conditions did not differ on the pre-test, $F(1,38) = 0.10$, n.s., or on the immediate post-test, $F(1,38) = 0.01$, n.s. The predicted difference between conditions became visible only on the retention test in which the control group significantly out-performed the experimental group, $F(1,38) = 3.63$, $p < .03$, $d = 0.62$. As the table shows, the performance of the students who trained with the PA tutorial decreased considerably in the three-week interval, whereas the performance of the students who had trained with the control tutorial even improved slightly.

Conclusion

This experiment shows that there is no such thing as a 'one design fits all' for paper tutorials. Where regular students were positively influenced by the presence of a PA, the opposite was true in the present study. For these students with low reading skills the presence of the PA was counterproductive for motivation and learning. They profited more from a tutorial that presented only the basic instructions.

The study further indicates that the children benefitted considerably from a tutorial that taught them to detect and format text elements such as paragraphs, enumerations, citations and headings. In another study one of the participating schools informed us that after completing their training the students more often employed some of the trained strategies in their report writing. This is, of course, the ultimate goal. To achieve success beyond the experimental situation it is probably needed that schools receive (additional) support for engaging in a systematic approach to implementing such a change. One way of doing so would be to agree upon and publish a set of guidelines for report writing and to follow-up by judging school reports for compliance to these guidelines.

References

Clark, R. E., & Choi, S. (2005). Five design principles for experiments on the effects of animated pedagogical agents. *Journal of Research on Educational Computing Research, 32*(3), 209–225.

Van der Meij, H., Op de Weegh, M. J., & Weber, I. H. M. (2009). Heeft een (papieren) medeleerling een meerwaarde in software handleidingen? *Pedagogische Studiën, 86,* 296–312.

Subsection 2.02

Learners' Writing Processes

Chapter 2.02.01

Explaining Knowledge Change Through Writing

Veerle Baaijen, David Galbraith and Kees de Glopper

Kellogg (1988) has shown that outlining improves text quality. According to Bereiter and Scardamalia's knowledge transforming model (1987) this is a consequence of how it helps writers to develop their understanding. Bereiter and Scardamalia (1987), who focus on the processes involved in writing, attribute the effects of writing on learning to explicit problem solving designed to satisfy rhetorical goals. However, this claim has not been directly tested.

Furthermore, alternative models of writing (Galbraith, 2009) claim that outlining can reduce, rather than enhance, the development of ideas and that effects of outlining vary as a function of individual differences in self-monitoring. Galbraith set out to investigate directly how writers develop their understanding through writing and found different patterns of knowledge change for both low and high self-monitors. However, within this context there has been no research directly examining the processes responsible for these differences.

The aim of this PhD-project is therefore to investigate how processes of writing relate to knowledge change. This first experiment investigated whether the development of ideas varied as a function of planning and self-monitoring and investigated both knowledge change and the processes responsible for it.

Method

Eighty-four students from the University of Groningen were recruited to participate in the experiment. They all received €10 for their participation. Participants were pre-selected using Snyder's revised 18 item self-monitoring scale (Snyder & Gangestad,

Learning to Write Effectively: Current Trends in European Research
Studies in Writing, Volume 25, 175–177
ISSN: 1572-6304/doi:10.1108/S1572-6304(2012)0000025042

1986). They were classified as high self-monitors (HSM, $n = 42$) if they scored between 11 and 18 on the scale and as low self-monitors (LSM, $n = 42$) if they obtained a score 0 and 8 on the scale.

Participants were randomly assigned to one of the four experimental groups: (i) HSM outline planning, (ii) HSM synthetic planning, (iii) LSM outline planning and (iv) LSM synthetic planning. They were asked to plan and write an article for the university newspaper discussing whether 'our growing dependence on computers and the Internet is a good development or not'. Participants in the synthetic planning condition were given 5 minutes to think about the topic and to write down a single sentence summing up their overall opinion. Participants in the outline planning condition were given 5 minutes to construct a structured outline. Following this initial planning phase, participants had 30 minutes to write a well-structured article for the university newspaper. During this phase, all participants were allowed to consult their written outlines. In addition, during writing keystrokes were logged with the use of Inputlog (Leijten & van Waes, 2006).

Participants carried out the experiment individually and they wrote their article on a computer with standard text-editing software. In order to assess the relationships between ideas before and after writing and to assess the development of understanding participants were asked — both before and after writing — to list all the ideas they could think of relevant to the topic (10 minutes), to rate the importance of these ideas and to indicate how much they felt they knew about the topic. In addition, after writing participants were asked to rate the extent to which ideas on the second list corresponded to the ideas on the first list on a 6-point scale ranging from 1 = identical point to 6 = no correspondence.

Ideas on the second list were classified as new ideas if participants did not identify a corresponding idea on the first list. In contrast, ideas from the first that persisted onto the second list were classified as preserved ideas. For both lists the number total words and average number of words per idea was calculated. This gave us the opportunity to investigate the development of ideas and the complexity (mean number of words per idea) of ideas produced before and after writing.

Preliminary Results

A two-way between subjects ANCOVA on post-knowledge with self-monitoring and type of planning as independent variables and prior knowledge as a covariate revealed a significant main effect of type of planning on subjective knowledge after writing [$F(1,79) = 5.750$, $p = .019$]. This reflects the fact that the mean knowledge score after writing in the synthetic planning condition is 5.0 (SD = .81) whereas the mean knowledge score after writing in the outline condition was 4.5 (SD = .94) compared to a pre-knowledge mean of 4.5. This is a new finding with potentially important implications in that it suggests that development of understanding occurs after synthetic planning but not after outline planning.

In addition, this result shows that the two types of planning have different effects. The key thing to note here is that this indicates that the synthetic planning condition possibly imposed less control on text production allowing participants to develop their understanding of the topic. This result is therefore compatible with the assumptions of Galbraith's (2009) dual process model.

The analyses of the effects of planning showed a reduction in complexity of preserved ideas in the outline planning condition, but not in synthetic planning condition [$F(2,154) = 3.456, p = .034$]. A possible explanation for this result is that in the outline planning condition writers construct a mental outline consisting of their initial ideas and that when these ideas are referred to after writing they are able to simply label these ideas held in memory. By contrast, in the synthetic planning condition no outline is constructed in memory and therefore, after writer, writers fully formulate ideas as for the first time.

Preliminary Conclusions

The main conclusion of our preliminary findings is that writers experienced increases in subjective knowledge after synthetic planning but not after outline planning. Given that these conditions also show differences in the complexity of preserved ideas this suggests that maintaining an outline during writing reduces the extent to which writers develop their subjective knowledge of a topic. This explanation will be further explored by analysing the relations between subjective knowledge and idea change. In addition, further analyses will also examine how these differences relate to text quality and writing processes. These analyses will be particularly important in resolving the question of why it is that outlining improves text quality (cf. Kellogg, 1988) but recording to our results does not lead to development of increases in knowledge.

References

Bereiter, C., & Scardamalia, M. (1987). *The psychology of written composition.* Hillsdale, NJ: Lawrence Erlbaum Associates Publishers.

Galbraith, D. (2009). Writing as discovery. *British Journal of Educational Psychology. Monograph Series II — Teaching and Learning Writing, 6,* 5–26.

Kellogg, R. T. (1988). Attentional overload and writing performance: Effects of rough draft and outline strategies. *Journal of Experimental Psychology: Learning, Memory, and Cognition, 14*(2), 355–365.

Leijten, M., & Van Waes, L. (2006). Inputlog: New perspectives on the logging of online writing. In K. P. H. Sullivan & E. Lindgren (Eds.), *Studies in writing: Vol. 18. Computer keystroke logging and writing: Methods and applications* (pp. 73–94). Oxford: Elsevier.

Snyder, M., & Gangestad, S. W. (1986). On the nature of self-monitoring. *Journal of Personality and Social Psychology, 51,* 125–139.

Chapter 2.02.02

Patterns of Meta-Cognitive Processing During Writing: Variation According to Reported Writing Profile

Marion Tillema, Huub van den Bergh,
Gert Rijlaarsdam and Ted Sanders

Writing involves tending to many cognitive processes at the same time, such as generating ideas, translating these ideas into language, monitoring the structure of your text, making revisions when needed, while keeping an eye on proper language use, keeping your rhetorical goals in mind and staying aware of your intended audience. These cognitive activities can be handled in different ways. Writers can, for example, generate all the ideas for a text at once and then start thinking about how to word these ideas. Alternatively, writers may continually alternate generating and translating processes (Van den Bergh & Rijlaarsdam, 2007). There are numerous other examples, but it is clear that there are many ways of organizing the ongoing cognitive activities over the process of task execution (Van Weijen, Van den Bergh, Rijlaarsdam, & Sanders, 2008).

Two main organizational patterns, both at opposite end of the spectrum, have regularly emerged in writing-related research: writing processes with a strong focus on planning activities and writing processes with a strong focus on revising activities (Kieft, Rijlaarsdam, & Van den Bergh, 2006; Torrance, Thomas, & Robinson, 1994, 1999). Planning-type writing involves thinking about how well a text matches your rhetorical goals before you start writing, and making few revisions. On the other end of the continuum, Revising-type behaviour involves thinking about how well a text matches your rhetorical goals after writing. Writers who apply a strict Revising approach, usually start writing almost immediately, and rely on subsequent revisions to produce coherent texts. Torrance et al. (1999) found cognitive processing during

Learning to Write Effectively: Current Trends in European Research
Studies in Writing, Volume 25, 179–182
ISSN: 1572-6304/doi:10.1108/S1572-6304(2012)0000025043

writing tasks to reflect Planning- and Revising-type profiles as measured by a questionnaire.

Organizing cognitive activities during task execution requires monitoring. Meta-cognitive control regulates the occurrence of the various cognitive activities during the execution of a writing task. A switch from the activity of wording ideas to the activity of revising, for example, is governed by meta-cognition. Organizational patterns of cognitive activities during writing, then, entail specific patterns of meta-cognition across task execution. Typical Planner-type behaviour, then, will be characterized by a peak of meta-cognitive activity at the start of writing tasks. Typical Reviser-type behaviour, on the other hand, will involve a peak of meta-cognitive activity towards the end of task execution.

Method

Fourteen- and 15-year-old students ($N = 16$) in their third year of pre-academic secondary education wrote three argumentative essays each in Dutch, their mother language, on topics such as 'camera surveillance in inner city areas' or 'legalization of soft drugs'. They performed these tasks under think aloud conditions. The students completed the essays during one session, with a short break between assignments. The topics were systematically balanced across participants. The essays had to be about half a page in length. The available time for each essay was 30 minutes.

The think aloud data were transcribed, fragmented and coded. One think aloud protocol (number of fragments = 518) was coded by two researchers. The inter-coder agreement (κ) was 0.85. The coding instruction distinguished between eight cognitive, writing-related categories and four meta-cognitive categories. Examples of cognitive categories are generating ideas, translating ideas into language and revising. As meta-cognitive categories, we identified monitoring, goal setting, structuring, meta-comments.

We considered the occurrence of verbalizations of meta-cognition as a function of time, or more precisely, as a function of the number of fragments elapsed since the start of task execution. The occurrence of meta-cognition over the writing process was statistically modelled by means of a polynomial regression model. As our data are hierarchically organized (protocol fragments are nested within tasks, which are in turn nested within students), we used a multilevel model.

In addition, the students completed the Writing Questionnaire developed by Kieft et al. (2006). This questionnaire measures reported writing behaviour. It asks participants how they would handle the fictitious task of writing an argumentative essay about the tobacco industry. The questionnaire consists of 36 statements about writing strategy. Thirteen of these items indicate Planning-type behaviour and 12 items pertain to Revising-type behaviour. The remaining 11 items are fillers. Participants received scores for both the Planning dimension and the Revising dimension. These scores were added to the statistical model, to explain inter-student variations in the occurrence of meta-cognition during task execution.

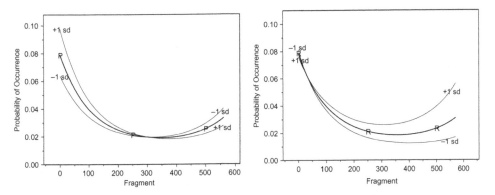

Figure 1: The occurrence of meta-cognitive activity over the writing process according to Planning scores (left) and Revising scores (right).

Results and Conclusions

Figure 1 shows the occurrence of meta-cognitive activity modelled according to Planning (left) and Revising (right) scores. Students with relatively high Planning scores on the Writing Questionnaire (one standard deviation or more above the average score) applied significantly more meta-cognition at the start of task execution than students with a Planner score around average. Students with relatively low Planner scores (one standard deviation or more below the average score) applied significantly less meta-cognition at the start of writing tasks than those with Planner scores around average. In addition, high Planner scores were related to a sharper decrease of online meta-cognition between the start and the middle part of task execution. Shortly after the middle part of task execution, high and low Planners generally applied equal amounts of meta-cognition. Towards the end of task execution, low Planners showed a sharper increase of applied meta-cognition.

High and low reported Revising behaviours were characterized by almost equal amounts of meta-cognition at the start of the writing process. Shortly after the start of task execution, there was a decrease of online meta-cognition for all reported behaviours. The lower the Revising score, however, the sharper the decrease. Towards the end of task execution, students with relatively high Revising scores on the Writing Questionnaire showed a sharper increase of online meta-cognition. The higher the Revising score, the more meta-cognition peaks at the end of writing tasks. In short, the higher the reported Planning-type behaviour, the more meta-cognition peaks at the start of task execution. The higher the reported Revising-behaviour, the more meta-cognition peaks at the end of the writing process. In subsequent research, we will investigate if the different patterns of meta-cognition across task execution reported in this study can explain differences in text quality.

References

Kieft, M., Rijlaarsdam, G., & Van den Bergh, H. (2006). Writing as a learning tool. Testing the role of students' writing strategies. *European Journal of Psychology of Education, 21*(1), 17–34.

Torrance, M., Thomas, G. V., & Robinson, E. J. (1994). The writing strategies of graduate research students in the social sciences. *Higher Education, 27*, 379–392.

Torrance, M., Thomas, G. V., & Robinson, E. J. (1999). Individual differences in the writing behaviour of undergraduate students. *British Journal of Educational Psychology, 69*, 189–199.

Van den Bergh, H., & Rijlaarsdam, G. (2007). The dynamics of idea generation during writing: An online study. In G. Rijlaarsdam (Series Ed.) and M. Torrance, L. Van Waes & D. Galbraith (Volume Eds.), *Writing and cognition: Research and applications* (Vol. 20, pp. 125–150). Studies in Writing. Amsterdam: Elsevier.

Van Weijen, D., Van den Bergh, B., Rijlaarsdam, G., & Sanders, T. (2008). Differences in process and process-product relations in L2 writing. *ITL Applied Linguistics, 156*, 203–226.

Chapter 2.02.03

Formulating Activities in L1 and L2 and Their Relation With Text Quality

Daphne van Weijen, Marion Tillema and
Huub van den Bergh

There have been many studies into the relation between cognitive processes during writing in the mother tongue (L1) and writing in a second or foreign language (L2). The results of different studies can hardly be called equivalent. However, many of the differences in results between studies can be attributed to methodological issues (van Weijen, 2009). In some studies, for instance, differences between languages are studied as between subject comparisons, while a within subject comparison is far more effective for analysing L1 and L2 writing processes (Roca de Larios, Murphy, & Marin, 2002, p. 31).

Second, if writing processes like planning, formulating, revising etc. are compared across languages, this usually concerns comparisons of frequencies (van Weijen, 2009). However, as task situations during writing continuously change, so does the probability of occurrence of cognitive activities. Indeed it has been shown that the orchestration of cognitive activities over the writing process is strongly related to aspects of the quality of the resulting texts (Van den Bergh et al., 2009).

In the present study, we focus on the orchestration of formulating activities during writing in L1 and L2, and their relation with text quality.

Method

First year university students of English ($N = 20$) wrote eight short argumentative essays while thinking aloud. All students wrote four texts in their L1 (Dutch) and

Learning to Write Effectively: Current Trends in European Research
Studies in Writing, Volume 25, 183–186
Copyright © 2012 by Emerald Group Publishing Limited
All rights of reproduction in any form reserved
ISSN: 1572-6304/doi:10.1108/S1572-6304(2012)0000025044

four texts in their L2 (English), on topics such as 'surveillance cameras', 'down-loading music', ' mobile phone use' etc. The assignments were counterbalanced, so that each assignment occurred as often in L1 as in L2.

The think-aloud data were transcribed and coded in terms of cognitive activities (van Weijen, 2009). Two raters coded the protocols. The interrater agreement (κ) varied from 0.84 in L1 to 0.95 in L2. Text quality was rated by two panels of raters, one for the L1 texts and one for the L2 texts. Each panel consisted of five raters, who rated text quality in a holistic way. The interrater agreement was satisfactory ($\alpha > 0.82$ for L1 and 0.83 for L2).

As observations of cognitive activities were nested within assignments, and assignments were nested within individuals, the results were analysed by means of multilevel modelling (Van den Bergh et al., 2009).

Some Results

The estimated occurrence of formulating activities is presented in Figure 1 (top row). Each line represents the average occurrence of formulating activities for one writer.

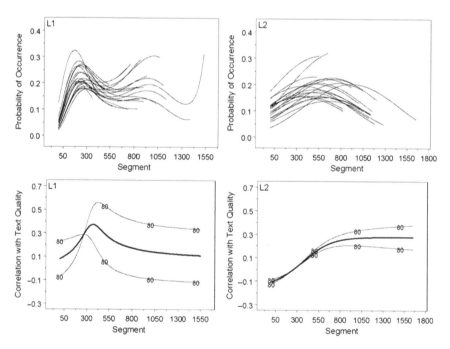

Figure 1: Top row: The probability of occurrence of formulating activities (*y*-axis) during the writing process (*x*-axis) in L1 (left) and L2 (right). Bottom row: The correlation between formulating activities and text quality in L1 (left) and L2 (right), average (solid line) and 80% confidence intervals due to task (80).

The probability of occurrence varies between writers as well as over time. The variation between writers is clearly larger in L2 than L1 at the start of the writing process. Towards the end of the writing process, however, the variation becomes larger in L1 than in L2.

Second, Figure 1 shows that the occurrence of formulating activities follows a more complex pattern in L1 than in L2. In L1, the orchestration of formulating activities over the writing process is more varied than in L2, as is reflected in the different number of peaks in both figures.

Not presented in Figure 1 are the differences in occurrence due to task. These appear to be comparable for L1 and L2; for formulating activities, differences due to assignment are much smaller than differences due to individuals. Nevertheless, assignment-related differences are time dependent as well; in both languages only 8–15% of the variance is attributable to the assignment. So, writers who give evidence of many formulating activities in one text also perform relatively many formulating activities in other texts.

In the second part of the analysis relations between the occurrence of cognitive activities and text quality are estimated. The results are also summarized in Figure 1 (bottom row).

Figure 1 shows that the correlation between formulating and text quality is somewhat different in both languages. Initially the correlation is negative in both languages, but gradually becomes positive as the writing process unfolds. In L1 it peaks around 0.37 and slightly decreases afterwards (but stays positive). Hence, writers who engage in formulating activities after the start of the writing process are likely to have written better texts. In L2 the correlation increases slowly over time, and stabilizes around 0.27 just past the middle of the writing process. This indicates that, in L2, writers who concentrate on formulating activities in the beginning of the writing process are likely to write poorer texts than writers who refrain from performing formulating activities in the beginning of the writing process.

Figure 1 (bottom row) also contains the 80%-confidence intervals due to task. These intervals show that the correlation between formulating and text quality can vary substantially in L1, but hardly varies in L2. In L1, for instance, variation in this correlation due to task ranges from –0.1 to 0.25 in the beginning and from −0.1 to 0.4 near the end of the writing process. For L2 differences due to task are minimal in the beginning, while it ranges from 0.15 to 0.35 near the end of the writing process.

Discussion and Future Research

The present study shows that the occurrence of formulating activities differs between L1 and L2. The occurrence of formulating activities in L1 follows a more complex pattern than the occurrence of formulating in L2. Furthermore, the correlation between formulating activities is more complex in L1 than in L2. Finally, this correlation appears to be highly task dependent in L1 but not in L2.

In subsequent research we will focus on comparisons of other cognitive activities in L1 and L2 writing such as planning, generating and revising, and on explanations for these differences, by taking differences in vocabulary, reading skill and other language skills into account (cf. Tillema, Van den Bergh, Rijlaarsdam & Sanders, this volume).

References

Roca de Larios, J., Murphy, L., & Marin, J. (2002). A critical examination of L2 writing process research. In G. Rijlaarsdam, S. Ransdell & L. Barbier (Eds.), *Studies in writing. New directions for research in L2 writing* (Vol. 11, pp. 11–47). Boston, MA: Kluwer Academic Publishers.

Van den Bergh, H., Rijlaarsdam, G., Janssen, T., Braaksma, M., van Weijen, D., & Tillema, M. (2009). Process execution of writing and reading: Considering text quality, learner and task characteristics. In M. Shelly, B. Hand & L. Yore (Eds.), *Quality research in literacy and science education: International perspectives and gold standards* (pp. 399–426). New York, NY: Springer.

Tillema, M., Van den Bergh, H., Rijlaarsdam, G., & Sanders, T. (this volume). Patterns of metacognitive processing during writing. Variation according to reported writing profile. In M. Torrance, D. Alamargot, M. Castelló, F. Ganier, O. Kruse, A. Mangen, L. Tolchinsky & L. Van Waes (Eds.), *Learning to write effectively: Current trends in European research.* Bingley, UK: Emerald Group Publishing Limited.

van Weijen, D. (2009). *Writing processes, text quality and task effects: Empirical studies in first and second language writing.* Utrecht: LOT.

Chapter 2.02.04

Relationship Between Text Quality and Management of the Writing Processes

Caroline Beauvais, Thierry Olive and
Jean-Michel Passerault

What determines quality of a text a student has composed? Actually, researches have already shown that text quality is related to the writer's level of verbal skill (McCutchen, 1986). Moreover, aside from verbal skills, writers' prior domain knowledge also makes an important contribution to writing achievement (Kellogg, 1987). However, more than knowing what to write in their text and how to formulate it, students have to know how to coordinate and regulate the attention paid to the writing processes (Kieft, Rijlaarsdam, & van den Bergh, 2008). Recent researches have suggested that online management of the planning, translating and revising processes plays a decisive role in text quality (Levy & Ransdell, 1995) and good and poor writers may be distinguished on the basis of how and when they use the writing processes during composition.

In this framework, two experiments were conducted to examine the relationship between online management of the writing processes and quality of the narrative and argumentative texts. In both experiments students composed a narrative and an argumentative text. While composing their text, participants were instructed to think aloud. The verbal protocols collected were categorized into four writing processes: planning, translating, reading and reviewing (Swarts, Hayes, & Flower, 1984). The pre-writing pause and writers' reaction times to secondary auditory probes (to assess cognitive effort of the writing processes) were also collected. Three sets of variables were analysed: first, variables related to general dynamic of composition (pre-writing pause, fluency); second, variables related to online management of the writing processes (cognitive effort, occurrences, total time spent in each writing process,

Learning to Write Effectively: Current Trends in European Research
Studies in Writing, Volume 25, 187–189
Copyright © 2012 by Emerald Group Publishing Limited
All rights of reproduction in any form reserved
ISSN: 1572-6304/doi:10.1108/S1572-6304(2012)0000025045

mean length of each writing process episode). Finally, two judges independently assessed content and style of the texts and a holistic quality score was then calculated on the basis of these scores.

The results of the first experiment confirmed that narrative and argumentative texts are composed with different strategies. Narratives are composed by frequently shifting between the writing processes, with a high fluency and short pre-writing pause. By contrast, argumentative texts require a slower rate, a longer pre-writing time and longer episodes of the writing processes. More precisely, whereas there are short and frequent episodes of planning when composing a narrative, argumentative composition involves less but longer episodes of planning. Furthermore, text quality is related to the use of these two strategies: in each text type, the more the writer uses the adequate strategy, the more the text quality.

The second experiment investigated more precisely how the relationship between text quality and the online management of the writing processes might be affected by a goal emphasizing text quality. Using the same triple task paradigm as used in the first experiment, students composed narrative and argumentative text under two goal quality conditions: a quality goal condition in which the instruction given to students emphasized the quality of both style and content of the text to compose (i.e. the two components of the text quality assessment scale). This condition was compared with a standard goal condition in which any explicit expectations about quality were formulated before text production.

As expected, and replicating the findings of Experiment 1, different patterns in the online management of the writing processes were observed in the narrative and argumentative compositions. Students who received the quality instructions rather than the standard ones composed texts that were assessed as being of a better quality. Contrary to our expectations, no change was observed in the orchestration of the writing processes, suggesting that students used the same strategies to compose their texts whatever level of quality they were seeking to achieve. The only change in the online management of the writing processes in this condition was an increase in the length of the pre-writing pause in the quality-based goal condition. This minimal change resulted in increased quality.

In sum, what emerges from these studies is that students change and adapt their writing strategy according to the constraints of the writing task. Educationally speaking, the present study addresses issues related to writing acquisition and to skilled writing. The findings from the two experiments described here suggest that topic knowledge and language skills cannot fully account for skilled writing. As we have seen, skilled writers — like the university students who took part in these two experiments — are skilful at managing the writing processes, as they are able to shift between strategies according to task demands. It has been shown that instructions designed to improve self-regulation strategies can be of benefit to students. The present study therefore highlights the importance of teaching students about the procedural differences between different types of text. It is well known that one possible way used to enhance writing performance is to teach self-regulatory procedures that include goal setting in the course of the writing task. They need to learn how to set goals by analysing the writing situation before they set pen to paper and to practice composing different types of text with different goals.

References

Kellogg, R. T. (1987). Effects of topic knowledge on the allocation of processing time and cognitive effort to writing processes. *Memory and Cognition, 15*, 256–266.

Kieft, M., Rijlaarsdam, G., & van den Bergh, H. (2008). An aptitude-treatment approach to writing-to-learn. *Learning and Instruction, 18*, 379–390.

Levy, C. M., & Ransdell, S. E. (1995). Is writing as difficult as it seems? *Memory and Cognition, 23*, 767–779.

McCutchen, D. (1986). Domain knowledge and linguistic knowledge in the development of writing ability. *Journal of Memory and Language, 25*, 431–444.

Swarts, H., Flower, L. S., & Hayes, J. R. (1984). Designing protocol studies of the writing process: An introduction. In R. Beach & L. S. Bridwell (Eds.), *New directions in composition research* (pp. 53–71). New York, NY: Guilford Press.

Chapter 2.02.05

Spanish Children's Use of Writing Strategies When Composing Texts in English as a Foreign Language

José María Campillo Ferrer, Sonia López Serrano and Julio Roca de Larios

As compared to research with adults, children's writing is not particularly visible as a field of inquiry in L2 writing research. According to Matsuda and De Pew (2002), the main reasons for this state of affairs include (i) scholars' lack of familiarity with children's learning environments, as L2 writing research has usually been carried out in higher educational contexts or, to a lesser extent, in secondary institutions; (ii) the range of external and internal official conditions that have to be met when dealing with children; (iii) the difficulties teachers usually face to bring research into line with their daily teaching routines; and (iv) the financial problems involved in carrying out this type of research.

In spite of these shortcomings, one research area which has begun to emerge in recent years is related to the use of L2 writing strategies by children. Graham and Macaro (2007) and Macaro (2007) initiated a research programme in the United Kingdom aimed at ascertaining how British schoolchildren employ formulation strategies when composing French texts. Methodologically, a very important contribution of this research has been the use of task-based data collection procedures and the elaboration of a number of coding categories to account not only for the repetition of lexical items and structures previously memorized by children but also for their novel recombination of L2 chunks.

In the present study we have used these procedures and categories in an attempt to answer the following research question: To what extent are the L2 writing strategies used by Spanish primary school children dependent on their level of L2 proficiency?

Learning to Write Effectively: Current Trends in European Research
Studies in Writing, Volume 25, 191–193
ISSN: 1572-6304/doi:10.1108/S1572-6304(2012)0000025046

Method

The study took place in a primary school situated in a middle-class area in the Southeast of Spain (Murcia). The sample consisted of 30 sixth graders who had been studying English since they were six (three hours per week) and, at the time of data collection, had received neither training in writing at school nor extra EFL lessons outside school. The children were grouped into three L2 proficiency levels (low, middle and high) according to an average score obtained from their performance on a number of tasks which included drills, fill-in-the-gaps, guided compositions and multiple choice tests.

The children were asked to write a free composition in English on an individual basis. No prior topic, aim or input was provided. The writing sessions took place in ordinary class hours and no time limitations to complete the compositions were set. After writing their compositions, each individual child was interviewed in Spanish by the first researcher by means of stimulated recall procedures which were intended to elicit the strategies they used. The protocols obtained were analysed through an adaptation of the categories developed by Macaro (2007).

Main Findings

The analysis of the data revealed the existence of both similarities and differences across groups. As for similarities, the data showed that most children limited themselves to thinking about the topic as the starting point for their writing. In consonance with prior studies in L1 and L2 writing (Bereiter & Scardamalia, 1987; Macaro, 2007), they spent very little time (less than a minute on average) before starting to write, which proved their overdependence on the ideas that came to their minds on the spur-of-the-moment. Another strategy common to the three groups was their use of the topic as the only device at their disposal to assure textual continuity and to link the sentences of their compositions. Finally, these children, regardless of their level of L2 proficiency, were found to be highly dependent on their mother tongue for the activation of most composition processes.

The differences found in the data have allowed us to elaborate two strategic profiles that should be understood as an attempt to describe how the children in the present study differentially activated their L2 writing strategies as a function of their L2 proficiency level. General speaking, the low- and mid-ability children had access to a limited repertoire of strategies and, as a result, were less successful than their high-ability counterparts in articulating their ideas on paper. In those cases in which the former managed to convey meaning in their L2 texts, they had no option but to rely on avoidance and compensatory strategies, resort to either formulaic words or set phrases retrieved from the last units covered in class or else generate word-for-word phrases or sentences via L1. When reviewing their texts, however, these children, probably because of the saliency of their mistakes, used more error detection strategies than the high-ability children, which means that they were able to perceive that there was something wrong with their texts, although not yet able to repair it.

The high-ability learners, in contrast, showed a wider repertoire of strategies. This was apparent in their activation of textual schemata to ensure coherence, their incipient use of communication strategies for upgrading purposes and their complex use of formulation strategies which included not only the retrieval of specific set phrases previously covered in class but also the construction of new phrases or sentences through both simple and complex processes of generation and recombination of constituents. They were also able to correct their texts, which we take as a clear indication that these children had a higher level of metalinguistic awareness than the other children.

Conclusions

This study, which was intended as an attempt to provide insights into Spanish young learners' use of strategies for writing purposes in English, has shown that children, in spite of having being taught a foreign language for a similar period of time, may spontaneously activate different L2 writing strategies as a function of the L2 proficiency they have developed. The main pedagogical conclusion to be drawn from this finding is that, as suggested by Chong (2002), schoolchildren should be exposed to instructional approaches that allow them not only to learn and use the L2 but also to improve their strategic practice.

References

Bereiter, C., & Scardamalia, M. (1987). *The psychology of written composition.* Hillsdale, NJ: Lawrence Erlbaum.

Chong, F. H. (2002). Children writing in English in the Singapore upper primary school: A case study of six 12-year-old students. LING 201: Linguistic Methodology Department of Linguistics and Modern English Language, Lancaster University.

Graham, S., & Macaro, E. (2007). Designing Year 12 strategy training in listening and writing: From theory to practice. *Language Learning Journal, 35,* 153–173.

Macaro, E. (2007). Do near-beginner learners of French have any writing strategies? *Language Learning Journal, 35,* 23–35.

Matsuda, P. K., & De Pew, K. E. (2002). Early second language writing: An introduction. *Journal of Second Language Writing, 11,* 261–268.

Chapter 2.02.06

The Effects of Dyslexia on the Writing Processes of Students in Higher Education

David Galbraith, Veerle Baaijen, Jamie Smith-Spark
and Mark Torrance

Undergraduates with dyslexia typically report that writing is the activity that they find most problematic in their studies. However, there has been very little empirical research into the specific problems dyslexic students encounter in writing. Previous research (e.g. Connelly, Campbell, Maclean, & Barnes, 2006) has focused almost exclusively on the written product or on relatively low-level processes (Wengelin, 2007). The present study aimed to deepen our understanding of the effects of dyslexia on writing by directly examining the writing process as well as the product. We were particularly interested in whether dyslexic students' difficulties with low-level processes lead to differences in high-level planning processes compared to non-dyslexic students.

Method

Twenty-eight undergraduates registered as dyslexic at a university in the United Kingdom were compared with 32 undergraduates matched for age, gender and academic discipline. Tests of intelligence and of reading and spelling skills showed that the two groups were of equal intelligence but that the dyslexic students performed significantly worse on the reading and spelling tests and on a test of working memory span.

Learning to Write Effectively: Current Trends in European Research
Studies in Writing, Volume 25, 195–198
Copyright © 2012 by Emerald Group Publishing Limited
All rights of reproduction in any form reserved
ISSN: 1572-6304/doi:10.1108/S1572-6304(2012)0000025047

All participants were asked to write an article for a student newspaper in which they discussed the pros and cons of legalizing euthanasia. This took place in three phases:

– Phase 1 (5 minutes): participants were asked to list all the ideas they could think of relevant to the topic.
– Phase 2 (10 minutes): participants were asked to construct an organized outline of the article they planned to write.
– Phase 3 (30 minutes): participants wrote the article themselves.

The articles were word-processed, and all key-strokes were logged using Inputlog (Leijten & van Waes, 2006).

During phase 3, half the participants in each group (15 dyslexics, 16 non-dyslexics) were asked to carry out the 'triple task' (Kellogg, 1988) at the same time as writing. The triple task involves participants responding as fast as possible to a tone presented at random intervals by pressing a foot pedal to stop the tone. Participants then have to classify the process they were engaged in at the time the tone sounded by pressing a button labelled with one of five categories of writing process: 'Planning to do', 'Planning to say', 'Writing', 'Reviewing', 'Other'. The time taken to respond to the tone indicates the effort currently being devoted to writing; the process classification indicates when, and how often, writers engage in the different kinds of writing process. Prior to the writing task participants were trained to classify their writing processes and baseline response times were collected.

The other half of the participants (13 dyslexics, 16 non-dyslexics) wrote as normal, free from interruption.

Results

All differences referred to below were significant at $p < .05$.

Dyslexics made more spelling mistakes than non-dyslexics. Even after texts were corrected for spelling and capitalization, their texts were rated as of much lower quality by two independent judges (inter-rater reliability $= .69$).

There were no differences in proportions of time which dyslexics and non-dyslexics spent on the different writing processes or in the effort they put into the processes. However, there was strong evidence that these processes were differently related to the quality of the final text. Non-dyslexics showed a negative correlation $(R = -.53)$ between amount of content planning during writing and text quality. This suggests that, for non-dyslexics, writers who were still generating ideas during the writing of the text itself wrote less well than writers who had completed idea generation during outlining. Dyslexics, however, showed a strong positive correlation $(R = .66)$ between amount of content planning and text quality. This suggests that dyslexic writers do not benefit from outlining in the same way the non-dyslexic writers do, and that they need either to reconstruct content during writing itself or that they write better when the expression of ideas in words takes place close to the point of idea generation.

There were no differences between the groups in length or quality of the outlines produced before writing. However, dyslexics introduced significantly more new ideas into their outlines than non-dyslexics. This was not related to the quality of the text for either group. Instead, for dyslexics, there was a positive correlation ($R = .45$) between the number of ideas from the initial list retained in the outline and text quality. This suggests that dyslexics were able to write more effectively when they had a relatively stable set of initial ideas to write about.

Both groups of writers consulted their outlines a similar number of times during writing. However, these consultations took place at different places in the text for dyslexics and non-dyslexics. Dyslexics consulted their outlines relatively more between words and between paragraphs, and relatively less between sentences, than non-dyslexics. For dyslexics, there was a significant correlation ($R = .44$) between the number of plan consultations made between sentences and text quality. This suggests that one difficulty dyslexics have with writing is in coordinating their initial goals as specified in their outlines with subsequent text production. They appear to plan at either too low a level (between words) or at too global a level (between paragraphs).

Students with dyslexia paused for much longer within and between words than non-dyslexics, replicating previous findings by Wengelin (2007). Relationships with text quality are still under analysis for this measure.

Theoretical and Educational Implications

These findings suggest that the problems dyslexics have with writing are not restricted to low-level processes related to spelling and punctuation. They appear to have greater difficulties than non-dyslexics in constructing a stable outline of their ideas before writing, to need to reconstruct content to be written about during writing itself rather than relying on content generated during outlining, and to have greater difficulty in coordinating their initial goals with appropriate levels of text production. This may be a consequence of (i) problems with low-level processes interfering with high-level processes or (ii) a direct effect of lower working memory capacity on planning processes or (iii) a combination of both these factors.

References

Connelly, V., Campbell, S., Maclean, M., & Barnes, J. (2006). Contributions of lower order skills to the written composition of college students with and without dyslexia. *Developmental Neuropsychology*, *29*(1), 175–196.

Kellogg, R. T. (1988). Attentional overload and writing performance: Effects of rough draft and outline strategies. *Journal of Experimental Psychology: Learning, Memory, and Cognition*, *14*(2), 355–365.

Leijten, M., & Van Waes, L. (2006). Inputlog: New perspectives on the logging of online writing. In K. P. H. Sullivan & E. Lindgren (Eds.), *Studies in writing: Computer key-stroke logging and writing: Methods and applications* (Vol. 18, pp. 73–94). Oxford: Elsevier.

Wengelin, A. (2007). The word-level focus in text production by adults with reading and writing difficulties. In G. Rijlaarsdam (Series Ed.) and M. Torrance, L. van Waes & D. Galbraith (Volume Eds.), *Writing and cognition: Research and applications* (Vol. 20, pp. 67–82). Studies in Writing. Amsterdam: Elsevier.

Chapter 2.02.07

Subcomponents of Writing Literacy: Diagnosis and Didactical Support

Joachim Grabowski, Michael Becker-Mrotzek, Matthias Knopp, Nicole Nachtwei, Christian Weinzierl, Jörg Jost and Markus Schmitt

Writing literacy, in the sense of the ability of text production, is a complex skill comprising many different cognitive, linguistic, motivational and affective subcomponents (Becker-Mrotzek & Böttcher, 2006). In the framework of educational and didactical research, these components were hitherto predominantly holistically studied and instructed, that is with respect to individual genres, where the typical composition tasks at school — narration, description/instruction, argumentation — play a central role (Becker-Mrotzek, 2007). In contrast, our aim is to identify overarching subcomponents of writing literacy where 'overarching' is related to abilities that become operative in all (or many) kinds of writing processes. In doing so, we concentrate on skills that (a) are compatible with linguistic insight, (b) correlate with the quality of text products and (c) are suitable for purposeful didactical measures.

Exemplarily, we will study three subcomponents: (a) the ability to take a partner's perspective and to adapt to the addressee's needs, (b) the differentiated and thematically adequate use of vocabulary and (c) the creation of coherence by the use of the respective linguistic means of cohesion. Two classes of each fifth and ninth grade will be studied in three typical German school types, namely Hauptschule, Realschule and Gymnasium. Analyses will intend to identify correlational patterns between the general writing ability and the above-mentioned subcomponents within the most central genres of narratives/reports, instructions/descriptions and argumentative tests. In addition to approved tasks and test

Learning to Write Effectively: Current Trends in European Research
Studies in Writing, Volume 25, 199–201
Copyright © 2012 by Emerald Group Publishing Limited
All rights of reproduction in any form reserved
ISSN: 1572-6304/doi:10.1108/S1572-6304(2012)0000025048

instruments, we will also conceive of new writing tasks specific for the subcomponents under investigation.

The delineated project is a cooperation of psychological, linguistic and didactical researchers, funded by the German Ministry of Education and Research (BMBF) for the first three years (10/2009–09/2012) within the programme 'Fostering Empirical Educational Research in the Field of Linguistic Diagnosis and Support'.

The long-term aim of the project is to develop a linguistically and psycholinguistically substantiated model of writing literacy which is relevant with respect to linguistic didactics and which includes abilities of how to use linguistic forms and structures and how to strategically leverage the respective processes. In contrast to the assumptions and approaches of traditional text composition didactics, we will describe and measure writing literacy not or not only by means of a progression through text types of increasing complexity nor on the basis of text products. Rather, we will look for ability components that are, with sufficient linguistic and psychological plausibility, relevant across text types (Grabowski, 2010). We expect that such subcomponents of writing literacy may exist earlier in students' development and school career than their ability to generate complete texts of a certain quality. Therefore, relevant subcomponents could be fostered and developed earlier than the production of full texts in which they are applied. Based on our general objectives, the following questions and consequences arise.

What are the linguistically manifest qualities of texts in which the relevant subcomponents of writing literacy become particularly clearly visible? This question emerges from the theoretical assumption according to which writing literacy is the result of the integration of component abilities which are, to varying degrees, required for all writing tasks — rather than the result of the gradual acquisition of text types of increasing levels of difficulty. Therefore, we will not in the first place study the holistic success on complex writing tasks, but the implementation of individual partial aspects relevant for writing literacy.

We further assume that such partial abilities are frequently overlooked or ignored when experienced teachers assess the quality of texts through global ratings, because they predominantly estimate those component abilities that are didactically central for the respective text type.

From a comparison of the various subcomponents realized in different text types, a question may be directed towards the mutual relationship between these partial aspects after they were theoretically isolated (partner orientation, management of coherence, lexical access). Do these partial abilities develop simultaneously on comparable levels? Or is there one particular leading ability on which subsequent partial abilities are based? Are these partial abilities universal, so to speak, or must they be considered functions of certain text types or writing assignments?

Finally, it appears worth to question whether subcomponents of writing literacy can be trained (Grabowski, Blabusch, & Lorenz, 2007). For example, is a general, transferring training of partner orientation ability possible across text types? — At the best, however, this last-mentioned group of questions must be left to a follow-up phase of the project.

References

Becker-Mrotzek, M. (2007). Aufsatz-und Schreibdidaktik [The didactics of writing and composition]. In K. Knapp, G. Antos, M. Becker-Mrotzek, A. Deppermann, S. Göpferich, J. Grabowski, M. Klemm & C. Villinger (Eds.), *Angewandte Linguistik. Ein Lehrbuch* (pp. 36–55). Tübingen: Francke.

Becker-Mrotzek, M., & Böttcher, I. (2006). *Schreibkompetenz entwickeln und beurteilen* [*Developing and assessing writing literacy*]. Berlin: Cornelsen.

Grabowski, J. (2010). Speaking, writing, and memory span in children: Output modality affects cognitive performance. *International Journal of Psychology*, *45*, 28–39.

Grabowski, J., Blabusch, C., & Lorenz, Th. (2007). Welche Schreibkompetenz? — Handschrift und Tastatur in der Hauptschule [Which writing ability? — Handwriting and keyboard in German Hauptschule]. In M. Becker-Mrotzek & K. Schindler (Eds.), *Texte schreiben* (pp. 41–61). Köln: Gilles & Francke.

Chapter 2.02.08

What Expert Writers Do When They Don't Solve Problems? Literate Expertise Revisited

Atle Skaftun and Per Henning Uppstad

Literate Expertise Revisited is the title of a project that will heed a 30-year-old call for the literacy-research community to contribute to a general theory of expertise across skill domains. This means that the project will challenge the widespread assumption that reading and writing are fundamentally different from other skills in that experts spend more time and effort than novices on representative tasks.

The project is founded in several years of critical inquiry into the concept of skill with an ambition to contextualize the strong and somewhat unbalanced emphasis on strategic behaviour and problem solving in theory of reading and writing as well as in the instructional practice. What literate experts do when they don't solve problems is less focused. We will explore the explanatory powers of everyday life expertise as a frame for understanding skills in general, and literate expertise in particular. In this perspective the tradition of expertise research is a highly relevant point of reference.

Scardamalia and Bereiter (1991) claim to show that expertise in writing, unlike expertise in other skill domains, is characterized by greater effort than 'novicehood'. They maintain that experts devote more time and energy to solving the tasks given to them than non-experts, while the case is the opposite in other domains. Their proposed explanation is that the increased use of time is linked to an increased cognitive load as a result of the complexity of the skill domain. On this basis, the authors assume that problem-solving strategies are crucial to expertise in reading and writing — which is quite different from the characteristics of expertise in other domains. The 2006 Cambridge Handbook of Expertise and Expert performance does not describe reading, but it does deal with writing. In his review of writing research Kellogg describes a wide range of characteristic features in professional writing expertise, spanning from problem solving to studies of flow states in writing. The

Learning to Write Effectively: Current Trends in European Research
Studies in Writing, Volume 25, 203–205
Copyright © 2012 by Emerald Group Publishing Limited
All rights of reproduction in any form reserved
ISSN: 1572-6304/doi:10.1108/S1572-6304(2012)0000025049

cognitive load of writing is treated as a particular feature to be dealt with by the writer, but is also an important part of the tacit background of the review: Writing differs from other skills because of the cognitive load involved (Kellogg, 2006).

The only substantial criticism levelled at Scardamalia and Bereiter's conception of expertise derives from a brief article by Mark Torrance published in 1996. In his article, Torrance addresses the tendency for circular reasoning between premises and conclusions which follows from the design of tasks. Torrance's main point is that this type of study design has a critical blind spot as regards the importance of familiarity with genre. The design typically invites young participants to exercise what he sees as their genre-specific expertise, while the adults are forced into a genre that is not (no longer) familiar to them. This means that, for the adult assumed to be an expert, the task is unfamiliar despite its assumed simplicity; it does not afford the expert performing his expertise.

Key logging studies has shown a long initial pause for adult writers, followed by a fluent writing behaviour while writing text to a picture series. Young writers pause less initially but have a significantly larger amount of long pauses during writing. This is most often interpreted as a difference of high- and low-level processing. However, the impact of text type on the process of writing — and further theorizing — has not been investigated. Interestingly, our own research group has found no long initial pause (average 6 seconds) when adults write a text about how they celebrate Christmas, a text type which is more familiar and straightforward for the adult than for instance the picture series.

In order to deal with the similarity between the novice performing adequately within the limited frame of, for example a school genre and the expert performance in a far more complex and open domain, we need a theory of development that explains both the similarities and the differences between the two performers. The phenomenological skill model (Dreyfus & Dreyfus, 2004) is but one possible frame of understanding. This model generally describes a developmental dynamics with effortless performance as a goal. Rules, maxims and problem-solving strategies are means for moving from the more limited overview of the domain onto being familiar with most of the situational complexes that might occur. The expert facing problems in this view will have to resort to strategies and planning in order to adjust the holistic response to the situation. But that does not make problem solving the normal condition for the expert; expertise is defined according to a human strive for balance between the intentionality of the individual and the affordance of his environment.

This understanding of expertise is general in that it is based on a philosophical understanding of the relation between individual and environment. Everyday expertise — that is the highly complex ways we relate to our surroundings on a biological, physical, cultural and discursive level — provides the optics for understanding also what we consider outstanding performance. More specifically it allows us to study reading and writing as skills alongside other skill domains.

The project will encompass writing tasks from three different domains: writing a story about everyday experience typical for school practice; writing in a familiar genre contextualized as everyday experience; and finally teachers' professional reading of and written response to students' texts. The first task has its design from earlier expertise research, and will provide empirical evidence to control Torrance's suggestion that the data demonstrates differing genre familiarity rather than different skill level. The second task will establish equal terms concerning familiarity with the genre for writers at different skill level and thus providing a basis for questioning the assumption that expert writers use more time and effort on the task than novice writers. The third study limits the scope to a specific professional domain in order to better be able to describe the development towards literate expertise within this domain. The hypothesis is that, when controlling for familiarity with the task or genre and keeping the complexity of the performance in mind, literate expertise is characterized by less time and less effort on the task relative to novice writers as is the case with expertise in other skill domains.

References

Dreyfus, H. L., & Dreyfus, S. E. (2004). The ethical implications of the Five-Stage Skill-Acquisition Model. *Bulletin of Science, Technology and Society, 24*(3), 251–264.

Kellogg, R. T. (2006). Professional writing expertise. In K. A. Ericsson, N. Charness, R. Hoffman & P. Feltovich (Eds.), *The Cambridge handbook of expertise and expert performance* (pp. 389–402). Cambridge: Cambridge University Press.

Scardamalia, M., & Bereiter, C. (1991). Literate expertise. In K. A. Ericsson & J. Smith (Eds.), *Toward a general theory of expertise: Prospects and limits* (pp. 172–194). Cambridge: Cambridge University Press.

Torrance, M. (1996). Is writing expertise like other kinds of expertise? In G. Rijlersdam, H. van den Bergh & M. Couzijn (Eds.), *Theories, models and methodology in writing research.* Amsterdam: Amsterdam University Press.

Chapter 2.02.09

Effects of Creative Writing on Students' Literary Response

Tanja Janssen

Previous research has shown that different kinds of writing may have beneficial effects on students' literary response and understanding (e.g. Boscolo & Carotti, 2003; Marshall, 1987). These studies focused on formal, academic modes of writing (essays, reviews) and/or personal writing (journals). Whether creative, imaginative writing may be beneficial as well has not been established.

Advocates of creative writing have repeatedly pointed out its value for literary reading. According to some, creative writing may lead to enhanced reading engagement and appreciation of literary texts, increased self-efficacy as readers of literature, deeper processing of literary texts, more knowledge of and insight into literary techniques. Also, it has been assumed that creative writing — as a pre-reading activity — may activate certain (meta)cognitive activities that are important for reading and understanding. In this view, creative writing may lead to positive changes in students' reading processes, which in turn may lead to better reading comprehension and recall (Denner & McGinley, 1992).

In the present study we examined the effects of one particular creative writing assignment: writing a story in the pre-reading stage, predicting the story to be read. In this assignment, students are asked to predict story content and form, by writing their own story on the basis of certain 'clues' about the story to be read. We examined the effects of this type of writing on two outcome variables: reading process and story appreciation.

The main question was: does story writing as a pre-reading activity have beneficial effects on students' literary response to short stories, compared to 'no writing'?

'Literary response' refers here to both the process and product of literary reading. Following Denner and McGinley (1992) and others, we expected that students who

Learning to Write Effectively: Current Trends in European Research
Studies in Writing, Volume 25, 207–209
Copyright © 2012 by Emerald Group Publishing Limited
All rights of reproduction in any form reserved
ISSN: 1572-6304/doi:10.1108/S1572-6304(2012)0000025050

wrote their own story before reading, would show a different reading process compared to students who do not write. In particular, students would relate the literary story to their own story and they would show more emotional engagement during reading.

Furthermore, we hypothesized that story writing before reading would be advantageous for the outcomes of the reading process, for students' appreciation of stories.

Method

An experimental design was used, with a control group and post-tests. Participants were 10th-grade students from different Dutch secondary schools (15–16 years old, pre-university and higher general education).

Participants were assigned to one of the following conditions:

an experimental condition in which students ($n = 18$) wrote their own story, before reading the original literary story under think aloud conditions;
a 'no writing' control condition in which students ($n = 35$) read the story while thinking aloud.

In both conditions students read two short stories, written by recognized authors of literary fiction. In the experimental condition, students completed two creative writing tasks, preceding their reading of each of the literary stories. In the writing tasks, certain clues were given about story content and genre, to be used by students in their writings. These clues consisted, for instance, of the title and the opening sentences; the task then was to complete the story, or to write a dialogue between the main characters. Students wrote their stories on a computer. They were given 45 minutes to complete the writing tasks.

Afterwards, they read the stories under think aloud conditions (about 15 minutes per story). The stories were presented, fragment by fragment, on a computer screen. Students could scroll forward and backward, as they liked. During reading they were asked to verbalize all their thoughts (see Janssen, Braaksma, & Rijlaarsdam, 2006, for the think aloud procedure).

In the control condition students just read the stories, under think aloud conditions, without any writing beforehand.

To get insight into students' reading processes, their think aloud responses during reading were recorded, transcribed and segmented into statements. Statements were analysed for the reading activities they revealed (e.g. retelling, inferencing, problem detecting, evaluating, emotional responding). The coding scheme was developed and tested in a previous study (Janssen et al., 2006). Percentages were calculated for each reading activity in the scheme.

After reading each story, students were asked to indicate their liking of each story on a 10-point scale.

Results

One-way analyses of variances revealed two significant differences in reading process between conditions: the experimental, creative writing group more often connected the literary story to other texts (i.e. their own story), and more often responded emotionally to the literary story during reading. Effect sizes were medium to large (Cohen's $d = .64 - .91$). No difference was found in meta-cognitive responses between the conditions.

Furthermore, we found that the course of students' reading processes over time (during the reading of the story as a whole) differed significantly between conditions. Connecting the literary story to other texts, for instance, occurred mainly at the beginning of the reading process in the experimental condition. As the reading progressed, the experimental students hardly referred to their own story or other texts at all. The control group showed an unchanging pattern of response, overall making few connections to other texts during reading.

Finally, the experimental creative writing group scored significantly higher on story appreciation than control students. The effect size was large ($d = 1.09$).

Preliminary Conclusions

Our conclusion is that creative writing (in the form of composing ones own story before reading) appears to positively affect students' literary response. The creative writing task not only seems to influence students' literary reading process (more emotional engagement, more intertextual connections), but also the outcome of this process: students' story appreciation. Some of these effects are large.

Possibly, the writing task made students curious about the original story, causing them to orchestrate their reading activities differently. The alteration of the reading process may in turn have led to higher appreciation of the literary text. However, further explorations of the exact mechanisms at work are necessary.

References

Boscolo, P., & Carotti, L. (2003). Does writing contribute to improving high school students' approach to literature? *L1 — Educational Studies in Language and Literature, 3*(3), 197–224.

Denner, P. R., & McGinley, W. J. (1992). Effects of prereading activities on junior high students' recall. *Journal of Educational Research, 86*(1), 11–19.

Janssen, T., Braaksma, M., & Rijlaarsdam, G. (2006). Literary reading activities of good and weak students: A think aloud study. *European Journal of Psychology of Education, 21*(1), 35–52.

Marshall, J. (1987). The effects of writing on students' understanding of literary texts. *Research in the Teaching of English, 21*, 30–63.

Chapter 2.02.10

Writing Summaries and Syntheses to Learn in Secondary and Higher Education

Isabel Solé, Mariana Miras, Marta Gràcia, Nuria Castells, Sandra Espino, Mar Mateos, Elena Martín, Isabel Cuevas and Ruth Villalón

The general aim of this research was to investigate how students use reading and writing as tools for learning in Secondary and Higher Education. We approached this general issue from a socio-cultural perspective, considering the psychological impact of literacy to be a consequence of the social practices in which students are engaged.

Some research supports the hypothesis that when reading and writing are used together, in hybrid tasks (Spivey & King, 1989), they become more powerful learning tools than when employed separately. This is due to the fact that students perform different roles (source-reader, note-writer, new text-writer, draft-reader; Tynjälä, 2001), which increases the epistemic potential of reading and writing. We were especially interested in two different hybrid tasks: writing a summary of a single text and writing a synthesis of multiple texts.

In a previous study (Solé et al., 2005) designed to identify and characterize reading and writing tasks assigned by teachers (214) and carried out by students (616) in order to learn academic contents, we founded that summarizing, a relatively simple hybrid task, is a task that students perform quite frequently; therefore, reading multiple texts and writing a synthesis of them is one of the tasks least frequently assigned and performed. This hybrid task requires high levels of elaboration, the integration of different texts and written composition and may lead to deepen knowledge.

Learning to Write Effectively: Current Trends in European Research
Studies in Writing, Volume 25, 211–214
ISSN: 1572-6304/doi:10.1108/S1572-6304(2012)0000025051

Using this conceptual framework, we analysed the relationships between personal variables (prior knowledge, reading and writing competence) and contextual variables (different types of hybrid tasks — summary and synthesis), on the one hand, and the processes performed by the participants and the products they created, on the other.

The questions we posed were: What are the cognitive processes students from different educational levels activate when they carry out tasks of different levels of complexity that involve reading and writing to learn? What are the relations between the prior knowledge students have, the processes they carry out, the written products they elaborate and the learning outcomes they achieve?

Method

To answer these questions a case study was carried out with 47 participants from different educational levels: 12 first-year secondary education students (12 year olds), 12 fourth-year secondary education students (15 year olds), 12 post-secondary education students (17 year olds) and 11 university students.

In all cases the teacher asked the whole class to write a summary or a synthesis after reading one or more texts on the Social Studies subject they were studying. While the rest of the class did the assignment as homework, the participants performed the task in the presence of the researcher.

The procedure included a pre-task questionnaire to assess prior knowledge and a short interview to determine task representation. Then, to access their mental processes, each student was recorded and observed while performing the task and asked to think aloud in order to understand the way they were constructing meaning from informational texts. The written products were also collected. Once the students had completed the summary or synthesis, they were asked to fill in a short learning questionnaire.

We analysed the written products to categorize them on several dimensions (selection of the main ideas, integration, coherence and cohesion mechanisms, elaboration and misinterpretations).

We used two approaches to analyse the processes: a 'macro' approach, which gave us an overview of the procedures employed by the participants in performing the task, including the sequence in which the procedures were used; and a 'micro' approach, embedded within the other, focusing on the students' verbalizations.

We created a single category system that enabled us to code the participants' verbalizations during the performance of the task both while they were involved in reading and while they were involved in composing. In this way we identified the planning operations (setting goals, global and local planning of formal aspects, content planning, etc.) and when they took place; the meaning construction processes (paraphrasing, elaborating, integrating information, etc.); and the checking and supervision processes students verbalized (supervising comprehension/production, formulating problems, verbalizing solution strategies, etc.). We were also able to identify erroneous elaborations (Integrated Category System (ICS); Mateos, Martín, Villalón, & Luna, 2008).

Results

The results obtained in this study are very extensive. Therefore here we present only the main conclusions.

The best products (summaries and syntheses) were associated with a pattern of procedures in which the students made more recursive and flexible use of reading and writing. On the other hand, the least elaborated products were associated with a pattern in which reading and writing were used in a more linear and routine fashion (Mateos et al., 2008).

Students from the different educational levels used inadequate procedures, such as writing without reading completely the text or texts. Also, a lot of students reproduced a learned sequence: reading, underlining, writing and revising, but did not re-read the text or texts.

Very different products were generated by students using quite similar cognitive and meta-cognitive processes.

The differences between the procedures used and the quality of the products generated seem to be related to the students' level of knowledge about the topic, as even students with high competence in reading and writing had difficulties when performing the summary and synthesis.

In the case of the synthesis, which was a more difficult task than the summary, the quality of the products differed from one educational level to another, with the students at the lower levels creating the products the furthest removed from a synthesis proper. The texts produced by these students were often juxtaposed summaries of the source documents and failed to integrate the information. Only at the higher levels did the attempted syntheses outnumber the products that could not be considered syntheses. The students at the higher levels of the educational system used more complex and appropriate procedures than the students at the lower levels, whose procedures were simpler and more direct (Mateos & Solé, 2009).

References

LEAC. (2007). Integrated Category System (ICS). Coordinated project BSO2001-3359-C02-01.

Mateos, M., Martín, E., Villalón, R., & Luna, M. (2008). Reading and writing to learn in secondary education: Online processing activity and written products in summarizing and synthesizing tasks. *Reading and Writing: An Interdisciplinary Journal, 21*, 675–697.

Mateos, M., & Solé, I. (2009). Synthesising information from various texts: A study of procedures and products at different educational levels. *European Journal of Psychology of Education, 24*(4), 435–451.

Spivey, N., & King, J. R. (1989). Readers as writers composing from sources. *Reading Research Quarterly, XXIV,* 7–26.

Solé, I., Mateos, M., Miras, M., Martín, E., Castells, N., Cuevas, I., & Gràcia, M. (2005). Lectura, escritura y adquisición de conocimientos en Educación Secundaria y Educación Universitaria. *Infancia y Aprendizaje, 28*(3), 329–347.

Tynjälä, P (2001). Writing, learning and the development of expertise in higher education. In P. Tynjälä, L. Mason & K. Lonka (Eds.), *Writing as a learning tool: Integrating theory and practice* (pp. 37–56). Dordrecht, The Netherlands: Kluwer Academic Press.

Subsection 2.03

Text Assessment

Chapter 2.03.01

CEFLING: Combining Second Language Acquisition and Testing Approaches to Writing

Maisa Martin, Riikka Alanen, Ari Huhta, Paula Kalaja, Katja Mäntylä, Mirja Tarnanen and Åsa Palviainen

The official aims and practices of language education and assessment in Europe are fundamentally influenced by the Common European Framework of Reference for Languages: Learning, Teaching, and Assessment (CEFR). The best known aspect of the CEFR is the six-level scale of language proficiency. In Finland the 'CEFR effect' is particularly strong, as the CEFR scales have been adapted for the National Core Curricula for schools, for adult education and for the National Certificates language examination. Even the citizenship requirement of skills in one of the national languages (Finnish or Swedish) is based on the CEFR (B1).

The CEFR scale describes language proficiency with communicative and functional goals and descriptors. These are obviously not language-specific and thus give the learner or teacher no pointers for what structures and words might be useful for reaching a given level. The CEFLING project addresses the question of how second language skills in a given language develop from one functional level to the next. It brings together two usually separate research fields: the study of second language acquisition and the study of language testing. It is a part of an informal European network called SLATE (Second Language Acquisition and Testing in Europe).

The focus area of the CEFLING project is the development of writing. Two languages are involved: Finnish as a second language (L1 varies) and English (L1 Finnish). The research questions are the following:

What combinations of linguistic features characterize learners' performance at the proficiency levels defined in the CEFR and its Finnish adaptations?

Learning to Write Effectively: Current Trends in European Research
Studies in Writing, Volume 25, 217–219
Copyright © 2012 by Emerald Group Publishing Limited
All rights of reproduction in any form reserved
ISSN: 1572-6304/doi:10.1108/S1572-6304(2012)0000025052

To what extent do adult and young learners who engage in the same communicative tasks, at a given level, perform in the same way linguistically? To what extent are the adult-oriented CEFR levels and their Finnish adaptations for young learners equivalent?

To what extent are the pedagogical tasks found in the teaching materials in the Finnish comprehensive school comparable with the tasks defined in the CEFR and the new curriculum?

What are the linguistic and communicative features that teachers and the National Certificates raters pay attention to when assessing learners with the help of the Finnish adaptations of the CEFR scales? How do these features relate to the linguistic and communicative analysis of the same performances?

The data consists of writing samples from adults (National Certificates test performances) and young learners (grades 7–9, ages 12–16). The tasks for both sets of data were similar. For the development of the tasks, see Alanen et al. in this publication. The samples were assessed by trained raters using both the CEFR scale and the National Curricula scale. The National Curricula scale breaks down the CEFR levels into smaller steps, for example A1 into A1.1–A1.3. The samples with the minimum of 67% inter-rater reliability (two ratings agree and one is at the most one level higher or lower) form the basic data. The basic data for Finnish consists of 671 samples from adults and 825 from young learners. For English there are 562 samples from young learners (adult data selection in process). The data has been coded in CHILDES format (Child Language Data Exchange System, http:// childes.psy.cmu.edu/).

At time of writing (Autumn, 2009) the analysis for RQs 1 and 2 is still underway. Several senior researchers and doctoral students each follow the development of certain structural or lexical features across the functional, CEFR-based proficiency levels. For each feature, three dimensions are studied: frequency (per 1000 words), accuracy and distribution. Both quantitative and qualitative methods are used. The theoretical starting points of the linguistic analysis vary somewhat but are primarily usage-based (construction grammar, conceptual semantics). Work on L2 English syntax focuses on the development of questions and negation. Vocabulary studies focus on the frequency, range and depth of lexis in the learners' writing across proficiency levels as well as on the development of word derivation skills and the ability to use formulaic expressions such as collocations, prepositional phrases in English and verbal structures in Finnish as well as metatextual phrases. The work for the RQs 3 and 4 is also proceeding, with the analyses of the task performance and the teacher and rater interviews.

At the moment the results are very tentative. However, it seems that the growth of the linguistic skills is not linear across the CEFR levels but there are bigger differences between some levels. Furthermore, the growth of the three dimensions is different: frequency and accuracy do not always grow similarly. An important finding is that practically any linguistic structure can be found at any level, even A1, but first with very limited distribution. This sheds new light on the SLA theories of the order of acquisition. The first results on the analyses of the rating data suggest that the two rating scales used in the study are quite comparable but that the qualitative findings from the interviews point out certain problems in usability of the scales and the specific descriptors of performance used in them.

Chapter 2.03.02

Designing and Assessing L2 Writing Tasks Across CEFR Proficiency Levels

Riikka Alanen, Ari Huhta, Maisa Martin,
Mirja Tarnanen, Katja Mäntylä, Paula Kalaja
and Åsa Palviainen

The CEFLING project (http://www.jyu.fi/cefling), funded by the Academy of Finland (2007–2009), was set up in 2006 for the explicit purpose of combining the research perspectives of language testing and second language acquisition. In the project, written L2 data were collected from young (aged 12–16) and adult L2 Finnish and L2 English. The overall aim of the project is to describe the features of language that L2 learners use at various levels of language proficiency as described by the CEFR scales.

Data elicitation, or what kinds of tasks are used to collect L2 data is a critical issue for both SLA and language testing research. Languages are learned by using them in various tasks inside or outside the classroom both in formal and informal contexts. Tasks in this very broad sense provide language learners/users opportunities for language learning. Language task is defined here as 'an activity which requires learners to use language, with emphasis on meaning, to attain an objective' (Bygate, Skehan, & Swain, 2001).

L2 data used in CEFLING come from two sources. First, the adult L2 data come from the National Certificate language examinations, a national language testing system run by the Centre for Applied Language Studies at the University of Jyväskylä. The tasks and the data from adult language learners have yet to be analysed systematically. Secondly, L2 data were also collected from seventh to ninth graders at school. A considerable amount of time and effort went into designing tasks suitable for eliciting L2 data from younger language learners. In what follows

Learning to Write Effectively: Current Trends in European Research
Studies in Writing, Volume 25, 221–223
ISSN: 1572-6304/doi:10.1108/S1572-6304(2012)0000025053

we will present an account of the procedures that went into designing and assessing these particular L2 writing tasks.

Our first requirement was that the tasks should be communicative and that they should have some measure of authenticity in terms of text types and processes needed in completing the tasks. A number of tasks used in the National Certificate language examination, which have been found reliable and valid for testing the proficiency of adult L2 learners, were reviewed to find a number of suitable candidates for data elicitation. Second, it was decided that task types themselves should be familiar to students so that they would find it easier to understand what was required of them. For this purpose, language course books used at school were reviewed. Finally, it was decided that the tasks should be aimed at the appropriate L2 proficiency level, that is they should be neither too easy nor too difficult: L2 users/learners in this instance were estimated to be at least at the level A1 and at B2 at the most.

Based on such considerations, a set of communicative writing tasks were designed for the project. The tasks were piloted by asking a small number of students to complete them. The results were then analysed and some changes were made as to the number of tasks and instructions. The final set of tasks consisted of five communicative tasks representing a variety of functions, text types and register: Task 1 was an informal email message to a friend, Task 2 was an informal email message to a teacher, Task 3 was a formal message to an internet store, Task 4 was an opinion piece and Task 5 was a story. Additional tasks were designed to elicit data on particular linguistic features (such as questions, relative clauses and word derivation) in L2 English.

Assessing the L2 learners' performance on the tasks was carefully planned, as well. The assessment criteria and procedures necessary for the reliable and valid rating of the tasks and task performances based on CEFR were prepared. The criteria used in assessment consisted of relevant CEFR scales for writing, including scales for written interaction, correspondence and notes, messages and forms, creative writing and thematic development, and overall written production. A team of raters for L2 Finnish and L2 English was selected and trained for the project. The raters were also given a set of benchmarks selected from the pilot performances; in the case of L2 English, they were also given benchmarks prepared by the Council of Europe.

A total number of 3427 performances were collected from seventh to ninth graders from schools. A number of scripts ($N = 1789$) were selected for assessment by a team of trained raters ($N = 9$ for English, $N = 4$ for Finnish). Each script was rated by four (L2 English) or three (L2 Finnish) trained raters. Only those scripts were selected for the analysis of linguistic features on which the raters were in sufficient agreement (three out of four raters for L2 English, two out of three for L2 Finnish). Thus, the final corpus for L2 English contained 562 scripts and for L2 Finnish 825 scripts.

The suitability of the tasks for users/learners at various CEFR levels was assessed by raters before data collection begun. These assessments were then compared with the ratings of the L2 learner performances. The findings so far indicate that the raters were for the large part in agreement about the difficulty of the tasks: for example, A2 was deemed within the range of all of the tasks. Similarly, various statistical analyses (e.g. multifaceted Rasch analyses) of the L2 users/learners' performance across the five communicative tasks reveal little variation in task difficulty across the five tasks (Alanen & Huhta 2009). Overall, these findings indicate that the task design was quite successful in eliciting L2 data across the proficiency levels from A1 to B2, but rather less so for advanced levels; however, this was only to be expected because of the young age of the participants. In sum, CEFLING is one of the few projects to date in which an attempt has been made to combine the methodological rigour of a theory-bound SLA research with an understanding of the need to define L2 performance according to a strictly defined set of standards based on a model of communicative language use.

References

Alanen, R., & Huhta, A. (2009). L2 learners' performance across L2 writing tasks: Comparing tasks and language proficiency through CEFR scales. Paper at TBLT 2009, 13–16 September, Lancaster, UK.

Bygate, M., Skehan, P., & Swain, M. (Eds.). (2001). *Researching pedagogic tasks. Second language learning, teaching and testing.* Harlow: Longman.

Chapter 2.03.03

What Is 'Improvement' in L2 French Writing?

Cecilia Gunnarsson

When evaluating the quality of the output, oral or written in L2 (second language), you do it in the terms of complexity and accuracy (cf. Wolfe-Quintero, Shunji, & Hae-Young, 1998). Improvement in L2 writing could therefore be expressed in an increase of complexity and accuracy. Nevertheless, recent L2 research shows that these evaluating tools are quite difficult to define and ambiguous to use (cf. Housen, Kuiken, & Vedder, forthcoming).

In a 30-month longitudinal study, we have used ScriptLog (Strömqvist & Malmsten, 1998) and a video-filmed thinking aloud protocol (TAP) to record the written production of five Swedish guided learners of L2 French during their last six semesters in high school (i.e. from low/intermediary to intermediary/advanced level of L2 French according to the Bartning & Schlyter (2004) evaluation criteria). The subjects produced 2 texts per each of the 6 recording periods (= 12 texts). Three kinds of narrative tasks were used: personal memory telling, summary of a film or a text studied in class and stories to be told from a series of pictures. The data from these recordings are used to analyse the 'improvement' of each subject in terms of complexity and accuracy. Complexity is evaluated by conventional measures for syntactic complexity (clauses per T-unit), and the findings presented here are based on data from one of the writing tasks — telling a personal memory. According to the Wolfe-Quintero et al. (1998) study, simple error counting has problems when measuring improvement in accuracy: (1) there is a risk for subjectiveness when defining an error and (2) an error could be the sign of a positive development in the subject. For these reasons, we have here opted for focusing on the use and development of four morphosyntactic phenomena: subject-verb agreement in the group of verbs on -ir, -re and -oir (in singular where the agreement can only be seen in written production but not heard in oral production), negation (ne V pas), clitic object pronouns (COPs) and the choice between passé composé and imparfait in the

Learning to Write Effectively: Current Trends in European Research
Studies in Writing, Volume 25, 225–227
ISSN: 1572-6304/doi:10.1108/S1572-6304(2012)0000025054

past tense. Based on structure complexity, subject-verb agreement and negation are considered to be simple structures and COPs and the choice between passé compose and imparfait are considered to be complex structures. Data from all texts and tasks were considered for the analyses of accuracy (see Gunnarsson, forthcoming for more details). As this is a corpus study of five subjects, there is not enough data to make quantitative statistics, therefore all analyses are qualitative.

The findings for complexity show very little improvement in the different subjects. Furthermore, when consulting the TAPs, we cannot find any signs of the learners being aware of complexity issues when formulating the text. It is possible that the learners in this study have not yet reached the linguistic level in their L2 French to start to manifest an explicit interest in complexity. On the contrary, the TAPs seems to confirm the claim that L2 writers are more preoccupied with low-level linguistic aspects (i.e. spelling, grammar and vocabulary) at the expense of more high-level linguistic aspects such as textual and pragmatic aspects which would promote complexity (Barbier, 2004). One could therefore assume that the improvement in text quality would be more significant in accuracy.

When evaluating the improvement in the four morphosyntactic phenomena we chose to study, we first of all notice important individual differences, albeit the differences appear to vary according to the studied morphosyntactic phenomenon. For the simple phenomena subject-verb agreement and negation, there are of course individual differences, but what is interesting to observe is that those who have the most correct production in the first recording continue to have it, albeit the increase of correctness is quite weak in all the subjects.

When it comes to the more complex morphosyntactic phenomena the picture is another. In COPs, the subjects having a less correct production in the simple structures have a more correct AND, more important, a more frequent production of COPs. Moreover these subjects use more COPs in the last recordings. Finally, the choice between passé composé and imparfait in the past tense occurs to be a good illustration of the multidimensional concept of accuracy. If we only consider correctness of the production, the subjects having a more correct production in the simple structures do have a more correct production in the first recordings compared to the others. This is challenged in the last recordings where one subject of the other group reaches the same level of correctness. Then we also have to take into account the variation between passé composé and imparfait. It is only when you use both tenses in a text that you get to give both foreground (passé composé) and back-ground (imparfait), which makes the texts more complex, showing a more mature writer. When variation between the tenses is considered, only the subjects with a less correct production in the simple structures use both past tenses, whereas the others do not. They tend to concentrate on a correct use of passé composé, which makes the texts a more unidimensional telling of 'what came next' and continue to do it all along the study.

These observations raise once again the question of how to measure improvement in intermediary L2 writing. Syntactic complexity seems to be quite useless as the L2 writers at this level are not concerned with high-level linguistic aspects. Which accuracy parameters should be considered? A correct production or a production with more complex grammatical structures? Could it be that some learners concentrate on accuracy in the terms of simple structures which are easier to control when writing while other learners concentrate on complexity, not in terms of clauses per T-unit, but in terms of a more complex grammatical structure? If this is the case, what is 'improvement' in L2 French writing?

References

Barbier, M.-L. (2004). Écrire en langue seconde, quelles spécificités? In A. Piolat (Ed.), *Écriture: Approches en sciences cognitives* (pp. 181–203). Aix-en-Provence: Publications de l'Université de Provence.

Bartning, I., & Schlyter, S. (2004). Itinéraires acquisitionnels et stades de développement en français L2. *Journal of French Studies, 14*, 281–299.

Gunnarsson, C. (forthcoming). The development of fluency, complexity and accuracy in the written production of L2 French. In A. Housen, F. Kuiken & I. Vedder (Eds.), *Dimensions of L2 performance and proficiency investigating complexity, accuracy and fluency in SLA.* Language Learning and Language Teaching Series. Amsterdam: John Benjamin.

Housen, A., Kuiken, F., & Vedder, I. (forthcoming). *Dimensions of L2 performance and proficiency investigating complexity, accuracy and fluency in SLA.* Language Learning and Language Teaching Series. Amsterdam: John Benjamin.

Strömqvist, S., & Malmsten, L. (1998). *ScriptLog Pro 1.04? User's manual.* Technical Report. Department of Linguistics, Göteborg University, Sweden.

Wolfe-Quintero, K., Shunji, I., & Hae-Young, K. (1998). *Second language development in writing: Measures of fluency, accuracy and complexity.* Honolulu: University of Hawaii.

Chapter 2.03.04

DESI — Text Production

Astrid Neumann

On comparison at the international level it was found that German students had average proficiency in the areas of language, particularly their native language. To overcome this education policy-makers in Germany started looking for reasons within the curricula or those resulting from teaching practices. Consequently, large studies were conducted to monitor the learning progress of students in different domains by comparing their results at the international and the national levels (PISA 2000, 2009). Furthermore, mandatory standards for the competence of the students were defined at the federal level to ensure that the set norms were met (Educational Standards for the Primary Level and the Secondary Level — lower and higher secondary track). Along with the implementation of the standards the development of empirical-based competence scales for different sub-domains was essential. The representative DESI study (German English Student Assessment International) in 2003/2004 provided fundamental spadework in the areas of language proficiency — German (native language competencies) and English (foreign language competencies).

The following article reports some fundamental results of testing writing competencies in German as part of the DESI study (German English Student Assessment International) — a representative and curricular-based study that tested German ninth graders. What areas are of interest from an international point of view? The process and the importance of coding the productions and the data collection as a precondition for applying models allowing mathematical corrections were the main focus before developing the competence levels and giving the results of students' writing proficiency in the German school system.

Learning to Write Effectively: Current Trends in European Research
Studies in Writing, Volume 25, 229–234
Copyright © 2012 by Emerald Group Publishing Limited
All rights of reproduction in any form reserved
ISSN: 1572-6304/doi:10.1108/S1572-6304(2012)0000025055

Coding

In DESI a coding schema was developed by using materials and results from the IEA Study of Written Composition in 1985 and additional linguistic aspects. It comprised holistic and analytical criteria. Possible solutions are obtained by setting pre-trials function as a benchmark so that coders have an orientation for their assessment of real students' texts. Each text was coded twice (double-blind procedure) by two raters who judged on the basis of more than 50 criteria. The results of the data collection (absolute agreement for the dichotomous variables was altogether 96%, for the polytomously scored judgements differed by one stage about 95% and reliabilities of the rating scales $\alpha = .82 - .84$) show that the proportion of measurement errors could be diminished to a high extent; thus, objective and reliable achievement data could be provided for analysis (Neumann, 2007). These features and the progress in computer technology made possible a statistical control of task difficulties and rater effects (by applying Multifaceted Rasch Models, Linacre, 1989). For a study like DESI, aiming at the description of proficiencies based on competence levels, an objective comparison by using standardized coding procedures had to be realized.

Competence Levels and Results

Structural analysis revealed that on a task level two sub-competencies[1] have to be activated in order to response to the tasks. Formal and content-related features that were coded dichotomously and text organization, style, word choice, the polytomously coded variables with five stages form the first one (called semantic-pragmatic sub-competence) and orthography, word grammar and sentence construction form the second one (called language systematic competence).

The competence levels were developed with predictors of difficulties: In addition to text-constitutive features from a rough classification into content and form and language elements other aspects of the tasks play a role when determining what is difficult to reach from all the coding criteria. The underlying method of determining competence scales implies that common features exist among all tasks that determine their difficulties. In this context the solutions of all tasks differ on an item level through the thematic orientation, the stimulus, the functional pragmalinguistic level, the form of verbalization and the act of communication. These features are the basis for predicting the item difficulties using the significant beta-weights of regression analysis to determine quantitatively the position of the cut-scores. So three distinctive areas of the scale could be identified, which formed the basis for the development of competence levels. If one combines these distinct set of features with the demands from the functional pragmatic and systematical linguistic system, competence levels

---

[1]This duality confirms the findings of the IEA Study of Written Composition as well as the suggested distinction between a composing and language competence.

for the identified sub-competencies could be defined (Neumann & Lehmann, 2008), as shown in Table 1.

For estimating competence gains new scaling methods were applied in DESI. On the basis of combining the two measurement points as 'virtual' persons, calculating item difficulties in a multidimensional model by including several control variables (latent regression) plausible values for all participants were estimated for each measurement point and their difference in learning gains, which is in semantic-pragmatic sub-competence 5 points (scala: MEAN 500/STDDEV 100) and in language-systematic 0 points.

All analyses and evaluation of learning improvement were done by underlying other writing and schooling factors. The intercorrelation between semantic-pragmatic competence and other language abilities (reading .25; argumentation .29; language awareness .31) shows that text production is a highly complex test procedure for aspects of pragmalinguistic competence, which includes receptive and productive abilities. For the other sub-competence, language system, the results from an orthography test correlate as expected in a similar magnitude (.36), and the increase in language awareness seems to be a key for development of better writing competencies (.29).

Other findings in DESI on individual and class levels confirm these results. Consciously dealing with language and a rich offer of structured and supportive learning opportunities, regardless of the demands of curricula for different school types, ensures cumulative learning in the area of language competencies.

Taken altogether, the following findings of the presented study are of considerable importance:

(1) Writing competence was represented as a two-dimensional construct confirming the results of many studies in writing.
(2) About two-thirds of the students showed acceptable results. However, within the segregated school system in Germany there are low-achievers at Comprehensive Schools ('Integrierte Gesamtschulen') and Secondary General Schools ('Hauptschulen') of which more than half of the texts are hardly or not understandable. A discussion about changing school structures now taking place in several federal states can only succeed with parallel work on forms and effectiveness of teaching German.
(3) With regard to this, the correlative and structural analytic analyses provided some results which suggest that learning about language awareness and a structured approach to deal with language phenomena lead to an increase in writing competence. Findings from language acquisition and foreign/second language research confirm that explicit instructions of language should be provided to older learners.
(4) By presenting results from the module text production of DESI this work was able to show that the measurement of writing proficiency in a large-scale assessment that applies text linguistic models and psychometric methods satisfying rater reliability can be achieved. Nevertheless, research in the measurement of writing competence is a future desideratum. Open test formats

Table 1: Description of the competence level — semantic pragmatic and language systematic competence and distribution of participants in DESI (in percent).

Level % S P/L S	Description semantic-pragmatic competence: Students can write texts with following characteristics	Description language systematic competence: Students can write texts with following characteristics
Mastery 0.1/0.3	Contentwise independent task management with differentiated representation of problem situation and development of solutions and consequences; orientation at general standards of written communication; linguistic-pragmatic executions are better than on level 3, without inconsistencies	Error-free texts in variable, varied, appropriately complex sentence structure
Level 3 13.2/7.5	Contentwise combination of more than in a text presented information within group-specific framework; orientation at text-type specific standards; in itself more conclusively, consistently, logically developed text; all substantial text elements contain demanded style (formally vs. personally) and addressee orientation of the argumentation with possibly existing paragraph arrangement for support, in that according to the letter form with accurate, goal-prominent, varied word choice; occasional inconsistencies can be found	Texts correspond to the orthographic conventions with occasional inconsistencies; word grammar is correct; varied, appropriately complex sentence constructions are characterized only by occasional inconsistencies in the punctuation
Level 2 57.6/54.3	Contentwise combination of information extracted from the task within group-specific framework; orientation at text-type specific standards; usually in itself more conclusively, logically developed text, in which the substantial text elements are to be recognized at least in beginnings and which possibly contains contradicting statements and beginnings of a paragraph arrangement, in mostly demanded letter form of appropriate style	Texts correspond to a large extent to the orthographic conventions; problems arise with foreign and technical terms and complex grammatical phrases; word grammar is characterized by occasional inconsistencies, which do not affect the comprehensibility; appropriate complex sentence constructions are used; however usually incorrect punctuation makes the legibility/understanding more difficult

Table 1: (*Continued*)

Level % S P/L S	Description semantic-pragmatic competence: Students can write texts with following characteristics	Description language systematic competence: Students can write texts with following characteristics
	(formally vs. personally) and addressee orientation with appropriate expression of emotionality; own, however limited, word material in essentially safe and appropriate use with occasional repetitions of word and over generalizations	
Level 1 23.3/35.1	Contentwise combination of graphic or in tasks explicitly presented items of information within individual framework and purchases to functional oral language; logically, incorrectly developed text, substantial text elements of a letter are missing, without paragraph arrangement, without and/or with incorrect addressee orientation, style not according to the desired letter form (formally vs. personally); with very limited word material, which is most taken from the writing impulse, with frequent repetitions of word and/or inadequate words and idioms	Texts are understandable up to individual, insulating passages; errors in orthography, punctuation and sentence construction load communication; word-grammatical conventions are kept to a large extent except for complexity problems
Below Level 1 6.0/3.0	Contentwise little meaningful text without/with minimum connection to information of tasks; very short texts without distinguishable text elements, inadequate style, very expressive vocabulary	Linguistic executions disfigure the sense of the text, elementary errors in the word grammar, the sentence structure consists most of lining up phrases and is usually without punctuation

allow an adequate representation of complex language and also cognitive competencies but these are bound to a considerable high amount of human and material resources; therefore these are not acceptable in the long run as further tests for standardization efforts in the setting in all federal states and for a practical transferability into the school life. The IQB, the German Institute for Educational Progress, which develops tests based on the German national standards for representative national comparisons, is faced with the complexity of testing a high number of students, and therefore considering this aspect it has declared that the development of appropriate coding strategies is a big challenge.

References

Linacre, J. M. (1989). *Many-facet Rasch measurement*. Chicago, IL: MESA Press.

Neumann, A. (2007). *Briefe schreiben in Klasse 9 und 11. Beurteilungskriterien, Messungen, Textstrukturen und Schülerleistungen* [*Writing letters in grade 9 and 11. Judgment criteria, assessment, text structure and student's competences*]. Münster: Waxmann.

Neumann, A., & Lehmann, R. H. (2008). Schreiben Deutsch [Text production in German]. In DESI-Konsortium (Ed.), *Unterricht und Kompetenzerwerb in Deutsch und Englisch. Ergebnisse der DESI-Studie* [*Teaching and learning in German and English classes*. Results of the DESI-study] (pp. 89–103). Weinheim, Basel: Beltz.

Chapter 2.03.05

Indicator Model of Students' Writing Skills (IMOSS)

Astrid Neumann and Swantje Weinhold

The planned research study discussed in this chapter aims at the development of an empirically based indicator model of students' writing skills in the German school system. Factors that influence writing achievements of the pupils at different levels of the instruction system are considered systematically. Methodically it concerns the triangulation of different research conceptions to develop a general model for effective writing instruction and support.

In the research on school effectiveness both teachers and scientists refer to multilevel output models, as set up by Weinert and Helmke for the instruction effectiveness. Meta analyses on school effectiveness (Bosker & Scheerens, 1997) thereby show temporally unstable effects, even within a class: effects for combined achievement tests are larger than those for single and for underprivileged and weak learners; and the effects vary between subjects. So it must be proceeded from a differential effectiveness term, which does (still) not appear in the above mentioned input–output models. So far Helmke and Klieme (2008) have adapted such a model for the linguistic instruction in order to be able to interpret results of the DESI study. Since the problem of the instruction reality for the total abilities in German and English (by means of a global factor) was modeled in the DESI study, within the planned research framework we want to examine more specifically which factors of influence have a large effect on the acquired writing abilities.

Figure 1 points out investigation possibilities in this framework concept. In this figure possibilities for testing the indicated components are listed in ellipses. Relations between them are to be tested in the project systematically.

In some of the indicated components and their correlations we can refer to those large research traditions of reading literacy, reading socialization and reading

Learning to Write Effectively: Current Trends in European Research
Studies in Writing, Volume 25, 235–237
Copyright © 2012 by Emerald Group Publishing Limited
All rights of reproduction in any form reserved
ISSN: 1572-6304/doi:10.1108/S1572-6304(2012)0000025056

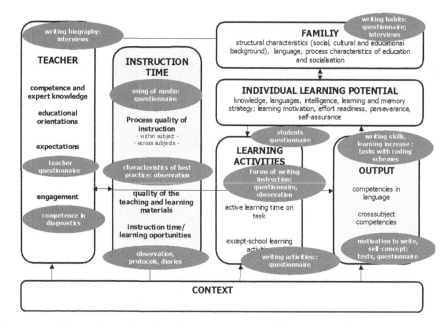

Figure 1: Adapted model of writing instruction effectiveness, following the model described by Helmke and Klieme (2008).

support (Garbe, Holle & Jesch, 2009) which have the advantage in relation to writing research to be able to examine receptive abilities with rather closed item formats. In contrast writing research must measure the text quality in open formats with more objective coding procedures. These formats have to integrate the partially strongly out-differentiated developmental and processing concepts from a didactical perspective of the last years (Fix, 2006; Weinhold, 2009) and empirical indicators of the instruction reality at different levels. Therefore still basic work has to be done, both on the level of the instruments and coding and on the analysis of multi-level structure models.

Despite the rather unsatisfactory starting situation from a language-didactical point of view it can be expected from the empirical-educational review that writing ability is acquired more strongly than reading ability in school framework. However intensity and quality, and particularly motivation to use and perfect writing ability, depend on the primary socialization instance family and competent handling on class level and this more clearly than on school and contextual conditions.

In the project quantitative and qualitative procedures for the estimation of writing achievement and different indicators of their development in the school context are to be developed. This way we want to use triangulation for description of an indicator model. Beyond that a multilevel structure model of the school writing (inclusive of first parameter estimations) is to be computed.

First the national and international literature on written composition and support and already existing materials and data from different schools are to be analysed, before a first indicator model can be estimated. Simultaneously further test instruments, questionnaires and video designs are to be developed with which the effectiveness of the model at schools of different educational tracks is to be examined.

The project is settled in the empirical specialized didactics of German language and will examine different procedures for measurement of writing skills and the pertinent indicators for their development in the school context. In addition the following preliminary work was conducted to develop the project.

Both authors worked intensively in several areas. The first author has experience in qualitative error analysis and conditions of instructional influence at the beginning of written language acquisition. The second author has experience in the quantitative measurement of writing competencies. Different coding procedures (holistically vs. analytically and in combination) were developed, which were applied to texts of different age groups and computation samples with consideration of more rater and task-specific characteristics.

Separately in each case, not yet categorized and evaluated project materials (test materials/questionnaires/reports) were raised, which can serve as the first work basis:

– questions on the writing motivation of the students (learning and training processes);
– writing motivation; motivation by authentic tasks;
– motivation to the task choice and 600 written students' texts;
– questions on writing biographies (students/parents/teachers);
– diagnostic competencies of instructors.

These materials must be completed and developed further in order to be able to investigate the relationships between separate factors with the help of multilevel structure analysis.

References

Bosker, R., & Scheerens, J. (1997). *The foundations of educational effectiveness*. Oxford: Pergamon.

Fix, M. (2006). *Texte schreiben. Schreibprozesse im Deutschunterricht* [*Text production. Writing processes in classes of German language*.]. Paderborn: Schöningh.

Garbe, C., Holle, K., & Jesch, T. (2009). *Texte lesen: Lesekompetenz-Textverstehen-Lesedidaktik – Lesesozialisation* [*Reading texts: Reading literacy –understanding – reading instructions – reading socialization*]. Paderborn: Schönigh.

Helmke, A., & Klieme, E. (2008). Unterricht und Entwicklung sprachlicher Kompetenzen [Instruction and development of language competencies]. In DESI-Konsortium (Ed.), *Unterricht und Kompetenzerwerb in Deutsch und Englisch. Ergebnisse der DESI-Studie* [*Teaching and learning in German and English classes. Results of the DESI-study*] (pp. 301–312). Weinheim, Basel: Beltz.

Weinhold, S. (2009). Effekte verschiedener didaktischer Konzepte auf den Schriftspracherwerb in der Grundschule [Effects of different instructional concepts on learning to write in German "Grundschule"]. *Didaktik Deutsch, 27*, 52–75.

Chapter 2.03.06

Assessment of Written Proficiency: Finnish-Speaking University Students Writing in Swedish

Åsa Palviainen

This paper presents SVE2JU, an ongoing research project at the University of Jyväskylä, Finland that focuses on Finnish-speaking university students, on their attitudes and motivation towards Swedish, and on their proficiency in written Swedish (Nordqvist Palviainen & Jauhojärvi-Koskelo, 2009; Palviainen, 2010). The State of Finland has two official languages, Finnish and Swedish. All Finnish-speaking students are obliged to study Swedish at comprehensive school. University students must also pass a National Certificate language examination in Swedish as part of their university degree. To obtain the certificate, a student must demonstrate a spoken and written proficiency equivalent of at least level 'B1' or level 'three out of six' on the proficiency scales provided by the Council of Europe's Common European Framework of Reference for Languages (CEFR).

The CEFR scale describes what learners can do in a foreign language in levels from beginning to advanced (A1, A2, B1, B2, C1 and C2). Finland has pioneered its use: in addition to the National Certificates language examination, CEFR has been adapted for the National Core Curricula of Finnish schools. The SVE2JU project was initiated in 2006 after university Swedish teachers began to report dramatically weakened language skills. These made it difficult, in turn, for students to pass the National Certification language examination and reach level B1. Moreover, although the CEFR plays a central role in the newest National Core Curricula, few descriptions exist of the linguistic features that correspond to the CEFR proficiency levels.

Learning to Write Effectively: Current Trends in European Research
Studies in Writing, Volume 25, 239–241
ISSN: 1572-6304/doi:10.1108/S1572-6304(2012)0000025057

The SVE2JU project part that focuses on written proficiency has two main aims. One, to examine whether Finnish-speaking students have the written Swedish skills requested by the State, namely at least level B1 on the CEFR scale. Two, to find the linguistic features and textual characteristics that teachers attend to when assessing student performances. Specifically, the project aims to discover the linguistic features typical to written performances at different proficiency levels.

A total of 666 students attending the compulsory course in Swedish at a Finnish-speaking university wrote an 100–150 word 'argumentative' text by hand on a topic given by the researcher. A sample of 490 essays, 70 texts from each of the 7 university faculties, were collected for assessment. Three experienced Swedish teachers trained in using the CEFR assessment scales evaluated the texts and reached an acceptable level of inter-rater reliability (Cronbach's α: .834). To search for textual characteristics and their relative weight in explaining the teachers' assessments, 122 of the texts (43 representing level A2, 43 level B1 and 36 level B2) were transcribed and coded in the CHAT-format (MacWhinney, 2000). The five measures included were clauses/t-unit (Complexity), errors/clause (Accuracy), words/clause (Fluency) (following Wolfe-Quintero, Inagaki, & Kim, 1998), number of words (Text-length) and vocd (Vocabulary diversity) (Malvern & Richards, 1997). Nominal regression analysis discovered to what extent the five measures predicted the assessments. An analysis of variance (ANOVA) was applied to investigate differences between the three levels.

In the assessment, 21 texts (4.3%) were marked A1, 238 texts (48.6%) A2, 195 texts (39.8%) B1 and 36 texts (7.3%) B2. A total 52.9% of essays were therefore marked levels A1 and A2, below the level required to pass the National Certificates language examination. This high percentage is alarming and indeed points to weak skills (for a more thorough discussion of its implications, see Palviainen, 2010). The five measures (Complexity, Accuracy, Fluency, Text length, and Vocabulary diversity) together predicted 87.7% of the assessments. A model of Accuracy and Text-length explained 81.3% of the assessments. The ANOVA showed significant main effects for Accuracy ($F(2) = 64.468$, $p = .000$), Fluency ($F(2) = 8.178$, $p = .000$), Text length ($F(2) = 34.484$, $p = .000$) and Vocabulary diversity ($F(2) = 8.724$, $p = .000$), whereas no effect was found for Complexity. Posthoc tests (Bonferroni) showed differences ($p < .05$) between all levels for Accuracy, Fluency, Text length and Vocabulary diversity, except between A2 and B1 for Fluency and between B1 and B2 for Vocabulary diversity.

The outcomes of the assessment procedure suggest, therefore, that a relatively large group of Finnish-speaking university students do not have sufficient Swedish writing skills according to the State requirements. Moreover, analysis of the assessments showed that the length of texts and their accuracy in terms of lexical and grammatical correctness played a major role for the three teachers when differentiating between performances and levels. Lexical variation seems important in distinguishing between level A2 on the one hand and levels B1 and B2 on the other, whereas higher fluency is an important feature of level B2 in comparison with lower levels. The next step of the project will carry out more detailed and qualitative analyses of the linguistic features typical of the different levels. These will include analysis of types of errors, lexical variation and of cohesive devices. Finally, the measure of complexity (clauses/t-unit) must be reconsidered and a more detailed analysis of complexity and mastery of linguistic structures at the different levels should be carried out.

References

MacWhinney, B. (2000). *The CHILDES project: Tools for analyzing talk* (3rd ed.). Mahwah, NJ: Lawrence Erlbaum Associates.

Malvern, D. D., & Richards, B. J. (1997). A new measure of lexical diversity. In A. Ryan & A. Wray (Eds.), *Evolving models of language*. Clevedon: Multilingual Matters.

Nordqvist Palviainen, Å., & Jauhojärvi-Koskelo, C. (2009). *Mitt i brytpunkten: Finska universitetsstudenters åsikter om svenska* [*In the middle of a crossroads: Finnish university students' views on Swedish*] In L. Collin & S. Haapamäki (Eds.), *Svenskan i Finland 11* (pp. 125–133). Turku: University of Turku.

Palviainen, Å. (2010). The proficiency in Swedish of Finnish-speaking university students: Status and directions for the future. *Apples – Journal of Applied Language Studies, 4*(1), 3–23.

Wolfe-Quintero, K., Inagaki, S., & Kim, H.-Y. (1998). Second language development in writing: Measures of fluency, accuracy, and complexity. Technical report No. 17. Second Language Teaching and Curriculum Center, University of Hawai'i at Manoa.

Chapter 2.03.07

Development of Written and Spoken Narratives and Expositories in Icelandic

Hrafnhildur Ragnarsdóttir

The aim of the current research is to study the development of text construction proficiency from late childhood to adulthood in two different genres (narratives and expository texts) and modalities (written and spoken). The findings reported in this paper are derived from the Icelandic part of a cross-linguistic study that includes six other languages (Dutch, English, French, Hebrew, Spanish, Swedish, see Berman & Verhoeven, 2002). Previous publications based on this research have addressed the effect of language-specific factors and typology on various aspects of text construction (e.g. Berman, Ragnarsdóttir, & Strömqvist, 2002; Ragnarsdóttir & Strömqvist, 2005; Ragnarsdóttir, Aparici, Cahana-Amitay, van Hell, & Viguié, 2002; Strömqvist et al., 2002). Manuscripts that are in progress will report on the writing process, based on analyses of the Icelandic ScriptLog files.

Method

Eighty Icelandic subjects participated in the study. They were equally divided between four gender-balanced age groups: 11-, 14-, 17-year-olds and adults. The adults were in the age range of 25–42 years, and had completed a masters or a doctoral degree.

All participants received the same elicitation task: a three-minute wordless video clip showing seven familiar, interpersonal conflict episodes staged in a culturally neutral high school setting. Participants were tested individually and each asked to produce four texts:

Learning to Write Effectively: Current Trends in European Research
Studies in Writing, Volume 25, 243–246
Copyright © 2012 by Emerald Group Publishing Limited
All rights of reproduction in any form reserved
ISSN: 1572-6304/doi:10.1108/S1572-6304(2012)0000025058

– A written and an orally produced personal narrative about an incident of a similar kind as shown in the video.
– A written and an orally produced expository text about the same kind of problems as shown in the video.

All four texts were transcribed in CHAT-format and coded for various linguistic and structural aspects. The main categories of dependent variables analysed so far are the following:

– Text length
– Words pr. clause
– Types of clauses: main, subordinate, finite/non-finite, etc.
– Vocabulary
– Lexical Diversity (VocD)
– Lexical density (content words vs. function words)
– Word length
– Verbal paradigm (use of tenses, aspect, mood, voice, person ...), (Ragnarsdóttir et al., 2002)
– Use of the generic pronoun 'maður' (e literal translation man, corresponding English pronoun one) and Swedish 'man' (Ragnarsdóttir & Strömqvist, 2005)
– Speed of writing, pauses, corrections, etc.

The independent variables are the following:

(a) Within-subject variables: Genre, Modality, Order (oral → written; written → oral).
(b) Between-subjects variables: Age, Sex, and Language.

Below, we present a summary of the results of a three-way ANOVA (Modality × Genre × Age) and Post hoc tests for Age on the distribution of text length, vocabulary, syntactic complexity and verbal paradigm. Significance level $p < .05$.

Results

Based on the different processing constraints of written and spoken text construction and comprehension, we expected modality to affect the scores on all measures of semantic and syntactic density. The findings confirmed this hypothesis in all cases. The percentage of content words was higher, and participants in all age groups used more diverse vocabulary in their written than in their spoken texts. This difference increased with age. Furthermore, mean word length, which is an indicator of lexical complexity and specificity, was higher in the written texts and, again, this difference increased with age. Spoken texts, on the other hand, were longer in all age groups, and contained longer clauses than written texts in the youngest age groups. As for syntactic complexity, there was no main effect of modality but a significant Genre × Modality interaction reflects a greater syntactic complexity of the written as compared to the oral modality of expository texts. The distributions of tense, aspect, mood and voice within the verbal paradigm, were similar in both modalities of the same Genre.

Contrary to modality, the verbal paradigm and syntactic complexity measures clearly differentiated between the two different genres in all age groups, while vocabulary did not. Narratives were predominantly in the past tense and subjects used aspectual marking more in narratives than in expository texts. Verbs in the expository texts, in turn, were in the present tense and subjects used subjunctive mood and passive voice more than in narratives.

The two Genres also differed in length, syntactic complexity and lexical density, reflecting the greater cognitive load of the expositories. Thus, expositories were shorter than narratives, but contained a higher percentage of subordinate clauses. A Genre × Modality interaction reflects the greater genre-difference in syntactic complexity in written texts. Expositories were also semantically more dense — higher in lexical density than narratives. Lexical diversity, on the other hand, was similar in both genres.

Age had a significant main effect on almost all the dependent variables, except the verbal paradigm which remained largely the same across age groups. The subjects produced longer texts with age, their syntactic complexity increased and progress was significant on all major vocabulary measures. Age × Genre interaction on Text length and Word length indicate that Expositories catch up with Narratives with age. Furthermore, Age × Modality interaction on Lexical diversity and Word length reflects the fact that written texts are the privileged arena for long-term vocabulary development.

Post hoc tests reveal that the most important developmental shift does not occur until late adolescence or even in adulthood. Another clear shift on most measures is between the youngest children and the other age groups, whereas, unexpectedly, there was no difference between the 14- and the 17-year-olds. Thus, on three important indicators of text quality, that is text length, percentage of subordinate clauses and VocD, Post hoc tests yield three subgroups: (1) 11-year-olds, (2) 14- and 17-year-olds and (3) Adults.

In contrast to our prediction and the results from other countries participating in this cross-language project, there was no indication on this level of analysis of a turning point in the development of complex text construction between the ages of 14 and 17 in the Icelandic sample. One possible explanation for this unexpected finding is that there may be a different curricular emphasis in the final years of obligatory education in Iceland. In fact, there is some indication that the National tests that are administered to children in 10th grade may induce teachers to overemphasize grammar, orthography and other lower-level aspects of writing and composition in their teaching in the final grades.

References

Berman, R. A., & Verhoeven, L. (2002). Cross-linguistic perspectives on developing text-production abilities. *Written Language and Literacy*, 5(1), 1–44.

Berman, R., Ragnarsdóttir, H., & Strömqvist, S. (2002). Discourse stance. *Written Language and Literacy, 5*(2), 255–289.

Ragnarsdóttir, H., & Strömqvist, S. (2005). The development of generic maður/man for the construction of discourse stance in Icelandic and Swedish. *Journal of Pragmatics, 37,* 143–155.

Ragnarsdóttir, H., Aparici, M. D., Cahana-Amitay, D., van Hell, J., & Viguié, A. (2002). Verbal structure and content in written discourse: Expository and narrative texts. *Written Language and Literacy, 5*(1), 95–126.

Strömqvist, S., Johanson, V., Kriz, S., Ragnarsdóttir, H., Aisenman, R., & Ravid, D. (2002). Towards a crosslinguistic comparison of lexical quanta in speech and writing. *Written Language and Literacy, 5*(1), 45–93.

Subsection 2.04

Learner and Teacher Variables

Chapter 2.04.01

What Do Portuguese University Students Say About Their Writing in Exams?

José Brandão Carvalho

Traditional ways of looking at writing at school have been changing. Nowadays, writing is no longer a mere testing tool; its role as a learning tool is being progressively stressed out (Björk & Räisänen, 1996).

According to Tynjälä, Mason, and Lonka (2001), writing enhances active learning as long as students are engaged in knowledge transforming processes. Therefore, it may be implied through the whole learning process: in the 'early' knowledge acquisition stages, writing may, for instance, be used to take notes during listening or reading tasks; in 'intermediate' stages, it enables students to structure and elaborate the information previously acquired; and finally, in the 'last' stages of the process, students write to express knowledge. In such contexts, writing is used for several purposes involving different genres: reports, literature reviews, essays, written answers in exams.

In most of these knowledge expression tasks, writing still keeps the traditional role of testing tool referred above. Nevertheless, the aim of writing in such contexts should not be the mere reproduction of students' factual knowledge in the subject. Writing to express knowledge is not only related to the way students have developed previous stages of the learning process, but is itself a task in which students may elaborate and transform knowledge.

Besides generic abilities, this writing requires specific capacities in order to fulfil the demands of communicative contexts following conventions according to the genres involved. Proficient writers are able to express their knowledge better than developing writers do. Their writing processes are success enhancing as far as knowledge is transformed and content adapted to a communicative context and an intended reader within a complex, goal-directed, problem-solving activity. On the

Learning to Write Effectively: Current Trends in European Research
Studies in Writing, Volume 25, 249–252
Copyright © 2012 by Emerald Group Publishing Limited
All rights of reproduction in any form reserved
ISSN: 1572-6304/doi:10.1108/S1572-6304(2012)0000025059

other hand, the knowledge telling process, usually followed by poor writers, tends to be less effective, consisting of a content retrieval based on cues, without any transformation in order to fulfil communicative goals. Composing this way is just generating appropriate content items and writing them down (Bereiter & Scardamalia, 1987).

The study

This study is a part of a broader study aiming at identifying students' literacy practices (Carvalho, 2008; Carvalho & Pimenta, 2007). Based on a questionnaire administered to a sample of about 1700 first- and fourth-year Portuguese university students from different scientific areas, it analyses their performance when answering questions in exams.

The construction of questionnaire items assumed that writing processes developed by mature writers differ from those performed by poor writers.

Students were asked about different aspects of their writing process: recalling knowledge from the memory; selecting information; organizing and structuring ideas; transcribing; revising the paper before delivering it to the teacher.

Questions had a four-degree Likert-scale format (never/sometimes/often/always) considering how frequently each situation described occurred.

Data analysis used descriptive (frequency distribution; means) and inferential (*t*-test; one-way ANOVA) statistical procedures.

Results

The data analysis enables the description of students' writing practices as well as comparisons between different grades and areas and concerning five different dimensions of the writing process.

Most students say that they do not usually start writing just after finding the first suitable idea. Only Medicine and Engineering students admit doing it frequently. The majority of students say that they usually analyse the questions before they start writing, trying to identify the aspects involved. Anyway, Science and Engineering students admit doing it less frequently than the others. When we compare freshmen with older students, we conclude that the latter demonstrate a more mature attitude revealing more thinking activity before starting to write.

Including as much information as possible is a practice reported by the majority of students, independently from their scientific area. First-year students admit doing it more frequently than their fourth-year colleagues. Considering rhetoric factors when performing a written task seems to be more frequent for Education and Psychology students, while Medicine students are those who consider these factors less relevant.

The draft sheet is mainly used to register the main topics of the answer. Child Studies, Humanities, Education & Psychology and Social Sciences students also admit using it frequently to elaborate a scheme/diagram integrating the main aspects involved in the question. Writing the answer in a draft sheet and rewriting it later does not seem a frequent practice.

Medicine students are the exception as far as the use of the draft sheet is concerned as only 29% admit using it frequently. Fourth graders report more elaborate practices than freshmen.

More than 50% of the students say that when they start writing, they go on without interruptions until the end. Science students seem to be the exception reporting a step-by-step transcribing process, with interruptions aiming at thinking about what is going to be written afterwards. Most students say they are concerned with formal aspects of language during the writing process. Despite concern with language being slightly higher in fourth graders, there seems to be no difference between first- and fourth-year students' transcription practices.

More than 50% of the students of the different scientific areas say that they usually evaluate what they are writing and eventually modify the text (content and form). Law students are the exception, as only 33% of them admit doing it often. Freshmen seem to be more concerned with revision than fourth graders.

Discussion

On one hand, students report some writing practices that might be considered as characteristic of proficient writers (thinking before starting to write; considering the communicative context; revising and modifying the text). However, and on the other hand, there are also some features of immature writing (transcribing without pauses; including as much information as possible), emerging from the student's answers.

Comparing literacy practices reported by students from different scientific areas, some relevant differences emerge, what might allow us to infer the existence of different literacy practices involving specific genres.

Finally, fourth graders reveal a more mature attitude towards writing in most aspects, except in what concerns revision. In fact, freshmen report more revision practices than their older colleagues.

References

Bereiter, C., & Scardamalia, M. (1987). *The psychology of written composition*. Hillsdale, NJ: Lawrence Erlbaum Associates.

Björk, L., & Räisänen, C. (1996). *Academic writing — A university writing course*. Lund: Studentlitteratur.

Carvalho, J. B. (2008). Acquiring, elaborating and expressing knowledge — A study with Portuguese university students. Zeitschrift Schreiben. Retrieved from http://www.zeitschrift-schreiben.eu. Accessed on 1.07.2008.

Carvalho, J. B., & Pimenta, J. (2007). Writing to acquire and express knowledge: A study with university engineering students. In G. Shiel, I. Stričević & D. Sabolović-Krajina (Eds.), *Literacy without boundaries* (pp. 327–330). Osijek: Croatian Reading Association. Retrieved from http://www.hcd.hr/datoteke/Zagreb_Conference_Proceedings.pdf

Tynjälä, P., Mason, L., & Lonka, K. (2001). Writing as a learning tool: An introduction. In P. Tynjälä, L. Mason & K. Lonka (Eds.), *Writing as a learning tool. Integrating theory and practice* (pp. 7–22). Dordrecht: Kluwer Academic Press.

Chapter 2.04.02

The Impact of Educational Experiences on Writing Processes and Products

Florentina Nicolás Conesa

Research in the field of writing has shown that strategy instruction can have positive effects not only on the quality of the texts produced but also on the writing process engaged in by students (Graham & Harris, 1989; Graham, Harris, & Mason, 2005). Drawing on these findings, the current thesis project departs from the assumption that improvements in students' texts as a result of writing instruction may be attributed to a change in learners' writing processes. However, there is not much research about the impact of strategy instruction on the relationship between composing processes and the final quality of the texts produced.

By writing processes we understand a number of writers' internal variables that can be classified into clusters of cognitive (mental actions linked to strategic performance) and meta-cognitive procedures (goals and beliefs about writing). We consider that these clusters are related to each other and to L2 proficiency and that they are necessary for the correct development of writing ability and the resulting written products.

The ultimate aim of the current thesis project is to deepen our knowledge about the development of a number of learners' internal variables thought to be related to the successful composition of academic texts. These variables include students' beliefs about the writing task, use of L2 writing strategies, goals about composing, L2 proficiency level and writing ability.

We will base our research on recent developments in the field of educational psychology and SLA research that operationalize language learning in relationship with learning products and processes (cf. Fidalgo, Torrance, & García, 2008; Graham & Macaro, 2008).

Learning to Write Effectively: Current Trends in European Research
Studies in Writing, Volume 25, 253–254
Copyright © 2012 by Emerald Group Publishing Limited
All rights of reproduction in any form reserved
ISSN: 1572-6304/doi:10.1108/S1572-6304(2012)0000025060

Our participants will be fourth-year students in a five-year-English Philology degree at a Spanish University in Murcia enrolled in an English for academic purposes (EAP) writing course. The teacher of the EAP course will also participate in the study by means of semi-structured interviews throughout the academic year.

Data collection procedures will include interviews with students and teachers of the degree, learners' journals, proficiency tests, timed-essays and assignments produced by students, learners' background questionnaires and classroom observation. Due to the diverse nature of these sources, data will be analysed through a mixed method approach, which involves the use of both quantitative and qualitative data analysis techniques. Inter-rater reliability in the analyses of data will also be sought.

With this longitudinal study, we expect to offer empirical evidence of the influence of contextually situated literacy experiences on (i) the dynamics of writing strategy use, (ii) the development of students' goals aimed at improving their writing in different academic settings, (iii) the changes in students' beliefs about the writer and the writing task, (iv) the development of L2 proficiency and (v) the evolution of composing ability. In addition, our research design will allow us to explore the possible relationship between the development of students' writing process and L2 proficiency, on the one hand, and their final written products, on the other, as a result of their literacy experiences. It is also important to highlight that one of our variables (writing beliefs) has not been extensively studied and that students' writing goals have not been analysed in relationship with L2 writing strategies and with the quality of products. Therefore, we expect to offer new empirical and theoretical evidence on these variables in foreign language writing.

References

Fidalgo, R., Torrance, M., & García, J. N. (2008). The long-term effects of strategy-focussed writing instruction for grade six students. *Contemporary Educational Psychology*, *33*, 672–693.

Graham, S., & Harris, K. R. (1989). Improving learning disabled students' skills at composing essays: Self-instructional strategy training. *Exceptional Children*, *56*, 201–216.

Graham, S., Harris, K., & Mason, L. (2005). Improving the writing performance, knowledge, and self-efficacy of struggling young writers: The effects of self-regulated strategy development. *Contemporary Educational Psychology*, *30*, 207–241.

Graham, S., & Macaro, E. (2008). Strategy instruction in listening for lower-intermediate learners of French. *Language Learning*, *58*, 747–783.

Chapter 2.04.03

Taking and Using Notes and Learning Approach in University Students

Sandra Espino and Mariana Miras

This research project forms part of a doctoral thesis and was designed to understand how reading and writing processes are used as learning instruments in educational contexts and the ways in which these instruments improve learning. From our perspective (Gràcia, Solé, Miras, & Castells, 2005; Solé, Castells, Gràcia, & Espino, 2006; Solé et al., 2005), note-taking is one of the most frequently used tools by students in higher education. The present study sets out to analyse some elements of this instrument, to identify the relation between certain variables involved in the conditions in which it is used, specifically the relation between the type of notes taken by students and the uses they make of them, on the one hand, and their learning approach, on the other, when they are working on a specific academic task.

An 'ex post facto' quasi-experimental design with three independent variables was used: type of task (synthesis), level of prior knowledge and learning approach (deep vs. surface). The dependent variables were students' representations of note-taking and the use of notes (reproductive, mixed or constructive), type of notes (literal vs. paraphrased and exhaustive vs. selective or incomplete), uses of notes (more elaborate vs. less elaborate) and learning outcomes after performing the academic task.

The participants were 55 third-year Psychology degree students at the University of Barcelona. Data-gathering began with the selection of an academic task. The task consisted of producing a synthesis in which students were required to make connections between different concepts and work up the information from various source texts, including their lecture notes. Before performing the task, students were given two questionnaires to complete: a standardized test (CEPEA) to assess their learning approach and a questionnaire specially devised for the purpose to assess

Learning to Write Effectively: Current Trends in European Research
Studies in Writing, Volume 25, 255–256
Copyright © 2012 by Emerald Group Publishing Limited
All rights of reproduction in any form reserved
ISSN: 1572-6304/doi:10.1108/S1572-6304(2012)0000025061

their representation of note-taking and its uses. The students' prior topic knowledge was controlled by means of another questionnaire. The notes taken by the students in one of their class sessions and the products handed in to the lecturer upon completion of the tasks were collected.

At the same time, a small sample of participants was selected on the basis of their learning approach (eight students with a surface learning approach and nine with a deep learning approach) and these students were monitored more closely and in greater detail. This closer monitoring consisted of conducting semi-structured interviews with them, collecting self-reports from them in which they were asked to specify the actual use they made of their notes while performing the task, collecting the materials they used (notes, rough drafts, outlines, etc.) and collecting the products handed in to the lecturer upon completion of the task.

We are currently analysing the data gathered and the preliminary results show two things. (1) The participants in the study have different learning approaches, although most of them display a deep learning approach (80%). (2) University students have different types of representation about note-taking and its uses. A high percentage of them have a constructive representation of note-taking and its uses (67.3%), 10.9% have a reproductive representation and 21.8% have a mixed representation.

The analyses carried out show a significant correlation between the learning approach and the representation of note-taking and its uses. Students with a deep learning approach tend to have a constructive representation ($\chi^2 = 10.729$, $p = 0.013$), while students with a surface learning approach have different types of representation (constructive, mixed and reproductive).

Different degrees of elaboration have been identified in the use of note-taking in the performance of the synthesis task (uses with a higher level of elaboration vs. uses with a lower level of elaboration).

The use of notes is an element to consider in relation to students' eventual learning outcomes. In the data analysed so far, we have observed a relation between a higher level of elaboration in the use of notes and better learning outcomes.

References

Gràcia, M., Solé, I., Miras, M., & Castells, N. (2005). Llegir i escriure per aprendre a ciències socials i naturals. Immersió Lingüística. *Revista d'Ensenyament Integrat de Llengües i Continguts, 7*, 108–114.

Solé, I., Castells, N., Gràcia, M., & Espino, S. (2006). Aprender psicología a través de los textos. *Anuario de Psicología, 37*(1–2), 157–176.

Solé, I., Mateos, M., Martín, E., Miras, M., Cuevas, I., Castells, N., & Gràcia, M. (2005). Lectura, escritura y adquisición de conocimientos en Educación Secundaria y Educación Universitaria. *Infancia y Aprendizaje, 28*(3), 329–347.

Chapter 2.04.04

The Effect of Beliefs on Writing Synthesis from Multiple Texts

Mar Mateos, Isabel Cuevas, Elena Martín, Ana Martín, Maria Luna, Gerardo Echeita, Mariana Miras, Isabel Solé, Nuria Castells, Sandra Espino and Marta Minguela

Most of the learning tasks students engage in are, to a greater or lesser extent, tasks involving reading and writing. At university and in secondary education, the tasks requiring students to consult, compare and integrate information from various diverse sources start to become more common and frequent than at lower educational levels (Mateos, Villalón, De Dios, & Martín, 2007; Solé et al., 2005). Exploring and integrating various sides of an issue in order to reach a reasoned written synthesis may require a particular way of conceiving the nature of knowledge and its acquisition through reading and writing; in other words, it may be affected by the type of epistemological, reading and writing beliefs the student holds. This is a topic that has so far been little explored and, when it has been, the role of epistemological beliefs, reading beliefs and writing beliefs has been analysed separately. That is why we set about investigating the role played by the three types of beliefs together when the learning task involves the co-ordinated use of reading and writing.

We assume that people develop a personal epistemology — that is a set of beliefs about the nature of knowledge and how it is acquired — that influences the way we acquire knowledge or, what amounts to the same thing, how and what we learn (Schommer, 1990). Schraw and Bruning (1996) and White and Bruning (2005) have distinguished two implicit models of reading and writing: the transmissional model, which involves the belief that meaning is transmitted from the writer and/or the text to the reader, and the transactional model, which involves the belief that meaning is

Learning to Write Effectively: Current Trends in European Research
Studies in Writing, Volume 25, 257–259
Copyright © 2012 by Emerald Group Publishing Limited
All rights of reproduction in any form reserved
ISSN: 1572-6304/doi:10.1108/S1572-6304(2012)0000025062

actively constructed by means of a transaction between the author, the reader and the text. Students with transactional beliefs about reading and writing produce better-quality written compositions than those with less transactional beliefs. Similar results have been found in respect of students holding sophisticated epistemological beliefs.

Based on the assumptions and approach outlined above, the general aim of this research line was to explore the role played by epistemological beliefs and beliefs about reading and writing in influencing the way secondary and university students approach tasks in which they have to integrate, in a written composition, conflicting or complementary information on a particular issue obtained from reading various different texts.

In a first study, the focus was on (a) analysing the relationship between general epistemological beliefs and beliefs about reading and writing held by 96 Psychology undergraduates and (b) the role played by these beliefs on the level of perspectivism-integration of knowledge displayed in a written argumentation task based on reading texts presenting conflicting perspectives on a hotly debated topic in education. Beliefs were assessed by administering the Epistemology beliefs questionnaire (Schommer, 1990), the Reader Beliefs Inventory (Schraw & Bruning, 1996) and the Writing Beliefs Inventory (White & Bruning, 2005). The written arguments produced before and after reading the texts were evaluated on the basis of the following criteria:

(1) The writer adopts a position giving arguments only in favour of his/her own view.
(2) The writer adopts a position taking arguments from both sources, but in order to argue in favour of only one of them.
(3) The writer considers the arguments and counterarguments of the different positions, and integrates them in a compromise solution between the two (adopts both positions, albeit establishing a hierarchy between them) or indeed proposes a wholly new alternative.

Our results support the idea that epistemological beliefs and reading and writing beliefs do not occur in isolation from each other: they are internally coherent. Specifically, the internal coherence is stronger in those students who conceive knowledge as integrated in complex conceptual structures. These students display pure models of transactional beliefs about reading and writing (high transactional beliefs and low transmissional beliefs). Furthermore, the evidence allows us to assert that those students who show more transactional reading beliefs produce syntheses with a greater degree of perspectivism and integration.

In a second study, we focused on the analysis on the relationships between reading and writing beliefs and the quality of a written synthesis, on the one hand, and between the quality of the synthesis and the degree of learning students achieve after producing it, on the other. Participants were 48 secondary school students who were asked to write a synthesis of three historical texts presenting complementary perspectives on the same topic. Reading and writing beliefs were assessed by administering the same beliefs inventories as in the previous study. The written products generated by the students were analysed in regard to three dimensions:

organization and coherence of the text, selection of the necessary information and integration of the information from the reference texts. The learning achieved was assessed by means of a questionnaire containing both closed- and open-ended questions in regard to three dimensions: recovering information, interpreting information and thinking about the topic in question. The results point to the fact that the syntheses produced by students with more transactional reading and writing beliefs are better organized and show a greater content integration than those produced by students with less transactional beliefs. The results also indicate that students who produce more integrated texts obtain greater benefit in terms of learning.

In summary, the results obtained so far suggest a relationship between epistemological, reading and writing beliefs, and the degree of integration of a written synthesis of information from different texts. The research currently under way is aimed at gaining a greater understanding of the role played by these beliefs when students are faced with reading and writing tasks with different objectives and when they have to produce syntheses in collaboration with their fellow students.

References

Mateos, M., Villalón, R., De Dios, M. J., & Martín, E. (2007). Reading-and-writing tasks on different university degree courses: What do the students say they do? *Studies in Higher Education, 32*, 489–510.

Schommer, M. (1990). Effects of beliefs about the nature of knowledge on comprehension. *Journal of Educational Psychology, 82*, 498–504.

Schraw, G., & Bruning, R. (1996). Readers' implicit models of reading. *Reading Research Quarterly, 31*, 290–305.

Solé, I., Mateos, M., Miras, M., Martín, E., Castells, N., Cuevas, I., & Gracia, M. (2005). Lectura, escritura y adquisición de conocimientos en educación secundaria y educación universitaria. *Infancia y Aprendizaje, 28*, 329–347.

White, M. J., & Bruning, R. (2005). Implicit writing beliefs and their relation to writing quality. *Contemporary Educational Psychology, 30*, 166–189.

Chapter 2.04.05

The Dynamics of Writing Beliefs and Composing Strategies

Florentina Nicolás Conesa

Scholars in educational psychology seem to agree on the importance of beliefs for language learning (cf. Hofer & Pintrich, 2002) on account of (i) the crucial role that students' conceptions are thought to play in the engagement in language learning actions and (ii) the widely held assumption that the relationship between beliefs and strategies is interactive in nature. It is generally posited that what learners believe to be effective significantly influences the strategies that they use in their learning process (Mori, 1999) and, conversely, that the efficacy with which students face their approach to learning seems to be dependent on the strategies that they apply. For this reason, researchers have examined students' beliefs about the nature of language learning and the efficacy of the strategies that they use.

Given the empirical evidence of the impact of educational experiences on the shaping of beliefs and the consequent use of strategies, the study of beliefs in language teaching and learning has become a central area of enquiry in second language acquisition research. However, it is also relevant to note that, in spite of the crucial role that they are thought to play, research on beliefs as they relate to language use (i.e. speaking, listening, reading and writing) is scarce. Our empirical study is an attempt to start filling this gap in research by focusing on the influence of instruction in shaping learners' beliefs about L2 writing and the implementation of composing strategies.

The study explored 32 foreign language learners' belief systems and writing behaviour during an academic year at a Spanish university. The participants were learners in the fourth and fifth year of a five-year English degree and differed in their previous writing experience and instruction. At the time of data collection, students in the fourth year were taking a compulsory English for academic purposes (EAP)

Learning to Write Effectively: Current Trends in European Research
Studies in Writing, Volume 25, 261–263
Copyright © 2012 by Emerald Group Publishing Limited
All rights of reproduction in any form reserved
ISSN: 1572-6304/doi:10.1108/S1572-6304(2012)0000025063

writing course aimed at improving their reading and writing skills. The fifth-year group, in contrast, had already done that EAP course the previous year. Therefore, previous writing instruction and experience constituted the independent variable of the study, whereas the dependent variables were the participants' beliefs about L2 writing and their self-reported use of writing strategies.

Quantitative and qualitative data were collected, the former by means of written questionnaires and the latter through an interview with the writing teacher. This interview was intended as a secondary source that could help in the interpretation of the quantitative data resulting from the analysis of the questionnaires.

The questionnaires were originally designed for a previous research project by a research team at Murcia University (Manchón, Murphy, & Roca de Larios, 2007). The Beliefs About Writing Questionnaire was developed from scratch by the research team, as no questionnaires of this type could be found in the literature. Based on various empirical studies, the researchers decided to focus on five dimensions of beliefs about writing.

The participants' use of writing strategies was measured with a writing strategy questionnaire that was designed on the basis of previous cognitively oriented research on writing processes and strategies, especially Roca de Larios, Murphy, and Marin (2002) and Manchón, Roca de Larios, and Murphy (2007).

A Pearson Chi-Square test was conducted to compare the data from the two groups of participants (i.e. the fourth- and fifth-year students). The test showed statistically significant differences between the two groups regarding their beliefs and writing strategies. Concerning beliefs, the differences included (i) self-efficacy beliefs, (ii) their views about human factors and their role in language learning and (iii) their beliefs about strategic use of feedback. Regarding writing strategies, the statistically significant differences referred to (i) textual concerns, (ii) use of L1 and backtracking strategies and (iii) the revision process.

Given the results obtained and the limited attention paid to beliefs in writing, this study can be considered a modest contribution to the investigation of individual differences in SLA, in general, and L2 writing research in particular.

Acknowledgement

The present research is funded by Fundación Séneca, Agencia de Ciencia y Tecnología de la Región de Murcia.

References

Hofer, B. K., & Pintrich, P. R. (Eds.). (2002). *Personal epistemology. The psychology of beliefs about knowledge and knowing*. Mahwah, NJ: Erlbaum.

Manchón, R. M., Murphy, L., & Roca de Larios, J. (2007). The dynamics of beliefs about foreign language writing: Listening to students' and teachers' voices. Paper given at symposium on Second Language Writing, Nagoya Gakuin University, Japan.

Manchón, R. M., Roca de Larios, J., & Murphy, L. (2007). Second and foreign language writing strategies: Focus on conceptualizations and impact of the first language. In A. Cohen & E. Macaro (Eds.), *Language learner strategies: 30 years of research and practice* (pp. 229–250). Oxford: Oxford University Press.

Mori, Y. (1999). Epistemological beliefs and language learning beliefs: What do language learners believe about their learning? *Language Learning, 49,* 377–415.

Roca de Larios, J., Murphy, L., & Marin, J. (2002). A critical examination of L2 writing process research. In G. Rijlaarsdam (Series Ed.), *Studies in writing,* vol. 11 & S. Ransdell & M. L. Barbier (Volume Eds.), *New directions in research on L2 writing* (pp. 11–47). Dordrecht: Kluwer Academic Publishers.

Chapter 2.04.06

Does the Quality of Teaching Determine Students' Achievement in Writing?

Deilis-Ivonne Pacheco-Sanz, Jesús-Nicasio García
and Carmen Díez

Interesting contributions lead us to consider which aspects are evaluated or not within the classroom; the variables which are used to relate the teachers' practices with the students' achievements; the results obtained; the theoretical and educative implications, the limitations and deficiencies of the studies, and suggestions for future research. Our research suggests several conclusions concerning the self-regulation of teachers' practice and its relationship with the students' achievement in the education of the written composition (Díez, García, Robledo, & Pacheco, 2009; Pacheco, García, & Díez, 2007, 2009).

According to the research, the education concerning writing that many of the students receive is inadequate because it focuses almost exclusively on the teaching of an inferior level of writing abilities, such as calligraphy and spelling, with few opportunities to actually write. Only a short amount of time is dedicated to the teaching of the necessary abilities and the strategies of writing, as it is assumed that these abilities can be acquired through informal and secondary methods of study. A great part of the quality of teaching that the students receive has a large effect as a fundamental determinant on their achievement in writing. Thus, the need arises to search for effective teaching written composition (García et al., 2009; Troia, 2006).

The objective was to study the teachers' practices in relation to the achievement of the students in the teaching of written composition. It is considered that teachers' practice is based on their beliefs, attributions, expectations and the sense of personal efficacy that they hold with respect to the education-learning process and that this is

Learning to Write Effectively: Current Trends in European Research
Studies in Writing, Volume 25, 265–268
ISSN: 1572-6304/doi:10.1108/S1572-6304(2012)0000025064

closely related to the students' achievement and the factors or components which modulate it.

Method

The participants were selected from two types of origin, although they were interrelated. On one hand, there was the sample of teachers taken from a previous study: 99 teachers from 30 public and private schools in the province of León, Spain, who teach in the area of language and are responsible for students with and without learning disabilities (LD) and/or low achievement. On the other hand, there were the students (of these teachers) who comprised the second sample. One hundred and eleven students from the third to sixth years of Primary Education were extracted (78 males and 33 females). Thirty-five of the students were diagnosed as having LD, 36 did not present LD and 40 had ADHD.

The instrument used was the PRAES. It evaluates the Role of the Teachers' Practice in Writing, with its respective questionnaires focusing on the evaluation of the opinions, approaches, activities or behaviours in the classroom and the teachers' self-efficacy as concerns what they actually do when they teach written composition to their students. We measured both the students' general achievement and intelligence, and their specific achievement in written composition.

The study, within a descriptive studies framework, consisted of two comparative and related samples, chosen simultaneously from 30 education centres; the samples were selected to complement each other. In fact, the research team is carrying out a series of studies in the province of León, Spain, which require samples of students from three different typologies: students with LD, without LD and with ADHD.

Results

Considering the measures of writing (product totals from the reader- and text-based measures) and the measures of the PRAES (totals from the scales and the subscales) as predicting variables and the type of students as predicted variables, we obtain statistically significant results. When the measures are taken only from writing, statistically significant results in the prediction of the type of students are also obtained.

However, when only the PRAES results are considered, they do give statistically significant results in the prediction of the typology of the students. In any case, this is interesting, as it does not support the idea of differences in the teachers' practices based on the typology of students. When the type of students is taken as a dependent variable or predicted variable taken from the set of the total measures of the writing product (students' achievement), in the hierarchic multiple regression step-by-step analysis we obtained one model with a statistically significant regression coefficient. When the variables from writing (the product totals from the reader- and text-based measures) as predicted variables and as predicting variables those from the PRAES are taken one by one, many give statistical significance albeit of a low level. However, this is interesting as they indicate a tendency, and given the nature of the different measures, this supposes results, which are very relevant from a theoretical point of view.

Discussion and Conclusions

The results obtained suppose, at least indirectly, the type of teachers' practices in the area of language. There were no significant differences in relation to the theoretical concepts and strategies applied in the teaching of the writing in the different school years from infant to primary. There were, however, differences based on the age, which is an indicator of some type of adjustment according to the students' level of development. Our results suggest that teachers tended to teach in ways that are consistent with their own theoretical preconceptions. This suggests poor self-regulation. In addition, it appears that they offer little differentiation in the treatment of teaching and learning writing for students with and without LD and/or low levels of achievement.

Acknowledgements

During this research project, we received competitive funds from the Ministry of Research, Science and Innovation — from the Spanish Government; project EDU2010-19250 (EDUC) for 2010–2013, in addition to European Union FEDER funds. We also acknowledge Excellence Research Group funds from Junta de Castilla y León (GR259) and European funds for 2009–2011 (BOCyL 27, April 2009), both awarded to the Director/Principal Researcher (J. N. García). We are very grateful to Rubén García-Martín for the data analysis of the orchestration processes and to Jenny Gunn for the English correction.

References

Díez, M. C., García, J. N., Robledo, P., & Pacheco, D. I. (2009). Habilidades sociales y composición escrita en alumnos con dificultades de aprendizaje y/o bajo rendimiento [Social skills and writing composition in students with learning disabilities and/or low performance]. *Boletín de Psicología, 95*, 73–86.

García, J. N., de Caso, A. M., Fidalgo, R., Arias, O., Pacheco, D. I., & Torrance, M. (2009). Investigaciones recientes en desarrollo e instrucción en composición escrita en el Sistema Educativo Español [Recent research in development and instruction in written composition in the Spanish Educational System]. *Aula Abierta, 37*(1), 91–104.

Pacheco, D. I., García, J. N., & Díez, C. (2007). La práctica de los profesores en la enseñanza de la composición escrita [The practice of teachers in the teaching of writing].

In J. N. García (Coord.), *Dificultades del desarrollo: Evaluación e intervención* (pp. 267–277, cap. 23). Madrid: Pirámide.

Pacheco, D. I., García, J. N., & Díez, C. (2009). Self-efficacy, approach, and teacher's practice in the writing teaching. *European Journal of Education and Psychology*, *2*(2), 5–23.

Troia, G. (2006). Writing instruction for students with learning disabilities. *Handbook of writing research* (Chapter 22, pp. 324–336). New York, NY: The Guilford Press.

Chapter 2.04.07

Perspective Taking: A Prerequisite of Communicative Writing

Markus Schmitt and Joachim Grabowski

Adapting information appropriately to the needs of an audience is a major component of successful communication. While in oral communication settings, a recipient may give feedback information, we find a more demanding situation with respect to writing. Here, the needs of the audience must be completely anticipated by the writer on her or his own, thus complicating the successful constitution of common ground. Of course, there has been research on this important aspect of writing. Such studies, however, most often investigate developmental and/or interventional topics (e.g. Holliway & McCutchen, 2004), leaving some other questions still unanswered. Which role do personal aspects play when a writer engages in partner-oriented text production? Which relevant prerequisites of communicative writing can be identified?

In the present study, it is assumed that personal properties of a writer do influence the quality of partner orientation during writing, which should also be observable in the final text product. Among a set of possible candidates, especially the ability of perspective taking can be regarded as an important prerequisite. Up to now, however, one finds only little work in this field. Thus, the main aim of this study was to empirically prove the predictive power of perspective taking skills for partner-oriented writing performance. To further investigate the topic, university students were chosen as a starting point for at least two reasons. Firstly, only in adult individuals personality traits have reached an acceptable amount of stability, which is important for reliable measurement. Secondly, adult — or at least skilled — writers should be more familiar with any kind of text genre, therefore minimizing possible differences in performance on this account.

Learning to Write Effectively: Current Trends in European Research
Studies in Writing, Volume 25, 269–271
ISSN: 1572-6304/doi:10.1108/S1572-6304(2012)0000025065

In psychological research, the construct of perspective taking itself has no clear definition yet, being often mixed up with the related construct of empathy. Additionally, the assessment of adult perspective taking has almost exclusively been based on self-reports gained from questionnaire measures like the interpersonal reactivity index (Davis, 1983). This type of data source, however, is known to potentially generate problems with respect to reliability and validity. Moreover, the available instruments do not account for all relevant facets of perspective taking. As a consequence, we here postulate a three-facet structure of perspective taking that differentiates between conceptual, visual-spatial and affective-emotional perspective taking, a structure that has already been reported elsewhere (Steins & Wicklund, 1993; also see Steins, 2000). A preliminary aim therefore was to develop a test battery of adult perspective taking that accounts for these aspects.

Method

To measure perspective taking in adults without using data from self-reports, we developed three computer-based item subscales representing the three facets (with 16–18 items each), using the mouse as input device. By this means, accuracy as well as response times could be gained. As an alternative to accuracy information, response time measures here can provide useful information about how adults differ in their perspective taking skills. Furthermore, this kind of data source should be a better predictor for writing performance than data from self-reports.

In a first empirical step, a test construction study was conducted. In individual sessions, $n = 33$ university students completed each of the three subscales as well as questionnaire measures of perspective taking. Furthermore, several relevant covariates were assessed: working memory capacity, verbal ability, visual-spatial ability and basic reaction speed. In a second step, $n = 26$ university students participated in a writing study, again in individual sessions. Here, participants had to complete the instruments of the first study mentioned above. Additionally, three rather short writing tasks had to be worked on. Individuals were asked to write instructional texts: two tasks should be addressed to third graders, and the third task was intended to instruct another adult person. For the resulting text products, overall writing time and text length were obtained as basic variables. Moreover, using expert ratings, several aspects of text quality were assessed.

Results

In the test construction study, all three subscales proved to be reliable (Cronbach's alpha being .86 to .89) and positively intercorrelated, with the highest coefficient between the conceptual and the affective-emotional facet ($r = .47$; $p < .01$; one-tailed test). This positive intercorrelation pattern holds even when the applied set of covariates is statistically accounted for. Interestingly, intercorrelations between the response time measures and the questionnaire data did not exceed .29 (n.s.).

The writing study revealed that the average duration for writing a short instructional text was 11 minutes and 30 seconds (SD = 2.48) with an average length of 181.52 words (SD = 38.72). Stepwise regression analyses were conducted with perspective taking measures and covariates as possible predictors. As expected, our response time measures of perspective taking (aggregated total score) proved to be a better predictor for several text variables than the usually assessed self-reports. With respect to basic text properties, the total score — together with age — best predicted writing duration ($\beta = .41$; $p < .05$) as well as text length ($\beta = .37$; $p < .05$). Regarding text quality, the total score was the best predictor for appropriateness of language use at all ($\beta = .65$; $p < .001$). In contrast, the questionnaire subscale 'perspective taking' did not significantly predict any of the text variables.

Discussion

We could show that adult individuals who better perform on our perspective taking items in terms of response time clearly need less time and less words to write instructional texts. Moreover, those texts have a significantly better quality with respect to an appropriate use of language, which can be regarded as a form of partner orientation during writing, particularly when children are addressed. Moreover, when solely using self-report data to assess adult perspective taking, no such results can be found. This indicates that a monomethodological approach is insufficient to make all the information observable that is relevant for the construct of perspective taking as a predictor of skilled writing performance. Further research could address questions concerning the influence of different text genres on the predictive power of perspective taking or interventional approaches to improve writing performance via improving perspective taking skills.

References

Davis, M. H. (1983). Measuring individual differences in empathy: Evidence for a multidimensional approach. *Journal of Personality and Social Psychology, 44*, 113–126.

Holliway, D., & McCutchen, D. (2004). Audience perspective in children's descriptive writing: Reading as the reader. In L. Allal, L. Chanquoy & P. Largy (Eds.), *Revision: Cognitive and instructional processes*. Amsterdam: Kluwer Academic Press.

Steins, G. (2000). Motivation in person perception: Role of other's perspective. *Journal of Social Psychology, 140*(6), 692–709.

Steins, G., & Wicklund, R. A. (1993). Zum Konzept der Perspektivenübernahme: Ein kritischer Überblick. *Psychologische Rundschau, 44*, 226–239.

Chapter 2.04.08

Development of Fluency in First and Foreign Language Writing

Eva Lindgren, Kirk Sullivan and Kristyan Spelman Miller

A writer's fluency affects how quickly a writer can produce text. Fluency has been defined in terms of number of words (Chenoweth & Hayes, 2001) or characters produced per minute (Lindgren, Sullivan, & Spelman Miller, 2008; Spelman Miller, Lindgren, & Sullivan, 2008). A complementary definition relates to how many words or characters a writer produces before interrupting the writing flow with a pause or a revision. Fluency has been considered in relation to theories of cognitive load. As writers become more familiar with writing, they automatize aspects of their writing, such as grammar and spelling, which reduces cognitive load on the working memory and enables higher fluency.

In two longitudinal studies, we examined fluency and revision behaviour in young adolescents' first (L1) and foreign language (FL) writing (Lindgren et al., 2008; Spelman Miller et al., 2008). The study of revision provides insight into the writers' foci during writing. The students, 13 years of age at the onset of the study, each wrote one text in each language per school year over a three-year period. The tasks were of an argumentative/persuasive character. All texts were composed on a computer and recorded by the computer, using keystroke logging (see Sullivan & Lindgren, 2006, for an overview). All revisions were analysed manually (Lindgren & Sullivan, 2006), and pauses and fluency measures were calculated from the automatic analysis functions provided by the software tool. Two experienced L1 and FL teachers graded all the texts.

The results indicate a strong relationship between fluency and text quality in both L1 and FL. As the writers grew more familiar with writing and language in years 2 and 3 of the study, their fluency also increased. There was higher fluency in L1 than in the FL texts, and the writers focused more on form, that is spelling and grammar

Learning to Write Effectively: Current Trends in European Research
Studies in Writing, Volume 25, 273–274
Copyright © 2012 by Emerald Group Publishing Limited
All rights of reproduction in any form reserved
ISSN: 1572-6304/doi:10.1108/S1572-6304(2012)0000025066

when they wrote in their FL. However, the writers did not focus less on content when writing in the FL than in the L1. The writers compensated for the greater demand on their working memories when using an FL by requiring a longer writing time. The writers seemed to have a concept of what constitutes a good text which they were able to apply to their texts regardless of the language in which they were writing. Another study of early teenage L1 and FL writing found that the FL stimulated writers to focus on, and revise more, style aspects of their writing.

In conclusion, these studies illustrate how L1 and L2 writing fluency increases as learners become more experienced, how quality is closely related to fluency, and how L1 and FL writing can feed into each other. Learners are able to transfer knowledge of writing between languages in order to produce texts of sufficient quality, and, under suitable writing conditions, compensate for a lack of fluency in the FL.

References

Chenoweth, N. A., & Hayes, J. R. (2001). Fluency in writing: Generating text in L1 and L2. *Written Communication, 18*(1), 80–98.

Lindgren, E., & Sullivan, K. P. H. (2006). Analyzing on-line revision. In G. Rijlaarsdam (Series Ed.) and K. P. H. Sullivan & E. Lindgren (Vol. Eds.), *Studies in writing,* Vol. 18, *Computer keystroke logging: Methods and applications* (pp. 157–188). Oxford: Elsevier.

Lindgren, E., Sullivan, K. P. H., & Spelman Miller, K. (2008). Development of fluency and revision in L1 and L2 writing in Swedish high school years 8 and 9. *International Journal of Applied Linguistics, 156,* 133–151.

Spelman Miller, K., Lindgren, E., & Sullivan, K. P. H. (2008). The psycholinguistic dimension in second language writing: Opportunities for research and pedagogy. *TESOL Quarterly, 42*(3), 433–454.

Sullivan, K. P. H., & Lindgren, E. (Vol. Eds.). (2006). *Studies in writing,* Vol. 18, *Computer keystroke logging: Methods and applications.* Oxford: Elsevier.

Chapter 2.04.09

Writing Counter to Personal Opinion: Can Advanced Communication Students Set Aside Their Own Understanding of a Field?

Denis Alamargot and Céline Beaudet

The production of persuasive texts in the workplace requires the writer to adopt an enunciative stance that reflects/reproduces the multitude of interests at whose intersection the writing task is being performed (Beaudet, 2003). The objective is not for the writer to transmit his or her own understanding of a field, as would be the case when writing a description, a set of instructions or an explanation; rather, the objective is to justify a specific position on request, in a pre-established sociodiscursive context. The question is to determine how a professional writer, and specifically a writer-in-training, can demonstrate apparent detachment when textually mediating a strongly biased area of knowledge which may also be in conflict with his or her own personal values or opinions.

Alamargot and Beaudet (2009) conducted an experiment designed to assess the impact of opinion on the temporal and linguistic characteristics of the texts produced. Seventeen Quebec students in undergraduate and graduate programmes in communications at the Université de Sherbrooke undertook the exercise of writing two different texts on the same subject, namely the threat to the environment, after having read two contradictory documents dealing with the economy and the environment: 'Gaz à effet de serre: le grand responsable, c'est l'homme' ('Greenhouse gases: Man is chiefly to blame') and 'Changements climatiques: la mise au point de nouvelles technologies' ('Climate change: The development of new technologies'). The participants, who had all received training on how to write in a professional situation, were asked to write two texts consecutively, one in which they would assume the role of a professional writer working for the association Friends of the

Learning to Write Effectively: Current Trends in European Research
Studies in Writing, Volume 25, 275–277
Copyright © 2012 by Emerald Group Publishing Limited
ISSN: 1572-6304/doi:10.1108/S1572-6304(2012)0000025067

Earth (in which they would defend the ecological viewpoint), and the other in which their role would be that of a professional writer working for the Bio-Petrol company (in which they would defend the industry's point of view). The time allowed to write the texts was not specified, but the length of the texts was specified (two handwritten pages each). They were not allowed to consult documentary sources during the writing task, but they were allowed to consult their reading notes and were encouraged to include their own personal opinions. A questionnaire completed before the writing task had revealed that all the writers were against the industry's point of view.

Two analyses of the texts were conducted. (i) A quantitative analysis (of the temporal course and distribution of ideas, markers, connectors, etc.) showed that the difference between the two texts (pros and cons) could be found essentially in the level of content (number of ideas) and in linguistic structuring (connectors, markers). In texts defending the writer's own opinion and understanding of the field, content was more emphatically developed, whereas texts that defended an opposing position were more encyclopaedic and factual, based on a limited number of ideas that were more strongly articulated by a greater number of connectors. On the other hand, results showed no effect of opinion on the temporality of production. (ii) A qualitative analysis of the argumentation confirmed the conclusions of the quantitative analysis. Writing a text that was counter to personal opinion led to the production of a shorter text with fewer ideas that were, however, more tightly connected. This is probably related to the fact that, unlike the situation where writers were supposedly working for Friends of the Earth, the participants were not able to resort to their own encyclopaedic knowledge of the issue or to their received ideas, as conveyed by the prevailing social discourse. The qualitative analysis seems to indicate that the participants, when writing for Bio-Petrol, wrote without planning an overview of the problem and the task, and relied instead on cohesion rather than coherence (thus emphasizing grammatical and syntactic aspects and the use of connectors).

Writing about a familiar issue generally reduces the length of pauses during the writing process (Dansac & Alamargot, 1999), as well as the cognitive cost of the processes involved, in particular the planning process (Kellogg, 1987). It seems here that the two texts were produced with the same temporality and ease. This absence of difference is probably due to the advanced expertise of the participants. At this stage of their training, they were able to acquire and proceduralize the strategies of elaborating text content, and thus were able to write in an optimal manner, without resorting to long periods of reflection or major textual revisions (Alamargot, Plane, Lambert, & Chesnet, 2010).

References

Alamargot, D., & Beaudet, C. (2009). Rédiger contre son opinion: Des étudiants avancés en communication peuvent-il faire abstraction de leurs connaissances du domaine? *Pratiques, 143/144*, 218–232.

Alamargot, D., Plane, S., Lambert, E., & Chesnet, D. (2010). Using eye and pen movements to trace the development of writing expertise: Case studies of a seventh, ninth and twelfth grader, graduate student, and professional writer. *Reading and Writing, 23*(7), 853–888.

Beaudet, C. (2003). Le rédacteur et la fabrication du sens d'un texte persuasive. *Communication: Information, médias, théories, pratiques, 22*(2), 44–61.

Dansac, C., & Alamargot, D. (1999). Accessing referential information during text composition: When and why? In M. Torrance & D. Galbraith (Eds.), *Knowing what to write: Cognitive processes in the generation, selection and development of ideas during text production* (pp. 79–97). Amsterdam: Amsterdam University Press.

Kellogg, R. T. (1987). Effects of topic knowledge on the allocation of processing time and cognitive effort to writing processes. *Memory and Cognition, 15*(3), 256–266.

Chapter 2.04.10

Peer Interaction in Students With/Without Learning Disabilities in Writing (LD, NLD and ADHD)

Carmen Díez, Deilis-Ivonne Pacheco-Snaz
and Jesús-Nicasio García

Different studies suggest that the social skills of students with learning disabilities (LD) are generally lower, and that they have problems with anxiety, probability of action and emotional skills (Koenig, Cicchetti, De los Reyes, Scahill, & Klin, 2009; Riggio & Yee Kwong, 2009). Learning disabilities in social skills should serve to highlight the importance of increased awareness among teachers and students to be able to integrate feelings (emotional competence), thoughts (cognitive competence) and actions (behavioural competence) and thus promote better adjustment, effort and motivation. Peer interaction influences social skills such as assertiveness, cooperation and self-control, anxiety levels, the capacity for action and performance in the area of language in students of primary education. The investigation studies 687 students from the fourth to the sixth year of Primary Education. We observed that students with LD gained lower scores on emotional skills and higher scores on anxiety levels and the students with ADHD and LD were those who scored highest on negative emotional skills. We observed statistically significant differences in the relationship between the condition of the students (LD, ADHD and without LD) and their performance in writing, for example the students without LD get better grades in writing than LD and ADHD students and that their perceptions about future grades are more optimistic.

Learning to Write Effectively: Current Trends in European Research
Studies in Writing, Volume 25, 279–282
Copyright © 2012 by Emerald Group Publishing Limited
All rights of reproduction in any form reserved
ISSN: 1572-6304/doi:10.1108/S1572-6304(2012)0000025068

Method

Six hundred and eighty-seven students aged between 9 and 12 years, studying from the fourth to the sixth year of Primary Education were studied. These students had been previously classified into three groups: LD, NLD (without learning disabilities) and ADHD.

The instrument used was called 'Social Skills in Students of Primary Education' and is composed of the student's identification data, psychometric and performance data, as well as three instruments to assess social skills: HHSS/MS to measure the emotional aspects, AN which analyses the degree of anxiety and AC which analyses the probability of action (Diez, García, & Pacheco-Snaz, 2007). In addition, instruments to measure specific achievement in written composition were employed.

Once constructed, the instruments were subjected to validation through the use of a questionnaire. Assessment of the social skills in children in primary education (HHSS) focused on the student (HHSS/A) and on the teacher (HHSS/P). The following stages were carried out: the design and sampling plan was piloted in one centre, thus allowing time to verify the implementation of this questionnaire in schools in the province of Leon. Then different schools were sampled, allowing for a representative group of students to be selected. This required the collaboration of schools, teachers, etc. whose selection criterion was to select children with low achievement and/or learning difficulties and/or educational failure.

The next step was the field work itself. It consisted of establishing telephone contact with the directors of the schools, in order to obtain permission to visit and apply the questionnaire to students from the fourth to the sixth grades of primary education. Then the research team travelled to the centres on the arranged dates for students to fill out the questionnaire at the same time.

The procedure followed for the study of the sample of students can be summarized in the following steps. First, general measures were applied to select the sample; we initially applied the instruments of social skills aimed at students (HHSS/A) with its subscales. This assess social skills from an emotional (EM) and anxiety (AN) perspectives, and also the the likelihood of action (AC). Once the field work was carried out and the questionnaires were collected, the data was then computerized and codified in an excel matrix.

Results

We carried out a non-parametric Kruskal-Wallis test. First, we observed statistically significant differences, in the relationships between the condition of the students and their performance in writing, the data indicates how those students with ADHD scored highest on the issue I speak too loudly, followed by students with LD, while those who have no difficulties of any kind achieved more appropriate scores with regard to this emotional social skill. When we analysed anxiety levels, we found statistically significant differences in students with ADHD and LD, who were those who showed the greatest problems.

When we looked at writing, we observed statistically significant differences in the performance in skills such as conversation ($p = .018$), socio-emotional ($p = .001$) and life skills and well-being ($p = .001$).

We saw how students with better grades in their language examination score higher on social skills such as conversation (RP LOW = 193.79 vs. RP HIGH 285.04), socio-emotional skills (RP LOW = 170.01 vs. RP HIGH 290.05) and life skills and subjective well-being (RP LOW = 133.18 vs. RP HIGH 282.32).

We observed statistically significant differences in the relationship between the condition of the students and their performance in writing; the data indicates how the students without learning difficulties achieve better grades in writing than the other two groups and their perceptions concerning their future grades are more optimistic. On the other hand, the grades of students with ADHD are the lowest and their future perceptions were also lower.

Discussion

The conclusions regarding the relationships between the condition of students with or without LD and social skills are the following: Students with ADHD and LD are those who scored highest on negative emotional skills. However, these two groups of students act most appropriately in other situations of social exchange, such as being aware of their shortcomings when faced with a specific topic.

We observed that students without LD achieve better grades in writing than the LD and ADHD students and their perceptions about future grades are more optimistic. In conclusion, we can highlight how the student's condition affects their social skills, at least indirectly, in their performance in the area of writing (Díez, Pacheco-Snaz, & García, 2008).

Acknowledgements

During this research project, we received competitive funds from the Ministry of Research, Science and Innovation — from the Spanish Government; project EDU2010-19250 (EDUC) for 2010–2013, in addition to European Union FEDER funds. We also acknowledge Excellence Research Group funds from Junta de Castilla y León (GR259), and European funds for 2009–2011 (BOCyL 27, April 2009), both awarded to the Director/Principal Researcher (J. N. García). C. Díez received a grant to finance the hiring of recently graduated research staff from the Junta de Castilla y León. We are very grateful to Jenny Gunn for the English correction.

References

Diez, C., García, J. N., & Pacheco-Snaz, D. I. (2007). Instrumento de evaluación de las habilidades sociales en los alumnos de Educación Primaria con y sin dificultades del desarrollo [Assessment instrument of social skills in students of primary education with or without developmental difficulties]. Instrumentos y programas de intervención en las dificultades del desarrollo (cap. 18, CD-ROM). Madrid: Pirámide.

Díez, C., Pacheco-Snaz, D. I., & García, J. N. (2008). Las habilidades sociales en el marco del EEES [Social skills in the context of the EEES]. In M. Hijano del Río (Ed.), *Las titulaciones de educación ante el Espacio Europeo de Educación Superior: Análisis de experiencias* (pp. 239–247). Archidona (Málaga): Aljibe.

Koenig, K., Cicchetti, D., De los Reyes, A., Scahill, L., & Klin, A. (2009). Group intervention to promote social skills in school-age children with pervasive developmental disorders: Reconsidering efficacy. *Yale Child Study Center, 39,* 1163–1172.

Riggio, H., & Yee Kwong, W. (2009). Social skills, paranoid thinking, and social outcomes among young adults. *Personality and Individual Differences, 47,* 492–497.

Subsection 2.05

Genre in Educational Contexts

Chapter 2.05.01

Academic Genres in French Humanities

Isabelle Delcambre and Christiane Donahue

Until recently in France, fairly little attention has been paid to studying university students' writing, although research about K-12 writing and about disciplinary knowledge, writing and epistemology is richly developed. Attention has been paid to specific aspects of university writing: note-taking, source use and integration, and error have been well-developed domains of inquiry, for example (Delcambre & Reuter, 2009). Far less attention has been given to students' writing experiences as they enter disciplines, in contrast to Anglo-Saxon research traditions about this subject (Donahue, 2008). We shall present below results from a recent study of students' writing in five disciplines at three French universities, exploring students' experiences at each stage of the curriculum.

Aims of the Study

The study we are engaged in, funded by the French National Research Agency, is entitled 'University Writing: Inventory, Practices, Models'.[1] This study is pursuing three major aims:

– to describe the links between writing practices and the university disciplines in which the students are engaging, that is to say, to identify differences between the kinds of writing students have to produce in various disciplines;

---

[1]ANR-06-APPR-019: 'Les écrits à l'université: inventaires, pratiques, modèles'.

Learning to Write Effectively: Current Trends in European Research
Studies in Writing, Volume 25, 285–288
Copyright © 2012 by Emerald Group Publishing Limited
All rights of reproduction in any form reserved
ISSN: 1572-6304/doi:10.1108/S1572-6304(2012)0000025069

– to question the smooth or difficult transitions they face as they progress through the curriculum, from the first to the fifth year, including their perceptions of what good writing is at these different levels;
– to analyse the specificities of research writing that advanced students encounter in writing situations, new for them, linked to their initiation into research activity.

According to the theoretical frame of Bakhtin's speech genre theory, one of our hypotheses is that disciplines, taught at the university, provide the contexts that shape the writing produced by the students and expected by the faculty. Thus, we consider these kinds of university writing to be genres of discourse, produced in different contexts: the institutional context (secondary vs. post-secondary, university vs. teacher-training institute …), the context of the year of study with its specific demands, the context of the discipline, etc.[2] The specificity of our study is its questioning of the disciplinary dimensions of writing within the narrow field of Humanities, instead of comparing disciplines far apart, as is frequently done (Humanities, Sciences, Sociology and Medicine, for example). If we can show differences between the kinds of writing within the field of Humanities, our disciplinary hypothesis is even stronger.

Method

The two research groups involved in this project have developed complementary research axes. The first, from the Théodile-CIREL research group at l'Université de Lille 3, collected student responses through an extensive questionnaire, and interviewed faculty, in order to examine how the writing of various disciplines is represented by these different stakeholders.

The second, from the LIDILEM research group at l'Université de Grenoble 3, targeted descriptions of the rhetoric of research writing in Literature, Linguistics and Education Sciences (Boch & Rinck, 2010) and identification of what distinguishes doctoral students' writing from that of renowned researchers.

The questionnaire mentioned above was distributed to 600 students in five disciplines (Literary Studies, Educational Sciences, Psychology, Linguistics and History), at five levels of the curriculum, in three different French and one Belgian universities. In addition, some interviews were done with students at the masters levels to investigate more deeply the perceptions of research writing practices, and five focus groups were conducted with faculty in the five disciplines of the study in order to see how they define their expectations about students' writing at the masters levels.

---

[2]If we analyse the texts written by the students, we should also mention the context of instructions and other classroom activities (Donahue, 2008).

We present here only the main results of the questionnaire (Delcambre & Lahanier-Reuter, 2009). This questionnaire aims to create an inventory of the types of writing students say they produce in these five disciplines, their explicit and implicit standards, their perceptions of the faculty standards, their writing and rewriting practices, measures put in place to guide them and the perceived efficiency of these aids. We shall focus here on the first three points.

The Influence of Disciplines

The pieces of writing considered as representative of their discipline by the students vary clearly according to the university discipline. For three disciplines, there is practically no piece of writing named by the students which is common to another discipline. For example, students in Literature cite essays, text commentaries and text analysis. Students in Educational Sciences overwhelmingly cite Masters theses and course project work. Linguistics students are more likely to cite internship reports.

The disciplines also influence the standards the students pay attention to when they are writing. We have highlighted response profiles (using ACP analysis) that are linked more or less to the disciplinary membership: in Literature, the students see their writing as a form of personal expression, while in Linguistics, they are more likely to construct a structured and readable text, to pay attention to the coherence of their written texts. These two disciplines, however, have something in common: the writing practices are less articulated with the reading practices; the students pay less attention to bibliographical references and to text reformulation. In Educational Sciences, we find an intriguing negative result: the students claim to have little concern for providing the correct answer in their written work.

Students' perceptions of faculty standards are also different according to disciplinary membership: History and Linguistics students think faculty evaluate the correctness of language (spelling, style) and the level of personal expression, while Psychology and Literature students think that the research question, argumentation and content organization are more important to faculty.

If some disciplines are clearly demarcated in the students' discourses, whatever the theme, others aren't. For example, Psychology and History students present less clear responses about their disciplinary writing (either they do not reply, or they cite a lot of different kinds of writing, without any one dominating), and in these two disciplines, there is no significant result about the students' standards. They are only clearly distinguished for the third theme, their perception of faculty standards.

The Influence of Levels of Study

In the earlier college years, the students do not name any shared genres of discourse, while the masters students name two shared genres: the Masters thesis and 'course project works'. However, we have established that the perceived standards evolve and change in tandem with the curriculum: at the beginning, the students say they pay attention to correct responses and think they are evaluated on the correctness of response and correctness of language. At the masters level, students say their writing is based on their readings and think they are evaluated upon the originality of their research, and the global coherence of their text. There is thus an interesting evolution from academic and linguistic norms to discursive and scientific ones.

Conclusion

These first results allow us to consider that, even if it is not always systematic, disciplines provide contexts that shape the writing produced by the students and expected by the faculty, even in very similar disciplines in the field of Humanities. These results question the usual conceptions of teaching to write as a technical, transversal or instrumental process (Daunay, 2007) and confirm the interest of the concept of disciplinary awareness (Delcambre & Reuter, 2009).

References

Boch, F., & Rinck, F. (Eds.). (2010). Enonciation et rhétorique de l'écrit scientifique, Lidil, 41.

Daunay, B. (2007). The evolution of the French field of Didactique de l'écrit: Theorizing the teaching practices of writing in the disciplines. *L1-Educational Studies in Language and Literature, 8*(2), 13–34. Retrieved from http://www.ilo.uva.nl/development/L1Education Research/. Accessed on 25 September 2009.

Delcambre, I., & Lahanier-Reuter, D. (2009). Écrits et disciplines dans l'université française: le cas des sciences humaines. In J.-M. Defays, A. Englebert, M.-C. Pollet, L. Rosier & F. Thyrion (Eds.), Les discours universitaires: formes, pratiques, mutations. Actes du Colloque international de Bruxelles (pp. 151–166). Paris: L'Harmattan.

Delcambre, I., & Reuter, Y. (2009). The French Didactics approach to writing: From elementary school to university. In Ch. Bazerman, R. Krut, K. Lunsford, S. McLeod, S. Null, P. Rogers & A. Stansell (Eds.), *Traditions of Writing Research*. London: Taylor & Francis.

Donahue, C. (2008). Ecrire à l'université. Analyse comparée en France et aux Etats-Unis. France, Villeneuve d'Ascq: Presses Universitaires du Septentrion.

Chapter 2.05.02

Comparing Genres of Academic Writing: Abstracts and Summaries

Cornelia Ilie

This is a presentation of an ongoing project whose aim is to distinguish the major features that are shared and that differentiate various genres of academic writing by using a rhetorical and discourse analytical approach. The paper discusses a number of multilevel distinctions between academic abstracts and academic summaries with regard to drafting and editing processes, as well as evaluating practices. Significant aspects of these two academic genres are investigated: focus (highlighting the importance of a research area and outlining relevant aspects of the investigated issue), goal (raising the reader's awareness and interest for a particular research issue and problematization), audience orientation (targeting junior and/or senior scholars, a national and/or international audience and so forth), contextualization in time and space (e.g. adjusting the discursive content and form for a particular occasion or moment in time — starting with an introduction of the subject, ending by summing up the results/conclusions; and for a particular socio-cultural space — a research seminar, a national/international scientific conference and so forth).

Although abstracts and summaries are basic academic genres in the sense that we often encounter them either as readers or as writers of academic texts, the similarities and differences between the two are under-researched. They are often mentioned and commented on in books on academic writing (Bhatia, 2004; Booth, Colomb, & Williams, 2003; Swales, 1990). Certain 'how-to' books for academic writers take a prescriptive approach (Cremmins, 1982). An in-depth study on this topic was carried out by Kaplan et al. (1994) who used five parameters to analyse abstracts submitted to a 'call for papers': thematic structure, clause structure, pragmatic moves, propositional organization and lexical cohesion. Their study is based on a teaching experience with graduate students in a course in written discourse analysis. However,

Learning to Write Effectively: Current Trends in European Research
Studies in Writing, Volume 25, 289–291
ISSN: 1572-6304/doi:10.1108/S1572-6304(2012)0000025070

the results cannot be generalized because they apply only to sub-samples of the whole corpus and have a pedagogical bias.

While there is no consensus about a universally acknowledged definition of an academic abstract, there are tacitly accepted practices for writing abstracts in various academic and professional settings in keeping with disciplinary conventions and constraints. As a rule, an abstract is conceived of as a very short outline of a research article, thesis, report, conference paper, etc. pertaining to a particular discipline, which is supposed to provide the essential ideas, methods and results in concentrated form.

The basic purpose of the abstract is to tell readers what to expect, that is to foreground the news value of the paper. It is often used to help the reader to quickly ascertain the writer's intention as to the purpose and scope of a piece of writing. This is why the abstract always appears at the beginning of a manuscript, acting as the point of entry for any scientific paper or report.

A summary is often regarded as a short final survey of a longer text, such as a research article, a conference paper or a book. It is expected to review the main ideas, methods and conclusions/results in a nutshell.

Unfortunately, non-specialists tend to use the terms abstract and summary interchangeably, which may often create a lot of confusion. In order to better understand the particular scope, structure and functions of these two genres, five basic parameters have been used to outline the distinctions:

(i) A first parameter concerns their respective length and selectivity: The abstract is normally very short (and selective: from two to three sentences to one paragraph), whereas the summary tends to be longer and normally contains an abbreviated version of the most important points in an academic study, paper, article, etc.

(ii) A second parameter concerns the authorial presence and evaluative attitude: The abstract is normally non-evaluative, whereas the summary often includes the writer's critical assessment and evaluative reasoning. The author of a summary is seen to convey an overall evaluation of the study and its ensuing results (new findings, confirmed or disconfirmed hypotheses, etc.).

(iii) A third parameter concerns time-related framing: The abstract is often written before the main text — directing the reader's attention to the prerequisites of the original investigation and thinking process; the summary is necessarily written after the main text and is based on the main text, directing the reader's attention to the results/finality of the investigation.

(iv) A fourth parameter concerns the position slots of abstracts and summaries in relation to the text they represent: Summaries are usually placed at the end of a chapter or an article, highlighting the major point of the piece and outlining significant findings. Abstracts are normally placed at the beginning of the text that they introduce and briefly describe in terms of aims, hypotheses, etc.

(v) A fifth parameter concerns the content and scope of abstracts and summaries: Abstracts have a restricted scope in that they state the research problem, indicate the key themes and anticipate the main issues developed in the text of the article, paper, etc. Summaries start by stating the context and the problem, continue by describing the research methodology or procedure and reporting the research, and close by reviewing the results/findings.

On accounting for specific research and on reviewing major research findings, academic abstracts and summaries have to comply with several discourse and metadiscourse conventions (Ilie, 2002). It is therefore important to understand the discursive and metadiscursive strategies used with regard to the academic writing process and to the written product. Hence, the study of conference abstracts and of article summaries across disciplines can be highly revealing of disciplinary discourse practices, particularly when the form and content of abstracts, for example are the basis on which gate-keeping decisions are made (as in the refereeing of conference abstracts).

From a rhetorical perspective, the abstract belongs to the deliberative genre through its future-oriented discourse: the author promises to do something and his/her commitment is linked to the quality of the main text. From a rhetorical perspective, the summary belongs to the forensic genre through its past-oriented discourse: the author reviews and evaluates what she/he has already done. At the same time, it also belongs to the epideictic genre due to the fact that the author emphasizes the value of the accomplished research. It is obvious that there are overlaps between abstracts and summaries. Thus, the academic practice of abstract writing often involves a number of features displayed by summaries, which explains why in many abstracts the verbs in the past tense co-occur with verbs in the present and the future tense.

The next step of the project will consist of examining larger samples of parallel corpora in order to map the sub-genres of abstracts and summaries in terms of form, content and purpose.

References

Bhatia, V. K. (2004). *Worlds of written discourse: A genre-based view*. London: Continuum.

Booth, W. C., Colomb, G. G., & Williams, J. M. (2003). *The craft of research*. Chicago, IL: University of Chicago Press.

Cremmins, E. (1982). *The art of abstracting*. Philadelphia, PA: ISI Press.

Ilie, C. (2002). Who's afraid of Paul Grice? The role of the cooperative principle in academic metadiscourse. *RASK, 16*, 3–32.

Kaplan, R. B., Cantor, S., Hagstrom, C., Kamhi-Stein, L. D., Shiotani, Y., & Zimmerman, C. B. (1994). On abstract writing. *Text, 14*(3), 401–426.

Swales, J. M. (1990). *Genre analysis: English in academic and research settings*. Cambridge Applied Linguistics Series. Cambridge: Cambridge University Press.

Chapter 2.05.03

Writing Cultures and Student Mobility

Otto Kruse

The organization of a common European Higher Education Area, as attempted by the Bologna Process, rests on national educational systems differing greatly in such important aspects as the role of independent learning, the implicit conceptions of student literacy, the expectations about critical thinking abilities and the connection between secondary and higher education. Writing, as a part of the teaching arrangements in higher education, is related to many of these aspects. Historically, the introduction of writing as a means of learning, as exemplified by seminar teaching, thesis writing, school essays or written examinations, provided new forms of independent learning and intellectual socialization (Kruse, 2006). The resulting genres are amazingly persistent through the course of history and easily outlast several centuries as Bazerman (1988) has shown with the research article.

Today, intercultural differences in writing practices in higher education are marked and tend to be a serious obstacle to student mobility. Confronted with the task of writing in another culture, students are likely to misunderstand the rationale of the genres and to fail meeting the expectations of their teachers. Educational genres like the seminar paper or the critical essay demand mastering the linguistic and formal requirements but also allow acquiring and rehearsing what is considered the appropriate way of academic thinking, arguing and communication in the respective culture. Educational genres are providing learning opportunities that help constructing, shaping and integrating knowledge and allow students developing rhetorical authority. Educational genres are part of the disciplinary socialization processes allowing the learners to try out new author roles and acquire an accepted academic habitus.

Academic writing culture may be defined as a set of rules, regulations, practices and attitudes regarding the usage of writing for learning and teaching. The terms

Learning to Write Effectively: Current Trends in European Research
Studies in Writing, Volume 25, 293–295
Copyright © 2012 by Emerald Group Publishing Limited
All rights of reproduction in any form reserved
ISSN: 1572-6304/doi:10.1108/S1572-6304(2012)0000025071

'genre practices' and 'writing practices' refer to the fact that genres in educational settings are routinely used in a recurring and regulated manner. Genres are embedded in teaching routines and serve defined functions of learning, reflection and communication within the study programmes. They are also used for examination and grading purposes. Traditionally, study programmes end with the submission of a final thesis which is seen as an important opportunity for independent learning but also as part of a passage ritual within academic socialization. Genre practices are regulated by detailed prescriptions determining the goals, length, time frame and grading criteria of the compositions.

Writing cultures exist at different organizational levels. Writing cultures are part of the disciplinary identities but may also be identified at the level of university type. Differences in national cultures have been documented by several cross-cultural studies (see, e.g. Foster & Russell, 2003) and they seem to persist in spite of the homogenization of higher education through the Bologna process. Genres, for these reasons, are a good focus for intercultural studies and genre knowledge can help transform writing experiences from one culture to another. Preparing students for exchange visits thus should be connected with teaching them the ways writing is handled in the guest culture. The following issues will be focused on: Which text genres are used? How are they are defined? How are they integrated in academic learning? How they are connected to writing practices? There also will be an investigation of how genre skills are taught, how they are valued by the faculty members and how their place in the respective curricula is defined.

The project's objective is to explore writing cultures at European universities and provide data helping to establish comparability and transferability of writing practices. Studying the contexts of writing is helpful to gain insight into the differences of the genres used in higher education, or, vice versa, studying genres is helpful to come to an understanding of writing cultures.

Project Design

The main methodological problem of the study is to secure comparability by creating unbiased measurement tools for the use in different cultures. The study of writing practices in Europe demands assessment tools in different languages which have to be pre-tested in different cultures to show stable reliability and validity measures across cultures.

Cultures cannot be measured directly but have to be inferred from observations. To understand cultures, it is necessary to gain an adequate data base to draw conclusions from. In this project, we will collect data from comparable disciplines at universities of different cultures which may allow drawing inferences to writing cultures. The following data will be gathered:

Student writing skills by a multilingual questionnaire
Attitudes of university teachers towards writing and writing practices used in class by a multilingual questionnaire

Interviews with faculty focusing on the genres used for teaching and the respective genre practices

Prescriptive materials on writing and writing regulations within study programs

At present, the project resumed its work and has been successful in developing the questionnaires and providing a base for multiple comparisons of attitudes towards writing and self-perceived writing skills in different languages/cultures. For a pre-test, questionnaires have been used to study differences in disciplinary writing in one university. Then, data on differences between study programmes in teachers' education in three different parts of Switzerland (French, German and Italian speaking) have been studied. The next step will be a collection of data in collaboration with partners from different European countries to make systematic comparisons of text genres, writing practices, text production skills, learning situations and transfer issues. An analysis of these factors is likely to reveal the challenges that students and young researchers face when studying or working abroad and writing papers in a new writing culture.

Conclusions

Differences in national writing cultures, as addressed in this project, are a little recognized but form a serious obstacle to student mobility. Development of measurement methods as a first step will provide a base for exploring writing cultures with comparable data. The results of the study are likely to support mobility programmes and will be used to develop tools like best practice guidelines, study recommendations and genre descriptions.

References

Bazerman, C. (1988). *Shaping written knowledge: The genre and activity of experimental article in science*. Madison, WI: University of Wisconsin Press.

Foster, D., & Russell, D. (Eds.). (2003). *Writing and learning in cross-national perspective. Transitions from secondary to higher education*. Mahwah, NJ: Lawrence Erlbaum.

Kruse, O. (2006). The origins of writing in the disciplines: Traditions of seminar writing and the Humboldtian ideal of the research university. *Written Communication: An International Quarterly of Research, Theory, and Application, 23*(3), 331–362.

Chapter 2.05.04

Students' Conceptions About Academic Writing

Ruth Villalón and Mar Mateos

In the course of the last decade, students' perceptions have received the attention of many researchers, as they play an important role in students' performance. In the field of writing in particular, students' task representations are essential to understanding how they tackle writing tasks. At the present time, it is thought that students' conceptions of writing itself may be a variable that can influence students' performance in writing-to-learn tasks. Different approaches have established two ways in which writing is conceived: as a tool for identifying and 'transmitting' or 'telling' knowledge, or as a dynamic and creative tool for 'transforming' and constructing new knowledge (Bereiter & Scardamalia, 1987; Ellis, Taylor, & Drury, 2007; Levin & Wagner, 2006; White & Bruning, 2005). Whereas the former conception implies a mechanical and linear process, the latter considers writing as a learning tool able to fulfil an epistemic function (Villalón & Mateos, 2009). These studies have shown that students' beliefs are related to the quality of the written texts they produce and seem to influence written composition. However, most of the work on this subject has been carried out with English-speaking undergraduates and has not taken into account the relationship between students' academic writing conceptions, other writing perceptions and their school performance.

In this context, our general aim is to explore the influence of a relatively unexplored variable — conceptions about writing itself — on the way in which students deal with writing-to-learn tasks. In particular, our research had three concrete objectives:

– to identify students' conceptions about writing at different educational levels;

Learning to Write Effectively: Current Trends in European Research
Studies in Writing, Volume 25, 297–299
Copyright © 2012 by Emerald Group Publishing Limited
All rights of reproduction in any form reserved
ISSN: 1572-6304/doi:10.1108/S1572-6304(2012)0000025072

- to research the influence of writing conceptions and other motivational variables, such as self-efficacy beliefs about writing, on academic achievement;
- to explore the relationship among students' writing conceptions, the texts they produce and the learning they acquire while performing a writing-to-learn task.

In order to achieve these objectives, three studies were carried out.

Method

In the first study, 202 students from lower secondary school, 163 from upper secondary school and 310 from university participated. All of them attended state-run secondary schools or universities in Madrid.

In the other two studies, sub-samples of secondary students took part: 273 students in the second study and 111 in the third one.

Writing conceptions were examined through a questionnaire designed for a wider research project (Villalón & Mateos, 2009). Answers were recorded on a six-point Likert scale ranging from 'totally disagree' to 'totally agree'. The questionnaire contained two scales for identifying the two writing conceptions. The reproductive scale contained 14 items and the epistemic scale contained 15 items. The Cronbach Alpha values for each scale were .78 and .72, respectively. Confirmatory factor analysis was used to test construct validity and the goodness-of-fit indices showed a good fit.

A new instrument for measuring writing self-efficacy was developed. The Alpha value for the whole questionnaire was .90.

Two passages about European Imperialism — a topic in the Social Studies curriculum — were selected and adapted from textbooks for the research. As they were presented to the students, oral instructions were given to explain the synthesis task.

Students' texts were rated according to seven criteria taking into account four dimensions: information inclusion, information organization, structure and formal aspects. The average inter-rater agreement was .70.

Students were given eight questions of different degrees of complexity to assess their learning. The average inter-rater agreement was .80.

The questionnaires were administrated by one of the researchers during one of the students' lessons. In a later session, they produced the synthesis and answered eight learning questions.

Different types of analysis were used to meet the goals that had been set. In the first study, Confimatory Factor Analysis and ANOVA were used; in the second study, bivariate correlations, linear regression and the Sobel test were used; in the third study, bivariate correlations and Confirmatory Factor Analysis were used.

Results

The results of the first study suggest that, although university students have a more sophisticated and complex conception of writing than secondary students, neither group has a fully epistemic conception. Furthermore, female students tend to hold a more sophisticated view of writing than their male peers.

The analyses of the second study indicate a relationship between writing conceptions and self-efficacy beliefs. The epistemic conception was related to a greater sense of writing competence and the reproductive conception was associated with lower self-efficacy scores. Furthermore, the data confirm the effect of both variables on academic achievement and suggest that self-efficacy beliefs partly mediate the role of epistemic and reproductive conceptions.

Finally, the results of the third study show that students who hold more epistemic writing conceptions tend to write products that receive better scores on the quality criteria and to learn more when they write a synthesis. On the contrary, students with more reproductive conceptions of writing tend to write products with poorer scores on the quality criteria and to learn less. Furthermore, the Confirmatory Factor Analysis supports the hypothesis that writing conceptions influence writing quality and that text quality in turn has a bearing on learning.

Taken together, these findings support the idea that writing conceptions play an indirect but important role in students' academic performance and learning through writing, so they should be taken into account in academic contexts.

Acknowledgement

The research project was funded under the FPI Programme by the Spanish Ministry of Science and Technology (FP2001-2230) and under the General Programme for the Promotion of Knowledge 2005–2008 by the Spanish Ministry of Education (SEJ2005-08434-C02-01/EDUC).

References

Bereiter, C., & Scardamalia, M. (1987). *The psychology of written composition*. Hillsdale, NJ: Lawrence Erlbaum Associates.

Ellis, R., Taylor, C., & Drury, H. (2007). Learning science through writing: Associations with prior conceptions of writing and perceptions of a writing program. *Higher Education Research and Development*, 26(3), 297–311.

Levin, T., & Wagner, T. (2006). In their own words: Understanding student conceptions of writing through their spontaneous metaphors in the science classroom. *Instructional Science*, 3(3), 227–278.

Villalón, R., & Mateos, M. (2009). Concepciones del alumnado de secundaria y universidad sobre la escritura académica. *Infancia y aprendizaje*, 32(2), 219–232.

White, M. J., & Bruning, R. (2005). Implicit writing beliefs and their relation to writing quality. *Contemporary Educational Psychology*, 30, 166–189.

SECTION 3

DOCUMENT DESIGN

Chapter 3.00.01

Introduction: Design of Written Professional Documents

Franck Ganier

Professional documents can be distinguished from other written texts (such as narrative or expository texts) on the basis of their purpose: these documents are designed in order to be used. They involve at least one writer and one or more readers, who may be users, clients, correspondents or colleagues. The intended recipients may be professionals or, in the cases of administrative documents or instructions for use, members of the public. In any event, it is crucial for both the organization and the user that the information they convey is efficiently communicated.

During the last 30 years or so, several studies have been conducted in a bid to identify the cognitive processes involved in the processing of such technical documents. These studies have led to a better understanding of these kinds of processes, differentiating them from those used to produce or understand other kinds of text, including narratives (novels, reports, etc.) and texts with a didactic purpose (textbooks, encyclopedias, etc.). They have allowed the development of models describing the processes and interactive mechanisms implied in the processing of these documents.

The main characteristics of the contributions presented in this section therefore deal with studies aimed to enhance the design and quality of technical documents. They focus on the following:

- Analyses of the main characteristics of these documents;
- Empirical knowledge of how professional documents are used and understood by their users;

Learning to Write Effectively: Current Trends in European Research
Studies in Writing, Volume 25, 303–306
Copyright © 2012 by Emerald Group Publishing Limited
All rights of reproduction in any form reserved
ISSN: 1572-6304/doi:10.1108/S1572-6304(2012)0000025073

- Empirical knowledge of user-centred methods allowing assessment of the quality of professional documents;
- Elicitation of professional writers' writing strategies.

On the one hand, some of these studies attempt to evaluate current knowledge, discuss theory, methods and practical issues, and build common research on the impact of document design in professional communication. This way, assessing the quality of professional documents from the writer's and the user's perspective makes it possible to identify the sources of problems and design suitable recommendations for professional writers (drafting, revising and improving technical documents). On the other hand, some of these studies rely on the assumption that writers need to develop composing strategies in order to design a suitable document.

Eight of the contributions to this section focus on the first topic. All of these aim to investigate how the impact of text design on the user can provide insight for the writer. The first two chapters aim to characterize procedural documents. In *Four Characteristics of Procedural Texts* Franck Ganier highlights some specific features of documents that aim to communicate procedures, such as how to use a VCR, bake a cake or put together DIY furniture. The presentation of these specific characteristics makes it possible to distinguish this kind of text from other kinds of texts, such as narrative or expository texts, and identifies cognitive processes implied in their processing. Four characteristics are thus detailed: the purpose of procedural texts, the complexity of their use, the constraints linked to these documents and the distinction between procedures to be carried out and procedures to be remembered.

Michaël Steehouder's chapter *The Anatomy of Procedural Instructions* focuses on two aspects that create optimal effects on the use and processing of procedural instructions: number of actions per step and how instructions are formulated. Presenting numerous examples, this author shows that our understanding of factors that enhance the quality of procedural instruction is lower than one might expect. Moreover, he argues that the simple rules of thumb presented in many textbooks are insufficient for truly professional practice and that developing research in this field can help to answer many significant questions.

The next two chapters deal with the use of procedural documents, focusing on constraints in play in the processing of procedural instructions and motivational elements that could help in the use of procedural documents.

Among all their characteristics, the purpose of procedural documents (such as instructions for use, recipes, online help systems) is to lead their users to carry out a task successfully. Despite this, the use of procedural documents is sometimes unsuccessful. In the chapter entitled *Some Constraints on the Processing of Procedural Instructions*, Franck Ganier proposes two constraints that could explain why the processing of procedural instructions sometimes proves difficult for the users. The first one concerns on the user/document/device interaction; the second one concerns the capacity-limited working memory of the users.

Nicole Loorbach and Joyce Karreman's chapter (*Textual Motivational Elements in Cell Phone User Instructions*) describes a study aimed at testing the effects of motivational elements in instructions for use. In an experimental setting, the authors investigated the effects of motivational elements such as textual or pictorial additions or modifications to instructions for use. In a study exploring the usability of a cell phone instruction manual the authors studied the effects of control steps versus personal stories about a co-user on users' understanding, motivation and confidence in using the cell phone.

The next two chapters show how the design of technical documents can rely on research results, including many aspects previously mentioned (characteristics of the documents, processing difficulties, etc.). In the chapter entitled *Enhancing the Design of Instructions for Use: A Contribution of Cognitive Psychology*, Franck Ganier argues that the design of instructions for use can be enhanced on the basis of research results about cognitive processes underlying the use of devices they accompany. He describes different steps that could help technical writers to take the user into account in order to design instructions for use in an optimal way.

In the chapter *Writing Easy-to-Read Documents for People with Intellectual Disabilities*, R. Ignacio Madrid, and co-workers consider the case of people with intellectual disabilities (PwID), presenting deficits at several levels (phonological awareness, word definition abilities ability to draw inferences and so forth). They define easy-to-read documents as containing only the most important information, presented in the most direct way, following a clear and logical sequence, and presenting pictures and illustrations aimed to support text. Asking whether easy-to-read documents really suit people with intellectual disabilities' needs, the authors present a research programme with two objectives: (i) to produce a new set of research-based easy-to-read guidelines for PwID and (ii) to develop methods and writing tools to help authors to produce easy-to-read materials.

The next two chapters focus on the use of new media in the workplace, such as hypertext and multimedia documents. R. Ignacio Madrid, José J. Cañas and Herre van Oostendorp's interest focuses on the use of hypertext documents. In their chapter entitled *Reading Strategies and Cognitive Load: Implications for the Design of Hypertext Documents*, these authors describe a research project aimed to test a hypertext comprehension model. In this model, they consider that users' processing characteristics have two components: (i) a behavioural component (their reading strategies) and (ii) a cognitive component (cognitive load imposed by the hypertext reading task). They assume these components influence each other, determining comprehension and learning. Results of three studies support this model and lead to recommendations aimed to enhance the design of hypertext documents.

In the chapter entitled *Designing Multimedia Documents for the Workplace*, Patricia Wright discusses the role that multimedia could play in communicating professional information in the work place. She describes an experiment investigating the preferences of adults users in the display of information (written or spoken text; static or animated graphics) for carrying out four procedural and one reference tasks. Results show differences depending on users' characteristics, and kinds of tasks.

The last contribution in this section (*Idée Suisse: Language Policy and Writing Practice of Public Service Media Journalists*) focuses on the production of documents aimed to communicate in a multilingual context. Taking a socio-linguistic perspective, Daniel Perrin, and co-workers investigated language use in journalism. They studied how a public service broadcasting company can promote public understanding by linking speech communities in a country such as Switzerland, with German-, French-, Italian- and Rumantsch-speaking parts. Different practices were identified through analysis of various types of data including completed texts, interviews with journalists, writers' verbal protocols and keystroke logs. They studied four different groups of stakeholders (media politicians, media managers, chief editors and journalists). From these results, the authors conclude that cycles of quality are to be implemented to enhance the language awareness needed to promote public understanding.

Research results generally show that written professional documents can vary in their quality and therefore affect the cognitive processing that they induce (Alamargot, Terrier, & Cellier, 2007). In order to adapt these documents so that they fit their users, studies reported in the present chapter show necessary to identify the main characteristics of these documents and to elaborate models of cognitive processes of the users implied in their processing. Moreover, this chapter shows that, in order to make document design more efficient, pooling together theoretical and methodological knowledge accumulated in research domains such as cognitive psychology, linguistics, information science, technical writing and information design would be of interest (a) to propose some methods aimed to quickly and easily help assessing the quality of these documents and (b) to conceive curricula aimed to train technical writers to design documents fitting users' needs and cognitive processes.

Reference

Alamargot, D., Terrier, P., & Cellier, J. M. (2007). *Written documents in the workplace.* Amsterdam: Elsevier.

Chapter 3.00.02

Four Characteristics of Procedural Texts

Franck Ganier

Procedural texts are part of our everyday life, whether teaching us how to use a VCR, put together a DIY furniture kit or bake a cake. These documents could help avoid both the difficulties users confront when faced with a new piece of equipment and the unnecessary costs to the manufacturers associated with setting up services dedicated to resolving these problems (employing technicians to answer hotlines or technical support services, returning devices to the manufacturer for analysis, etc.).

Having analysed and validated certain characteristics of comprehension and learning activities using procedural texts, researchers in the areas of psychology, linguistics and ergonomics have a better understanding of their functioning. That way, they are now able to propose some recommendations to be followed in order to design documents better suited to their users, or in order to evaluate their quality. Through the presentation of theoretical approaches concerning the learning of new procedures using procedural texts, this paper aims to summarize the specific features of these documents as well as the cognitive factors involved in their processing.

Ganier and Barcenilla (2007) identify a number of specifics of procedural texts when compared with other types of texts. The differences identified concern the purpose of these documents, the complexity of the situation of use, the efficiency constraints associated with this kind of document and the goal of the reader. Firstly, we shall examine the distinctions that can be made between procedural texts and other types of texts.

The Purpose of Procedural Texts: A Pragmatic Approach

Unlike narrative or expository texts — which are designed to entertain, inform or educate the reader — procedural texts have a more pragmatic objective. The readers' goal is to understand in order to act. That way, using procedural texts is therefore

Learning to Write Effectively: Current Trends in European Research
Studies in Writing, Volume 25, 307–309
Copyright © 2012 by Emerald Group Publishing Limited
All rights of reproduction in any form reserved
ISSN: 1572-6304/doi:10.1108/S1572-6304(2012)0000025074

not just a question of reading, but a complex and composite activity requiring the intervention of linguistic, cognitive and motor processes. For this reason, we prefer the term of 'user' to the term of 'reader'. This pragmatic objective of procedural texts has advantages for both users, researchers and professionals wanting to assess the efficiency of these documents. Thus, the completion of actions in the real world allows the users to evaluate the success of their actions using external criteria (it is more difficult for a reader to monitor his/her own comprehension or to detect incoherences with narrative or expository texts for example). Furthermore, the efficacy of the instructions displayed in procedural texts can be directly observed by external observers (such as researchers or human factors specialists), by using objective measures: time taken to complete the task, success or failure in the execution of the task, number and nature of errors, etc.

The Complexity of the Situation of Use: The Interaction between a User, a Document and a Device

Although the reading of a narrative or an explicative text involves an interaction between a reader (and his/her knowledge) and a text, the use of a procedural text suggests a more complex information-gathering context for the user. Indeed, in such a situation, s/he must process information taken from both the instructions and the device in an ever-evolving environment, as the device being used may well change form and state during the task. This complex interaction generally results in alternating between the document and the device, which might induce to present information aimed to facilitate this switching activity.

The Constraints of Procedural Texts

In the case of narrative or explicative texts, written inaccuracies or errors may lead to inconsistencies, which can either go unnoticed or simply be interpreted as a case of misunderstanding on the part of the reader. These inconsistencies do not involve risks that could prove harmful to the reader. However, for users of procedural texts, errors or inaccuracies in the document can have more serious consequences and, in extreme cases, cause accidents (a device wrongly put together, an appliance calibrated to the wrong setting, or a dangerous product used in the wrong way, etc.). As a great number of the ethical and social issues concerning the effectiveness of the instructions rely on the way in which they are understood, it is essential for these documents to be well written, both in terms of clarity and correct language (Fayol, 2002).

Procedures to be Carried Out and Procedures to be Remembered

Many researchers agree that reading is a flexible and active process which evolves depending on the reader's goals (Mills, Diehl, Birkmire, & Mou, 1995). Thus, a number of different strategies may be involved in the reading of different kinds of texts insofar as the readers' goals are distinct. For example, Sticht (1977) introduces a distinction between 'reading to learn', where the goal is to understand and to remember content, and 'reading to do' where the goal is to use the document in order to carry out a task. Mills et al. (1995) studied the relationship using procedural texts. In an experiment aimed to differentiate between the processes involved in 'reading to learn' and 'reading to do', these authors found that the participants who were asked to remember the text developed a more accurate representation of the text (a propositional representation) and were able to recall more information than those who were asked to perform the task described in the text. However, the participants asked to carry out the task were able to draw up a much more complete situational model and were thus able to perform the task more easily than those who were asked to remember the text. These results show that the purpose of reading influences the kind of representation built from reading the text. Moreover, this distinction allows us to distinguish between texts presenting procedures to be carried out immediately (such as assembly instructions, recipes) and texts presenting procedures to remember (i.e. to be carried out with a delay, such as first aid manuals). Turning on the assessment of such documents, the former might induce task performance testing, by contrast, the latter might induce memory testing.

Conclusion

This paper aimed to present four of the main characteristics of procedural texts. These characteristics are likely to affect the way procedural texts (and instructions they display) are dealt with by users, as well as they are studied by researchers, designed by technical writers or assessed by human factors specialists. Considering these characteristics should allow professionals to make a better design of these documents, enhancing their quality and leading to a better use in daily like as well as in industrial settings.

References

Fayol, M. (2002). Les documents techniques: bilan et perspectives. *Psychologie Française, 47*, 9–18.

Ganier, F., & Barcenilla, J. (2007). Considering users and their uses of procedural texts: A prerequisite for the design of appropriate documents. In D. Alamargot, P. Terrier & J.-M. Cellier (Eds.), *Improving the production and understanding of written documents in the workplace* (pp. 49–66). Amsterdam: Elsevier.

Mills, C. B., Diehl, V. A., Birkmire, D. P., & Mou, L.-C. (1995). Reading procedural texts: Effects of purpose for reading and predictions of reading comprehension models. *Discourse Processes, 20*, 79–107.

Sticht, T. G. (1977). Comprehending reading at work. In M. A. Just & P. A. Carpenter (Eds.), *Cognitive processes in comprehension*. Hillsdale, NJ: Erlbaum.

Chapter 3.00.03

The Anatomy of Procedural Instructions

Michaël Steehouder

Procedural instructions are extremely important in professional engineering writing since they form the core of user guidelines, manuals and other genres. Although novice engineers may be familiar with procedural instructions by prior experience, it is necessary to teach them to reflect on requirements and the broad repertoire of linguistic and visual means that can be applied when designing instructions.

Several criteria play a role in decisions about the content and form of procedural instructions, all of them related to particular goals. Traditionally, researchers have paid attention the way errors and mistakes can be prevented (effectiveness), and how time and effort can be minimalized (efficiency). In educational settings, understanding the system, and retention of instructions have also been important requirements. And especially in the past decade, motivational aspects, including confidence of the user, have been considered.

Many aspects of procedural instructions have been analysed or empirically tested to increase our understanding of factors that create optimal effects (cf. Van der Meij, Blijleven, & Jansen, 2003). Among them are for instance level of detail, number of actions per step, formulation of actions, sequence of steps, role of lay-out, in particular to support adequate switching and the use of diagrams and tables. Two of them will be elaborated here.

Number of Actions Per Step

Procedural instructions are usually numbered lists of steps that have to be carried out in order to complete the purpose of the instruction. Intuition may say that each step conveys one action. However, practice shows that this is not the case, as is shown by

Learning to Write Effectively: Current Trends in European Research
Studies in Writing, Volume 25, 311–313
ISSN: 1572-6304/doi:10.1108/S1572-6304(2012)0000025075

a yet unpublished corpus analysis by Steehouder and Ligt, which revealed a variety of combinations, such as

- Alternatives without condition (Insert a number (1 to 999) or press on XX on the remote control)
- Alternatives with condition (When the contact is turned on, push switch one, otherwise, pull it upwards)
- Actions on the same object (Remove and replace the broken bulb)
- Actions on related objects (Remove the mat and the plastic cover)
- Actions that can be seen as run (Push the memory card completely in the slot and close the cover)
- Action with a routine prerequisite (Turn the camera on and put the switch on Capture)
- Navigation sequences (Press MENU on the remote control and select TV-menu > Installation > Decoder > Channel)
- Simultaneous actions (Keep the brake pedal pushed down and select the position R, E or M)

These examples suggest that actions can be combined into one step if there is enough coherence between them. In that case, the combination can easily be remembered by users when switching from the text to the technical artefact on which the action have to be carried out. Combined actions diminish the burden of frequent switching between instruction and device, and thus increases efficiency. However, strong coherence is needed to prevent that users forget elements during switching, which would harm effectiveness.

Further research is needed to find the principles that create the aforementioned coherence. It is likely that linguistic coherence (sentence constructions and connectives) plays a role, but I expect that coherence of the content is more important. A candidate for a theory is an adaptation of Aristotle's principles of the dramatic unity: the unity of time, place and action.

Formulation of Instructions

There is strong empirical evidence that using the imperative increases the effectiveness of procedural instructions. However, other forms are used frequently in practice, such as modal verbs (you may … , you should … , you can …) or even the passive (The remainder of the toner should be discarded in the special boxes).

Several functional deviations of the imperative have come to light in our research of conversations via telephonic helpdesks (e.g. Steehouder, 2007). Helpdesk agents apply several strategies that might help clients to understand and follow their instructions better, such as:

Referential instalments: the user is lead to the object of the action before the action itself is mentioned (… and then you see a number of tag pages and the third one is number: there you may click on …).

Over-specifications: elements are described with apparently redundant extra features — which ensures that no misunderstanding can occur (You see that green box in the lower left of the screen, the one with 'start' on it? There you have to click on.)

Again, empirical research is needed to see whether such formulations do increase the effectiveness of instruction, without negatively affecting their efficiency of the user's motivation.

The examples show that our understanding of factors that enhance the quality of procedural instruction is lower that one might expect. The more complex technical systems are, the more expertise is needed about how to optimally instruct users. The simple 'rules of thumb' that we find in many textbooks, and that are applied in daily practice, are insufficient for a truly professional practice. The research agenda in this field show a broad variety of significant questions for analytic and empirical studies.

References

Steehouder, M. (2007). How helpdesk agents help clients. Paper presented at the International Professional Communication Conference (IPCC), Seattle.

Van der Meij, H., Blijleven, P., & Jansen, L. (2003). What makes up a procedure? In M. J. Albers & B. Mazur (Eds.), *Content and complexity. Information design in software development and documentation* (pp. 129–186). Mahwah, NJ: Erlbaum.

Chapter 3.00.04

Some Constraints on the Processing of Procedural Instructions

Franck Ganier

The very purpose of procedural documents is to accurately conduct a sequence of actions to complete a task. This characteristic supposes that their use requires an adequate interpretation of the instructions displayed in these documents (Ganier, 2004). Moreover, the processing of these instructions (from their reading to their application) might not exceed our cognitive system capacity. The goal of this paper is to present some constraints dealing with the processing of procedural instructions. The first one involves factors implied in the drawing of inferences from the user–document–device interaction; the second one is linked to our capacity-limited working memory.

The User–Document–Device Interaction Constraint: Three Sources for Drawing Inferences

When an individual undertakes a task using procedural instructions, s/he elaborates a mental representation of the task based not only on the instructions, but also on the device which s/he is using, as well as existing declarative and/or procedural knowledge retrieved from long-term memory (Ganier, 2004). One of the main causes of difficulties when using procedural instructions lies in the discrepancy between the characteristics of the mental representation drawn from the instructions, and the characteristics of the representation which direct the execution of the action (the 'action plan'). To satisfactorily build an action plan that will allow to perform the task accurately, users often have to resort to inferences. In order to draw such inferences, they have to derive new information from their own prior knowledge, from the device

Learning to Write Effectively: Current Trends in European Research
Studies in Writing, Volume 25, 315–317
Copyright © 2012 by Emerald Group Publishing Limited
All rights of reproduction in any form reserved
ISSN: 1572-6304/doi:10.1108/S1572-6304(2012)0000025076

itself, and from the information given in the instructions (be they fragmentary or complete; Ganier, 2004). Several studies have clearly shown that an individual's prior knowledge — be it knowledge about the device or reading skills — can affect learning in a number of different domains. For example, experts are able to make inferences and to create interpretations of a situation described in text or pictures more easily than novices. Thus, possessing appropriate prior knowledge allows users to come up with an appropriate action plan even if the interpretation of the information found in the procedural document is incomplete or flawed. However, using instructions in order to carrying out a task is usually conducted by individuals learning new tasks and who thus have little or no prior knowledge in the domain (Kern, 1985). That way, only two remaining information sources can help users to make inferences: the device and the instructions for use. The device can constitute a source of information which can be used to help action planning. For example, the shape of the controls on the device, or even of the device itself, might suggest the way in which it could be used, and for what purpose. Norman (1991) refers to these properties as 'affordances', he defines them as 'the perceived and actual properties of the thing, primarily those fundamental properties that determine just how the thing could possibly be used' (Norman, 1991, p. 9). Thus, affordances would be a helpful basis to avoid making incorrect inferences. Unfortunately, most of the time, the document design process takes place once the device has been setup. Thus, when the user's prior knowledge and the device itself can't provide a helpful basis for inferences, the only one remaining source of information can be provided by procedural instructions. The difficulty is in knowing how to present the information aiding to build an accurate representation of the situation so that action planning may be drawn up as effectively as possible, at the lowest possible cost to the cognitive system.

Working Memory Constraints

Wright (1983) suggests that the transfer of information from instructions to actions or sequences of actions can have an impact on the load imposed on working memory. Working memory is involved in every aspect of any task, and it reveals to be an essential factor in the processing of instructions, particularly in storing the user's goal, the meaning of instructions and the resulting action plan (Ganier, 2004). The importance of working memory in the processing of instructions is highlighted in Engle, Carullo, and Collins's (1991) research, which found that the complexity effect observed when instructions are presented orally is of greater difficulty for children with a short working memory span than those with a large one. These results confirm other findings, which show that the processing of instructions requires a great deal of the user's mental capacity. This cognitive demand is revealed by a 'switching activity' and a fragmentation of the instructions to be carried out: when following instructions, users switch from the instructions to the device. Furthermore, they divide the described actions into basic actions, which in no way correspond to the size of the instructions. Thus, this way of breaking down the information could be seen as a necessary accommodation, which enables the users to reduce processing costs in working memory.

Conclusion

The constraints in mental processing caused by the capacity-limited working memory indicate that the user has meta-cognitive control over a number of psychological processes, such as not trying to memorize too much information at once, and keeping track of his/her place in the text when leaving the document to carry out the action. Recognition of this phenomenon could raise writers' awareness of the importance of the spatial layout of information. Indeed, research has shown that numbered instructions in list form are read more quickly than the same information in paragraphs. Varying the format of instructions, notably by adding pictures, should reduce the inherent cognitive costs involved in constructing a mental image from a text.

Turning on the second constraint, each of the three information sources described in this paper (the user–the instructions–the device) plays an important role in the comprehension of procedural documents and the completion of the described tasks. When using procedural instructions, individuals with more extensive prior knowledge in the particular domain tend to organize information better and make less mistakes than those who have less prior knowledge. Unfortunately, most of users generally lack of prior knowledge when using a new device. Moreover, the device itself sometimes lacks in presenting information aimed to guide the user's actions. Instructions are rarely wholly explicit: they can be ambiguous, vague or even fragmentary. If these three sources of information are lacking (i.e. the necessary knowledge to carry out appropriate actions is not available), users must attempt to make up for these shortcomings by using problem-solving processes, at the risk of acquiring only inconsistent levels of success.

References

Engle, R. W., Carullo, J. J., & Collins, K. W. (1991). Individual differences in working memory for comprehension and following directions. *Journal of Educational Research, 84*, 253–262.

Ganier, F. (2004). Factors affecting the processing of procedural instructions: Implications for document design. *IEEE Transactions on Professional Communication, 47*, 15–26.

Kern, R. P. (1985). Modeling users and their use of technical manuals. In T. M. Duffy & R. Waller (Eds.), *Designing usable texts* (pp. 341–375). London: Academic Press Inc.

Norman, D. A. (1991). *The design of everyday things* (Titre original (1988): *The psychology of everyday things*. New York, NY: Basic Books). New York, NY: Doubleday.

Wright, P. (1983). Manual dexterity: A user-oriented approach to creating computer documentation. *Human Factors in Computing Systems: CHI'83 Conference Proceedings*, 12–15 December, Ann Janda Editor Boston, MA (pp. 11–18).

Chapter 3.00.05

Textual Motivational Elements in Cell Phone User Instructions

Nicole Loorbach and Joyce Karreman

For a long time, user instructions were considered as purely instrumental documents: Instructions had to enable readers to perform tasks with an accompanying device. And even though this still remains the main purpose of user instructions, views on how to accomplish this have changed over the years. The traditional view seemed to assume that when the instructions were correct, readers would automatically be able to use the accompanying device well (Moore, 1997). According to current views, the instructions should motivate readers to keep on reading once they have started doing so (Horton, 1997). This new approach to technical communication is being adopted by a vastly growing group of practitioners in the field, but relatively little research has been conducted so far to test for the effects of this approach. We executed a number of studies to test for the effects of motivational elements in user instructions (Loorbach, Karreman, & Steehouder, 2007, 2009). This short paper is a summary of our most recent study.

Motivating readers of user instructions seems to be especially important for users who are less experienced with the device in question. Since senior users belong to a group that is known for being less experienced with relatively new technology devices, we decided to test for effects of providing motivation in user instructions by letting seniors (60–70 years) use instructions for a cell phone. In an experimental study, we enhanced user instructions for a cell phone to study the effects of so-called 'motivational elements'. Motivational elements are textual or pictorial additions or modifications to user instructions with the aim of motivating the reader, without changing the content of the actual instructions.

We tested for effects of two specific types of motivational elements aimed at increasing users' confidence in performing tasks with a cell phone: (1) control steps

Learning to Write Effectively: Current Trends in European Research
Studies in Writing, Volume 25, 319–321
ISSN: 1572-6304/doi:10.1108/S1572-6304(2012)0000025077

and (2) personal stories about a co-user. Control steps were provided at the end of procedures to allow users to check if these procedures were performed correctly. We expected control steps to stimulate 'enactive mastery experiences' (cf. Bandura, 1997). These steps should either take away possible doubts about whether or not having performed a procedure correctly or be a confirmation of indeed having succeeded. All personal stories described how Mrs. Damhuis, a 68-year-old woman, had struggled a bit with the instructions, but always succeeded in reaching her goal. Each story was accompanied by a picture of Mrs. Damhuis in the described situation. We expected the stories to allow for 'modelling' or 'vicarious experiences' (cf. Bandura, 1997), so users will feel stimulated that they too can perform certain tasks with the telephone.

Fifty-nine seniors performed three tasks with either a control version or one of the two motivational versions of an instruction manual for the Nokia 1100, a cell phone. The first motivational version contained control steps; the second motivational version contained personal stories. One of the three tasks was very difficult, since the accompanying instructions were incomplete in all versions of the instruction manual. We believed that such a difficult task could inform us about users' persistence in trying to deal with setbacks during task performance. In other words, we expected motivational elements to be most welcome when users are challenged in reaching their goals. In this study, we tested for the individual effects of control steps and personal stories on the usability of the user instructions, on senior users' motivation and their confidence in using the cell phone.

We measured the usability of the user instructions according to ISO's three usability aspects effectiveness of task performance, efficiency of task performance and satisfaction with the user instructions. Results showed positive effects of both control steps and personal stories on one of the aspects, namely effectiveness of task performance: seniors using either motivational version of the user instructions succeeded more often at the very difficult task than seniors using the control version without motivational elements. This positive effect of both types of motivational elements is promising, since it is likely that difficult situations like this one also happen during seniors' real-life interactions with cell phones.

Contrary to our expectations, no differences existed between the conditions for both self-reported and observed motivation of senior users. And even though seniors' confidence scores also did not differ between the conditions, we did find an interesting effect for the self-efficacy aspect of confidence for all 59 users combined. For each of the three tasks, our study shows that if seniors succeeded at reaching their goal, their self-efficacy scores for that particular task were (statistically significantly) higher after the task than before. In other words, our study confirmed Bandura's assumption that enactive mastery experience is a main source of users' self-efficacy; that experiencing success at a specific task increases people's judgements of their capabilities to again succeed at this task in the future. We found positive influences of control steps and personal stories on senior users' effectiveness in performing tasks with inadequate instructions. This may not only affect the usability of the user instructions, but users' confidence as well by increasing users' experiences with success. Future research should shed more light on this issue.

References

Bandura, A. (1997). *Self-efficacy: The exercise of control.* New York, NY: W. H. Freeman and Company.

Horton, W. (1997). *Secrets of user-seductive documents: Wooing and winning the reluctant reader.* Arlington, VA: Society for Technical Communication.

Loorbach, N., Karreman, J., & Steehouder, M. (2007). Adding motivational elements to an instruction manual for seniors. *Technical Communication, 54*(3), 343–358.

Loorbach, N., Karreman, J., & Steehouder, M. (2009). Boosting seniors' confidence by enhancing user instructions. *IPCC conference*, July 2009, Hawaii.

Moore, P. (1997). Rhetorical vs. instrumental approaches to teaching technical communication. *Technical Communication, 41*, 163–173.

Chapter 3.00.06

Enhancing the Design of Instructions for Use: A Contribution of Cognitive Psychology

Franck Ganier

Whether trying to use a new software, assembling a bookcase or washing a car in an automatic washing station, we all know from personal experience that carrying out a task while following instructions for use is not always as simple as it seems and can prove unsuccessful. Errors or failures resulting from the use of instructions often lead to incriminate the device — or its manufacturer — rather than the instructions themselves. Thus, improving procedural documents displaying instructions for use proves to be an extremely important issue for both the user and the manufacturer.

Research conducted in the domain of cognitive psychology provides a vast corpus of data concerning the way in which new procedures are learned and about the understanding and recall of text and/or pictures (Ganier, 2004). Applying this data to the domain of technical writing could prove to be of real interest, as it would provide a frame of reference when deciding which design solutions might prove the most appropriate for drawing up instructions adapted to users' needs.

From the Study of Cognitive Processes to the Design of Instructions for Use

Some decisions concerning the way instructions are designed cannot be made without first considering who they are designed for. The first step when designing instructions is to determine who will be using them (i.e. the characteristics of the users), and the questions the users might ask themselves when confronted with the device. Gathering concrete data concerning the information required by the users (through survey questionnaires or individual interviews) should reveal users' knowledge of and beliefs

Learning to Write Effectively: Current Trends in European Research
Studies in Writing, Volume 25, 323–325
ISSN: 1572-6304/doi:10.1108/S1572-6304(2012)0000025078

about the device as well as its characteristics and the different ways they think it might be used. The second step deals with studying cognitive processes involved in using and understanding instructions. Indeed, comprehension of instructions is the first step of a series to be completed prior to performing a task. To be able to carry out the described action, the user must first draw up an action plan from the comprehension process (Dixon, 1987; Ganier, Gombert, & Fayol, 2000). There are many different ways of presenting the information needed to carry out the procedures, which can either facilitate or impede the way the user plans to act. Dixon (1987) suggests that the mental organization of such action plans can be studied accurately by observing the order in which the actions are carried out. Several studies have shown that in some cases, the surface format of the instructions can affect the way users re-encode the initial instructions (Dixon, 1987; Wright, 1996). The transformation from the reading of the instructions to the execution of the task is thus facilitated if the order in which the instructions are presented matches the order of the actions to be carried out. This is known as the 'use-order principle' (Wright, 1996).

In a complementary approach, to take the user and his/her prior knowledge and skills into account, we must first consider the document's content, as well as the format in which the information will be presented and the most appropriate level of detail. Since the 1980s, as the use of pictures became more and more common in procedural documents, researchers studying instruction comprehension began to pay an increasing amount of attention to picture-only or mixed instructional formats (Ganier et al., 2000). Results of these studies generally show that, when compared to text-only and picture-only formats, the mixed format yields the best performances: participants perform the tasks more quickly and more accurately, with fewer errors. When presented together, these formats complement one another thus facilitating the elaboration of a representation from reading the instructions (Ganier et al., 2000). Users must also be provided with some representation of the desired outcome (as a heading or a picture) so that they can check that the task at hand coincides with that outcome (Ganier, 2004).

Conclusion: A Strategy for the Optimal Design of Instructions for Use

In order to help users, it is important to provide them with the best possible conditions for reading, understanding, remembering and applying the instructions with the least cognitive effort. An optimal design strategy should thus first present general information — or organizational information — facilitating the elaboration of a representation of the desired goal. This organizational information would allow the user to compare the final result with the evolution of the task by evaluating the similarities between the result and the goal, and by a process of auto-correction (Ganier, 2004). In terms of information content, the procedural document should present instructions according to user's level of knowledge about the device and the procedure (this is more and more feasible with electronic documents). In terms of information display, the procedural document should describe each step of the procedure, and preferably be presented using the mixed 'text + picture' format. Providing a structured presentation of numbered instructions in association with pictures should, one the one hand, facilitate the location of instructions when alternating between reading the instructions and using the device and, on the other, prove useful when coming up with a procedure and/or a functional mental model. Therefore, comprehension can be aided by adding pictures to the information to be carried out, which enables participants to elaborate accurate mental models. Further information regarding possible errors and how to overcome them should also be included.

Using a strategy such as this does not however fully guarantee the quality and usability of procedural documents. Indeed, the application of these recommendations is only one of the steps of producing a document suited to its users. Devising a truly suitable document must also involve testing it on a sample group — and thus almost certainly modifying it — before it can be published. Ganier (2007) gives an example of a procedural document designed on the basis of these recommendations that proved to be more efficient than the one usually sold with domestic appliances.

References

Dixon, P. (1987). The structure of mental plans for following directions. *Journal of Experimental Psychology: Learning, Memory and Cognition, 13*, 18–26.

Ganier, F. (2004). Factors affecting the processing of procedural instructions: Implications for document design. *IEEE Transactions on Professional Communication, 47*, 15–26.

Ganier, F. (2007). Comparative user-focused evaluation of user guides: A case study. *Journal of Technical Writing and Communication, 37*, 305–322.

Ganier, F., Gombert, J.-E., & Fayol, M. (2000). Effets du format de présentation des instructions sur l'apprentissage de procédures à l'aide de documents techniques. *Le Travail Humain, 63*, 121–152.

Wright, P. (1996). The comprehension of written instructions: Examples from health materials. In D. Wagner (Ed.), *Literacy: An international handbook*. New York, NY: Garland Publishing Inc.

Chapter 3.00.07

Writing Easy-to-Read Documents for People With Intellectual Disabilities

R. Ignacio Madrid, Vicenta Ávila, Inmaculada Fajardo and Antonio Ferrer

The ability to access written information is fundamental for people to be able to take part in mainstream life. However, some people can have problems understanding text due to learning or cognitive disabilities, lack of sufficient formal education, social problems or aging processes.

In the case of people with intellectual disabilities (PwID), language processing, which includes reading, is one of the most affected areas, even behind social interaction and general intelligence.

The provision of easy-to-read versions of documents is proposed to help people with cognitive and learning disabilities to better understand written information. In this context, an easy-to-read document is defined as one that contains only the most important information, written and presented in the most direct way so that the largest possible audience can understand it. The contents should follow a clear and logical sequence, and all unnecessary ideas, words, sentences or phrases should be avoided or removed. Presentation is also very important: Photographs, pictures or symbols should support the text wherever possible in order to aid understanding. However, are these recommendations valid for PwID?

Several sets of guidelines have been proposed previously to help authors write easy-to-read materials (e.g. the IFLA guidelines for easy-to-read materials; Tronbacke, 1998). However, existing guidelines have some problems that affect their effectiveness in providing such easy-to-read content.

First, there is little research about comprehension processes of PwID and most of the guidelines are based only on common sense. For instance, PwID have deficits at

Learning to Write Effectively: Current Trends in European Research
Studies in Writing, Volume 25, 327–330
ISSN: 1572-6304/doi:10.1108/S1572-6304(2012)0000025079

several levels: phonological awareness, decoding processes, receptive and expressive vocabulary repertory, word definition abilities, syntactic processing or ability to make inferences. However, the extent to which those processes are involved in reading comprehension is not clear. Only a few studies have dealt with this issue, finding a counter-intuitive lack of correlation between expressive vocabulary and syntaxes and reading comprehension (Verhoeven & Vermeer, 2006). On the other hand, inference making abilities seem to be most directly related to reading comprehension in intellectual disability (Bos & Tierney, 1984). These findings support use of guidelines intended to facilitate inference making (e.g. use of connectives) rather than those for lexical processing (e.g. use of high frequency words). Therefore, there is a lack of empirical support for the idea that those sets of guidelines produce more understandable documents for PwID when compared with original documents.

Second, the guidelines lack a clear set of tools and instructions to help journalists, web content managers and editors improve the readability of the information they provide.

To cope with these two problems in the production of easy-to-read documents, our research has two objectives:

Produce a new set of research-based easy-to-read guidelines for PwID
Develop methods and writing tools to help authors to produce easy-to-read materials

Towards a New Set of Easy-to-Read Guidelines for PwID

As mentioned above, in spite of this lack of evidence, most of the design guidelines for easy-to-read text recommend the use of frequent vocabulary and syntactic simplifications which, according to the scarce literature available, might not be as helpful as coherence textual markers (e.g. use of connectives) for PwID. Indeed, the available easy-to-read guidelines do not report the results of the empirical validation, if any, conducted to select them. Therefore, we have designed two empirical approaches to investigate psycholinguistic indexes which could predict reading comprehension for PwID and then to propose a new set of empirically validated guidelines. These two empirical approaches based on traditional research with non-handicapped people are:

– Linguistic analyses of simplified texts and correlation with reading comprehension indexes (e.g. Crossley, Greenfield, & McNamara, 2008). This approach, widely used by linguistics researchers, aims to find out which linguistic variables are useful for predicting text readability and consists of asking people to read a set of texts and then to answer comprehension questions. Then, a set of linguistics variables is measured for the texts and both linguistic and comprehension results are correlated. In order to arrive at a valid construct, the key to this approach lies in selecting a comprehensive set of linguistic indexes based on theories of reading comprehension which consider not only superficial features of text such as number of words per sentence or syllables per word but also deeper factors of textual coherence such as overlapping vocabulary or use of connectives. Again, a valid set of comprehension metrics (e.g. text based and inference questions) based on cognitive models of reading comprehension must be selected.

- Direct manipulation of psycholinguistic factors. This approach consists of comparing individuals' reading comprehension scores after reading authentic texts versus texts simplified according to one or several linguistic levels (lexical, syntactic or textual). This is a theory-based approach as well and its strength is that the factors of interest are directly manipulated.

Using these two approaches, we attempt to ensure that only those linguistic variables which are really predictive of PwID's reading comprehension will be incorporated in easy-to-read guidelines and writing tools.

Development of Writing Tools

One way of providing support to those involved in the production of easy-to-read materials is through the automation of the process of creating easy-to-read versions of existing documents.

Preliminary work (Bautista, Gervás, & Madrid, 2009) has tested the feasibility of a semi-automatic method to summarize text to improve readability. The study explored whether automatic conversion processes based on natural language processing techniques might succeed in providing easy-to-read fast drafts. The proposed conversion processes — that take the existing guidelines as a reference — were applied to a small set of example texts, and validated numerically by the application of a suite of readability metrics. Future work on the development of writing tools will be based on the new set of guidelines developed by our research, focusing on the reading needs of PwID.

Acknowledgements

Most of the work presented here is a result of the research contract with the ONCE Foundation in the context of the LECTURA FACIL Project, which is partly supported by the Spanish Ministry of Industry, under the AVANZA programme. The opinions expressed in this paper are those of the authors and are not necessarily those of the ONCE Foundation or of the Spanish Ministry of Industry.

References

Bautista, S., Gervás, P., & Madrid, R. I. (2009). Feasibility analysis for semiautomatic conversion of text to improve readability. In M. Jemmni (Ed.), *Proceedings of the second international conference on ICT and Accessibility* (pp. 33–40). Hammamet: Art Print.

Bos, C. S., & Tierney, R. J. (1984). Inferential reading abilities of mildly mentally retarded and nonretarded students. *American Journal of Mental Deficiency*, *89*(11), 75–82.

Crossley, S. A., Greenfield, J., & McNamara, D. S. (2008). Assessing text readability using cognitively based indices. *TESOL Quarterly*, *42*(3), 475–493.

Tronbacke, B. I. (Ed.). (1998). *Guidelines for easy-to-read materials*. IFLA Professional Reports, 56. The Hague: IFLA.

Verhoeven, L., & Vermeer, A. (2006). Literacy achievement of children with intellectual disabilities from diverse linguistic backgrounds. *Journal of Intellectual Disability Research*, *50*(10), 725–738.

Chapter 3.00.08

Reading Strategies and Cognitive Load: Implications for the Design of Hypertext Documents

R. Ignacio Madrid, José J. Cañas
and Herre van Oostendorp

Hypertext documents are pieces or nodes of information connected to each other through hyperlinks. The information that they contain can be read and comprehended in a similar way as linear texts, but they remove part of the responsibility from the authors to the readers since they have to develop their own reading strategies. This chapter describes a research project focused on the use of hypertext documents, analysing how readers process hypertext and how its design can accommodate readers' cognitive restrictions to enhance comprehension and learning.

The main goal of this research project was to test a hypertext comprehension model (see Figure 1). In this model, user variables and hypertext system variables interact to determine users' processing characteristics, which have two components:

– A behavioural component: reading strategies – Hypertext reading strategies can be defined as implicit rules that readers follow to select which parts of a set of hypertext documents to read and in which order. Our research has focused on two reading strategies: the coherence strategy (reading the hypertext node semantically most related to the previously read one in order to maintain text coherence) and the interest strategy (reading first the most interesting nodes for the user, and postponing the less interesting ones). Research has demonstrated that readers using these two reading strategies follow different reading orders and, as a

Learning to Write Effectively: Current Trends in European Research
Studies in Writing, Volume 25, 331–334
ISSN: 1572-6304/doi:10.1108/S1572-6304(2012)0000025080

consequence of that, focus on different aspects of the text, affecting comprehension and learning (Madrid & Cañas, 2007).
– A cognitive component: cognitive load – Cognitive load is related to how much load is imposed on the reader's cognitive system by the hypertext reading task. It increases when readers' cognitive abilities are low or task difficulty is high. When cognitive load is too high, readers' comprehension can be hindered.

Both behavioural and cognitive components influence each other determining comprehension and learning. Performing different reading strategies leads to different levels of cognitive load and, on the other hand, the availability of cognitive resources is related to the selection and development of reading strategies. The next section summarizes the main results of three studies in this research project.

In Study 1 we explored the cognitive factors and reading strategies involved in comprehension with hypertext navigation tools.

Interactive overviews are frequently used to give orientation and provide access to the main set of hypertext documents. However, the way in which readers use and benefit from these navigation tools seems to depend on their abilities and experience.

In this study, we tested the relation between a set of cognitive abilities and the reading strategies that readers follow when using an interactive overview, and their effect on comprehension. Results showed that readers' spatial abilities predict the reading strategies they follow: readers with higher spatial abilities accessed more different pages, spent less time using the overview and followed a reading order more related to the structure suggested by the interactive overview, which in turn for all these strategies was related to better comprehension.

In Sudy 2 (Madrid, Van Oostendorp, & Puerta-Melguizo, 2009) we explored the effect of number of links and navigation support on cognitive load and learning.

Does the number of links included in a hypertext system determine readers' cognitive load and comprehension? Is it possible to help readers to reduce cognitive load and to enhance learning by providing navigation support? These two questions

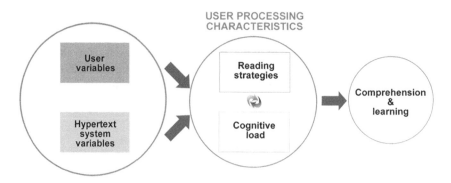

Figure 1: Hypertext comprehension model proposed.

were examined in a investigation in which novice readers used an hypertext either with four or eight links per page in which navigation support was provided or not. Navigation support was provided by signalling the two links that were semantically more related with the text just read which helps readers to develop a coherence strategy. Results showed that using link suggestions was beneficial for learning, but no effect of the number of links per page was found. Moreover, the effects of system variables on cognitive load were mediated by the reading order that participants selected: those readers that performed a more coherent reading order learned more and suffered less cognitive load than those who followed a less coherent one.

In Study 3 (Madrid & Cañas, 2009) we explored the effect of prior knowledge and reading strategies on cognitive load and learning.

This experiment compared the effect of two different reading strategies (coherence vs. interest) on cognitive load and reading comprehension, both for low and high prior knowledge readers. The interest reading strategy caused more cognitive load during hypertext reading than the coherence strategy for all readers. Regarding comprehension and learning, the coherence strategy showed to be better for low prior knowledge readers, while both strategies lead to similar results for high prior knowledge readers.

Theoretical and Practical Implications

The studies described above supports the hypertext comprehension model depicted in Figure 1. It stresses the importance for readers' comprehension and learning to select an appropriate reading strategy and to keep cognitive load not too high.

Furthermore, both the development of reading strategies and cognitive load depend on the interaction of user and system variables. Some practical implications to enhance hypertext reading comprehension through hypertext documents design can be drawn:

– Give support to appropriate reading strategies: All studies showed the importance of the coherence of the reading order, especially for readers with low prior knowledge. From a design perspective, hypertext designers can influence the coherence-building process despite the fact that hypertext users select the reading order by themselves. Some techniques include providing an interactive overview explicitly showing the semantic relation between hypertext nodes (Study 1) or giving link suggestions based on semantic similarities between sections of hypertext documents (Study 2).
– Take into account readers' characteristics: Hypertext documents designers can accommodate the system to readers' cognitive constraints and preferences. Study 1 suggests that interactive overviews are useful to provide readers' guidance, but their spatial complexity have to be limited to avoid readers with less spatial abilities get disadvantaged. Study 3 also suggests that when readers' prior knowledge level is known in advance, the hypertext designer can also support the use of a specific reading strategy.

Acknowledgement

This research was funded by research projects SEJ2004-05430 and SEJ2007-63850 from the Spanish Science and Education Ministry to first and second authors.

References

Madrid, R. I., & Cañas, J. J. (2007). How reading strategies affect comprehension of texts in hypertext. In D. Alamargot, P. Terrier & J.-M. Cellier (Eds.), *Improving the production and understanding of written documents in the workplace*. Amsterdam: Elsevier.

Madrid, R. I., & Cañas, J. J. (2009). The effect of reading strategies and prior knowledge on cognitive load during hypertext reading. *The Ergonomics Open Journal*, *2*, 124–132.

Madrid, R. I., Van Oostendorp, H., & Puerta-Melguizo, M. C. (2009). The effects of the number of links and navigation support on cognitive load and learning with hypertext: The mediating role of reading order. *Computers in Human Behavior*, *25*(1), 66–75.

Chapter 3.00.09

Designing Multimedia Documents for the Workplace

Patricia Wright

One of the common reasons for writing in the workplace is to provide people with advice and instructions on how to carry out various procedures; another reason is to disseminate information that people will keep and refer to as needed (e.g. handbooks). Communicating this kind of information has been the focus of much of my research during the past decade (e.g. Wright, 2000) which has explored how information design factors can change the ease with which people can use the material for its intended purpose. This approach to document design starts with readers' needs, both in terms of content and with respect to cognitive limitations and their preferences for the way information is presented. When documents in the workplace are made available online, writers have a rich multimedia design space within which to support readers. The digital document does not have to be the file that was printed from Microsoft Word or Adobe Acrobat, but as yet we know little about the design factors that could help people use written materials online to accomplish a variety of work-related tasks.

Among the recent design features that we have explored are issues of graphic animation, which can sometimes influence people's preference for written or spoken instructions. This has led us to examine the uses of audio as an optional addition to, not necessarily a replacement of, written text in documents incorporating graphics to different extents (Wright, 2006). So a variety of reference and procedural tasks are being studied, with the tasks differing in factors such as whether the tasks are themselves on-screen or in the physical world because this may change how much people try to remember in their read-then-do segments.

Learning to Write Effectively: Current Trends in European Research
Studies in Writing, Volume 25, 335–337
Copyright © 2012 by Emerald Group Publishing Limited
All rights of reproduction in any form reserved
ISSN: 1572-6304/doi:10.1108/S1572-6304(2012)0000025081

Method

The 128 paid adult volunteers participating in these studies have been chosen to reflect specific groups within the general public. They include fluent readers of working age, adults who class themselves as poor readers, adults for whom the text is not in their first language and older adults who may be experiencing sensory or cognitive challenges.

The recruitment of participants in this research involves placing advertisements in local newspapers and making contact with specific groups in order to invite volunteers between the ages of 18 and 80, to come to the university and provide us with feedback about our talking computer (Wright, 2006).

Throughout the study the information is presented on a 38 cm touch screen so that no prior familiarity with computers is needed. A two-hour session begins with three very short tasks such as finding an entry in a displayed phone list and entering this number on a displayed keypad. These tasks enable the comparability of the four categories of adults to be assessed so that any differences in their performance on subsequent tasks are not mistakenly attributed to category membership when they might arise from sensory or cognitive differences. These preliminary tasks include written and spoken text, static and animated graphics, and provide indices of participants' visual acuity and manual co-ordination, working memory span and visual-spatial ability.

The preliminary tasks are followed by an interleaving of four procedural tasks and three reference tasks. In all of these tasks there is an onscreen menu that lets people determine how the information is displayed. This panel gives control over the text and the graphics, and offers a voice option. The menu is available throughout the tasks and people can change their settings at any time. The procedural tasks include a mechanical assembly task with a metal valve, an information resequencing task done either entirely on screen or partly on screen and partly on paper, the setting of an alarm on a virtual mobile phone, and the onscreen rearrangement of a Tangram display. The reference tasks include answering questions by referring to predominantly graphic route information on a map (this route is either animated or static); answering questions by referring to a document giving information in various formats on the physical features, living and hunting characteristics of wild big cats (lions, etc.); answering questions about British universities by consulting a predominantly verbal document.

One of the main research interests is in the choices made by the volunteers about how they want the information displayed in different tasks. In addition, accuracy, time and debriefing comments by participants are noted for all tasks. In order to check whether people's choices would be reflected in their performance, a few of the tasks (including the map and university tasks) have been done by other adults who had no choice about how the information was presented (Wright et al., 2008).

Results and Discussion

The analysis that has been conducted so far suggests that the performance and preferences of adult fluent readers often differ from those of people in the other groups. For example, the older readers more often selected audio (Wright et al., 2008) and so too did those who were not fluent readers (Wright et al, 2009). It is important for writers to appreciate the differences within an audience as heterogeneous as the general public because these subgroups can represent a sizable minority whose information needs can be met by digital documents once the need to do so is recognized.

Analysis has also suggested that across all four groups, spoken text was more often selected in procedural tasks than in reference tasks (Soroka et al., 2006). This serves to emphasize the usefulness of being able to characterize the reading and writing tasks undertaken in the workplace, so that guidelines and advice on writing workplace documents can be tailored to specific contexts.

Acknowledgements

I acknowledge with thanks the financial support of an Economic and Social Research Council Award L328253011 as part of the P@CCIT (People at the Centre of Communication and Information Technologies) programme which was also funded by the Economic and Physical Sciences Research Council and the Department of Trade and Industry. Invaluable help was also received from Anthony Soroka who wrote the software and Steve Belt who collected almost all the data. The project steering group included Professors Pham and Dimov from the Manufacturing Engineering Centre at Cardiff University, Professor De Roure from Computer Science at the University of Southampton and Professor Petrie now at the Computer Science Department in the University of York.

References

Soroka, A. J., Wright, P., Belt, S., Pham, D. T., Dimov, S., De Roure D. C., & Petrie, H. (2006, August). User choices for modalities of instructional information. *Proceedings of 4th international IEEE conference on industrial informatics*, INDIN'06, Singapore (pp. 16–18).

Wright, P. (2000). Document-based decision making. In J.-F. Rouet, J. J. Levonen & A. Biardeau (Eds.), *Multimedia learning: Cognitive and instructional issues* (pp. 31–43). Amsterdam, NL: Pergamon.

Wright, P. (2006). Talking computers and diversity in older audiences. *Gerontechnology, 4*, 187–189.

Wright, P., Soroka, A. J., Belt, S., Pham, D., Dimov, S., DeRoure, D., & Petrie, H. (2008). Modality preference and performance when seniors consult online information. *Gerontechnology, 7*, 293–304.

Wright, P., Soroka, A., Belt, S., Dimov, S., Petrie, H., & De Roure, D. (2009, July). Effects of language fluency on modality choices by adults when following online explanatory demonstrations. *Proceedings of IEEE institute of professional communication conference*, Hawaii.

Chapter 3.00.10

Idée Suisse: Language Policy and Writing Practice of Public Service Media Journalists

Daniel Perrin, Marcel Burger, Mathias Fürer,
Aleksandra Gnach, Michael Schanne and Vinzenz Wyss

Public service broadcasting companies are among the most important broadcasting companies in Europe. In Switzerland, there is one such company: SRG. As a media enterprise, SRG is subject to market and competitive forces. As a public service institution, though, SRG has a federal, societal, cultural and linguistic remit to fulfil. We reconstructed this remit, from a socio-linguistic perspective, as the remit to promote social integration by promoting public understanding.

Promoting public understanding in a highly multilingual country means, at first sight, promoting discourse across the language boundaries: discourse between the German, French, Italian and Rumantsch parts of Switzerland. From a socio-linguistic point of view, however, the 'language boundaries' concept has to be refined. Urban and rural, poor and rich, lay persons and experts, immigrants and residents, ... different speech communities speak different linguistic varieties and interact with different views of the world. Thus, promoting public understanding means linking speech communities with other speech communities, both between and within the German-, French-, Italian-, and Rumantsch-speaking parts of Switzerland.

The various stakeholders of public broadcast regulation might not share a corporate view of the societal and linguistic remit. In fact, we assumed that politics, management and journalists interpret the remit in different and partially contradictory ways, due to partial ignorance and according to specific interests. Thus, our interest in these stakeholders' practices focused on promoting public understanding is: How do they do and how do they want to do what they have to do?

Learning to Write Effectively: Current Trends in European Research
Studies in Writing, Volume 25, 339–341
Copyright © 2012 by Emerald Group Publishing Limited
All rights of reproduction in any form reserved
ISSN: 1572-6304/doi:10.1108/S1572-6304(2012)0000025082

Investigating this main question requires an inter and transdisciplinary approach: We combined knowledge from linguistics and sociology with methodology from writing research to investigate language use in journalism. This complex approach is reflected in the research theory applied and developed, the research process, the project modules and the methodology.

The project architecture leads to a corpus with three types of data: First, it comprises documents such as meeting minutes of managers' decisions or copies of media text products, which merely had to be collected. Second, it contains transcriptions of interviews with politicians, managers and journalists, as well as verbal protocols of journalist's retrospective comments about their text production processes; they were obtained for the purpose of the research project.

However, the most important part of the corpus encompasses data from tracing natural text production processes: video recordings of newsroom conferences and workplace conversations and keystroke loggings of writing processes in the newsroom (Perrin, 2003, 2011). In order to record these data, the researchers and the project participants had to solve major organizational, legal, technical and psychological problems: The organizations and individuals under investigation had to agree to the computer logging of production processes; privacy and data security had to be assured; the computer editing systems had to be prepared for continuous and non-intrusive logging. For the case of the idée suisse project, this preparation phase took about a year.

Some Findings

Media politicians, media managers, chief editors and journalists — for all four groups of stakeholders under investigation, norms and policies in the context of the remit of promoting public understanding seem to be important. However, we have found strong discrepancies within and between the groups. According to most media politicians under investigation, the remit of promoting public understanding commits media in general and SRG in particular; according to SRG managers, it commits media other than SRG or actors other than the media. Managers' statements tend towards the following propositional reconstruction: 'Public media are not the institutions to solve social and pedagogical problems'. This would mean: SRG fails to do what it says it will and what it is expected to do. Bad end of the story?

Looking more closely at the situated activity, at the writing processes of the journalists under investigation allowed us identify emerging practices — ways out of the conflicts, towards language use meant to meet both public and market expectations. We identified these good practices and their most important counterpart, the critical situations. Whereas critical situations denote exemplary findings of which circumstances could lead to failure in promoting public understanding, good practices stand for potential success in terms of the journalists', chief editors', managers' and politicians' criteria reconstructed in the project.

One example of good practice is what we call the background-recency split. It emerged in an experienced journalist's conflict of basic practices: The journalist had to bring together recent pictures with the need to provide background information. He decided not to compromise, he decided not to overburden the pictures with inappropriate text and the audience with incomprehensible information, but to reach two goals properly in two texts:

- Distinguish between two stories: the recent story and the background story.
- Tell the recent story in the news text, because it fits the recent pictures available.
- Tell the background story because not all of the audience is up-to-date on this item.
- Tell the background story in the anchor text because there are no pictures.

For the news item itself, he takes into account recency, the market and the pictures available. For the anchor woman's introductory moderation, he keeps to the background information he expects to be useful for the less informed of the audience. This is how he practices promoting public understanding.

Interpretation and Transfer

This practice goes against widespread practices in his newsroom. Normally, the journalists leave writing introductory moderations up to the anchor. Thus, the practice is part of the journalist's hidden knowledge: a good practice of an experienced, but isolated professional. It deserves to be detected and to be transferred to the whole media organization, as a situational alternative to the widespread practice of leaving the production of the introduction to an anchor who might have less thematic competence.

How to reach the public and promote public understanding? — Since we located the crucial knowledge (of how to meet market forces and public demands at the same time) at the bottom of the organization, we call the knowledge transfer that we now have to promote a knowledge transfer from the bottom. Cycles of quality will be implemented, which are continuous processes to enhance the language awareness needed to promote public understanding.

References

Perrin, D. (2003). Progression analysis (PA). Investigating writing strategies at the workplace. *Journal of Pragmatics, 35*(6), 907–921.

Perrin, D. (2011). "There are two different stories to tell" — Collaborative text-picture production strategies of TV journalists. *Journal of Pragmatics, 43*(7), 1865–1875.

SECTION 4

TOOLS FOR STUDYING AND SUPPORTING WRITING

Chapter 4.00.01

Introduction: Tools for Studying and Supporting Writing: Technological Advances in Writing Research

Luuk Van Waes and Anne Mangen

The use of computers as writing instruments has not only had a profound effect on writing practice, but has also opened up new possibilities for writing research. During the last decade, for instance, several digital writing tools have been developed that enable precise logging and fine-grained analysis of emerging writing processes. Most of these tools also combine eye movement recordings (eye tracker) with recordings of the writing activity itself. Because very little is known about the interplay of the processes of reading from sources and reading an emergent text, these programs open an important window on the interaction between reading and writing.

In the first part of this section four different logging tools are presented, in combination with different approaches to the analysis of data collected using these programs. In the second part of the section other aspects of writing technology and the use of digital media are discussed. The main focus is on the interaction between reading and writing and the effect of handwriting versus typewriting in the organization of the writing process. Taken together the papers make a strong case for further interdisciplinary research, for the development of both theory and research methods.

Logging Tools

In the first part of this section different logging tools are introduced. The related chapters describe the tools and briefly summarize one or more studies in which the tools have been used. *Eye and Pen* is the first tool that is described. *Eye and Pen* uses

Learning to Write Effectively: Current Trends in European Research
Studies in Writing, Volume 25, 345–349
Copyright © 2012 by Emerald Group Publishing Limited
All rights of reproduction in any form reserved
ISSN: 1572-6304/doi:10.1108/S1572-6304(2012)0000025083

a digitizing tablet making a synchronous recording of handwriting and eye movements during written composition. This enables the researcher to collect data about visual information fixated during pauses as well as during the actual writing act. Alamargot present three studies illustrating the wide range of research objectives that can be addressed using this logging device.

EyeWrite is the second program that is presented. In contrast to reading research, the use of eye tracking is relatively new in the domain of writing research. The main reason for this is a technical one. When composing on a computer editing, line-wrapping and scrolling words do not retain their initial position on the screen. Therefore, methods used in reading research in which a static text is read will not work in this context. *EyeWrite* provides a technical solution to this problem. As Torrance explains, the program creates a logging environment that records where writers look within their emerging text. This provides a way of visualizing reading during writing offering multiple possibilities for research in this domain.

A third program, *ScriptLog*, is a keylogging program. Johansson et al. describe a study that uses ScriptLog combined with other software to explore reading during writing in comparison with reading static texts. They show that reading during text production consists of several different reading patterns not found in regular reading (e.g. many more backward movements within the text).

The last tool presented in this section is *Inputlog*. In contrast to the other logging programs, this logging tool does not record writing activities in a custom-designed word processor, but logs all keyboard and mouse events in whatever Windows environment. Also dictated text — using Dragon Naturally Speaking as a dictating device — can be captured. Leijten and Van Waes describe the main functions of the program and also illustrate how the program generates a revision analysis for texts produced in MS Word.

Comparing the fluency in second-language (L2) and in mother-tongue (L1) writing processes is a central concern in the writing research community, and an area in which the use of keylogging tools might provide considerable advantages. In her contribution, Mutta investigates how fluency in writing activity is linked with pausing behaviour in writers composing their first and a foreign language. The study employs ScriptLog in combination with verbal protocols to collect data both on writers' online writing process and on the writers' own verbalizations of sequences of thought.

Reading and Writing|Handwriting and Typewriting

Digital writing technologies — most prominently, the computer — alter the processes involved in written text production at many levels and in many different ways. Research on the differences between handwriting and typewriting is still in its infancy, and studies assessing the potential benefits and constraints of one and the other writing condition report conflicting findings. With regard to the optimal use of new writing technologies for pedagogical purposes, questions concerning advantages and disadvantages of handwriting and typewriting are of major importance. The research projects included in the section below represent some crucial first steps of exploring this urgent and complex topic.

Handwriting and typewriting may be compared in a number of ways. In research different levels and phases of the writing are addressed to compare both writing modes: from targeting the neural pathways involved to studying the potential effect of input mode on rhetorical aspects of written text production. From a neuro-scientific point of view, handwriting and typewriting are clearly distinct modes of writing involving very different sensorimotor processes. Whereas handwriting requires that the writer perform a movement which completely defines the shape of each letter, typewriting involves locating and pressing keys on a keyboard. Both modes of writing create an association between a specific character and a pointing movement, but in typewriting there is nothing in the movement itself informing the writer about the visual shape of the character. In their paper *Handwriting versus Typewriting: Behavioural and Cerebral Consequences in Letter Recognition*, Velay and Longcamp report findings from behavioural experiments showing how learning to write letters or characters by handwriting or by typewriting gives rise to different recognition performances on subsequent visual letter recognition tests. Neuro-imaging experiments using fMRI further confirm that handwriting memory facilitates the visual discrimination between characters and their mirror images for longer periods than typewriting memory.

The physical movements during handwriting and typewriting differ in terms of trajectories and acceleration patterns. Additionally, the two input modes differ with regard to the relation between the spatial location of the writer's physical input, his/her visual attention and the visual feedback provided by the emergent text. In handwriting, the visual attention of the writer is closely aligned with and in spatiotemporal contiguity with the physical text production. In typewriting, however, there is a spatial (and potentially temporal) dissociation between the visual feedback on the monitor and the location of the physical movement of typing. Comparing handwriting and typewriting at a global text production level, Johansson et al. ('text production in handwriting vs. computer') focus on how this difference in visual feedback from the emerging text in the two writing modes influences text production processes in terms of pause proportion and to what extent writers read their own emerging text.

The next research project, *The Visual Writer*, also studies the interplay between visual perception and text production. Posing the research question, 'What is the role of visual feedback in the writing process', Oxborough explores the role of visual feedback during typewriting by comparing two writing conditions: with and without visual feedback. Data is collected by combining eye tracking and keylogging methods, and the project aims at providing new knowledge about which functions of the writing process are lost or hard to uphold when the writer is deprived of visual feedback, as well as how writers adapt to this deprivation condition during writing. In addition, the project described will study changes in visual attention from a developmental perspective, by comparing writers of different ages and different levels of experience.

In *Computer Capture of Writing Under Keyboard and Handwriting Conditions*, Spelman Miller reports a study investigating idea generation and formulation (translation) in both handwriting and keyboard conditions among novice academic writers. Taking a discourse-focussed approach, the author supplements the grammatical approaches typically focusing on morphological and syntactic status of letter and word sequences produced. In this project data from *Inputlog* is complemented by data collection from writers using a digital tablet and the Eye and Pen software. These data are analysed in terms of distribution and sequencing of processes, and their relationship with the textual output.

Memory for word location in reading is well documented, and recent research has also indicated the existence of word-location memory in writing. In *Memory for Word Location: Studies in Writing*, Le Bigot et al. present a synthesis of four experiments conducted in order to advance our comprehension of this kind of memory in writing. The four experiments all followed a two-phase procedure, wherein the subjects first wrote (by hand) one-page texts, and in the second phase had to indicate (on a blank sheet of paper) the location of some of the words contained in this text. The experiments addressed three issues: first, they show the existence of memory for word location in writing; second, they analyse the nature of the resources involved in the construction of the text representation supporting this kind of memory and third they examine the kind of information that is involved in the construction of this representation. Taken together, the studies provide evidence for the existence of memory for word location in writing while at the same time providing further knowledge about what processes are engaged in this kind of memory. An interesting question in the light of the present discussion concerns the impact of typewriting and facilities such as word processing on the memory for word location.

Computers provide a range of new options for text production and presentation, of which PowerPoint is one prominent example. As both students and professors will attest, this presentation mode entails a sketchy, fragmented form of writing which is typically dependent on and integrated in an oral presentation. Observing how different PowerPoint is from more conventional text production, Paoletti (*Writing with PowerPoint*) poses several intriguing research questions: what criteria do university lecturers apply when composing PowerPoint slides? For instance, do they distinguish between a face-to-face and a stand-alone presentation (which can be used independently of the oral presentation)? And, how do the writers cope with the risk of misunderstanding among students? Paoletti's study uses structured interviews in order to collect data on university lecturers' opinions of, and experience with, using PowerPoint for conference paper and thesis presentation, and in lectures.

One Step Forward

Writing research has always been characterized by interdisciplinarity. New technological devices used in writing and writing research have only increased the need to integrate developments in related research areas into writing research. Perrin and Wildi's chapter *Modelling Writing Phases* is a fine illustration of this need for interdisciplinary collaboration, in this case with statisticians. As described above, the logging of writing process result in large data collections that are sometimes hard to analyse. In their research Perrin and Wildi collected data in different natural settings, resulting in three extensive corpora of educational and professional writing. In their chapter they suggest a method to explore these kinds of data by introducing new statistical techniques that facilitate different types of analyses. Based on advanced statistical methodology they try to provide a solid foundation for good practice models of writing processes.

García-Martín and García (*Design of An Open Corpus and Computer Tool for Writing Development and Instruction Among 8 to 16 Years Old Students With and Without Learning Disabilities*) also collected an extensive computerized corpus of writing data, in this case texts from students with and without Learning Disabilities. They approach their data more from a developmental and comparative perspective. Leaning on concepts taken from psychology and linguistics they propose (automated) techniques for analysing this kind of data and gain more insight into the quality, productivity, structure and coherence of written texts.

In *Developing Writing Through Observation of Writing Processes using Keystroke Logging* Lindgren and Sullivan show that logged data can also be used to assist learners to develop their writing skills. Their chapter integrates recent insights from pedagogy about observational learning by creating a situation in which writers can focus on how they write. Using keystroke-logging tools writers can observe their own process (and discuss it with peers). The studies they present illustrate that both younger and more adult students benefit from this type of intervention.

In the final chapter (*The Haptics of Writing: Cross-Disciplinary Exploration of the Impact of Writing Technologies on the Cognitive-Sensorimotor Processes Involved in Writing*), Mangen and Velay examine the specific role of the physically tangible writing device (pen on paper; computer mouse and keyboard; writing tablet). The researchers claim that a good understanding of what is entailed in the digitization of writing mandates an outspoken transdisciplinary approach. In their chapter they explore interesting perspectives for writing research by integrating theories and methods from fields such as experimental psychology, cognitive neuroscience, phenomenology and philosophy of mind.

Taken as a whole, the contributions of this section indicate that the development of digital writing tools has had a major impact on writing research, and has contributed to substantial scientific progress in the field theoretically, methodologically and empirically.

Chapter 4.00.02

Eye and Pen: A Device to Assess the Temporal Course of Writing Production — Three Studies

Denis Alamargot

Chesnet and Alamargot (2005) proposed a new method for studying the time course of written production from source, by considering reading during writing and the relationships between these two activities. The 'Eye and Pen' device makes a synchronous recording of handwriting and eye movements during written composition. We argue that it complements existing online methods by providing a fine-grained description of the visual information fixated during pauses as well as during the actual writing act. This device can contribute to the exploration of several research issues, since it can be used to investigate the role of the text produced so far and the documentary sources displayed in the task environment (Alamargot, Chesnet, Dansac, & Ros, 2006).

By now three main pilot studies have been conducted in order to understand the course of processing during text production from source, actually: (i) the visual processing during writing pauses, (ii) the visual processing in parallel with handwriting execution and (ii) the impact of the compositional expertise on these pausing/parallel processing.

In the first pilot study, Alamargot, Dansac, Ros, and Chuy (2005) investigated the influence of working memory capacity on the dynamics of text composition from source, notably the strategy used by writers to consult the sources and the text produced so far. Twenty-five graduate students composed a procedural text explaining how to assemble a model turbine. They were free to consult a documentary source, featuring captioned pictures of turbine parts and assembly steps, at any time. Graphomotor and eye movements were recorded using 'Eye and Pen' software with an eye tracker and digitizing tablet. Results showed that writers with high working memory capacity used a different strategy to explore the visual source, making longer

Learning to Write Effectively: Current Trends in European Research
Studies in Writing, Volume 25, 351–353
ISSN: 1572-6304/doi:10.1108/S1572-6304(2012)0000025084

pauses and producing more detailed procedures. The role of working memory in text composition from source is discussed with regard to the number of units that have to be held in memory in order to achieve communicative goals.

In the second study, Alamargot, Dansac, Chesnet, and Fayol (2007) show that parallel processing can occur before and after pauses during a procedural text production. Although writing pauses can be considered as main location of high-level processes, the latter can also occur in parallel with graphomotor execution. When a writer composes a text from source documents, the combined analysis of eye and pen movements made it possible to identify some of these parallel processes and infer their nature. Results show (1) that parallel processes differ in nature according to whether they precede or follow a writing pause and (2) that the frequency and duration of parallel processing phases depend partly on the writer's cognitive capacities (as assessed by graphomotor execution, Working Memory Writing Span, lexical fluency and domain knowledge).

The third study, conducted by Alamargot, Plane, Lambert, and Chesnet (2010) aimed at using eye and pen movements to trace the development of writing expertise by a 7th, 9th and 12th grader, graduate student and professional writer (see also Alamargot & Lebrave, 2010). This study was designed to enhance our understanding of the changing relationship between low- and high-level writing processes in the course of development. A dual description of writing processes was undertaken, based on (a) the respective time courses of these processes, as assessed by an analysis of eye and pen movements and (b) the semantic characteristics of the writers' scripts. To conduct a more fine-grained description of processing strategies, a 'case study' approach was adopted, whereby a comprehensive range of measures was used to assess processes within five writers with different levels of expertise. The task was to continue writing a story based on excerpt from a source document (incipit). The main results showed two developmental patterns linked to expertise: (a) a gradual acceleration in low- and high-level processing (pauses, flow), associated with (b) changes in the way the previous text was (re)read (eye movements).

To conclude, the study of the commitment of reading during writing provides important information about the dynamics of writing processes based on visual information. By now, the investigations we made focused on the strategy of text production from source, and mostly on the text content planning. It is possible to use the same dispositive to investigate lower level of processing, as the formulation process. Forthcoming research will concern the management of grammatical flexions, actually the role of the previous trace for subject-verb agreement.

References

Alamargot, D., Chesnet, D., Dansac, C., & Ros, C. (2006). Eye and Pen: A new device to study reading during writing. *Behavior Research Methods, 38*(2), 287–299.

Alamargot, D., Dansac, C., Chesnet, D., & Fayol, M. (2007). Parallel processing before and after pauses: A combined analysis of graphomotor and eye movements during procedural text production. In M. Torrance, L. V. Waes & D. Galbraith (Eds.), *Writing and cognition: Research and applications* (pp. 13–29). Amsterdam: Elsevier.

Alamargot, D., Dansac, C., Ros, C., & Chuy, M. (2005). Rédiger un texte procédural à partir de sources: relations entre l'empan de mémoire de travail et l'activité oculaire du scripteur. In D. Alamargot, P. Terrier & J. M. Cellier (Eds.), *Production, compréhension et usages des écrits techniques au travail.* Toulouse: Octarès.

Alamargot, D., Plane, S., Lambert, E., & Chesnet, D. (2010). Using eye and pen movements to trace the development of writing expertise: Case studies of a seventh, ninth and twelfth grader, graduate student, and professional writer. *Reading and writing, 23*(7), 853–888.

Alamargot, D., & Lebrave, J. L. (2010). The study of professional writing: A joint contribution from cognitive psychology and genetic criticism. *European Psychologist, 15*(1), 12–22.

Chesnet, D., & Alamargot, D. (2005). Analyse en temps réel des activités oculaires et graphomotrices du scripteur. Intérêt du dispositif 'Eye and pen'. *L'année psychologique, 105*(3), 477–520.

Chapter 4.00.03

EyeWrite — A Tool for Recording Writers' Eye Movements

Mark Torrance

Written production differs from speech in that it generates a permanent, visible trace. This not only affects the nature of the communication that is achieved through text, but also the processes by which it is produced. Writers are able to review what they have said in a way that is impossible in speech. This can occur at a local level — the detection of typos in the word currently being written, for example — or more globally, allowing more substantial changes to be made before the text seen by readers. The text produced also has the potential to act as external memory, providing information about what parts of the writers intended message have already been inscribed, and possibly cueing further content generation.

Little is known, however, about the detail of how writers use visual input from the text that they have already produced. What is needed is a method for recording where writers look within their text.

Figure 1 shows a short sequence of eye movements from a writer composing a text about global warming. She writes 'world' at the end of the clause 'Global warming has been increasing the temperature of the world', then pauses, looks back and forth within the sentence she has just written, and then appends 'in recent years'. This short paper describes a method by which this kind of data can be captured.

Several manufacturers produce eye trackers that are capable of recording fixations to word-level accuracy (and possibly higher) with text displayed in normal sized font on a computer screen, and without the need to constrain the writer's head. Interpreting the data generated by tracking writers' eye movements is, however, more problematic. Methods used in reading research based on pre-defining areas of interest within a static text will not work here. Except for very constrained tasks each participant will produce different text. Moreover, when composing by typing

Learning to Write Effectively: Current Trends in European Research
Studies in Writing, Volume 25, 355–357
ISSN: 1572-6304/doi:10.1108/S1572-6304(2012)0000025085

multi-sentence texts on a computer (our focus here), editing, line wrapping and scrolling all mean that words do not retain their initial position on the screen.

The data reported in Figure 1 could be extracted 'manually' by overlaying fixation information on a screen-dump video of the developing text. This functionality is provided by the software that accompanies all commercial eye trackers. However, serious theory building and testing requires analysis of a very large number of fixations across samples of writers. For example, several studies have found that writers pause for longer at sentence boundaries than at word boundaries (e.g. Chanquoy, Foulin, & Fayol, 1996). We have a strong theory about what tends to occur during these pauses. One possibility is that they tend to be associated with looking back within the existing text. It would be useful to know, therefore, both how often this is the case, and where in the text-produced-so-far these fixations tend to occur. It is also useful to know not just the location of the work that is being fixated, but exactly what that word is. This then permits exploration of, for example, word frequency and length effects, which in turn gives insight into the level to which fixated words are being processed. Manually extracting the data needed to address these kinds of questions from a video overlay would be prohibitively time consuming.

EyeWrite (Simpson & Torrance, 2007) takes the form of custom code running within SR Research's Experiment Builder programming environment. It therefore only works in conjunction with SR Research's EyeLink eye trackers, although the principles on which it is based could easily be adopted in other software/hardware contexts. It has two components: a basic editor which collects eye movement and keystroke data while writers compose text, and an analysis program that takes output from the editor and generates a data file. The data file describes three types of event — fixation onsets, character key-presses and cursor key-presses (all cursor movement is by cursor key). Each of these events is associated with a timestamp, accurate to a few milliseconds. For fixations, the data file gives fixation duration, distance of fixation (in characters, words, sentences, paragraphs) from the last-typed character, the text that is being fixated and a number of other useful variables. For key-presses the data file gives the key that is being pressed and its location (relative to start of text), time since last key press and several other variables.

The program works on a relatively straightforward principle. The screen is understood as a grid (of variable size depending on line spacing, font size and the dimensions of the typing window, all of which can be varied). Characters are displayed in a non-proportional font such that each character occupies exactly one

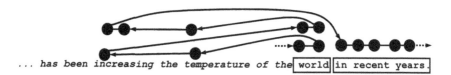

Figure 1: Eye movement during composing. Black circles represent short periods during which the writer's gaze was fixed on the text. All fixations were on the text but are shown above for clarity.

grid square. Grid squares are indexed from zero to the total number of characters in the text produced so far. Addition or deletion of a character, line wrapping and scrolling all change which character is associated with which grid square. For example, returning back to correct a typo in the third word of a text will change the character associated with each grid square subsequent to the location at which the new character was added. Therefore, at any particular point in time the character in that square, and the characters in all other squares, are known. Grid squares have invariant screen co-ordinates. Therefore, if we know the co-ordinates of the point on the screen at which a writer is gazing — information that is provided directly by the eye tracker — we know exactly which character (and word, and sentence) is being fixated at any particular time.

The resulting data allows us to explore short episodes during composition, as illustrated in Figure 1. Crucially, however, it also allows relatively swift generation of aggregate data that summarizes activity within and across many compositions. For example, preliminary findings from research using EyeWrite (Torrance & Wengelin, 2010; Wengelin et al., 2009) provides some insight into why pausing tends to occur more at sentence than at word boundaries. We found that, compared to eye movements at word boundaries, eye movements that occur immediately after the completion of a sentence are more likely to show gaze shifting to text already produced and also that the text that is looked at during these fixations tends to be at a greater distance from the last-typed character (i.e. further back within the text).

References

Chanquoy, L., Foulin, J. N., & Fayol, M. (1996). Writing in adults: A real-time approach. In G. Rijlaarsdam, H. van den Bergh & M. Couzin (Eds.), *Theories, models and methodology in writing research* (pp. 36–44). Amsterdam: Amsterdam University Press.

Simpson, S., & Torrance, M. (2007). EyeWrite (Version 5.1).

Torrance, M., & Wengelin, A. (2010). Writers' eye movements. In C. Bazerman, R. Krut, K. Lunsford, S. McLeod, S. Null, P. Rogers & A. Stansell (Eds.), *Traditions of writing research* (pp. 394–405). New York, NY: Routledge.

Wengelin, A., Torrance, M., Holmqvist, K., Simpson, S., Galbraith, D., Johansson, V., et al. (2009). Combined eyetracking and keystroke-logging methods for studying cognitive processes in text production. *Behavior Research Methods, 41*(2), 337–351.

Chapter 4.00.04

Reading During Text Production

Roger Johansson, Victoria Johansson, Åsa Wengelin
and Kenneth Holmqvist

The reading of one's own emerging text is an activity with different goals than, for instance, reading to understand and interpret a text written by someone else. The goal of text composition is to create a coherent and satisfactory text dependent on several variables, such as genre, audience and topic. Therefore, the reading of one's own emerging text is rarely performed in a straightforward fashion from the beginning to the end and it is unclear what cognitive processes underlie the activity of reading during writing.

Since no definitions of reading during ongoing text production have been established, we have in the current study chosen to compare it with the reading of a finished text written by someone else, to at all be able to get a sense of how these activities relate to each other. These comparisons are not intended to define the concept of reading during one's own emerging text. It will only be used as a means to at all be able to evaluate and explain how the concept of reading during ongoing text production works, and to investigate if it at all is meaningful in this context to use the established concept of reading and its' traditional eye movement measures (Johansson, Johansson, Wengelin, & Holmqvist, 2008).

Method

Twenty-eight university students, 13 females and 15 males participated in the experiment. As reported in Johansson, Wengelin, Johansson, and Holmqvist (2010) the gaze behaviour during text production is heavily influenced by typing skill and how much you can/do look at the monitor during the writing. Therefore the

Learning to Write Effectively: Current Trends in European Research
Studies in Writing, Volume 25, 359–361
Copyright © 2012 by Emerald Group Publishing Limited
All rights of reproduction in any form reserved
ISSN: 1572-6304/doi:10.1108/S1572-6304(2012)0000025086

participants were as in Johansson et al. (2010) separated into 'monitor gazers' and 'keyboard gazers'.

Each participant wrote one expository text about typical problems in a school setting — the text-production task — using the keystroke-logging software ScriptLog (cf. Strömqvist, Holmqvist, Johansson, Karlsson, & Wengelin, 2006), and read one very similar text on the same subject written by someone else — the reading task.

The recording of eye movements and text composition was synchronized as described in Wengelin et al. (2009).

Analysis

Apart from regular forward reading, eye movement patterns that looked like backward reading and irregular patterns moving both forward and backward were frequently found in the eye movement data from the text-production task. Additionally, eye movements following the inscription point were frequent for the monitor gazers. These patterns were virtually not found in the reading task, where regular forward reading was the only systematic eye movement pattern found. Therefore, task comparisons were only performed on regular forward reading. Another important aspect of reading during one's own emerging text is that reading is frequently performed in parallel with typing (especially for monitor gazers). Forward reading in the text-production task was therefore also broken down into reading in pauses and reading while writing (cf. Johansson et al., 2010).

Eye movements in reading consist of a series of rapid jumps from one word to another. It is between these jumps, in the fixations, that information is acquired. The most common measure in reading studies is the duration of these fixations, which is assumed to be an indicator of cognitive processing (Rayner, 1998). Comparisons of fixation durations are the main focus in this study. However, also regressions are considered. Regressions are single eye movements that move backward on the same line, to previous lines or within the word currently being fixated. In traditional reading research regressions are assumed to occur when the reader is having difficulty in lexically activating a word or do not understand the text (Rayner, 1998).

Results

ANOVAS revealed significant differences for average fixation durations between the text-production task and the reading task ($p < 0.001$). Further, an interaction effect between the tasks and gazer type (monitor/keyboard) revealed that this difference was almost entirely explained by fixation durations for monitor gazers who read while they were writing. In average the fixation duration in these cases was 389 milliseconds, while the averages in all the other cases ranged between 231 and 249 milliseconds, which are typical durations in traditional reading research (Rayner, 1998).

Additionally, it was found that regressions to previous lines were significantly ($p<0.001$) more frequent in the text-production task (mean: 8.7%) than in the reading task (mean: 1.5%). Post hoc tests also revealed that regressions to previous lines were significantly more frequent ($p<0.001$) for reading while writing than for reading in pauses. No significant differences were found for regressions on the same line or within words.

Discussion

Based on eye movement patterns we have shown that reading during text production appear to consist of several different reading patterns not found in regular reading of static texts (e.g. backward reading, irregular patterns moving back and forth and following the inscription point). A detailed analysis of regular forward reading revealed that fixation durations were significantly longer in the text-production task for monitor gazers who read in parallel with their writing. We propose that this result indicates that more cognitive capacity is needed because two processes — text composing and reading — are active at the same time. Additionally, regressions to previous lines in the text were much more frequent in the text-production task, especially when reading occurred in parallel with typing. It is unlikely that these regressions were triggered by problems related to text comprehension (as they would be in traditional reading research). We suggest that they are instead caused by a need to check for coherence or to make revisions.

On the basis of these results we propose that the reading of one's own emerging text is a very different activity than the regular reading of static texts and that the established eye movement definitions from traditional reading research (e.g. Rayner, 1998) must be interpreted differently.

References

Johansson, R., Johansson, V., Wengelin, Å., & Holmqvist, K. (2008). *Reading during writing: Four groups of writers*. Working Papers 53 (pp. 43–59), Department of Linguistics, Lund University, Lund, Sweden.

Johansson, R., Wengelin, Å., Johansson, V., & Holmqvist, K. (2010). Looking at the keyboard or the monitor: Relationship with text production processes. *Reading and Writing: An Interdisciplinary Journal, 23*(7), 835–851.

Rayner, K. (1998). Eye movements in reading and information processing: 20 years of research. *Psychological Bulletin, 124*(3), 372–422.

Strömqvist, S., Holmqvist, K., Johansson, V., Karlsson, H., & Wengelin, Å. (2006). What keystroke logging can reveal about writing. In K. Sullivan & E. Lindgren (Eds.), *Computer key-stroke logging and writing: Methods and applications* (pp. 45–72). Amsterdam: Elsevier.

Wengelin, Å., Torrance, M., Holmqvist, K., Simpson, S., Galbraith, D., Johansson, V., & Johansson, R. (2009). Combined eye-tracking and keystroke-logging methods for studying cognitive processes in text production. *Behavior Research Methods, 41*(2), 337–351.

Chapter 4.00.05

Inputlog 4.0: Keystroke Logging in Writing Research

Mariëlle Leijten and Luuk Van Waes

Logging programs enable researchers to accurately register and reconstruct the writing processes of writers who compose texts on the computer (Leijten & Van Waes, 2006; Sullivan & Lindgren, 2006). The basic concept of the different logging tools that have been developed is more or less comparable. First, the keystroke logging tools register all keystrokes and mouse movements. During the writing process these basic data are stored for later processing. Unlike other methods (e.g. think-aloud protocols) online data collection by keystroke logging tools is relatively non-obtrusive. Therefore, it ensures an ecologically valid research context. In this article we briefly describe Inputlog, a logging tool for writing process research developed for Windows environments. We present the most important characteristics of Inputlog 4.0, and shortly illustrate the program's functionality.

Inputlog allows researchers to record writing process data, generate various data files, integrate various types of data from other programs and playback the recorded session. The most distinguishing characteristics of Inputlog to date are its integration with Microsoft Word, the possibilities to identify and log in other Windows environments, the parsing technology, the standard XML structure of the output and the integration of speech recognition (Dragon Naturally Speaking, Nuance).

In this paper we elaborate briefly on the program's main functions. A more detailed description can be found in the online manual (www.inputlog.net).

Learning to Write Effectively: Current Trends in European Research
Studies in Writing, Volume 25, 363–366
Copyright © 2012 by Emerald Group Publishing Limited
All rights of reproduction in any form reserved
ISSN: 1572-6304/doi:10.1108/S1572-6304(2012)0000025087

Record a Writing Session

Inputlog enables researchers to record data of a writing session in Microsoft Word and other Windows based programs (e.g. Internet Explorer, Mozilla, PowerPoint, etc.). Inputlog logs every keystroke, every mouse movement and click, and-if available-speech input from Dragon Naturally Speaking. Furthermore, all the windows that a writer opens in different programs are identified and logged (see Figure 1). So, if a writer uses Google when writing a report, Inputlog logs the URL of the web page accessed together with a time stamp. This enables researchers, for instance, to take writers' search behaviour into account or to monitor writing from multiple online sources.

Generate Data Files for Statistical, Text, Pause and Mode Analyses

Inputlog 4.0 offers five different data analyses. The output files are all XML-based files, which can be converted to Excel files or exported to SPSS for further analyses.

1. General file: An XML file containing basic logging information of the writing session in which every line represents an input action (keyboard, mouse click or movement and-if present — speech, window information); for every input action, the session information is stored together with an identification of the start and end time of the input (key in and key out), the pause time that followed it, and — for a mouse operation — the xy-value of the screen position (see Figure 1).
2. Linear text: A plain linear text in XML-format containing the complete linear production of the text (keyboard and speech) including mouse movements and pauses. The threshold for the pause length can be adapted to meet the requirements of a particular study.

Output	Position	Doc length	Start Time	End Time	Pause Time	Pause Location	X	Y
document1.doc - Microsoft Word			0	0	0	7		
T	2	2	5500	5547	5500	5		
e	3	3	5860	5954	360	1		
s	4	4	6079	6172	219	1		
t	5	5	6485	6579	406	1		
SPACE	6	6	9813	9922	3328	2		
Movement			14297	16282	4484	7	174	893
Left Button			16313	16469	31	2	174	893
Internet Explorer			16313	16313	0	7		
www.google.com			16313	16313	0	7		
u			28907	28985	2063	7		
n			29141	29235	234	1		
i			29407	29469	266	1		
v			29704	29782	297	1		

Figure 1: Example of general file of Inputlog.

3. Summary data: An XML file containing basic statistical information of the writing session on a more aggregated level. Several process characteristics are shown, such as the number, mean and standard deviation of characters, words, sentences and paragraphs produced, pause times (based on the threshold entered in the interface) and the use of the different writing modes.

4. Pause analysis: An XML file containing analyses of every non-scribal period. The threshold for the pauses can be adapted to any user defined level larger than 1 millisecond. Pause data are generated on a more general level: number of pauses, mean and standard deviation of pause length, and on a more specific interval level in which the writing session is divided into 10 equal timeslots. Finally, pauses are summarized per word, sentence and paragraph location.

5. Revision analysis: An XML file containing a basic analysis of the revisions that have taken place during the writing session. At the moment the revision analysis of Inputlog reports: number of revisions, type of revisions, level of revisions, number of words and characters involved in the revision operation, as well as the location of the revisions in relation to the point of utterance.

Integrate Various Types of Data from Other Programs

Inputlog's third tab is Integrate. This module allows researchers to merge different XML output files from other logging and observation programs. At present, Inputlog's output can be integrated with Dragon Naturally Speaking and EyeWrite. The integration results in a single XML file or Excel file that can be used for further analysis.

Playback the Recorded Session at Different Speeds

The final tab of the Inputlog interface is the play function. A recorded writing session can be replayed using, the IDF file as a source file. In the basic version of Inputlog researchers can replay the logging file as it was recorded. However, it should be noted that the screen settings should be exactly the same before and after logging. In the Light, Minimal, Plus and Full versions the text can be replayed in a separate module that consists of four windows:

1. Text process window: The writing session can be replayed at different speeds. It can be played back exactly as it was recorded (in real time) or at a default speed, during which each inter-key interval is limited to 150 ms. It can also be replayed revision by revision.

2. Revision data window: The revision data is represented in an Excel-like matrix, showing the main characteristics of each revision. All variables — given and added — can be changed and saved.

3. Linear representation window: The linear representation of the text is based on the S-notation by Kollberg and Severinson (Severinson Eklundh & Kollberg, 1996).

4. Graphic representation window: Finally, we have opted for a graphical representation of the writing process. The graphical representation is a visual representation of the number of characters that are produced and deleted at each moment during the writing process. The cursor position and the pauses longer than a predefined threshold value are also shown. The graphical representation is based on a combination of Perrin's (2003) progress analysis and Lindgrens' (2007) interactive representation via a Geographical Information System.

Conclusion

This article briefly describes the main functions of Inputlog 4.0. We wanted to show how the program might be a valuable tool for researchers interested in using keystroke logging as a method for writing process research. At the moment the program is mainly used by researchers interested in cognitive processes, developmental writing, translation studies, L1 and L2 writing processes, etc. However, in our opinion the use of keystroke logging should not be limited to research. It can also be of great value as a pedagogical tool, because it makes pupils and students aware of the process characteristics of writing (see also Sullivan & Lindgren, 2006). For example, the replay function in keystroke logging programs can be used to elicit certain writing strategies in order to make writers more aware of their own approach to a writing task. If possible this should be done in combination with introspective interviews as a basis for a discussion with peer writers. Also, giving students the opportunity to look at the way in which professional writers develop their ideas while writing and show them their technical and strategic expertise, might be a very inspiring activity in a training or educational.

We welcome all writing researchers and tutors to try the program. Inputlog is freely distributed for academic research purposes and can be downloaded from the website www.inputlog.net.

References

Leijten, M., & Van Waes, L. (2006). Inputlog: New perspectives on the logging of on-line writing. In K. P. H. Sullivan & E. Lindgren (Eds.), *Computer key-stroke logging and writing: Methods and applications* (Vol. 18, pp. 73–94). Oxford: Elsevier.

Lindgren, E. (2007). GIS for writing: Applying geographic information system techniques to data-mine writing's cognitive processes. In M. Torrance, L. Van Waes & D. Galbraith (Eds.), *Writing and cognition: Methods and applications* (Vol. 20). Oxford: Elsevier.

Perrin, D. (2003). Progression analysis: Investigating writing strategies at the workplace. *Journal of Pragmatics, 35*(6), 907–921.

Severinson Eklundh, K. S., & Kollberg, P. (1996). Computer tools for tracing the writing process: From keystroke records to S-notation. In G. Rijlaarsdam, H. Van den Bergh & M. Couzijn (Eds.), *Models and methodology in writing research* (pp. 526–541). Amsterdam: Amsterdam University Press.

Sullivan, K. P. H., & Lindgren, E. (2006). *Computer key-stroke logging and writing*. Oxford: Elsevier Science.

Chapter 4.00.06

Fluency in Second-Language and in Mother-Tongue Writing Processes

Maarit Mutta

New technology has enabled a more precise analysis of writing processes when using chronometric studies, for instance, in analysing online processes in writing. The limited capacity forces the writer to choose which processes s/he favours when producing a text rapidly under great pressure. The analysis of verbal fluency is closely related to the writer's textual organization at micro- and macro-structural levels. The writer tries to control the processes of conceptual, internal representations and ideas, and then convert them into language, which means manifold ideas being converted into linear text.

My research deals with the fluency of writing processes in Second Language compared with the fluency of writing processes in the mother tongue (Dervin, Johansson, & Mutta, 2007; Mutta, 2006, 2007, 2009). The aim of my research was to investigate how fluency in writing activity is linked with pausal behaviour in the foreign and native language writer's processes of writing from the point of view of how it is manifest through their writing profile.

The corpus consisted of texts written in French by 11 Finnish university students of French (L2) and 6 native speakers of French (ERASMUS students) (L1) from different study fields. All Finnish students were female, their age varying between 20 and 23 (mean age = 21.6 years). Ten students studied French as their major subject, one had Swedish as a major and French as a minor subject. The French ERASMUS students, on the other hand, included four female and two male students between 20 and 24 years of age (mean age = 21.7 years). Their main subjects varied from political science to SLA studies, which means that their group was very heterogeneous. The Finnish students consisted mainly of third year students who participated in a course during which they were to write an academic dissertation of about 15 pages in

Learning to Write Effectively: Current Trends in European Research
Studies in Writing, Volume 25, 367–369
Copyright © 2012 by Emerald Group Publishing Limited
All rights of reproduction in any form reserved
ISSN: 1572-6304/doi:10.1108/S1572-6304(2012)0000025088

French. The ERASMUS students were recruited from several departments in the university. All students participated in the test voluntarily, and furthermore, the Finnish students received feedback on their end product by native teachers. The number of participants reveals that our study was a case study, but on the other hand, the amount of data collected on pausal behaviour by means of the ScriptLog tool was so large that we could draw some generalizable conclusions regarding L2 and L1 pausal behaviour.

Both groups participated in a test that mainly consisted of two parts: (a) an essay (between c. 150–200 words) written on ScriptLog, which is a tool for experimental research on the online process of writing and (b) an oral stimulated recall type verbal protocol where students verbalize in their mother tongue sequences of thought relevant to their task. In other words, each participant wrote one French essay (L2 or L1) and in addition to this, five of the Finnish students wrote one essay in Finnish (L1). Moreover, these Finnish students and all the French students verbalized retrospectively on what they had done just before. In other words, the participants had as a stimulus their own writing appearing on the screen online just after finishing the writing activity. The duration of each verbalization was directly related to the duration of each writing session. The participants were left alone in the test place, and could manipulate the recorder buttons themselves. They were asked to say what they were doing during the writing session and to comment on any relevant items. They could themselves choose which part of the text they wished to comment on. In other words, what received their conscious attention in the writing process. Verbalizations were supposed to reveal some hidden cognitive processes during writing activity, even if not all processes are verbalizable, for instance automaticized processes, that is implicit knowledge and cognitive operations leading to another cannot be detected.

They formed three different groups, namely (1) a group which wrote in L2 (= French), (2) a group which wrote in L2 (= French) and in L1 (= Finnish) who in addition verbalized these sessions, and (3) a group which wrote in L1 (= French) and verbalized the session. The writing sessions were carried out by means of the ScriptLog computer program. This means that all the writing processes were recorded so that afterwards we could analyse the pausal behaviour as well as the end product. The verbalization sessions were audio taped and transcribed.

The results indicated statistical differences between the groups in pausal behaviour, but there also was a lot of individual variation. I could moreover measure a personal pause length for every writer by means of the Hidden Markov Model. The results give support to earlier research findings that L2 writers more often make longer pauses in every location throughout the process than writers in their L1. Nevertheless, there was also a difference between the mother tongues, Finnish and French: the Finns made longer pauses, but the French had more difficulties with lower-level cognitive activities (e.g. orthography) and therefore paused more often within a word. Finally, the different writing profiles did not predict the level of success in the final result (i.e. product). The results showed moreover that at the processing level writing approaches speaking, even if the result is quite different.

References

Dervin, F., Johansson, M., & Mutta, M. (2007). Écriture académique: collaboration multimodale et "co-constructions identitaires" en FLA. In E. Piccardo, G.-L. Baron & A. Gohard-Radenkovic (coor.) Mobilités virtuelles et mobilités géographiques dans l'apprenTICEage : problèmes, enjeux et prespectives. Revue du GERFLINT. Synergies Europe 2/2007: 93–106. Grenoble: IUFM de l'Académie de Grenoble.

Mutta, M. (2006): Yksilölliset taukoprofiilit vieraan kielen kirjoitusprosesseissa. In P. Pietilä, P. Lintunen & H.-M. Järvinen (toim.) Kielenoppija tänään — Language Learners of Today. AFinlA:n vuosikirja 2006. Suomen soveltavan kielitieteen yhdistyksen (AFinLA) julkaisuja n:o 64. Jyväskylä, 379–396. [Individual pausal behaviour profiles in foreign language writing]

Mutta, M. (2007). Un processus cognitif peut en cacher un autre: Étude de cas sur l'aisance rédactionnelle des scripteurs finnophones et francophones. Annales universitatis turkuensis. Série B, tome 300. Turku : Turun yliopisto. Disponible aussi à partir du site https://oa.doria.fi/handle/10024/29185

Mutta, M. (2009). Comportement pausal de scripteurs français et leur parcours stratégique. In D. Alamargot, J. Bouchand, E. Lambert, V. Millogo & C. Beaudet (Eds.), Proceedings of the International Conference « de la France au Québec : l'Ecriture dans tous ses états », Poitiers, France, 12-15 November 2008, [http://www.ecritfrancequebec2008.org/]

Chapter 4.00.07

Handwriting versus Typewriting: Behavioural and Cerebral Consequences in Letter Recognition

Jean-Luc Velay and Marieke Longcamp

Fast and accurate visual recognition of single characters is crucial for efficient reading. The issue of the contribution of handwriting movements to visual perception of characters is of primary importance when one considers the striking change arising in our writing habits with the extended use of computer keyboards, and the progressive disappearance of traditional handwriting from our everyday lives. Computers are now being increasingly used at school, even by very young children in kindergarten. If children happen to learn how to write with a keyboard before they master handwriting, this may affect the way they perceive written language.

From the sensorimotor point of view, handwriting and typing are clearly two distinct ways of writing, and these writing methods may well involve distinct central processes. Handwriting learning requires the writer to perform a movement that completely defines the shape of the letter in order to build an internal model of the character. Once the learning is completed, there exists a unique correspondence between a given printed letter and the movement that is used to write this letter.

Typing is a complex form of spatial learning in which the beginner has to build a 'keypress schema' transforming the visual form of each character into the position of a given key in keyboard centred co-ordinates, and specify the movement required to reach this location. Therefore, learning how to type also creates an association between a character and a pointing movement. However, since the trajectory of the finger to a given key largely depends on its position before movement, the relationship cannot be very specific. Moreover, there is nothing in this pointing movement that informs about the orientation of the characters. The visuomotor

Learning to Write Effectively: Current Trends in European Research
Studies in Writing, Volume 25, 371–373
ISSN: 1572-6304/doi:10.1108/S1572-6304(2012)0000025089

association involved in typewriting should therefore have little contribution to its visual recognition.

Behavioural Studies

We investigated this handwriting/typing distinction in two behavioural studies, one in children and one in adults. First, we trained two groups of 38 pre-readers (aged 3–5 yeras) to copy letters of the alphabet either by hand or by typing them. After three weeks of learning, we ran two recognition tests, one week apart, to compare the letter recognition performances of the two groups. The results showed that in the older children, the handwriting training gave rise to a better letter recognition than the typing training (Longcamp, Zerbato-Poudou, & Velay, 2005).

We then trained adult subjects to write new characters either by copying them or by typing them on a keyboard (Longcamp, Boucard, Gilhodes, & Velay, 2006). After three weeks of training we ran a series of tests requiring visual processing of the characters' orientation. Tests were ran immediately, one week after, and three weeks after the end of the training period. Results showed that when the characters had learned by typing, they were more frequently confused with their mirror images than when they had been written by hand. This handwriting advantage didn't appear immediately, but mostly three weeks after the end of the training.

Behavioural and fMRI Study

The previous behavioural results suggest that the stability of the characters' representation in memory depends on the nature of the motor activity produced during learning. However, the neural basis of this motor contribution had to be investigated. It was the aim of the following study to further explore the contribution of acquired writing knowledge to visual recognition of characters by linking behaviour with brain function and (re)organization (Longcamp et al., 2008). For that purpose, we taught adult subjects how to produce sets of unknown characters either by traditional pen and paper writing or with a computer keyboard, exactly as it was done previously. Following learning, we tested their ability to explicitly recognize the orientation of the newly learned characters and, in addition, we measured their brain activity using fMRI.

The behavioural data confirmed that handwriting memory facilitates the discrimination between characters and their mirror images for longer periods than typewriting memory. Activations associated with discrimination of handwritten with respect to typed characters were assessed. This analysis revealed a restricted set of regions, mostly left lateralized, including bilateral inferior parietal lobules, the left Broca's area, the left dorsal pre-motor cortex, the left post-central gyrus and the medial posterior regions of both hemispheres. When the opposite comparison was performed (i.e. areas more activated by typed than handwritten characters), a single activation was evident in the right supra-marginal gyrus (BA40).

These fMRI results showed that, after learning, the difference in recognition performance between characters learned by handwriting and characters learned by typewriting is related to different neural pathways. They did not inform about the functional changes occurring during learning, however. This was the aim of another study in which we investigated the neural substrates involved by repeated writing of unknown characters using fMRI. We attempted to identify the brain areas that were engaged during handwriting at different times when we learn how to write new characters. Despite the difficulty of studying writing under the neuro-imaging conditions, preliminary results pointed to the parietal and inferior frontal lobes as 'writing centres' (Velay, Longcamp, & Anton, 2007). This study is still in progress with right- and left-handed writers. As a whole, these results might have implications for written language education and rehabilitation.

References

Longcamp, M., Boucard, C., Gilhodes, J. C., Nazarian, B., Anton, J. L., Roth, M., & Velay, J. L. (2008). Learning through hand- or type-writing influences visual recognition of new graphic shapes: Behavioral and functional imaging evidences. *Journal of Cognitive Neuroscience, 20*(5), 802–815.

Longcamp, M., Boucard, C., Gilhodes, J. C., & Velay, J. L. (2006). Remembering the orientation of newly learned characters depends on the associated writing knowledge: A comparison between handwriting and typing. *Human Movement Science, 25*, 646–656.

Longcamp, M., Zerbato-Poudou, M. T., & Velay, J. L. (2005). The influence of writing practice on letter recognition in preschool children: A comparison between handwriting and typing. *Acta Psychologica, 119*, 67–79.

Velay, J. L., Longcamp, M., & Anton, J. L. (2007). Brain areas activated by repeated writing of unknown characters. In J. Phillips, D. Rotgers & R. Ogeil (Eds.). Proceedings of the *13th Conference of the International Graphonomics Society* (pp. 92–96). Melbourne, Australia.

Chapter 4.00.08

Text Production in Handwriting versus Computer Typing

Roger Johansson, Victoria Johansson and Åsa Wengelin

There are several interesting differences between handwriting and computer typing (cf. Grabowski, 2008). For instance, the physical movements during handwriting consist of different trajectories and acceleration patterns depending on the written letter and the writer's visual attention is typically at the same location as the physical production of the text. Movements in computer typing, on the other hand, consist of less dynamic patterns and are executed on spatially different targets. Additionally, there is also a dissociation between the feedback displayed on the monitor and the location of typing execution. As was shown in Johansson, Wengelin, Johansson, and Holmqvist (2010) computer typists can access the visual feedback from their emerging texts to different degrees depending on how skilled typists they are.

The present study is an explorative study that compares global differences in text production patterns between computer typing and handwriting with the main objective to study how the different visual feedback from the emerging text in these two input modes influences the text production process. In this report, the two input modes are studied in regards of pause proportion and to what extent the writers read their own emerging texts.

Method

Ten university students, six females and four males, participated in the experiment. To get a more homogenous and comparable group we only included right-handed participants (in regards of visual feedback in handwriting) and those who mainly looked at the monitor while typing (Johansson et al., 2010).

Learning to Write Effectively: Current Trends in European Research
Studies in Writing, Volume 25, 375–377
Copyright © 2012 by Emerald Group Publishing Limited
All rights of reproduction in any form reserved
ISSN: 1572-6304/doi:10.1108/S1572-6304(2012)0000025090

Each participant wrote two expository texts about two typical problems in a school setting (bullying and cheating). One text was produced in the synchronized combination of keystroke logging and eye tracking as described in Wengelin et al. (2009). The other text was produced on a writing tablet with the eye and pen software (Alamargot, Chesnet, Dansac, & Ros, 2006), which makes it possible to analyse pen traces synchronized with eye movement data. The handwriting task and typing task were balanced for order.

Proportion of pauses (in relation to total time on task) was measured for pauses longer than 2 seconds (cf., Wengelin, 2006). The reason to analyse the time when the writer is not 'writing' is because this time is often related to important cognitive processes (Wengelin, 2006). For example, the writer may plan for future text segments, reflect on her text, review and/or read her own text.

Since eye movements were recorded during both texts it is also possible to study how much the writer reads her emerging text. As described in Johansson et al. (2010) reading in a text production task consists of several complex eye movement patterns on the text. However, only comparisons of the proportion of regular forward reading will be reported in this study.

Results and Discussion

A within subjects ANOVA revealed no significant difference in pause proportion between the two input modes. For proportion reading a significant main effect ($p = 0.05$) revealed that during computer typing the participants spent significantly more of their time reading (mean: 8.4%) than during handwriting (mean: 5.2%).

The results from our comparisons of handwriting and computer typing in expository writing indicate that writers do not differ in pause proportion between these two input modes, but reading is to a higher extent performed in computer typing.

This study was a first exploration of how these two input modes and their different visual feedback of the emerging text affect text production. Larger studies and further analyses on both text level and eye movements have to be performed to detect more detailed differences. For example, are individual differences more important than general differences between handwriting and computer typing? What is the impact of the different possibilities to revise between these two input modes? How do pause and reading distribution relate to syntactic aspects of the text?

References

Alamargot, D., Chesnet, D., Dansac, C., & Ros, C. (2006). Eye and pen: A new device to study the reading during writing. *Behavior Research Methods, Instruments and Computers, 38*(2), 287–299.

Grabowski, J. (2008). The internal structure of university students' keyboard skills. *Journal of writing research, 1*(1), 27–52.

Johansson, R., Wengelin, Å., Johansson, V., & Holmqvist, K. (2010). Looking at the keyboard or the monitor: Relationship with text production processes. *Reading and Writing: An Interdisciplinary Journal, 23*(7), 835–851.

Wengelin, Å. (2006). Examining pauses in writing: Theory, methods and empirical data. In K. Sullivan & E. Lindgren (Eds.), *Computer key-stroke logging and writing* (Vol. 18, pp. 107–130). Studies in Writing. Amsterdam: Elsevier.

Wengelin, Å., Torrance, M., Holmqvist, K., Simpson, S., Galbraith, D., Johansson, V., & Johansson, R. (2009). Combined eye-tracking and keystroke-logging methods for studying cognitive processes in text production. *Behavior Research Methods, 41*(2), 337–351.

Chapter 4.00.09

The Visual Writer

Gunn Helen Ofstad Oxborough

The aim of the master thesis 'What can key logging and eye tracking reveal about revision? — an exploration of aspects of revision from established definition of revision' (Oxborough, 2007) was to explore the notion of revision using key logging and eye tracking methods. The research questions challenged established theories where revision was defined as change in the text. The research assumption for the project was that revision also could involve no change, and empirical data involved identification of revision as a behaviour closely related to reading and monitoring the text, which in some cases lead to change in the text and sometimes not.

The research approach in the master thesis was explorative and allowed for a dynamic exploration of the data and the writing process as it unfolded in real time. One of the conclusions from the study was the need for further study of the inter-action between perception and production in order to understand the complexity and dynamics of the writing process more fully.

The topic of the master thesis is now developed into a PhD project, The Visual Writer, where the interplay between visual perception and text production will be studied. The main research question is: 'What is the role of visual feedback in the writing process?' The focus on visual feedback must be understood in the context of visual attention, a concept which here is defined as the visual behaviour associated with the language process during writing.

In order to explore the role of visual feedback in the writing process, visual feedback will be studied during two conditions of visual feedback: when visual feedback is present and when visual feedback is prevented. The experimental set-up, using eye tracking and key logging combined, allows for investigation of the following two hypotheses:

Which functions are lost or hard to uphold during the deprivation condition?
How do persons adapt to the deprivation condition?

Learning to Write Effectively: Current Trends in European Research
Studies in Writing, Volume 25, 379–381
Copyright © 2012 by Emerald Group Publishing Limited
All rights of reproduction in any form reserved
ISSN: 1572-6304/doi:10.1108/S1572-6304(2012)0000025091

1. Research assumptions regarding which functions are lost or hard to uphold during the deprivation condition includes (1) revision of content, (2) planning before and during writing, (3) fluency in sentence boundaries and (4) spelling mistakes.

   (1) Revision is assumed to be hard to uphold and frequently lost without feedback in all age groups. A consequence of the lack of revision is found in the level of lexical diversity and density which is thought to be lower during the condition without visual feedback, than with feedback.

   (2) Planning during writing differs between subjects of different ages and experience, as studies like the Frog Story (Strömqvist & Verhoeven, 2004) has shown, where the young writer typically uses little time to plan before starting to write, whereas the experienced writer uses longer time. This difference is thought to change, and the initial assumption is that all writers will use more planning time before or immediately after they start writing. Another assumption is that writers will apply different strategies that demand planning to different degrees, and that this will be a consequence of the lack of visual feedback and not experience.

   (3) Fluency in sentence boundaries is thought to suffer, with the consequence being a lack of bridges between sentence content.

   (4) Spelling mistakes are thought to be hard to correct, both because the writer cannot orient in the words misspelled and because no visual detection is available. One assumption is that the lack of opportunity to correct spelling mistakes favours the young writer, where focus on low level processes can be turned towards high level processes, as construction of content.

2. Research assumptions regarding the second hypothesis 'How do the subjects adapt to the deprivation condition?' focus on (1) revision, (2) planning and (3) shift in the nature of communication.

   (1) Revision of content is thought to become more verbal, where correction will be added, as it is in speech, due to the difficulties in correcting larger fragments of text.

   (2) Planning is thought to become longer before starting to write in all age groups, and during writing to be restricted to sentence boundaries or when a complete idea is written.

   (3) Shift in the nature of communication is thought to occur in the sense that an aspect like thinking for writing (Strömqvist, 2009) no longer apply, and where the text is more similar to spoken communication than written communication.

Developmental Perceptive on the Role of Visual Feedback

In addition to the research described above, the role of visual feedback in the writing process is approached through developmental changes in the role of visual feedback. Change in visual attention will be studied by comparing writers of different ages and experience, and the aim is to gain insight into the variability that the role of visual attention and feedback can have in the writing process. The research assumptions regarding possible change in the role of visual feedback and attention are based on a connectionism tradition and theories regarding development, where general development means acquiring skills and applying new strategies. The study will also use the deprivation condition as a research condition. The importance of studying these changes can be understood in the context of Slobin's (1977) statement that 'the study of language during it's unstable or changing phases is an excellent tool for discovering the essence of language itself'.

References

Oxborough, G. H. O. (2007). *What can key logging and eye tracking reveal about revision? — An exploration of aspects of revision from established definition of revision.* Master thesis, University of Stavanger, Norway.

Slobin, D. I. (1977). Language changes in childhood and in history. In J. Macnamara (Ed.), *Language learning and thought* (pp. 185–214). New York, NY: Academic Press.

Strömqvist, S. (2009). *Språkets Öga, om vägarne mellan tankar och ord.* Studentlitteratur, Lund Universitet, Sweden.

Strömqvist, S., & Verhoeven, L. (Eds.). (2004). *Relating events in narrative — Typological and contextual perspectives.* Mahwah, NJ: Lawrence Erlbaum Associates Publishers.

Chapter 4.00.10

Computer Capture of Writing Under Keyboard and Handwriting Conditions

Kristyan Spelman Miller

For several decades research comparing pen and paper and keyboard writing has indicated an array of interesting but contradictory findings concerning the impact of medium on writing process and written product. Most obviously, the facility offered by the word processor to modify text has led to interest in the nature of revisions, be they global, higher-level or local, lower-level edits, and the relationship between these and the quality of the final product. Investigations into differences in planning in word processing and paper conditions also suggest that the writing environment has an impact on the nature and timing of planning behaviour and the distribution of other strategies.

However, given the considerable time which has elapsed since Owston, Murphy, and Wideman (1992) study of word processing, the changes to features of word processors and the way in which today's writers interact with technology, our current research revisits the comparative study of writing in pen and paper and keyboard conditions. By employing computer capture tools, our study addresses the theme of technological advances in writing tools, building on 10 years of writing research using computer keystroke methodology and innovations in the digital capture of handwriting. Our approach takes an essentially discoursal view on the data produced.

Our current study of novice academic writers, first year undergraduates in UK Higher Education, investigates idea generation and formulation (translation) in both handwriting and keyboard conditions. The practical motivation for this is an interest in the literacy practices of young academic writers within a so-called 'new media age'. The use of word processing as the principal writing condition for such writers is in conflict with handwriting as the main condition for examination writing. Clearer

Learning to Write Effectively: Current Trends in European Research
Studies in Writing, Volume 25, 383–385
ISSN: 1572-6304/doi:10.1108/S1572-6304(2012)0000025092

understanding of the activity of writing under both conditions may inform academic and pedagogic practices. This understanding clearly relates to theoretical and empirical explorations of the cognitive demands of writing in different conditions. As Olive, Favart, Beauvais, and Beauvais's (2009) research demonstrates, the impact of factors such as learner awareness of genre on the cognitive effort and fluency of writing offers fertile research ground for furthering theoretical explanations of processing constraints.

In our study of novice academic writers, we focus on the production of argumentative/evaluative texts in handwriting and keyboard conditions in order to compare:

- the management of planning, translating and revision in terms of process sequences
- the nature and frequency of planning
- the nature and frequency of revisions
- the fluency of writing
- the quality and quantity of idea units
- the organization of ideas to meet rhetorical goals
- the presence of authorial stance.

The study therefore combines a focus on defining the nature and sequences of processes with the impact on text quality over different media conditions. Text quality is investigated in terms of idea units and discourse structure in relation to rhetorical goals.

Methodology

Computer keystroke logging is a well-documented research tool. Spelman Miller (2005, 2006) reviews the application of this tool to capture data on the planning, formulating and revising processes of individual writers. As Sullivan & Lindgren (2006) outline, studies using keystroke logging address a number of different writer and task conditions including first and second language writers, writers across different ages, with and without reading and writing disabilities and on different tasks. Keystroke recording allows access to detailed data related to planning, translating and revising activity: the location, distribution and sequencing of processes, and their interaction with textual output. Traditionally, output is considered in grammatical terms, that is the morphological and syntactic status of the letter and word sequences produced. An alternative approach is to consider the text span from semantic, pragmatic and discoursal perspectives.

In previous studies of online writing using keystroke logging pausing and revising are considered from the perspective of the thematic function of the output (Spelman Miller, 2005, p. 304). Certain textual stings are identified as serving topic-related functions in determining the discourse structure of the text, for example in signalling maintenance or shift of topic in response to rhetorical goals. Planning and revision activity around these key devices provides an interesting perspective on the writer's management of connectivity and coherence of text, how s/he responds to the requirements of genre, and how s/he positions her/himself within the writing. Voice, or authorial stance, is of particular interest in the construction of academic text.

The current investigation of keyboard writing (using Inputlog software) is complemented by data collection of the same academic writers composing parallel evaluative academic essay tasks by hand using a digital tablet and Eye and Pen software. Eye and Pen enables the recording of pausing, formulation and revision activity in handwritten text on a graphics tablet. These data are then analysed in terms of distribution and sequencing of processes, and their relationship with the textual output. Discoursal aspects of the output may therefore be compared with that of the keyboard writing in relation to the writer meeting her/his rhetorical goals.

References

Olive, T., Favart, M., Beauvais, C., & Beauvais, L. (2009). Children's cognitive effort and fluency in writing: Effects of genre and of handwriting automatisation. *Learning and Instruction, 19*, 299–308.

Owston, R., Murphy, S., & Wideman, H. (1992). The effects of word processing on students' writing quality and revision strategies. *Research in the Teaching of English, 26*, 249–276.

Spelman Miller, K. (2005). Second language writing research and pedagogy: A role for computer logging? *Computers and Composition, 22*, 297–317.

Spelman Miller, K. (2006). Pausing, productivity and the processing of topic. In K. P. H. Sullivan & E. Lindgren (Eds.), *Computer keystroke logging and writing: Methods and applications* (pp. 131–150). Studies in Writing. Oxford: Elsevier.

Sullivan, K. P. H., & Lindgren, E. (Eds.). (2006). *Computer keystroke logging and writing: Methods and applications*. Studies in Writing. Oxford: Elsevier.

Chapter 4.00.11

Memory for Word Location: Studies in Writing

Nathalie Le Bigot, Jean-Michel Passerault and
Thierry Olive

Almost all of us have experienced memory for word location after writing a text. When searching information in a text we have previously written, it is not necessary to reread the entire text to find information because we remember more or less accurately where an idea we have written is located in our text. Memory for word location has been investigated in reading and is now well documented (Fischer, 1999). Recently existence of such memory for word location was also studied as regards the writing activity (Le Bigot, Passerault, & Olive, 2009). This chapter proposes a synthesis of experiments we conducted in order to better comprehend this kind of memory in writing.

The same general procedure was used for the four experiments presented here. Studies were conducted in two phases: in the first phase, participants wrote one-page long text, and in the second phase, participants had to locate on a white sheet of paper some of the words contained in the text they had produced in the writing phase. In order to examine the construction of text representation supporting memory for word location, different writing conditions were manipulated to measure the impact of such differences on location performances. Number of words that were correctly located (being not outside a pre-defined zone surrounding the target word) evaluated memory for word location.

Three issues were addressed. The first objective was to show the existence of such memory. Le Bigot et al. (2009, exp. 1) demonstrated this existence by showing that participants who first composed a text and were then asked to locate words extracted from their text performed above a chance level established using a computer

Learning to Write Effectively: Current Trends in European Research
Studies in Writing, Volume 25, 387–389
ISSN: 1572-6304/doi:10.1108/S1572-6304(2012)0000025093

simulation and better than participants who did not compose a text but were told the subject of the text.

The second objective was to analyse the nature of resources involved in the construction of the text representation supporting memory for word location. For that purpose, the nature of processes engaged during writing in the construction of such text representation was tested using a dual-task paradigm. Results showed that participants who performed a visual concurrent task while writing had lower recall of words location extracted from their text than participants who performed a verbal, or spatial or none concurrent task. This result suggests that memory for word location is mainly supported by a visual representation of the text.

The third objective was to examine the kind of information that is involved in the construction of this representation. The visual nature of the representation supporting memory for word location suggests that writers construct a mental image of their text by visually processing the written trace of the text. Therefore, another experiment was conducted in order to test whether the visual feedback provided by the written trace is necessary for memory for word location. Three conditions were compared: the first condition, in which writers were able to see the written trace of the text they were composing; the second condition which prevented the writers from seeing the written trace (composing with an inkless pen); and the third condition, in which participants composed their text with no visible trace but they were also subjected to continuous visual noise. This visual noise was expected to disturb visual working memory. Results showed that memory for word location only decreased with visual noise. It is suggested that the written trace is not necessary for constructing the visual representation of the text that supports memory for word location, as writers can construct this representation through visual and kinesthetic feedback during the handwriting process.

Even when they did not see the visual feedback provided by the written trace, writers did, however, continue to access some visuospatial information about the physical structure of their texts. They notably could look at their pen moving across the sheet of paper to visually represent their text. Therefore, the fourth experiment addressed word location performances when no access to visuospatial information about the physical structure of the text is available. In such text production condition, participants can only rely on temporal cues about their text to locate words. Three conditions were tested: one condition assessed chance level; the second one is a standard writing condition in which participants are able to see their text and the third condition assessed location performance when no access to visuospatial information about the physical text. In this last condition, participants read aloud their text to the experimenter who transcribed the text on the sheet without participants being able to see it (dictation condition). Results showed that participants who were able to see the text and thus can construct a visuospatial representation of the text are better to locate words than the one who just can rely on temporal information. Moreover, participants in the dictation condition located words above chance level, showing that they reconstructed location information only from temporal text content representation.

These studies allow underlining the existence of a memory for word location in writing and clarifying the process engaged in such memory. While composing their text, writers engage visual resources to construct the physical text representation and they mainly rely on this representation to locate words in their text. They can also rely on a temporal representation of their composition to reconstruct the location information. Therefore, these findings provide insight into the multidimensional aspect of the representation of a text that has been produced and the processes involved in constructing it. One crucial issue concerns the role of this type of memory in the good achievement of writing process. Obviously, it may facilitate text revision by providing cues for quickly accessing information that has already been written (Piolat, Roussey, & Thunin, 1997). Another important question concerns the impact of writing with computer in the construction of the text representation supporting memory for word location. Such research may indeed be useful to in the development of word processing tools and interfaces.

References

Fischer, M. H. (1999). Memory for word locations in reading. *Memory, 7,* 79–116.

Le Bigot, N., Passerault, J. M., & Olive, T. (2009). Memory for words location in writing. *Psychological Research, 73,* 89–97.

Piolat, A., Roussey, J. Y., & Thunin, O. (1997). Effects on screen presentation on text reading and revising. *International Journal of Human-Computer Studies, 47,* 565–589.

Chapter 4.00.12

Writing with PowerPoint

Gisella Paoletti

In order to communicate with an audience during a conference's talk or a lecture it is becoming increasingly popular to use a fragmented, simplified and shortened form of writing, through a presentation manager like PowerPoint (or Presenter, or Impress and so on).

Such a form of writing concerns texts which generally are not self-sufficient and which will be integrated orally through expansions, comments, explanations, etc. by a presenter. These written texts might have two different forms and designs: one synthetic form for a synchronous face-to-face presentation and one extended form for an asynchronous, stand-alone presentation (Farkas, 2006; Gold, 2002).

PowerPoint (or .ppt) became popular because it is considered a useful tool for communication. Audiences — and students in particular — appreciate it (Bartsch & Cobern, 2003; Blokzijl & Naeff, 2004), because it seems to facilitate and enhance comprehension during lecture listening, because it makes the selection of important ideas explicit, because it highlights hierarchies and connections between ideas, showing the outcome of the speaker reprocessing of the material (Paoletti, Rigutti, & Guglielmelli, 2008).

The problem that I want to address is that, as a consequence of the program characteristics and of the well-known designing guidelines and best practices suggestions (like the famous no more than 6 words × 6 rows), .ppt might be very sketchy, schematic even when it is used asynchronically, without the oral integrations of the speaker, when it is read through some University platform or on a social software like SlideShare. Guidelines and even literature on the topic suggest that the written texts should be shorter — every point like a key-word-less cohesive and coherent than a normal text.

Learning to Write Effectively: Current Trends in European Research
Studies in Writing, Volume 25, 391–393
Copyright © 2012 by Emerald Group Publishing Limited
All rights of reproduction in any form reserved
ISSN: 1572-6304/doi:10.1108/S1572-6304(2012)0000025094

Method

In this investigation I am gathering information on the ways University lecturers write the text of their presentation and on their conceptualization of the functions of .ppt for lecture presentation. Which criteria do they follow during writing? Do they distinguish between a face-to-face presentation and a stand-alone presentation to be used when the oral integration is lacking? How do they cope with the risk of students' misunderstanding?

By means of a structured interview I collected the opinions of a pool of 10 University lecturers. The interview started from the vision of a .ppt which presented and exemplified a list of standards or design criteria regarding both the formats to be used to write a clear page/slide and the design which can be used to highlight the organization of the content and enhance comprehensibility. Subjects have been asked to express their agreement/disagreement with the standards, referring their comments to three different contexts of use of .ppt: a .ppt for a conference or a thesis presentation (that is a face-to-face presentation with strict time constraints) and a .ppt for lecturing (less strict time constraints, either face-to-face or distant presentation). They have also been asked to show and share with the interviewer one .ppt presentation they used during a lecture (therefore a 'good' one).

Preliminary Results

The analysis of the interview transcripts showed that some standards presented in guidelines and literature on .ppt are shared by the subjects. These standards seem to concern every kind of presentation (face-to-face and distant, short and long presentation) and are the format norms which guide the choice of font, colour and other low level details. Other standards are more controversial, for example the standard recommendation of simplicity versus the need to use complex graphs and pictures, or the standard requirement of selection and ordering of topics in contrast with the desire to freely organize exposition according to the need of the moment: some lecturers didn't agree with these statements.

Subjects overtly agreed with the format's standards (size, colour, type of font, font/background colours) even if the analysis of the .ppt they had previously used during lecturing showed that they often infringed those rules, for example by adopting a inappropriate choice of font/background colours, which made hard the discrimination of the written words, in the surplus of written text and graphs into a page/slide, slide which seems to be considered as an information unit and therefore is stuffed with many elements of information.

Agreements on the standards for an optimal selection, organization and presentation of content were more conditional. It is agreed that .ppt should highlight the logical superstructure of ideas, and the search of a difficult but needed equilibrium between synthesis and clearness of writing. Relevant factors seem to be time constraints and presenter experience.

Subjects stated that during a thesis presentation or in a conference (short time, expert audience), the writer must write and present very few main points, showing his/her results in a few words or short phrases. As the receiver is an expert, .ppt can be schematic, quick, formulated by key-words. In these contexts the low cohesion of the written text is not believed to cause misunderstandings. Moreover, the use of multimedia displays (pictures, animations) is considered potentially counter-productive especially when the presenter is a novice, because it takes away time and because sometimes it doesn't add informative content while consuming attentive resources.

For classroom lectures, subjects believe that there are less constraints on time (which is longer) and on the selection of content which can be chosen at the moment.

For longer presentations it is possible to show more complex data and displays. Tables, data, graphs have to be displayed in their entirety because they are otherwise incomplete.

Moreover, during a lecture, it is possible to digress, deciding on the spot the sequence of information so much that many subjects prefer transparencies to .ppt because the last imposes a strict ordering.

In such a context the lecturer (expert) takes advantage of the opportunity offered by .ppt to highlight the content structure, uses the tool to add relevant material which is not published on course manuals. However nobody mentioned a clear distinction between a face-to-face presentation and a stand-alone presentation. Therefore, .ppt published on the web as study material has a hybrid form: it highlights the structure of material, its hierarchical organization (therefore adhering to .ppt literature standards), but infringes other norms by adding extensive definitions and explanations (as one lecturer said: 'I saw that they don't study manuals and so I write more and more'), furthermore graphs and tables are not accompanied by a written comment.

Future development of this investigation will concern the restructuring of the interview. Questions will be added to analyse more in depth the more controversial and crucial standards. Another line of research will regard the effectiveness of the design criteria collected and analysed.

References

Bartsch, R., & Cobern, K. (2003). Effectiveness of PowerPoint presentations in lectures. *Computers & Education*, *41*, 77–86.

Blokzijl, W., & Naeff, R. (2004). The instructor as stagehand: Dutch student responses to PowerPoint. *Business Communication Quarterly*, *67*, 70–78.

Farkas, D. (2006). Toward a better understanding of PowerPoint deck design. *Information Design Journal Document Design*, *14*(2), 162–171.

Gold, R. (2002). Reading PowerPoint. In N. J. Allen (Ed.), *Working with words and images: New steps in an old dance* (pp. 256–270). Wertport, CT: Ablex.

Paoletti, G., Rigutti, S., & Guglielmelli, A. (2008). Presentation manager and Web2.0: Understanding Online presentations. In J. Zumbach, N. Schwartz, T. Seufert & L. Kester (Eds.), *Beyond knowledge: The legacy of competence* (pp. 287–289). Berlin: Springer.

Chapter 4.00.13

Modelling Writing Phases

Daniel Perrin and Marc Wildi

Until now, writing has been described in the research literature as the interplay of situations, strategies and phases — with phases being identifiable temporal procedural units with typical dominant writing actions such as 'formulating' or 'source reading'. Phases are recognized as essential for the success of writing processes. At the same time, most scientific approaches to writing base their phase concepts and phase descriptions on introspection, experiments or single case studies.

The methodology for a rigorous, objectively verifiable analysis of the structure of writing processes and therefore for an empirically testable explanation of the nature and interplay of phases in writing processes has not yet been developed. This is exactly what the research project outlined here aims to do: to explore and to model writing phases based on statistical methodology and thus to provide a solid foundation for good practice models of writing processes — a conditio sine qua non for systematic education in writing (Perrin & Wildi, 2010).

The research question is (1) What are the crucial phases of real-life writing (and their embedded reading) processes? The main subordinate questions (2) What are the key features of the different phases? and (3) What are the main factors determining them? Answering these questions means (a) identifying, (b) describing and (c) explaining the phases of writing processes.

(a) On the identification level of the project, the aim of the research is the theoretically and empirically sound exploration of writing processes in exemplary domains: education, academia, professions.
(b) On the description level, the modelling will be empirically based on information about phases as the crucial structural features of writing processes and on background conditions such as the writing task (i.e. intention, topic, structure),

Learning to Write Effectively: Current Trends in European Research
Studies in Writing, Volume 25, 395–397
ISSN: 1572-6304/doi:10.1108/S1572-6304(2012)0000025095

the task context (e.g. time, collaboration patterns) and the experience of the writers (e.g. school grade or professional status as novice or expert).

(c) On the explanation level, these background conditions can be operationalized in the statistical modelling approach by inclusion of suitably defined explanatory variables. Depending on the particular data structure, our task will be to identify or to adapt existing — or to develop new — statistics that match the data structure and the research purpose(s) as closely as possible (customization principle, see Perrin et al., this volume).

Methodology and Data

In order to answer the research questions, the crucial methodological problem to be solved is: How to identify the phases, features, and factors in an analysis of representative corpora? This aim requires a unified and co-ordinated development of writing research and signal extraction theories and tools — a new interdisciplinary approach of applied linguistics with mathematics.

The research project is based on one of the most extensive data collections of writing processes in natural settings: three representative corpora from three domains of educational and professional writing. Corpus I includes all of the writing processes produced for a Swiss newspaper, the 'Tagesanzeiger', by 190 journalists between the years 2000 and 2002; corpus II the writing processes produced in the myMoment research project by 206 first to fifth graders between 2004 and 2006 and corpus III the writing processes produced in undergraduate and professional development courses by approximately 120 translation students and 50 professional translators between 2007 and 2010.

The data are available in a so-called time series format which allows the use of particular statistical techniques beyond those normally associated with corpus linguistics. Specifically, writing phases can be characterized by time intervals during which the writing process is characterized by more or less homogeneous dynamics in the observed series. These homogeneous dynamics can be related to patterns which are to be isolated (recognized or extracted) from the ground noise (i.e. the purely idiosyncratic part). The interesting extracted phases can then be analysed in order to assess the underlying writing process based on new formal (statistical) measures (criteria).

Need for Interdisciplinary Collaboration

Neither of the disciplines involved is able to reach the research goal with its own means. Applied linguistics and mathematics have to co-operate and to cross their disciplinary borders on three levels of the project: (a) theory, (b) methodology and (c) application.

(a) On its theoretical level, the project addresses writing research: Never before has the key concept of the writing phase been shaped both theoretically and empirically. However, this concept is crucial for most of the existing models of the writing process. They might have to be revisited and revised according to a new empirically sound model which is intended to be the project output to writing theory — based on new and customized, problem-specific statistical tools.

(b) On its methodological level, the project addresses scientists both in writing research and in applied statistics: For the first time in writing research, formal statistical analyses will be developed and applied in order to model natural writing processes and their key components, the writing phases. The project output on this level will thus be an innovative and interdisciplinary application of statistical modelling, precisely shaped (statistical customization) by extensive domain knowledge.

(c) On its practical level, the project addresses the appliers of writing research: Due to the project, it will be possible to link good practice in writing to sound empirical insights into the crucial interplay of writing phases. The planned project output on this practical level includes pragmatic deliverables such as general and domain-specific descriptions of good practice — and ready-to-use tools for the diagnosis of writing behaviour. Again, these tools can only be developed through interdisciplinary collaboration of linguistics and mathematics.

Expected Outcome

Developing the intended methodology and applying it to the three corpora will allow systematic modelling of writing processes in educational and professional settings. These background conditions can be suitably operationalized in the statistical modelling approach. Expected results will allow us (a) to deduce empirically and theoretically based models of good practice in writing processes in specific settings and therefore (b) to systematically evaluate competence and progress in (professional) writing. Both (a) and (b) are the conditiones sine qua non for the design of systematic writing courses, training and coaching. Practical deliverables of the project will include task- and domain-specific good practice models of writing processes.

Reference

Perrin, D., & Wildi, M. (2010). Statistical modeling of writing processes. In C. Bazerman (Ed.), *Traditions of writing research* (pp. 378–393). New York, NY: Routledge.

Chapter 4.00.14

Design of an Open Corpus and Computer Tool for Writing Development and Instruction among 8 to 16 Years Old Students With and Without Learning Disabilities

Esther García-Martín and Jesús-Nicasio García

We aim, in this study, to create an open monolingual corpus in Spanish for the study of the development of writing composition between typologies of students with and without LD and with and without ADHD between 8 and 16 years of age, both from a developmental and comparative approach. We pursue the building of a computerized open corpus containing written language texts by Spanish students. These texts have been compiled by the research team since 1994 in which thousands of students have been studied (at least 7232) and between 14,000 and 20,000 texts have been gathered to date and that figure will continue to grow.

For this research project we were engaged in the building of a computerized open corpus, containing the texts written by students between 8 and 16 years of age which were collected by our research team since 1994 (García-Martín, García, Pacheco, & Díez, 2009). This open corpus which will continue to grow will allow us to create a tool for the automatic evaluation and analysis of those texts, focusing on both text-based assessment (productivity, structure and coherence) and reader-based assessment (quality).

Similar tools exist in other languages, as in English, implemented by Biber (Biber, Conrad, & Reppen, 1998) and allows for the extraction of markers of relational and referential coherence. Its application permits very interesting comparative analysis and results in students with and without LD to be obtained (Gregg, Coleman, Stennett, & Davis, 2002).

Learning to Write Effectively: Current Trends in European Research
Studies in Writing, Volume 25, 399–401
ISSN: 1572-6304/doi:10.1108/S1572-6304(2012)0000025096

For our specific purposes, the corpus will allow us to carry out developmental and comparative studies. It will also lead to the dissemination and retailing of the tool, with the aim of achieving its generalization among teachers in their classrooms. This will allow for an easier computerized analysis of the text, as well as the analysis of the productivity, the quality, the structure and the coherence. This will be done considering the level, the age, etc., implementing programs and computerized instructional sequences and strategies, according to level of each student in each moment.

A total of 7232 Spanish students, between 8 and 16 years of age, with and without LD and with and without ADHD took part in this research project. They were randomly assigned to either the experimental or control conditions to allow for the study of the development of writing composition between typologies of students, both from a developmental and comparative approach. The writing levels (quality and productivity) and the students' general achievement were considered. We also studied other psychological variables related to writing (processes and different factors: planning, reflexivity, motivation and self-efficacy, self-knowledge and self-regulation), and variables such as social skills or the role of the teacher's practice in the teaching of writing, and those which modulate the achievement of the students.

Between 14,000 and 20,000 written texts have been collected, since 1994 in paper format plus the texts that will be collected for future studies. Each texts contains about 100 words giving a total of about 2 million words. This should be sufficiently representative of the type of language being studied, as it is a generally considered that over 1 million words is an adequate quantity number to assure representativeness in corpora for specific purposes, that is dealing with a sub-language as opposed to general language corpora (see the special issue of the JWR Schlitz, 2010).

Firstly, we will have to scan or type all the texts into a computer so that all the information in available in electronic format for the storage and retrieval of information. Proof reading is required to eliminate typing or scanning errors. The texts will be codified following Biber's model. Contextual information about the text is necessary to arrange the texts according to the different student variables (age, gender, intellectual level, writing level, school year, typology ...).

The design selected will be that of a special purpose corpus geared towards a specific type of study. It is therefore domain or genre specific, and represents a sub-language. It will include texts written by students and will be used for the study of writing compositions from a psychological point of view.

It will contain written language and will be monolingual containing original Spanish language. It will be open, as texts will be added constantly. It could be considered as a developmental corpus, as it contains child language acquisition texts in their mother tongue. We have examples in other languages such as the International Corpus of Learner English (ICLE).

This type of corpus studies has been very popular among linguistic researchers in recent decades as it provides the possibility of storing large amounts of data in an electronic form, but most of the studies are limited to a descriptive level. With this study, not only will we be applying the corpus methodology to another discipline, but also bridging the gap that exists between theory and application that is in high demand in other areas such as translation studies (see the special issue of the JWR Schlitz, 2010).

In this way, the corpus we aim to build will be used for two main purposes, on one hand, for the empirical study of real data and, on the other hand, for applied purposes (see Deane, & Quinlan, 2010), namely to build a computer tool that will allow for an automatic analysis of the texts as well as their evaluation and correction.

Furthermore, a possible study that could derive from this present one could be the comparative study of writing between native Spanish students and learners of Spanish as a foreign language.

Acknowledgements

During this research project, we received competitive funds from the Ministry of Research, Science and Innovation — from the Spanish Government; project EDU2010-19250 (EDUC) for 2010–2013, in addition to European Union FEDER funds. Excellence Research Group funds from Junta de Castilla y León (GR259), and European funds for 2009–2011 (BOCYL 27 April 2009). Both awarded to the Director/Principal Researcher (J.-N. García).

References

Biber, D., Conrad, S., & Reppen, R. (1998). *Corpus linguistics: Investigating language structure and uses.* Cambridge, UK: Cambridge University Press.

Deane, P., & Quinlan, T. (2010). What automated analysed of corpora can tell us about students' writing skills. *Journal of Writing Research, 2*(2), 151–177.

García-Martín, E., García, J.-N., Pacheco, D. I., & Díez, C. (2009). Design of an open corpus and computer tool for writing development and instruction among 8 to 16 years old students with and without learning disabilities. *International Journal of Developmental and Educational Psychology*, INFAD, Revista de Psicología, Contextos Educativos Escolares: Familia, Educación y Desarrollo, *XXI* (1), 2, 107–116.

Gregg, N., Coleman, C., Stennett, R. B., & Davis, M. (2002). Discourse complexity of college writers with and without disabilities: A multidimensional analysis. *Journal of Learning Disabilities, 35* (1), 23–38, 56.

Schlitz, S. A. (2010). Introduction to the special issue: Exploring corpus-informed approaches to writing research. *Journal of Writing Research, 2*(2), 91–98.

Chapter 4.00.15

Developing Writing Through Observation of Writing Processes Using Keystroke Logging

Eva Lindgren and Kirk Sullivan

Observational learning has proved to be an excellent method to help writers develop their writing skills. By observing another writer producing text, or one's own text developing on the computer screen (Lindgren & Sullivan, 2003), writers are able to focus their full attention on how a text is produced without also having to focus on the writing task itself.

Several studies of writers (for an overview see Sullivan & Lindgren, 2006) have used keystroke logging as a tool for observation of the writing processes. Keystroke logging (see Sullivan & Lindgren, 2006) is a computer-based method that comprised several software tools. They share the feature of recording every keystroke and mouse activity during writing. Afterwards the entire writing session can be replayed and writers can observe, in detail, how they went about writing a text.

In studies of young adolescents' (13–14 years of age) writing, an observation session in which a peer and a teacher were present was found to increase awareness of language, style and content. One intervention study (Lindgren, Sullivan, & Stevenson, 2008) studied 10 writers who wrote texts in their mother tongue Swedish and their foreign language English. Half of the texts were descriptive and the other half argumentative. All texts were written on the computer and recorded using keystroke logging. After half of the writing sessions the writers observed their own writing process and that of a peer. They were invited to comment on and discuss their actions. They were invited to revise all their texts a few days later. Experienced teachers marked all the texts and all the changes made during writing were analysed to provide insight into writers' focus during writing. The intervention, observation, proved more successful for the weaker writers. It also promoted different discussion

Learning to Write Effectively: Current Trends in European Research
Studies in Writing, Volume 25, 403–404
Copyright © 2012 by Emerald Group Publishing Limited
All rights of reproduction in any form reserved
ISSN: 1572-6304/doi:10.1108/S1572-6304(2012)0000025097

and improvement depending on whether the observed text was descriptive or argumentative and the language of the text.

Adult writers have reported that they experience observation through keystroke logging as a useful tool for their writing development. The method raised adult writers awareness of highly individualized aspects of their own writing such as spelling, cultural features necessary to solve the particular writing task and a need to write faster so as not to loose track of the overall writing goals (Sullivan & Lindgren, 2002).

The same methodology has been shown to promote university students' translation skills. The students individually translated texts from their mother tongue, Swedish, into the foreign language of study, English, before observing the keystroke logs of the translations together with a peer. Later the students were invited to revise and improve, in pairs, one of their translations. Individually, they also filled in a questionnaire about their experiences of the intervention. The majority of the students claimed their awareness of translation strategies and language features had increased as a result of the intervention (Lindgren, Sullivan, Deutschmann, & Steinvall, 2009)

These studies, and others, show that observational learning using keystroke-logging tools can assist learners develop their writing skills. By providing a situation in which writers can focus on how they write that is separated from the writing session where the writing task also has to be solved, reduces the risk of overloading writers' working memories, thus providing capacity for writers to reflect, discuss and develop their writing skills.

References

Lindgren, E., Sullivan, K. P. H., Deutschmann, M., & Steinvall, A. (2009). Supporting learner reflection in the language translation class. *Journal of Information Communication Technologies and Human Development*, *1*(3), 26–48.

Lindgren, E., Sullivan, K. P. H., & Stevenson, M. (2008). Supporting the reflective language learner with computer keystroke logging. In B. Barber & F. Zhang (Eds.), *Handbook of research on computer enhanced language acquisition and learning* (pp. 189–204). Hershey, NY: IGI Global.

Lindgren, E., & Sullivan, K. P. H. (2003). Stimulated recall as a trigger for increasing noticing and language awareness in the L2 writing classroom: A case study of two young female writers. *Language Awareness*, *12*, 172–186.

Sullivan, K. P. H., & Lindgren, E. (2002). Self-assessment in autonomous computer-aided L2 writing. *ELT Journal*, *56*(3), 258–266.

Sullivan, K.P.H., & Lindgren, E. (Eds.). (2006). Studies in writing. In *Computer keystroke logging: methods and applications* (Vol. 18). Oxford: Elsevier.

Chapter 4.00.16

The Haptics of Writing: Cross-Disciplinary Explorations of the Impact of Writing Technologies on the Cognitive-Sensorimotor Processes Involved in Writing

Anne Mangen and Jean-Luc Velay

Writing is a complex cognitive process relying on intricate perceptual-sensorimotor combinations. In studies of writing, the particular role of the physically tangible writing device (pen on paper, computer mouse and keyboard, digital stylus pen and writing tablet, etc.) is rarely addressed. Today, most of our writing is done with digital writing devices rather than writing by hand. The switch from pen and paper to mouse, keyboard and screen entails major differences in the haptics of writing, at several distinct but intersecting levels. Handwriting is by essence a unimanual activity, whereas typewriting is bimanual. Handwriting is also a slower process than typewriting. Moreover, the visual attention of the writer is strongly concentrated during handwriting; the attentional focus of the writer is dedicated to the tip of the pen, while during typewriting the visual attention is detached from the haptic input, namely the process of hitting the keys. Hence, typewriting is divided into two distinct, and spatiotemporally separated, spaces: the motor space (e.g. the keyboard) and the visual space (e.g. the screen). Another major difference pertains to the production of each character during the two writing modes. In handwriting, the writer has to graphomotorically form each letter — that is to produce a graphic shape resembling as much as possible the standard shape of the specific letter. In typewriting, obviously, there is no graphomotor component involved; the letters are 'ready-made' and the task of the writer is to spatially locate the specific letters on the keyboard. Finally, word processing software provides a number of features all of which might

Learning to Write Effectively: Current Trends in European Research
Studies in Writing, Volume 25, 405–407
ISSN: 1572-6304/doi:10.1108/S1572-6304(2012)0000025098

radically alter the process of writing for professional as well as for beginning writers. An understanding of what is entailed in the digitization of writing mandates a transdisciplinary approach in which perspectives from fields such as experimental psychology, cognitive neuroscience, phenomenology and philosophy of mind are brought to bear on the field of writing (and reading) research — theoretically and methodologically. This ongoing transdisciplinary research project is an attempt at charting a new course in writing and reading research, influenced by the 'embodied cognition' paradigm. (Embodied cognition denotes a theoretical current in psychology, biology, neuroscience, phenomenology and philosophy of mind, focusing on how perception and motor action are closely connected and reciprocally dependent, and how they interact with and shape cognitive processes at different levels.)

In a series of cross-disciplinary theoretical and empirical studies, we pursue the following research questions:

- Why, in what ways and with what implications are writing with digital technologies (keyboard, e-book stylus) different than writing by hand with pen on paper?
- What implications might these differences have for children's learning, and for our reading and writing behaviour and experience? Entailed in this question complex are, moreover, wider implications surrounding the role of the hand-brain relationship in learning and cognitive development overall.

As evidenced by research in neuroscience, writing is a process that requires the cross-modal integration of visual, proprioceptive (haptic/kinaesthetic) and tactile information. The acquisition of writing skills involves a perceptual component (e.g. learning the shape of the letter) and a graphomotor component (e.g. learning the trajectory producing the letter's shape). Research has shown that sensory modalities involved in handwriting, for example vision and proprioception, are so intimately entwined that strong neural connections have been revealed between perceiving, reading and writing letters in different languages and symbol/writing systems. (Longcamp, Anton, Roth, & Velay, 2003) When writing by hand, motor commands and kinesthetic feedback are closely linked to visual information at a spatial as well as a temporal level, while this is not the case with typewriting.

Various data converge to indicate that the cerebral representation of letters might not be strictly visual, but might be based on a complex neural network including a sensorimotor component acquired while learning concomitantly to read and write (Longcamp et al., 2003). Close functional relationships between the reading and writing processes might hence occur at a basic sensorimotor level, in addition to the interactions that have been described at a more cognitive level. Viewed in this light, there are ample reasons to study how the changing technologies of reading and writing alter, on the one hand, the processes of reading and writing *per se*, and, on the other hand, how they might fundamentally impact the relationships between reading and writing on several levels and in different phases of reading and writing acquisition. If the cerebral representation of letters includes a sensorimotor component elaborated when learning how to write letters, how might changes in writing movements affect/impact the subsequent visual recognition of letters? More precisely, what are the potential consequences of replacing the pen with the keyboard?

The visuomotor association involved in typewriting — locating and striking a certain key on the keyboard — should have little contribution to its visual recognition. Thus, replacing handwriting by typing during learning might have an impact on the cerebral representation of letters and thus on letter memorization. In two behavioural studies, Longcamp et al. investigated the handwriting/typing distinction, one in pre-readers (Longcamp, Zerbato-Poudou, & Velay, 2005) and one in adults (Longcamp, Boucard, Gilhodes, & Velay, 2006). Both studies confirmed that letters or characters learned through typing were subsequently recognized less accurately than letters or characters written by hand. In a subsequent study (Longcamp et al., 2008), fMRI data showed that processing the orientation of handwritten and typed characters did not rely on the same brain areas. Greater activity related to handwriting learning was observed in several brain regions known to be involved in the execution, imagery and observation of actions, in particular, the left Broca's area and bilateral inferior parietal lobules. Writing movements may thus contribute to memorizing the shape and/or orientation of characters.

In the first article (Mangen & Velay, 2010), we discuss how digital writing technologies and devices, by radically altering the hand movements and hence the haptic feedback, might have an impact on future writing skills. Future research projects may include employing Eye and Pen in order to focus on the role of the physicality (e.g. coarseness, texture and friction) of print paper versus the intangibility of the digital (e-paper) during handwriting with pen and with digital stylus, respectively.

References

Longcamp, M., Anton, J.-L., Roth, M., & Velay, J.-L. (2003). Visual presentation of single letters activates a premotor area involved in writing. *NeuroImage, 19*(4), 1492–1500.

Longcamp, M., Boucard, C., Gilhodes, J.-C., & Velay, J.-L. (2006). Remembering the orientation of newly learned characters depends on the associated writing knowledge: A comparison between handwriting and typing. *Human Movement Science, 25*(4/5), 646–656.

Longcamp, M., et al. (2008). Learning through hand- or typewriting influences visual recognition of new graphic shapes: Behavioral and functional imaging evidence. *Journal of Cognitive Neuroscience, 20*(5), 802–815.

Longcamp, M., Zerbato-Poudou, M.-T., & Velay, J.-L. (2005). The influence of writing practice on letter recognition in preschool children: A comparison between handwriting and typing. *Acta Psychologica, 119*(1), 67–79.

Mangen, A., & Velay, J.-L. (2010). Digitizing literacy: reflections on the haptics of writing. In M. H. Zadeh (Ed.). *Advances in haptics* (pp. 385–402). Vienna: InTech.

Author Index

Subject Index

List of Volumes

Volume 10: Contemporary Tools and Techniques for Studying Writing
Thierry Olive, C. Michael Levy (Eds.) 2001
Paperback, ISBN 1-4020-0106-1; Hardbound, ISBN 1-4020-0035-9

Volume 11: New Directions for Research in L2 Writing
Sarah Ransdell, Marie-Laure Barbier (Eds.) 2002
Pages 281; Paperback, ISBN 1-4020-0539-3; Hardbound, ISBN 1-4020-0538-5

Volume 12: Teaching Academic Writing in European Higher Education
Lennart Björk, Gerd Bräuer, Lotte Rienecker, Peter Stray Jörgensen (Eds.) 2003
Pages 240; Paperback, ISBN 1-4020-1209-8; Hardbound, ISBN 1-4020-1208-X

Volume 13: Revision: Cognitive and Instructional Processes
Linda Allal, Lucile Chanquoy, Pierre Largy (Eds.) 2004
Pages 248; Hardbound, ISBN 1-4020-7729-7

**Volume 14: Effective Learning and Teaching of Writing: A Handbook
of Writing in Education**
Gert Rijlaarsdam, Huub van den Bergh, Michel Couzijn (Eds.)
2nd ed., 2004, X, Pages 670; 21 illus.; Hardcover, ISBN 1-4020-2724-9;
Softcover, ISBN 1-4020-2725-7

**Volume 15: Writing in Context(s): Textual Practices and Learning
Processes in Sociocultural Settings**
Triantafillia Kostouli (Ed.) 2005
Pages 280; Hardcover, ISBN 0-387-24237-6; Softcover, ISBN 0-387-24238-4

Volume 16: Teaching Writing in Chinese Speaking Areas
Mark Shiu Kee Shum, De Lu Zhang (Eds.) 2005
Pages 276; Hardcover, ISBN 0-387-26392-6

Volume 17: Writing and Digital Media
Luuk Van Waes, Mariëlle Leijten, Chris Neuwirth (Eds.) 2006
Pages 380; Hardcover, ISBN 0-08-044863-1

Volume 18: Computer Key-Stroke Logging and Writing
Kirk Sullivan, Eva Lindgren (Eds.) 2006
Pages 248; Hardcover, ISBN 0-08-044934-4

Volume 19: Writing and Motivation
Suzanne Hidi, Pietro Boscolo (Eds.) 2006
Pages 346; Hardcover, ISBN 0-08-045325-2

Volume 20: Writing and Cognition
Mark Torrance, Luuk Van Waes, David Galbraith (Eds.) 2006
Pages 392; Hardcover, ISBN 0-08-045094-6

Volume 21: Written Documents in the Workplace
Denis Alamargot, Patrice Terrier, Jean-Marie Cellier (Eds.) 2008
Pages 336; Hardcover, ISBN 0-08-047487-8

Volume 22: Voices, Identities, Negotiations, and Conflicts: Writing Academic English Across Cultures
Phan La Ha, Bradley Baurain (Eds.) 2011
Pages 233; Hardcover, ISBN 0-8-5724719-0

Volume 23: Research on Writing Approaches in Mental Health
Luciano L'Abate, Laura G. Sweeney (Eds.) 2011
Pages 250; Hardcover, ISBN 978-0-85724-955-5

Volume 24: University Writing: Selves and Texts in Academic Societies
Montserrat Castelló, Christiane Donahue (Eds.) 2012
Pages 300; Hardcover, ISBN 978-1-78052-386-6